AF521503

India-West Asia Trade in Ancient Times

(6th Century BC to 3rd Century AD)

India-West Asia Trade in Ancient Times

(6th Century BC to 3rd Century AD)

Giridhari Prasad Das

New Century Publications
New Delhi, India

NEW CENTURY PUBLICATIONS
4800/24, Bharat Ram Road,
Ansari Road, Daryaganj,
New Delhi-110 002
Tel.: 23247798, 65396605
Telefax: 011-41017798
E-mail: indiatax@vsnl.com
www.newcenturypublications.com

Editorial office:
34, Gujranwala Town, Part-2,
Delhi - 110 009
Tel.: 27247805, 27464774

Copyright © 2006 by the author

All rights reserved. No part of this book may be reproduced, stored in a retrieval system, or transmitted in any form or by any means, mechanical, photocopying, recording, or otherwise without the prior written permission of the publisher.

First Published 2006

ISBN: 81-7708-125-x

Published by New Century Publications and printed at Singhal Print Media, New Delhi -110 005

PRINTED IN INDIA

About the Book

The commercial intercourse between India and West Asia can be traced out from antiquity. If one leaves out the commercial relations between West Asia and India in the Bronze Age phase (3rd Millennium B.C.), then in the historical period a clear picture of this trade can be presented from 6th century B.C. with continuity.

The economic history of Indian subcontinent was initially dominated by the study of agrarian economics. The recognition of significance of trade became a topic of interest among the historians in the later phase. To discuss the trade of a subcontinent like India, spreading from the Himalayas to Kanykumari, is not an easy task.

A commercial intercourse between the two lands cannot be weighed on the basis of exchange of goods only. Therefore, researchers focus not only on trade but also consider allied topics like social, political and cultural matters. The present book examines various trade related activities at different levels including social bars, which were an impediment in the path of development of trade. Therefore, the social attitude of trade and traders and the attitude of ruling classes towards the foreign trade are also highlighted in this book.

The book covers the period from 6th Century BC to 3rd Century AD. The trade of India and West Asia during this period varied from one region to another. Specifically, the work seeks to explain (a) how the forces of exchange of commerce became an important part of the study of Indian trade history, (b) the impact of political relations on trade, in addition to exchange of goods, (c) the elaborate arrangement of Mauryas to get control over trade and exchange of cultural ingredients and (d) exchange of goods, market places, system of transport and communication etc. in commercial relations during the period under study.

Author's Profile

Dr. Giridhari Prasad Das completed his M. Phil. and Ph. D. degrees from the Centre for West Asian and African Studies, School of International Studies, Jawaharlal Nehru University (JNU), New Delhi. He specializes in economic history, particularly trade and commerce, of ancient India. Dr. Das has participated and presented papers on these subjects at national and international conferences. Presently, he is a lecturer in National Institute of Law, Faridabad, Haryana.

Preface

Trade and commerce are important determinants of the economic condition of a country. India's prosperity, which attracted many foreign conquerors, was largely due to foreign trade. The commercial intercourse between India and West Asia can be traced out from antiquity. If one leaves out the commercial relations between West Asian and India in the Bronze Age phase (3rd Millennium B.C.) then in the historical period a clear picture of this trade can be presented from 6th century B.C. with continuity. When the fragmented politics of India attracted Cyrus, the Persian invader not only wanted to satiate the desire of the territorial aggrandizement but also to capture the untold wealth of India.

A new epoch in the history of Indo-West Asian trade came after the coming of Sakas, Partians and Kushana. The craze of Roman people for Indian luxurious goods caused consternation in the heart of Roman emperor as well as geographer like Pliny. A large number of towns and urban centres sprang up due to the growth of trade. The trade brought the material prosperity in addition to cultural prosperity. The art, architecture, mathematics, science sculpture and culture etc, were influenced by coming in contact with West Asian people. Though the trade continued with an unabated zeal through ups and downs during different periods under different monarchs, the utmost profit of the trade went to Kushanas, who acted as the intermediary of Central Asian Trade. The Silk route which passed through Indian Subcontinent gave a suitable opportunity to the Indian merchants to take an active part in the Silk trade. The coinage of the Kushana Empire was greatly influenced by the coins of the Roman who were much interested in this trade. After Kushanas the trade started to decline during second century A.D. and got diverted towards Southeast Asia.

All that is glorious, majestic and beautiful naturally influences human mind and it is perhaps due to natural instincts that Indian mid felt the powerful impact of the achievements of West Asians in trade and culture. It was a sort of give and take which was perfectly natural between the two sister civilizations. In the Discovery of India, Nehru observed, "Few people have been more closely related in origin and throughout history then the people of India and Persia". How true!

The geographical continuity of North-West of India with Eastern Iran and the contracts, during the Bronze Age of the Indus Valley with a fairly advanced culture Mediterranean, is now well known. Trade by sea between India and West Asia goes back to antiquity. There is a large volume of evidences, numismatic and literary, bearing witness to the varying fortunes of a continuous trade. Strabo, Pliny, Ptolemy, the anonymous author of the "Periplus of the Erythrean Sea" (a voyage or sailing chart of the Red. Sea), clearly mark the different stages of increasing knowledge of the East, which was spreading to the West Asia. A large number of Indo-Roman coins found in different parts of India, give a crystal clear picture of trade.

From pre-historic times, three great trade routes have connected India with the West. The easiest and probably the oldest of these was the Persian Gulf route running from the mouth of Indus to the Euphrate. Then there was overland route, from the India passes to Balkh, down the Oxus to Caspian, passing through Caspian Gates and reaching at Antioch. Lastly there was circuitous sea route, down the Persian, Arabian coasts to Aden, up the Red Sea. West Asia comprises the countries like Iran, Iraq and Saudi Arabia and Asia Minor. Basically in Indo-Roman trade, theses countries were acting as middlemen. It will be a futile attempt for scholar if he tries to think of Indo-West Asian trade without going much deeper into Indo-Roman and Indo-Greek trade. Because their was no clear-cut demarcation between these trading activities.

Indo-West Asian trade can be clearly traced out from 6th century BC onwards. It has been claimed that the word "Sindhu" found in the library Ashrubanipal` (C668-626 B.C.) is used in the senses of Indian cotton and the word is used to be much older, belonging in reality to the Akkadian tongue, where it is expressed by ideographs meaning "vegetable cloth". India's cotton trade with West Asia was very old. Logs of Indian teak have been found in the temple of Moon at Mugheir (the "Ur of the Chaldees") and in the palace of Nebuchadenzaar, both belonging to 6th century BC and it was known that the trade in teak, ebony ,sandwood and blackwood between Barygana and the Euphrates was still flourishing up to 2nd century AD. In the6th Century BC, the chief ports like Tamralipti, Bharaukacha and Suppara, exported various kinds of birds and beasts, including curiously enough horses, ivory, cotton goods, jewels. Emigration was not uncommon.

In 606 BC, after the overthrow of the Assyrian empire, and Babylon which look the plae of Nineveh became crowded with the merchants from distant Tarshish and Indians from Punjab who came to sell their wares. In Jataka there are many stories about this trade. A Babylonian colony may have sprung on the borders of India. For Strabo tells us that the followers of Alexander found at Taxila a marriage market conducted on the well-known Babylonian principle. In the 5th Century B.C. , Ophir was an enter pot on the shores of Arabia, where Indians and Phoenicians brought their wares and bartered. Again the substances, which originally came from Dravidian ports, were cinnamon, ginger, berly-stone etc.

Alexander opened the floodgates of Indo-West Asian trade during 4th Century BC. Trading depots were founded all along the course of Indus as the Macedonian army moved towards the mouth of river. Bukephola and, Nickaea were built on the bank of Hydaspes. Alexandria was an important spot where the Akesines joined the mainstream; and Patala at the head of Indus-delta. Again the Royal Road of Persia linked the different trade centres of India (i.e. Taxila, Kanauj, Hastinapur, Prayag) as well as West Asia, which facilitated India's ancient international trade. Goods from the golden Chersonese and beyond, silk from the Seres, Gangetic muslins, spices from Arabia, all poured into the bazaars of Pataliputra. Greek girls were frequently imported to Barygaza and a guard of Yavana Woman" was stock feature of Raja's court in Indian dramas.

*During the First Centuries of Christian Era, the trade between India and West Asia was basically indirect and direct trade was very little. Athenaeus tells us that in the procession of Ptolemy Philadelphus, Indian woman, Indian hunting dogs and Indian cows, among other strange sights; also Indian spices carried on camels; were seen.

The articles imported by Rome were spice, pepper, ginger, cardamom, aromatic nut, slaves and eunuchs. Roman interest in spice and other plant products increased enormously in 1st Century A.D. Among the products pepper held chief place, which was called "Yavanpriya" or "favourite of the Yavanas", according to an old Tamil poem. In the time of Periplus, black and white pepper from the district of Cottonara of South India was brought down to the ports of Muziris and Nelycynda, whence it was transported by Greek merchants in very large vessels. Among the spices, cinnamon was in high demand among the Romans, which was used, "as perfume, as an incense, as a condiment and as a medicine". Again the costly spikenard oil which was in high demand among the Romans as an ingredient in cookery and drugs and rich ladies of Rome used to anoint guests at banquet with it.

Among the animals, which were exported, mention may be made of apes, monkeys, Nilgiri langurs, tiger, yak, rhinoceroses, parrots and peacocks etc. For obvious reasons they must have been carried largely along land routes. The testimony of Roman writers shows knowledge of at least three species of Indian parrots. The ladies not only on the fingers and ears but also on the shoes largely used Indian Muslin and pearls, which posed a great danger to the Roman economy. The Indians imported slaves, singing girls to be employed by Indian Kings or to be kept in the harem, fine red coral of the Mediterranean, flax cloth, gold, copper, tin, lead, orpiment, metal lamps and vases, glass and glass objects. Among the animal products of western origin coral held the chief place. It occurs repeatedly in the Indian list of gems, and its high value in the eyes of Indians as referred by Pliny that the men of India no less appreciated it than the Indian pearls by Roman women. As to agricultural products, large quantities of dates were exported to Barygaza, the first being most prized. Among aromatic, medicinal and other plant products, Barbaricum imported storax and frankincense and Baryagaza imported storax and sweet clover. Storax, which was probably derived from the sap of a tree native to Asia Minor, was used for medicinal purpose. Gold and silver plate was imported into Barbaricum while Barygaza obtained gold bullion from Persian Gulf (probably from mines in East Arabia). Very costly silverware, topaz was imported into Barygaza for king's use.

Mauryan period of Ancient India set up a new milestone in the trade relation by not only importing valuable goods but also exchanging embassies. It opened up a new era in trade as well as political arena. Bindusara a man of wide interests and tastes had asked Antiochus-I of Syria to send sweet wine, dried figs and a sophist. The Syrian king replied that, while he was sending the figs and wine but Greek laws forbade the selling of sophists. The classical writers testify to Bindusara's fascination for the Greeks. His son, Ashok maintained the relations and extended further by exchanging with them ambassadors. Dr. Smith has suggested that Dionysus, the envoy of Ptolemy Philadephus of Egypt presented his credentials to Ashok rather than Bindusara. Ashoka appointed many Yavana officials in his government including Tushapa as the governor of Saurashtra. He exchanged the ambassadors with Antiochus of Syria, Ptolemy Philadelphus of Egypt, Antigonus of Macedonia. Alberuni, the celebrated Muslim scholar observed the traces of Buddhism in Khorasan, Persia, Iraq and Syria which were undoubtedly the result of Ashoka's missionary zeal. His rock edicts are borrowed from the rock edict style of Darius. The palace of Patiliputra was also an imitation of Greek style. Again the presence of Indian women, animal and spices in the procession of Philadelphus, as described by Athenaeus. Suggests a close connection between the two countries. We know from Strabo that Myos Hormos became a great centre of India's Trade.

During the period of Kushanas, the trade reached at its peak. Regular contacts and exchange of embassies, gave a boost to this trade. The prosperity enjoyed by the Kushana empire was mainly due to brisk trade of Indian merchants between Roman and Chinese empire.

In South India, Chola, Chera and Pandya kingdoms were conducting very active trade with Rome. Muziris, the trade centre was crossed with Greeks and Arabian vessels; the Greeks brought the imperial products in large ships and exchanged them for Indian gods. But much money had to be brought as well as to make up the balance and to create a basis for exchange in India. At that time, the Chera kingdom was famous for its pepper while Pandya was famous for pearl. A Tamil poet, Nakkirar, exhorts a Pandya prince to drink in peace the cool and fragrant wine brought by Yavanas in their good ships. Wine was a luxurious item, which was largely imported into India.

From a series of recent studies, it is becoming increasingly clear that many of the supposed finds of Roman pottery are in fact indigenous Indian ceramic products. Red Polished Ware (RPW) once considered a Roman import, is in fact an Indian product, which originated in Gujarat (Rao-1970). At Amreli, Black Polished Ware preceded RPW in first century B.C., identical with RPW in composition and technique and differing from it only in colour. As the technique of production was used in Gujarat prior to any Roman imports to the region, it is reasonable to conclude that RPW is not a direct imitation of Roman Samiana Ware, which superficially resembles it. While the technique of roulette must have been acquired from earlier Hellenistic Meditarranean Ceramic Wares or metal work. The Rouletted Ware found in India was a regional product of the South East Asia and has been dated from Second Century B.C. to 1st Century A.D. at Arikamedu (Begley 1986: 47-54) The mould made ware of western Deccan has clear analogies in shape and decoration with Hellenistic pottery and metal work, as Begley has shown. M.W. from Nevesa is dated to 1st Century BC. So the foreign Prototypes must be earlier and antedate of Roman imports. Moreover, M.P. itself is a local product made in Western India.

In India, Roman bronzes have only been found at Kolhapur and Akota. Most of the Kolhapur bronzes are dated to the first century AD. (De Puma 1991:92-95). But rather surprisingly he considers that Poseidon statuette from Kolhapur was manufactured in third century BC and Wire Strainer of Etorusean in Roman Etrusean type is even earlier and that both bronzes reached in India long afterwards either as scrap metal or as an antiquarian export.

However, recent excavation at Qalat-al-Baharein, the capital of main land of Gulf, are providing thick layers of 6th –4th Century BC settlement and clear traces of an Achaemenid settlement in the region, even though no tangible remains of any Indian trade could be found. Such notices of exchanges with the East have to found in the presence of Indian ivory, wood from Caramania, Sind and Gandhar in Darius' palace in Susa and from Ctesias' knowledge of Indian steel and from the depiction of Indian dress and cotton on the Apadana friezes in Persepolis and from some indisputable written records. For example, following a step initiated by his predecessors, Nebuchadnezzar who founded the city of Teredon near Basrah in the Shatt-al-Arab, known as Diodurus by Arrians who adds that the merchants brought frankincense and other aromatics there. Excavation at Failaka, Leukos Limen and MyosHormos provide a good idea of India's trade with West Asia.

Trade has been defined as "the mutually appropriative movement of goods between hands". This movement may be within continuous social units (internal trade) or between groups across cultural boundaries (external trade). It has been further categorized into gift trade, administered trade and market trade. Basically the ancient trade, which was different from modern trade, can be defined properly within the fou walls of anthropological trade. According to author. Goa presented Polanyi man like other animals as naturally self-sufficient. But with the advance of culture, man's needs grew in monstrous proportion, which led the people to depend on each other to fulfill their needs and this gave a way to trade. According to Aristotle, "Trade is natural when it serves the survival of community by maintaining its self sufficiency". Polyanyi regarded the commercial trade as unnatural form of trade; natural trade was gain less, since it merely maintained the self-sufficiency. One may assume very clearly that replacing the barter trade by moneyed trade brought the profit motive among the people. Again trade appears as a two-way movement of goods through the market and money as quantifiable goods used for indirect exchange in order to facilitate the movements. Here market appears the locus of exchange while the trade is the actual exchange and money as the means of exchange.

The book is organised into five chapters.

Chapter 1 deals with the trails of trade from very antiquity. It also refers about the trade routes, goods of trade etc. with a glimpse. A brief discussion about these areas, objectives, methodology is also made in this chapter.

Chapter 2 starts with the invasion of Darius and Alexander. It also describes about the different political and socio-economic respects of their invasions.

Chapter 3 focuses on trade during the Maurya period. Lack of evidences does not throw much light on trade relations. But in political sphere, the exchange of embassies gives an idea that the people of India and West Asia were very close. Again in cultural front many similarities are found between Indian art, architecture and sculpture with West Asian counterpart. Ashoka's untiring effort to propagate the idea of Buddhism in distant lands brought more closeness among the people. These things have been vividly discussed in this chapter.

Chapter 4 provides a detailed picture of India's trade with West Asia is presented. The trade routes, goods of export and import, business organizations are also discussed vividly. The flourishing trade of South India with Rome is also discussed.

Chapter 5 records main conclusions of the work.

September 1, 2006 Giridhari Prasad Das
Faridabad, Haryana

Contents

Preface vii

1. Introduction 1-32

2. Trade during the Pre-Mauryan Period 33-97

3. Trade during the Mauryan Period 98-153

4. Trade during the Post-Mauryan Period 154-311

5. Conclusions 312-322

Bibliography 323-350

Dedicated to

My Beloved Parents

1

Introduction

The geographical continuity of North-West India with Western Iran and West Asia is a well-known fact. The cultural contacts and commercial interactions between India and West Asia go back to a very remote antiquity.[1] There is a growing volume of evidences, field archaeology, numismatic and literary evidence bearing witness to the varying fortunes of a continuous trade. Strabo, Pliny, the anonymous author of the "Periplus of the Erythrian Sea" clearly mark the different stages of increasing knowledge of the East which was spreading in the West Asia. Various archaeological evidences and a large number of coins, which are found in different parts of India, give a crystal clear picture of the trade.

Trade during Indus Valley Civilization (C2500 BC-1800 BC)

India's commercial interactions with West Asian countries can be traced back from the days of Indus-Valley civilization[2] and prior to this. The extensive researches on the famous pre-Harappan site at Mehergarh (in Bolan Valley, Pakistan) strongly indicate the availability of non-local objects at Mehergarh.[3] It is likely that the people of Mehergarh through exchange procured these objects.[4] This would suggest the beginning of exchange related functions in pre-Harappan context (around fifth Millennium B.C). It was the river basins of India where the civilizations appeared in a highly commercialised form. The fertile soil of river basin, navigation, fishing, shipping created a very favourable condition for trade. Navigation created a new class of sailors as traders. The fishing centres turned into mercantile towns.[5] It was really a cradle of commerce. The traders had sufficient knowledge of navigation, land routes, the deserts of Rajasthan and Arab world also.[6] They maintained a close commercial contact with the outside worlds like Sumer.[7] They exported goods both by land routes and sea routes to the West Asian countries.

Some evidences point out the fact that there was trade between India and West Asia during the period of Indus Valley civilization. The seal of Tell Asmar[8] is, however, certainly of Indian workmanship. The appearance of elephants, rhinoceros and crocodile *(gharial)* clearly supports the commercial relations between them. The representation on a seal of a mast less ship with a central cabin and steersmen seated at the rudder indicates that the people of Indus-Valley were fully acquainted with the maritime activities. The boat has a sharply upturned prow and stern, similar to the archaic representation on early Minoan seals, cylinders of Sumer and pre-dynastic pottery of Egypt. Mackay thinks that the Indus Valley was in close contact with Sumer and Elam by sea-route also.[9] Indus ports thus appear to have been great commercial ports carrying on trade with Ur, Kish, and Lagash and also with Egypt.[10]

A round seal (type 'h') found in the pre-dynastic cemetery at Ur and described and illustrated by Lagrain,[11] undoubtedly resembles some of the Indus seals in the material and shape. The fish of course commonly appears on the Mohenjodaro seals, it is common there as in the Sumerian Signatory but the scorpion has yet to be identified amongst the Indus-Valley pictographs[12] and one very notable example occurs on an axe head of Eighteenth Dynasty. The occurrence of a humped bull at both Mohenjodaro and Susa implies the communication between these two civilizations and further suggests that the inter communication took place by land rather than river.[13] Another seal bearing the figures of antelope was perhaps imported from Elam to India.[14] The most interesting seal portrays a hero grappling a tiger on the either side of him by throat was found at Harappa.[15] The seal recalls a scene on the ivory handle of knife from Geobelel-Ark in which human figure is at the grips of lions.[16] This scene may be identified with the exploits of Eabani or Enkidu[17] who was represented in Sumerian legend as fighting with lions & bulls in forest.

The different marks on seals point out the trade routes followed by the traders. Seals with animals on other designed motifs indicate the trademark for land routes whereas the seals with ship or boat motif indicate the trademark of sea-borne trade. An interesting fragment of a vessel was found in a low stratum at Mohenjodaro. This is of light green steatite.[18] The carving is very much similar to that found in different sites of Mesopotamia. It, therefore, definitely came to India by way of import from Mesopotamia. Other objects found at Harappa and Mohenjodaro, for example, beads of unusual shape can be linked up with the conditions of the West such as Egypt .The cloth must have been exported to Mesopotamia since, in the back of one seal still preserves its imprint. The texts from Lagash reveal that the garments were being traded for Dilmun copper.[19] The commercial tablets often refer to the transport by water or by, cattle and assess.[20]

Trade was sufficiently well organized to secure regular supplies not only of food stuffs from the fertile regions but also of gold, silver, copper, tin, lead. They might have been imported from the neighboring countries to the north and west, namely from Persia and Afghanistan.[21] On the other hand the manufactured goods including beads, knobbed pottery, vases and cloth were exported to Mesopotamia, Egypt and other countries. The ornaments include, fly amulets, such as were common in early Dynastic Mesopotamia, a pin with double scroll head, parallel to the double spiral headed pins which are distributed from the Indus-Valley through Annnan and Hissar-II & III to Troy, the cyclades and the Balkans.[22] Harappa was exporting timber, copper, gold, ivory, stones and beads.[23] Romila Thapar has pointed out that this is in keeping with the patterns of trade, existing in the ancient period when Indian enterprise across the sea was limited to the sale of Indian goods where there was demand and not involved to any large extent in acquiring the vital commodities unalienable in the sub-continent.[24]

The excavations at Lothal, point out that the city was a

harbour where sea-borne trade might have been originated. On the other hand, the Sumerian trader undertook the sea voyages over the Persian Gulf to Bahrain and Oman and reached at the Indus-Valley and at other coastal towns of India.[25] The natural coastline, fine harbours, navigable rivers, fertile lands, provided a conducive atmosphere to the growth of intensive trade. Other important small port towns of Indus Valley were Chahnudaro, Suktagendor, in the distant outposts.[26] The possibility can not be ruled out that some of the Sumerians and Iranian merchants had temporarily taken residence at Harappa and Mohenjodaro in connection with the trade, as indicated by some of the graves, excavated by Wheeler at Harappa.[27] Similarly it can be presumed that there might have been a colony of Indian traders in the city of Sumer.[28] To keep up the trade links with terminal markets, to dispose of their goods and to collect the return cargo by caravans, a good number of guards were provided. The island of Bahrain commanded the shipping dam of the Persian Gulf, which led among the coast of Persia right up to the mouth of Indus. It has, therefore, been argued that in 3rd millennium B.C., Bahrein merchants were handling the trade and transshipment between India and west. The traders were using the southern routes by sea and land for westerly connections.[29] The location of Harappan sites indicates the use of several minor Kirthar passes as well as the Bolan and Gomal passes but not the Khyber Pass.[30]

In another excavation it is found that Harappan shells and etched carnelian beads are found in Mesopotamian royal burials. Several small monkey figurines occur in Mesopotamia, although the monkey is not native to Western Asia.[31] The animal, which some Harappans may have taken abroad as pet, appears to have held fascination for Mesopotamians, who used the figurines as amulets.[32] Mesopotamian clay tablets refer to certain varieties of wood and gold and lapis lazuli coming from Meluha; ivory too was a Harappan items used in Southern Mesopotamia.

But Mortim Wheeler suggests that in the cemetery at Harappa, a grave with wooden coffin and reed shroud is in the Mesopotamia not the Harappan tradition.[33] Mesopotamians appear to have been charmed by the Indian monkeys and peacocks and presumably some Harappans saw the Bacterian camels in Kalibangan or Mahenjodaro (even if they did not fancy it for its is just depicted on one figurine at Shortughai and possibly one copper tablets of Mohenjodaro).

It Ras al Junayz (Oman) where occurred Harappan type jars, two scratched with Harappan signs, as well as pottery painted with motiffs resembling Harappan designs, there well may have been a sea port.[34] Some of the bronze mirrors of Bactria, late 3rd Millennium type, occur sporadically at Harappan sites and in upper Gulf, Kulli region, Mesopotamia and Elam.[35]

On the basis of above findings it may be concluded that there was a good trade between two civilizations. And its indelible impacts are found at different places in different forms.

Trade in Vedic Period (C1500 BC– 600 BC)

The collapse of Indus-Valley civilization did not bring an end of commercial relations between the two civilizations. It continued in the Vedic period about which the Vedic literature provides references. The merchants offered prayers and oblation to seek the divine grace for success in trade.[36] At that time the navigation was very much difficult and dangerous and shipwrecks were probably a common occurrence, the daring merchants nonetheless ventured regularly on a sea voyage with hundred oars ships.[37] Therefore, it was prayed when a merchant goes out for business, Vaisyanara may kindly look after the children and other relatives of foreign going merchants.[38] The traders were moving in all directions, to different foreign countries. The international trade was regulated and controlled by a certain section of Dasyu society. They were no other than Panis who were referred to as Dasyus. They held a prominent place in the field of commerce and trade. They were mighty and intelligent people and accumulated fabulous wealth through extensive international trade and commerce.[39] They made India a great centre of the world. Archaeology corroborates the fact by exploring many world famous cities, which were well surrounded by vast and productive villages[40] with flourishing agriculture[41], which produced sufficient surplus.[42]

The material life of Rig Veda was steeped in cattle keeping and animal breeding activities. There is little doubt that cattle wealth *(godhana)* constituted in most important aspect of social wealth if Rig Vedic days.[43] The Rg Veda was acquainted with regular sea faring, which is claimed on the basis of expression of sataritranau *and* the praise of *Samudra* by a person going, through it.[44] Various references about the trading activities in Atharva Veda clearly establishes the fact that there must had been a flourishing trade.

About the trade relations between India and west Asia, some evidences clearly point out the fact, the trace of this intercourse is found in the cuneiform inscriptions of the Hittite Kings of Mitanni in Kappadokia belonging to fourteenth and fifteenth centuries.[45] Again these kings bore Aryan names and worshipped the Vedic gods, Indra, Mitra, Varuna and Asvins whom they call by their Vedic title Nasatya. This clearly presents the fact that there was a close contact between these people. But we cann't precisely determine how, with the Aryans of Vedic Age, who were at that time dwelling in Punjab.[46] It has been claimed that the word "Sindhu"[47] found in the library of Assurbanipal (668-626 B.C) is used in the sense of "Indian cotton" and the word is said to be much older, belonging in reality to the Akkaddian tongue, where it is expressed by the ideographs meaning a Vegetable cloth".[48] It is believed that Ashurbanipal was a great cultivator who had sent for Indian plants, including the "Wool bearing" trees.[49] At any rate we know that the cotton trade of western India is of great antiquity. The Indians, when the Greeks first came in contact with them were dressed in wool grown on trees".[50] The night and Dawn are compared as 'two female weavers" in Rig Veda. The similar type of comparison is available in Arabic and Hebrew sources. Again the logs of Indian teak have been found in the temples of the Moon at Mugheir (the Ur of Chaldeas) and in the palace of Nebuchadnezzar, both belonging to sixth century B.C.[51] These evidences are enough to presume that there was a flourishing trade between these two sub-continents.

A Brief Review of Trade

A dramatic change in the political relations between India and West-Asia came with the invasions of Cyrus,(C558B.C.-529B.C.) Darius (C521B.C.-486B.C.) and Alexander(C327B.C.-486B.C.) They not only controlled some parts India but also broke the isolation of India in the world arena. The political relations gave a boost to trade and cultural relations. Alexander opened the flood gates of Indo-West Asian trade during 4th century B.C. Alexander planned to invade India not with a view to establishing the Greek rule but to control the commerce of India.[52] Trade centers were established all along the course of Indus on important land routes. Bukephala and Nikaca were built on the banks of Hydaspes, Jhelum, Alexandria on the Indus at the confluence of the Indus and Chenab at Patala, at the head of Indus delta.[53] Nearchus, the admiral in charge of Greek fleet, explored the way to Persian Gulf.[54] Culturally, India and Greece are the legacies of Alexander's campaign.[55] India received from Greece the lessons of astronomy, Gandhra art. Whether Indian art and architecture was influenced by Greek style of art and architecture or not is difficult to determine. India on the other hand influenced Greece with her philosophy and religion.[56]

The foundation of Mauryan (C321B.C.-184B.C.) Empire brought a substantial change in commerce. Though Mauryan Empire extended beyond the Hindukush, it led to the expansion of India's foreign trade and it brought a change in the economic structure of India. Trade regulations were carefully planned, suited to a well-organized economy and trade was brought under the state control with the appointment of Panyadhyaksha, the Superintendent of Trade.[57] It was the duty of Government to maintain a balance between the interest of the state and traders, traders and customers. The state officials were entrusted with different duties to carry out trade smoothly and stringent punishment was given to the people for violation of trade rules and regulations.[58] During this period, the state itself engaged in trade on fairly extensive scale. For the first time in the economic history of the world, Kautilya introduced the policy of 'mixed economy' in which private sector ran side by side.[59]

The presence of Megasthenes, the ambassodar of Selecus, in the Mauryan court point out the fact that the international commerce during the Mauryan period had gained momentum. In another instance, Bindusara, the second Mauryan king, asked Antiochus-I to send, wine, dried figs and a Greek philosopher.[60] The greatest impact of West Asian culture was felt during this period. The Mauryan administration, building art, architecture, sculpture, medicine, all were influenced by the culture of West Asian people and Acheimenids. From the above facts it can clearly be presumed that there must have been a developed trade though the foreign sources, numismatic as well as archaeological sources don't throw much light on the volume of trade.

After the fall of Mauryan Empire, in early 2nd century B.C, the foreign trade through land routes was very much disturbed. On the ruins of imperial structure of Mauryas, there arose a number of cities republican or tribal and monarchical, such as, Taxila, Panchala, Mathura, Kausambi etc. The trade routes now came under the control of more than one state, which proved quite detrimental to the free flow of commerce.[61] The traders from the distant lands had to pay tools to so many kingdoms that it became a costly affair. This sea-borne trade reached at its peak during the time of Satavahanas (1st C.B.C.-3rd C.A.D.).[62] These commercial activities continued right up to the second century A.D. Foreign trade now shifted to south and south India participated vigorously in commercial activities of India with the west. This is clear & evident from the account of Egyptian trade and commerce with East Africa and India as given in the Periplus of the Erythrean Sea ships of the western countries loaded with merchandise visited Indian ports of Broach,Dravida country, Supara (Sopara) and Kalyana (near Mumbai).[63]

A great change in trade relations with the West Asian countries came during the second and third centuries A.D. But with the rise of Gupta Empire, at the heart of Indian Empire moved inland towards central India and a cultural development set in with a distinctive Indian character. The emergence of the Sassanian Empire in 227 B.C., also checked the direct communication between the two areas. A sea change in the trade relations came during the Kushan(1st C.A.D.-2nd C.A.D.) period which included Afghanistan, Bactria and much of Central Asia composing the various peoples like Indo-Greeks, Parthians, Scythians, Iranians and Chinese and other. The spread of Buddhism to Central Asia and the cosmopolitan culture of Kushanas(1st C.A.D.-2nd C.A.D.) created a fertile ground for the advancement of trade.[64]

An area around the Mediterranean Sea enclosed the vast Empire of Rome. The northern frontier was bordered by Hardian's wall between England and Scotland and the rivers Rhine and Danube on the continent. The Eastern border ran across the territories of Modern Turkey, Iraq, Syria, Lebanon, Jordan and Israel.[65] The vast Empire of Rome opened the ample opportunities of trade with different countries in different directions in order to meet the needs of the people. The prevalence of peace and a strategic position due to its geographical importance, it became the focal point of attraction of the merchants. But one of the strange thing in this trade was, Indian merchants seldom met their Roman counterparts. The very reason was that the intermediaries who took maximum advantage of Indo-Roman trade. The intermediaries of Indo-Roman trade were the Alexandrians, Greeks, Syrians, Jews, Parthians, Armenians and Arabs who controlled the land routes leading to east.

The trade of West Asia with India was not confined to North India only but it was spread up to South India also. Three main South Indian areas like Pandyas, Cholas and Cheras were also actively involved in this trade.[66] They were carrying the commercial relations mainly through the waterways. Among the most important ports of south India were, Muziris, Nelcynda, Uraiyur, Kollchi, Puhar etc., which mainly controlled the trade.[67] It marks the presence of large number of foreigners in the South Indian states who were employed in different works of state. From the beginning of Roman Empire,the Pandyan people had probably taken the leading part in encouraging the Romans to come and trade for what they sent, as we have seen, as embassy to Augustus. In another interesting fact, the Tamil poet Nakkirar exhorts, a Pandya prince brought the cool and fragrant wine, to drink in peace, by the Yavana merchants. From the beginning, Pandya people had taken much interest in Indo-Roman trade and encouraged the trade. Agaru or Uraiyur was the main centre of muslin in South-Indian, which was attracting a large number of Greeks to collect this. A large number of gold coins chiefly struck by Roman emperors have been found in South India.

Among other trade centers, Muziris was the main centre, it attracted large number of Greek and Arab vessels. At that time, the Chera Kingdom was famous for its pepper while Pandya was famous for pearls.[68] Sixty eight hoards of Roman coins have so far been unearthed in the sub-continent, not less than fifty seven of then found in the south of Vindhyas.[69] So a flourishing trade relation was there in between South India and Roman Empire.

India, "the Queen of Eastern Sea" was famous for different goods, which were exported to different parts of the world. Among the export goods the most important forest products were ebony, teak wood, sandalwood, bamboo are important.[70] Various Narioles types of consumer goods such as wheat, rice, clarified butter, seasame oil, honey, capal, lac, indigo, purple were also exported to the Mediterranean countries.[71] Among the animals, which were, favourite items of West were apes, monkeys, Nilgiri Langurs, tiger, yak, rhinoceroses, parrots, peacocks etc. The spice was the favourite item of the West Asian people which mainly comprised the pepper, spikenard, cloves, costus, bdellium, cardamum, aloe and saffron. The vegetable products like palm wine, castor, sugar were the important which reached in the Mediterranean countries. The gold, silver, copper, iron, steel was the main items of export in metal.[72] The ladies not only in the fingers and ears but also on the shoes largely used Indian muslin and pearls, which posed a great danger to the Roman economy.

The list of goods, which were imported by India from the

West Asian countries, was comparatively small. The most important products of import were, Arabian incense, sweet clover, cinnamon etc.[73] some of the consumer goods which were also imported by the Indians were figs, dates, beverages, wines; were less in number in comparison of goods which were exported from India. Among the metals and mineral products, tin, lead, gold, silver, glass asphalt antimony, orpiment etc.,[74] were important. Some of the precious stones like Topaz, pearls, corals etc. were coming to India. The horses of Arabian countries were a favourite item of Indians. And sometimes the merchants of West Asian Countries presented horses to the Indian rulers.[75] Again India took the advantage of existing slave trade in western markets and imported the slaves into India in 1st C.A.D.[76]

The trade between India and West Asian countries created a very favourable condition for India because the trade was in favour of India. About this Pliny commented, "In one year" does India drain us no less than 550 million sesterces (22,000,000)"[77] Again he remarked, "at the lowest computation India, the Seres and the Arabian Peninsula with drew from our Empire 100 million sesterces every year, so dearly we pay for our luxury and our women."[78] This indicates that the Indo-West Asian trade was infavour of India and this view is further supported by the excavations of Roman coins at different places in hoards. The Roman people were paying a heavy price for Indian goods because the Arabs, Phoenicians, Syrian, Persians merchants were playing the role of intermediary and demanding a high price for Indian goods. Again, due to the lack of price control mechanism in Roman market just like Indian markets provided the Roman merchants a golden opportunity to satiate their parsimonious attitude.

Routes

According to Warmington, there were three main routes from Puteoli to the Middle East.[79] Robbers and pirates endangered the trade routes connecting India to West Asia on land. The sea route was equally dangerous due to stormy weathers, presence of pirates. Therefore, the caravan traders were taking the help of private army from guilds to protect their goods from external attacks. From pre-historic times, the great trade routes have connected India with the West. Among these routes, running form the mouth of Indus to Euphrates and at Euphrates the roads branch off to Antioch and Levantine ports.[80] There was the overland route from India passes to Balkh and from Balkh to the Caspian sea. And this route reaches at Antioch by way of Hekatompylos and Ktesiphone.

Finally there was a circuitous route, down the Persian and Arabian coasts to Aden up the Red Sea to Suez and from Suez to Egypt on the one hand and Tyre and Sidon on the other.[81] Except these main routes, there were many routes, which were followed by different traders in different times. The Roman merchants usually preferred the Red Sea route instead of land routes to India. Indian traders were following both the routes but the land routes were more favourable to them because Indian ships were not strong enough to stand against the bad weather of Sea. The caravan traders were taking all precautions before journey. Sometimes they take the help of Sthalniyamaka, to guide in the route, which had enough experience in this field. Again they were taking care of various things like the possibility of roads being ruined, water would become scarce, there would be no food and grass for bullock and availability of fresh vegetables.[82] The sea merchants were taking care of monsoon, the direction of winds, precautions against sea pirates, food, water etc. The direction finding birds were helping a lot to the merchants to find the direction.[83] Despite of so many difficulties, the traders braved all the hurdles in order to bring the closeness between the two sub continents. These traders in Ancient India were not only mercenary traders but also the ambassadors of Indian culture who were though working for their own profits, carrying the cultural ideas with them to distant lands. Crossing the geographical boundaries they helped the human society to come closer.[84]

Along the trade routes various trade centers grew which attracted the goods from nearby regions. Therefore it was easy for the traders to collect different goods, which were cheap at different points. Most of the important trade centers of India were, Barygaza, Ujjaini, Muziris, Soppara, Pataliputra, Kalyana, Poduca, Kaveripattanam, Tamralipti etc.[85] Most of these places were situated on the sea-shore because sea route was quite cheap for the traders. Vast coastline of India was a blessing in disguise for India's trade development. It may be one cause for the underdevelopment of transportation system on land routes. Because carts, chariots were the sole means of carrier of goods from Harappan times till the medieval period. During this period the boat making technology had changed a lot.

Cultural Development

The cultural connections developed during this period are clearly felt in different walks of life. Indian art and architecture is highly indebted to the western impact. Gandhara art is a glaring example of this. Art, architecture, sculpture, painting, all are more or less influenced by the western impact.[86] In the sphere of language, the similarity between, Brahmi and Kharosti clearly established a deep cultural interaction between these two sub continents.[87] The impact of Persian, Iranian and Assyrian people on Indian culture was largely felt during the Mauryan period. The Mauryan Royal palace, high ways, Ashokan pillars, cave architecture had felt the indelible impact of West Asian Culture. Indian coinage was largely influenced by the coinage of Roman system. India has equally influenced the astronomy, mathematics, philosophy etc. though cultural exchange was not on equal terms, India was much more influenced by the Western system.

As a profession, the trading and commercial activities were given due importance in ancient Indian society. It is a well accepted fact that economic pursuit in ancient India was associated with the Vaisya community. This class in mentioned as Gahapatis in Buddhist literature and as Gahavais in the Jaina canons.[88] The Vaisyas provided the economic support to elaborate structure of the society. As a class they amassed huge fortunes, acquired mostly in trade by sea and caravans. In Vedic times, this trading community was called as Panis.[89] The importance of trade can be realized from this that there was a special community to take care of the trade. This community was transferring the trade secrets to the future generation and they were keeping the secrets of the trade confined among them.

Various organizations, which grew up to smoothen the process of trade, among them the guild, was the most important organization which provided not only training to the workers but also social status to the workers of guild.[90] Probably, guilds were mainly responsible for the production of goods for the international markets because their style of production was quite innovative and a large number of people were employed to produce a huge quantity of goods for the market. Therefore, it may be presumed that the role of guilds in the growth of trade was immense. The guilds were acting as banking organizations also. They were providing loans for trade and were keeping the deposits of the people by paying interests. It was the duty of guild to determine the quality of goods and to fix the price of goods.[91] Usually the state authority did not interfere into the function of the guilds. Guilds played a predominant role in the trade activities by providing good quality of goods.

Geographical Knowledge

The trade relations between two sub-continents cann't be perceived thoroughly unless we don't have good geographical knowledge about the West Asian Empires in ancient period. The physical confirmation of West Asia is favourable to the growth of large Empires. The vast plain which extends from the foot of Niphates and Zagros to the Persian Gulf, the Red Sea, the Mediterranean, there are no natural fastness.[92] Similarly, only not quite to the same extent, in the upland region which succeeds to this plain upto the east and there is a deficiency of natural barriers. The upland and lowland powers are generally pretty, evenly balanced. In this geographical area, the Egyptian territory was bounded on the South and West by Nubian and Sahara deserts, on the East by Gulf of Suez and Red Sea.[93] The Persian Empire stretches in the north extending from lower Danube, North-East to the Black-Sea; thence North and East of the Caspian to the Central Asia.[94] The Assyria and Chaldean Empire was situated on a plateau bounded by the mountains on the north and east, desert on the west and Akkad on the South.[95] These Empires were always fighting among themselves in order to establish a vast Empire at the cost of others. In different times, the West Asian region had passed to the foreign hands like Alexander, Roman Empire. The Roman Empire had included the vast area of West Asia comprising modern Turkey, Iraq, Syria, Lebanon, Jordan and Israel.[96] Therefore in this work the Roman Empire is frequently mentioned because the main seat of Empire was West Asia.

To construct the maritime history is a difficult task for the historians. Very little definitive evidences is available to us to draw a picture of trade. Some of the foreign literary accounts like Pliny's Natural History, Strabo's Geography, Arrian's Indika and Periplus of Erythraian Sea throw much light on India's foreign trade. But the authenticity of these sources is questioned because most of the authors provide the information's from the secondary sources. Again the contradictory statements given by these authors create the hurdles for the historians to construct the concrete history. Indian sources also provide some information's about this. These sources are, Jataka stories, Buddhist, Jaina sources, Arthasastra, etc. which provide the information about the Indo-West Asian trade. These sources are not enough to draw the picture of India's foreign trade. A real progress has been achieved in this direction after the archaeological excavations of different places. These sources provide a good account of trade and numismatic sources which are also helpful in this context. Most of the items of India's foreign trade are perishable and this in the main difficulty to determine the origin of goods of export.

Reasons of this Trade

The vast geographical area of India was sufficient enough to cater the needs of the people, having fertile soil, rich forests and, rich flora and fauna. After all, the economic activities of ancient times were not solely determined not only by the economic structure but more significantly by cultural values.[97] The cultural values of India did not provide a fertile ground for the development of trade. The attitude of Brahminical tradition towards international trade was unfavorable because it was destroying the basic fabric of caste system by pollution of indigenous people coming in contact with foreigners, in their views.[98] Again the accumulation of wealth was criticized in different scriptures. These types of attitude inhibited the development of trade. In spite of so many obstacles, India's foreign trade flourished in a great extent.

The very basic reason for a well-documented trade relationship with West Asian countries are the surplus production of goods, which were badly needed by the people of West. Due to infertile lands of West Asia, they were always in need of food grains, which mainly compelled them to carry a direct trade with India.[99] The Indian mineral products, food products, forest products, were quite good in comparison with other products. Again the geographical continuity and political nexus activated this trade. The establishment of the Roman Empire and the increasing prosperity of the Roman nobility created a heavy demand for India's luxury goods and gave a further fillip to Indo-Roman trade connection in the early centuries of Christian era.[100] Rome enriched by the spoils and tributes from so many foreign lands and had acquired a taste for luxuries of every kind. The capital of the greatest Empire ever established in Europe was filled with the people who had inherited the great wealth and whose sole occupation was enjoyment of these riches. The retiring generals found their villas, dull, rustic and old fashioned made all the more unbearable because they had brought back with them masses of coinage, bullion and slaves. They had developed expensive tastes and they did so with feverish haste and great display. Common emulated the fashion determined by the elites.[101] This increased the demand for Indian luxurious goods in Roman markets to the highest level. The unprecedented demand of luxurious goods was beyond the reach of India and that's why

India sometimes exported the Chinese silk and other products to Rome.

Ancient Trade Mechanism

The trade during ancient times was totally different from the modern times. In modern times, the profit motive, division of labour, the market system and the transportation system are major determinants of trade and commerce. Though these forces were prevalent in ancient times, these were in rudimentary forms. Basically the trade in ancient times can be defined within the four walls of anthropological trade. According to author, Polanyi, man like other animals was presented by God as naturally self sufficient. But with the advancement of culture, men's needs grew in monstrous proportion, which led the people to depend on each other to fulfill the needs. And this gave way to trade.[102] According to Aristotle, "Trade is natural when it serves the survival of community by maintaining its self- sufficiency". Polanyi regarded the commercial trade as unnatural form of trade; natural was gainless, since it merely, maintained the self-sufficiency.[103] One may assume very clearly that replacing, the barter trade by money trade brought the profit motive forefront. Again trade appears as a two way movement of goods through markets and money as quantifiable goods used for indirect exchange in order to facilitate the movements. Here, market appears as the locus of exchange and money as the means of exchange. The market is generating the institutions of which trade and money are functions. The trade may be within the contiguous social units (i.e., internal trade) or between the groups across the cultural boundaries (external trade).

With the growth of agriculture, the rural economy gradually transformed. The surplus production gave rise to trade and commerce. Because the human needs are unlimited and he constantly searches the goods, which are beyond of his reach. The diversity in geographical distribution of wealth renders it necessary for man to obtain from distant areas, those commodities which are not produced within its locality. Thus the foreign trade, that is the trade between the geographically separated groups, has dominated practically all societies.

Again the trade usually starts when a producer has the capacity to produce more items than his immediate needs, the excess products are generally meant for transaction at the exchange center. Therefore, it is duty of a trader who establishes a link between the producer and a consumer. In he ancient Indian societies, the trade mechanism was basically operated through the forces like demand, supply and price fixes markets. This is a complex inter play of various forces including the state based polity and an administrative structure.[104] The prime mover of trade in a state society is the classical law of comparative advantage. For the advancement of economy, the specialization in crafts, productions, occupations and professions was necessary. As a person is unable to meet his own requirements in an advanced society, he/she depends upon other to cater his/her needs and this in the dragging force of national and international trade.

Thus the anthropologists, particularly economic anthropologists would try to situate trade in an overall human culture. Marxist ideas, which have immensely influenced the study of economic history, give priority to economic factors and forces as determinants of social forms. Some of the recent studies of many own-European and simplex societies point out the importance of social and cultural forms of economic development and growth. Persons, for example, considers social systems as having functional sub-systems: economics as perceived as an adaptive sub-system.[105]

In this context, the idea of Polanyi, the founder of substantivist school is more acceptable than the formalist school of economists. The substantivist position considers trade to be relatively peaceful method of acquiring goods, which are not locally available.[106] According to Polanyi, the market trade is to be associated with modern industrial capitalist economy. He discounts any possibility to market trade with supply, demand and price mechanisms in pre-capitalistic societies. The market, or open market is the price setting mechanism, which is of recent origin. Market trading requires large number of buyers and sellers and perfect competition, which is reached when distinct relations between prices, supply, demand and transactions are worked out. Substantivists think that market is different to a market place. Therefore, they precisely designate the trade in early societies as market less trade though there were market places.

With the passage of time, the facets of trade and commerce changed and it was transformed from a simple business to a complex business. Here some efforts are made to present the determinants of ancient trade which are totally different from modern trade and commerce.

Review of Literature

Primary Sources: Among the early literature primarily included *The Periplus of the Erythrean Sea* an anonymous mariner's account of early maritime trade with the Indian subcontinent. It finds out the routes of trade and gives a detailed picture of Indian ports. Both the *Periplus* and the *Natural History* of Pliny contain useful references between India and West. They provide an elaborate account of the advantages and disadvantages of the ports along the coasts of the sub continent; the mechanism of exchange between traders from India and the West; and the provenance of goods transported to the ports for export. Pliny is more useful for information on the uses of commodities imported into Rome and their comparative prices in the market. The colossal Geography of Strabo written about A.D. 19 contained exhaustive and accurate information primarily about Egypt and is of much less value for the Indian sub-continent. Strabo has based his account of India on earlier writers like Megasthenes and Nearchus and deals with diverse subjects like customs, division of castes and Alexander's campaign.

The *Guide to Geography* by Claudius Ptolemy, written in the middle of second century A.D., has very little narrative. It contains a series of tables of names and places followed by figures giving latitude and longitudes. These are of little use to us as they are based on a distorted map of India, which makes the west coast turn around a little below Bombay and run eastward, practically eliminating the peninsular region. Again a soldier physician who wrote his *Materia Medica* around 65 A.D. provides considerable information on spices used in pharmacology.

Secondary Sources: The monographs, which considerably influenced early studies, were those of G. Rawlinson, *Intercourse between India and Western World from the earliest times to the fall of Rome*, R.E.M. Wheeler, *Rome beyond the Imperial Frontiers* and M.P. Charlesworth, *Roman Trade with India: A Resurvey*. The Objective of all these works remained same -- to provide justification for the commercial enterprise of European nations in general scanty evidences and biases prevented these works to unravel the truth. But E.H. Warmington's work, *"The Commerce between the Roman Empire and India"* traces out the relations of India and West from Indus Valley up to Sixth century AD. Just like others he also gave support to the Western exploitation of Indian resources in particular. As Warmington put it: "The West: the little changing people of the East allowed the West to find them out. We have then, on the one side of the Orient, then as now, a disjointed aggregate of countries but without the uniting force of British rule which she now has and while open to commerce, contented generally to remain within her borders and to engage in agriculture." He outlined that the trade between India and West was basically indirect which gave a boost to Indian handicraft industries. Again he pointed out about the barter system, which creates the controversies, but the possibilities can't be over looked. His indications are the collapse of trade led the political and economic disintegration of the Empire. It is very difficult to accept because it may be one factor amongst the various factors responsible for the down fall of the Empire.

But G.F. Hourani's book, *"Arab seafaring in the Indian Ocean in Ancient and Early Medieval Times"* only gives an overview of trade with scanty evidences. He has made little use of known facts of commercial intercourse between different countries.

On the basis of ceramic evidences and excavations at Arikamedu, Wheeler in *Rome beyond the Imperial Frontiers* pointed out that the Rouletted ware was new to South India. On the basis of this, it is determined that Rouletted ware was imported from Mediterranean region and Arikamedu was a Roman settlement super imposed on a purely native and local culture.

Amongst the various books published recently J.I. Miler approached the subject differently. He started by listing spices described in classical literature and used not only as condiments in food but as ingredients in ointments, drugs as preservative and as incense. In his book, "The Spice Trade of the Roman Empire", he has identified the botanical names of the plants and demarcation of the natural habitat of the plant leading to the demarcation of fortunes not only to Indian Subcontinent but also to South East Asia and China. It has been suggested that the Indians from Konkan coast, in their own ships sailed for ports at the mouth of the Red Sea, while Southern Arabians were the carriers from Malabar and possibly also from Sri Lanka and the Greeks were the caries from India to Egypt.

Bernadi in his book *"The Economic problems of the Roman Empire at the time of Decline"* exploded the myth, which was often quoted by Pliny regarding the drain of wealth, and it became the sole cause of downfall. He pointed out that the decline was an internal process though drain of money contributed a lot in this matter but was not solely responsible.

Prakash Chandra Prasad in *Foreign Trade and Commerce in India* tried to bring out the importance of foreign trade in Ancient India and the place it occupied in the economic development of human Civilization from 3rd Millennium B.C. to 1st century A. It also provides an overview without making a deeper analysis.

In this book, *"Trade and Trade Route in Ancient India"* by Moti Chandra deals with the problems related to ancient Indian merchants, their trade and trade regulations. He established a very intimate relationship between trade and politics and tried to elucidate contemporary political conditions in different periods of Indian history. His use of precious material facts and methodology for discovering the new facts, create the new edifice of Indian history and culture.

The book, *"Ancient India: A study of cultural contacts"* by Nalinee M. Chapekar, emphasizes cultural contacts from very ancient times of Rig Veda period. In his views, Iranians are perhaps the only people who primarily maintained the relations with Indians before their coming to India. India in the beginning developed political contacts with Greece, commerce with Rome and cultural contacts with Iran. He traced out the impacts of Iranians on every walk of Indian people.

Seeley and Turner have brought another interesting thing to light in their article "Metallurgic investigations of three early Indian coinages" that the isotope ratios of coins of Kura Kings of Deccan were closely matching with Sardinian and Spanish lead sources exploited by Romans. Also the silver coins of Nahapana show a striking similarity with the pre-Nero-Silver issues not only in their fitness but also in the lead and gold content.

P.J. Turner's, *"The Development of trade between the Roman Empire* and the *East under Augusts"* outlined that initially the silver coins were preferred more for the eastern trade. But the introduction of gold coins got an edge over silver coins. There was distinct shortage of gold from the period of Nero's reforms of the currencies to Trajan's time.

The spurt of trade bore resemblances with many Indian goods including Roman lamps as pointed by Himansu Prabha Ray in *Monastery and Guild under Satavahanas*. Again she pointed out that due to the trade, the territories of South India not only flourished economically but the traders also contributed richly to Buddhist Sanghas. The term yavanas, which was referred for Greeks by Buddhist Sanghas in the later phase, included all foreign traders who made rich donations to the Buddhist Sanghas.

Vimla Beghley's book *"The Ancient Port of Arikamedu-New Excavation and Researches* is basically based on excavation at Arikamedu between 1989-92. According to her, the trade with the

Mediterranean basin seems to have been at its height between 50 B.C. and 50 A.D. She believed that the ancient settlement at Arikamedu was continued and towards the end of the 2nd Century A.D. (or slightly later) the site was abandoned. But she also suggests that some commerce with Mediterranean World continued till 7th Century A.D. by South Indian rulers like Cholas and others. She has gone through he detailed findings of Arikamedu and has given some new perceptions about the glorious Indo-Roman trade.

Rome and India the Ancient Sea Trade presents new evidences about the dating, provenance and distribution of classical imports to India that such as terra-sigillara, amphoras, glass and bronzes, which indicate that, previously held assumption about the trade must be revised. Further the detailed analyses of pottery presented, here suggest that the trade network along the eastern coast of peninsular India and Sri Lanka was more widespread than previously suspected. Questions related to routes and navigation from Red Sea to the Western Coast of Peninsular India are critically examined through the various sources from primary text to textual and archaeological sources by Vimla Begley and Richard Daniel De. Puma. Tradition and Archaeology – Early Martime Contacts in the Indian Ocean by Himanshu Prabha Ray and Jean Franco's Sales concentrate on two broad themes covering archaeological evidence of maritime links and technological studies of watercraft involved in trade and communication. The inter-disciplinary dialogues provide new insight on early sea faring in the Indian Ocean and questions to several existing theories that have continued to be repeated in archaeological and historical writings. She pointed out, "Trade didn't cease with decline of Empire: instead there were relocations in routes and changes in the participant involved."

R. Champaklakshmi in Trade, Ideology and Urbanisation in South India 1300 BC to 1300 AD focuses on two major periods of urbanisation in South India – the early historical period and the early medieval period prior to the rise of Vijaynagar Empire. The author, R. Champaklakshmi discusses urbanism not merely in terms of economy and demography but also a function of Chola imperialism and Bhakti ideology. Again she pointed out that early urbanism was not the result of forces of an inner growth but was of a secondary generation induced by inter regional trade and maritime trade between South India and the Mediterranean West.

The book of Himanshu Prabha Ray, *Archaeology of Sea-Faring: The Indian Ocean in the Ancient Period* attempts to compile recent archaeological research on sea faring instead of chronological narratives of maritime contacts. Her attention has been centred on material remains as indicators of contacts rather than on the communities themselves, especially the coastal communities settled along the Indian Ocean littoral. She has referred the maritime trade in Indian Ocean with glimpses without making a thorough analysis.

In comparison to these works, my research work is quite innovative. Some of the old books like purples of Erythran Sea, National History, guide to Geography were mainly dependent on secondary sources whose artificially is sometimes questioned. Again they did not have good idea about the geographical position of India. The books of H.G. Rawlinson, R.E.M. Wheeler, M.P. Charles worth provide scanty evidences and biases prevented, this authors to present the fact. They basically derive the facts from numismatic sources; foreign accounts neglecting the archaeological anthropological and paleo botanical sources. In this connection the works of Himanshu Prabha Roy, Vimala Vegley, R. Champaklakshmi are quite praise worthy. They have made an effort to present the facts with the help of archaeological sources. But they also neglect the paleo-botanical and anthropological data. In this work, the paleo-botanical, anthropological and archaeological facts were presented with due importance. Again these earlier works mainly concentrate on Roman Empire putting negligible importance on West Asia traders' role in this trade. But the present work mainly concentrate on West Asia traders and their rule. An economic transaction or trade relation can't be viewed singularly without weighing its impacts on social and cultural organizations. While earlier works have failed to present a holistic picture but here an effort is made to present these things with special importance.

Methodology

As history is concerned with the recreation of his significant features of the past with the help of numerous fragmentary evidences usually called the sources. In the writing of history, the primary sources always play predominant role to prepare the base and synthesise the facts. Therefore priority is given to collect to every kind of primary sources varying from inscriptions, numismatic sources, textual evidences and foreign accounts etc. Archaeological data is the main stay of the work. Some of the recent excavations of Myos Harmas, Leukas Limen, Berenice, Leuke Kome in the Gulf and Arikanedu, Kohlapur, Arikamedu, Paithain etc. throw more light on this topic. Again emphasis is given on the use of archaeological materials including field archaeological evidence, epigraphic, numismatic and art historical sources -- the latter ones throwing lights on material culture. Anthropological data is given priority to appreciate the possibilities of exchange among relatively simpler societies.

Among secondary sources the books and journals are important. Old as well as new edition books dealing with Ancient India's trade will be the main source. Libraries of Indian Archaeological Survey of India, Achieves of India, National Museum and ICHR provide a large number of books relating to this. I have made a sincere effort in this direction of collect and collate all the informations regarding the research. Again the museums like National Museum Calcutta Museum, Pondicherry Museum provided a lot of information and broaden the knowledge on this topic.

The journals like Art and Letters, Antiquity, American Journal of Archaeology, Journal of Economic and Social History of the Orient, Journal of Royal Asiatic Society, Calcutta are the backbone of research. The articles of these journals not only provide good data but also present the new methodology adopted to derive the conclusion. Some of the excavation reports available in those journals are valuable source for the work. Every effort has been made to collect and collate all the latest information in this topics work.

Finally the help of different professors and researchers, who are dealing with trade related matters, is taken into account. The authors usually commit mistakes like biasness in the interpretation of history. Best efforts are made in this direction to keep these mistakes at abeyance.

This topic is chosen for research because trade and commerce is an emerging area of research. The trade and commerce between two lands not only bring economic prosperity but also cultural prosperity by establishing a cultural proximity among the people. In this work, in addition with economic exchange the cultural exchange are given priority. If the Indians are considered as the successors of the Iranian people who has migrated during the Vedic phase and established the Indian culture, then it evokes a sense of interest to know about the relations of these people with Indians after segregation. Again it is obvious that when the two civilisations like Mesopotamia and Indus Valley sprang up in the same Asiatic soil, there must be some relations among these people and it is the bounden duty of historians to explore the facts and to present in a picturesque manner. Considering of as a challenge to historians, an attempt is made in this regard to broader the sphere of knowledge of general people and to bring the curiosity abysmally low. The historians pay West Asia as an area of research in Ancient period toward attention. Most of the works relating to trade and commerce in ancient India concentrate on Roman Empire, and South-East Asia, which was the focal point of attraction of ancient traders. The authors of Indo-Roman trade sometimes highlight the trade with West Asia with a negligible importance and most of the works are done on the basis of foreign accounts where the archaeological, anthropological, epigraphic data are least used. Therefore, taking all these facts into account an innovative effort has been made in this direction with all latest available data to examine this area from a new angle of view.

Some of the historians label the period between the Rig Vedic Age and the rise of Mauryan Empire as 'Dark ages' in history. The Indian people were dubbed as isolated people and living in their world with a frog mentality. In this connection the pronouncement of V.A. Smith that the Macedonian invasion was the sheet anchor of Indian history emerged as the outcome of impact of the West.[107] This Macedonian invasion was regarded as the boon in disguise by breaking the shackles of isolation of India and opened the ways in brisk contacts, commercial and cultural contacts of the Sub continent with West.[108] This logic of colonial historians to justify and validate the colonial role for the advancement and betterment of Indians is understandable in some extent. But the validity and authenticity of the statement is challenged on the ground that India was nevertheless isolated. Its contact with West Asian countries can be traced from Indus valley period and prior to this.[109] But colonial historians have turned a blind eye or underscored this fact in order to substantiate their point of contention. The invasion of Alexander and Cyrus brought India into the vision of Western people. But this theory has been challenged here and it has been proved that this theory does not contain much water. This was a misconception of some historians who had committed it without making a threadbare discussion of every fact. The trade and commerce with West Asian people had been continued from Indus Valley civilisation with many ups and downs till the third century A.D. and touched the lowest ebb in this period. But this trade again revived in 11th century A.D. and continued smoothly.

The basic aims and objectives of this work are to understand the different stages through which the commercial relations between the Indian sub continent and West Asia developed and declined. Again an attempt has been made to classify different types of primary source materials such as archaeological report, textual evidence, epigraphy and numismatic etc and to collate information bearing upon the theme. In this context it is also essential to understand the pattern of change is commercial relations by analyzing the movements of different items, which entered commercial exchange, and by studying their origins, procurements and relative values etc. It is also important to understand the social organization of commerce by studying, as far as possible, the composition of people involved in trade and interactions between different groups. The trade between India and West Asia was carried by different group of merchants and how they were competing among themselves to garner more profits is also discussed. Again the impact of trade on economy polity, society and culture is attempted to study.

End Notes

---

[1] Majumdar, R.C., *A comprehensive History of India*, Vol. III, Part – II, p. 1361.

[2] Mathew, K.S., *Mariner, Merchants and Oceans: Studies in Maritime History*, pp. 1-4.

[3] Budget Allechin and F.R. Allchin, *The rise of civilization in India and Pakistan*,

[4] Ranabir, Cahkrabarti, *Traders Early India*, Oxford, 2001, p.10.

[5] Chandra, Prakash, *Foreign Trade and Commerce in Ancient India*, pp 15-17.

[6] Ratngar, Shereen, *Trading contacts between India and Western Asia in Second Millennia B.C.* (Thesis), pp. 6-19.

[7] Mukherjee, R.K., *History of Indian Shipping*, pp. 58-63.

[8] Mackay,E.J.H., *'The Indus civilization' PI. M.* 16, 11

[9] Ibid.

[10] Ray, H.P., Himanshu Prabha, *The winds of Change: Buddhism and early maritime contacts with South East Asia*, pp. 1-8.

[11] *Museum Journal University of Penn*, 1929, 3, 4. pp. 305-6.

[12] Mackay,E.J.H., *Further excavation at Mohenjodaro,* Vol. I, p.327.

[13] Marshall, J., *Mohenjodaro and Indus civilization*, pp. 347.

[14] Gadd, C.J., *Seals of Ancient Indian style found at Ur*, pp. 28-56.

[15] Vats, *Excavations at Harappa*, p. 59.

[16] *Ancient Egypt*, 1917, p. 29.

[17] Vats, *Excavations at Harappa*, p. 59.

[18] Mackay, E.J.H.,*The Indus civilization*, p. 1-2.

[19] Lamborg ,Karlovsky, C.C., and Joshi, M., "Shahr-i-Shokta and Tepe Yahya: Tracks on Early History of the Iranian Plateau", *E.W.*, 23, pp. 21-57.

[20] King, L.W., *History of Babylone*, p. 235.

[21] Marshall, J., *Mohenjodaro and Indus civilization*, pp. 45-68.

[22] Ibid, Vol. II, p. 588.

[23] Ratnagar, Shereen, *op. cit.*, p. 385.

[24] Ibid.

[25] Chandra, Prakash, *Foreign Trade and Commerce in India*, p. 20.

[26] Goetz, H., *Arts of the World*, p. 27.

[27] Childe,,*New light on the most Ancient East*, p. 170.

[28] Ratnagar, Shereen, *op. cit.*, p. 384.

[29] Ibid.

[30] Mc. Pharson, Kenneth, *The Indian Ocean*, pp. 21-32.

[31] Ratnagar Shereen- *Understanding Harappan civilization in the Greater Indus Valley*, p.53.

[32] Ibid p.53

[33] Ibid p.54

[34] Chakrabarti, Ranabir, *Trade in Early India*, p.110

[35] Ibid p.110

[36] *Rig Veda*, III, p. 183.

[37] Chandra, Prakash, *Foreign Trade and Commerce in Ancient India*, p. 20.

[38] *Atharva Veda*, III, 15, 7.

[39] Chandra, Prakash, *op. cit.*, p. 21.

[40] Wheeler, M., *The Indus civilization*, p. 8.

[41] Gordon, H., *The pre-Historic background of Indian culture*, pp. 35-55.

[42] Stuart, Piggot, *Pre-Historic India*, p. 153.

[43] Ranabir, Chakrabarti, *Trade in Early India*, Oxford, 2001, p.43.

[44] *Rig Veda*, IV, 50, quoted from Ranbir Chakrabarti, *Trade in Early India*, p.43.

[45] Rawlinson, H.G., *The Commercial Intercourse between India and the Western World*, p. 2.

[46] These names were discovered by Prof Hugo Winckler on a cuneiform tablet at the Hittite capital of Boghazkoi, in 1907.

[47] *Cambridge History of India*, No. I, pp. 72-6.

[48] Sayee, *Hibbert Lectures*, 1887, p. 138 and Max & Muller, *PhysicalReligion ,p.25.*

[49] Rawlinson, H.G., *op. cit.*, pp. 1-4.

[50] Herodotus- III, p. 106.

[51] Watt, C. *Commercial Products of India*, p. 67.

[52] Rawlinson, H.G., *Intercourse between India and Western World*, p. 34.

[53] Chandra, Prakash, *Foreign Trade and Commerce in India*, pp. 26-30.

[54] Arrian, *Expedition of Alexander*, VI, 5, pp. 2-9.

[55] Bevan, *Cambridge History of India*, p. 345.

[56] Ashana, Shashi, *History and archaeology of Indian contacts with other countries*, pp. 154-168.

[57] Mukherjee, Radha Kumud, *History of Indian Shipping*, pp. 70-81.

[58] Ibid.

[59] Samasastry, *Arthasastra* (Kautilya), II, 16, pp. 30-32.

[60] Rawlinson, H.G., *Intercourse between India and Western World*, p. 39.

[61] Chandra, Prakash, *Foreign Trade and Commerce in India*, pp. 28-34.

[62] Ibid.

[63] Ray, H.P. *The winds of change: Buddhism and Maritime links of Early South Asia*, pp. 51-53.

[64] Saletore, B.A. *India's Diplomatic Relations with Other Countries*, pp. 45-73.

[65] Bunbury, E.H. A history of ancient geography among the Greeks and Romans from the earliest ages to the fall of Roman empire pp 48-51.

[66] Warmington, E.H., *The commerce between the Roman Empire and India*, p. 58.

[67] Saletore, R.N., *Early Indian Economics*, pp. 341-362.

[68] Chakraborty, Haripada, *Trade and Commerce in Ancient India*, pp. 32-46.

[69] Ray, H.P., *The Winds of Change*, pp.79-83

[70] Saletore, R.N., *Early Indian Economies*, p.197,

[71] Rawlinsan, H.G., *op.cit*, pp.86-92

[72] Warmington, E.H., *op.cit*, pp.268-272.

[73] Saletore, R.N., *Early Indian Economics*, p.129.

[74] Chakraborty, Haripada, *Trade and Commerce in Ancient India*, pp. 285-291.

[75] Saletore, R. N., *op.cit.*, p. 179.

[76] Tarn,W.W., *Greeks and Bacrtians in India*, pp. 355-360.

[77] Saletore, R. N. *op. cit.*, p. 272.

[78] Pliny, *Natural History*, IV, BK-VII, 41(18) p. 197.
[79] Warmington, E.H., *The Commerce between the Roman Empire and India*, p. 5.
[80] Rawlinson, H.G., *Intercourse between India and Western World*, p. 1.
[81] Ibid.
[82] Das, Deepak Ranjan; *Economic History of Deccan*. P. 236.
[83] Chandra, Moti, *Trade and Trade Routes in Ancient India*, p. 62.
[84] Ibid, p. 60.
[85] Singh, Ajay, Kumar, *Indo-Roman Trade*, pp. 30-42.
[86] Asthana, Sashi, *History and Archeology of India's Contact with other Countries*, pp. 170-186.
[87] Rawlinson, H.G.,"Foreign Influence in the Civilization of Ancient India" *Journal of Bombay Branch Royal Asiatic Society*, vol. 23, p. 227.
[88] Chandra, Prakash, *Foreign Trade and Commerce in Ancient India*. P. 11.
[89] Ibid, p. 12.
[90] Coomarswamy, A. K., *Indian Craftsman*, p. 59.
[91] Nigam, Shyamshundar, *The Economic Organization of Ancient India*, pp. 130-148.
[92] Rawlinson,H.G., *Manual of Ancient History*, p. 23.
[93] Upadhyaya, B.C., *The Ancient World*, pp. 24-32.
[94] Sykes, P., *History of Persia*, p. 119.
[95] Rawlinson,H.G., *op. cit.*, p. 25.
[96] Ray, Himansu Prabha, (ed.) *Archaeology of Sea-faring*, p. 5.
[97] Ray, H.P., *The winds of change: Buddhism and the Early Maritime Links of Early South East Asia*, 1994, p. 1.
[98] Ibid, p. 2.
[99] *History of Mankind, Cultural & Scientific Development* Vol. I II, 1956, pp. 36-42.
[100] Smith and Moorehead, *A Short History of Ancient World*, pp. 56-69.
[101] Paul, Louis, *Ancient Rome at Work*, pp. 236-239.
[102] Polanyi, K.C.M., Arensberg and H.W. Pearson (ed.) *Trade and Market in the Early Empires*, pp. 250-257.
[103] Ibid. 15.
[104] Chakrabarti, Ranbir, *Trade in early India*, p. 13.
[105] Ibid. 15.
[106] Polyani, K., C.M. Arensberg and H.W. Pearsons (ed.) *Trade and market in the early empires*, pp. 56-67.

[107] V.A. Smith, *Early History of India*, quoted from Ranabir Chakrabarti, *Trade in Early India*, p.5.

[108] Chakrabarti, Ranabir, *Trade in Early India*, p.6.

[109] Ibid, p.10.

2

Trade during the Pre-Mauryan Period

Introduction

The trade between India and West Asia was continuing from the time of Indus Valley and prior to this also. From the time of Rig-Vedic period, the trade between two civilizations continued to increase slowly. If Aryans are accepted as the original inhabitants of Europe, then the Iranians and Aryans are two branches of the tree. Due to the geographical separation, the trade relation was hampered to a certain extent but the cultural continuity was maintained. But the trade enlivened these relations with passage of time. Trade relations between the two lands are not measured with exchange of goods only. The cultural transformation is a by-product of this relation. So knowingly or unknowingly the cultural migration took place through these trade relations and made the culture of India mosaic.

The invasion of Cyrus, Darius and Alexander gave a new turn to the continued relations. They not only controlled some parts of India but also broke the isolation of India. Indians learned the system of administration and it further created a fertile ground for the growth of trade. The journey of Skylax and Nearchus opened the new routes of trade. In this way the trade and cultural relations increased further.

The period between Rig-Vedic Age and the rise of Muaryan Empire was labeled as "Dark Age"[1] in the Indian history mainly because of lack of sufficient materials to reconstruct its course.[2] The meagre-archaeological evidences available in foreign lands, especially in Western Asia, points to the limited amount of commercial and cultural intercourse between India and western neighbours.[3] From Sixth century B.C. onwards, we reach on firmer grounds as far as socio-economic-political history of India. [4] The foreign invasion like Cyrus, Darius and Alexander brought more proximity. The political relations gave a boost to trade and cultural relations. Especially the invasion of Alexander was well documented in the world history. It was a turning point of Indian history. He was accompanied by a number of Greek historians and their writings provide valuable data to reconstruct the trade relations between India and the West. Among the Indian sources the Jataka stories provide most indirect references about India's knowledge about foreign lands and India's relations with other countries with Egypt and Mesopotamia.[5] The archaeological sources also supplement these facts with more proofs and authenticity.[6]

On the basis of available evidence, the historians fail to draw a clear picture of this trade. Again to present the commercial data of individual regions is undoubtedly a difficult task. But it is my sincere effort to collect the every possible evidence to present a full picture of trade as well as cultural relations.

In the sphere of religion, culture and other spheres like astronomy, language, and the perceptible changes were brought about by the contacts with West Asia. Again the trade with West Asia brought the prosperity and wealth to India. Indian goods were highly praised in the West while Indian demands for their goods were quite less. This led the trade to create a favourable situation for India. Therefore, India was known as the queen of Eastern Sea.

Location of West Asian Empires

The physical conformation of Western Asia is favourable to the growth of large empires. The vast plain which extends from the foot of Niphates and Zagros to the Persian Gulf, the Red Sea and the Mediterranean, there is no natural fastness; and the race, which was numerically or physically superior to the other races inhabiting it readily, acquires dominion over the entire region. Similarly, quite to the same extent, in the upland region, which succeeds to this plain upon the east, there is a deficiency of natural barriers and the nation, which once begins to excel its neighbours, rapidly extends its influence over a wide stretch of territory. The upland and lowland powers are generally evenly balanced and maintain a struggle in which either side gives way; but occasionally the equality becomes deranged. Circumstances give to one or to the other an additional strength; and the result is, that its rival is overpowered. Then an empire of still greater extent is formed, both upland and lowland falling under the sway of the same people.[7]

Ancient Egypt

Hecatacus, the ancient Greek geographer, rightly called Egypt as "The gift of Nile". The river rises in the vicinity of the Great Lakes of Equatorial Africa and flows about 4000 miles in a northerly direction for over 1600 miles without a tributary. Every year, in the beginning of June the water rose from twenty to forty feet. The stream overflows channels and inundates the surrounding countryside for an average width of thirty miles. After the middle of the October, the flood rapidly subsides and leaves a heavy deposit of rich alluvial soil. Silt precipitated at the river's mouths, has resulted in the formation of a greater delta, through which the river has cut a number of channels to the sea. Thus the Nile has wrested a long narrow strip of arable land from the surrounding desert; this fertile region, aggregating approximately 10,000 square miles in area was the land of Pharaohs.[8]

Another geographical consideration, which has been over emphasised perhaps, was the relative isolation of Egypt in Ancient times. Bounded on the South and West by Nubian and Sahara deserts on the East by Gulf of Suez and the Red Sea, the country was joined to Asia on the northeast by the Isthmus of Suez and the peninsula of Sinai. This was vulnerable point; Hyksos, Assyrians and Persians came into the land by this route and subjugated it. Yet only well organised and disciplined powers could attack Egypt successfully. She was sufficiently isolated to preclude conquest by incursion of barbarian nomads. Proximity to Asia in the northeast facilitated the commercial contacts with opportunities for cultural infiltration.[9]

During 6th century B.C., Egypt had become the part of Assyrian and Persian Empire. Only after the temporary renaissance of Nineteenth Dynasty, the decline of Egypt proceeded more rapidly than ever. The foreign possessions were intrievably lost; civil war was frequent until virtual chaos ensued. In this weakened condition, Assyrians and Persians occupied the land of Egypt and swayed their hegemony. But the heavy march of Alexander the Great compelled Egypt to remain under his control. With the division of Alexander's empire, Ptolemy (323-283 B.C.) seized the control of Egypt, his dynasty endured until the defeat of Antony and Cleopatra in 31 B.C. with the end of the Ptolemiac Kingdom. Egypt became a subject of Rome.[10]

Persian Empire

A number of people, who were called Semites, were living on the edges of the Arabian Desert from the beginning. Corresponding with the grasslands of the "Fertile Crescent" there are vast stretches in the north extending from lower Danube, North-east to the Black sea; then North and east of the Caspian, into Central Asia. Great extremes of temperature prevailed, with the result that agriculture was almost precluded. The nomadic populace from time immemorial had wrested a livelihood from the pasturage of extensive herds of cattle, following the grassy lands, north in summer and south in winter. Shortly after the introduction of copper, nomads in the steppes of east of the Caspian began a great westward migration either because of Mongolian pressure from the east or failure of grazing facilities. During the course of migration, some ultimately pushed southward and occupied the Iranian plateau on the east border of "Fertile Crescent". This group was formed primarily of the peoples who became known as the Medes and Persians.[11]

The Medes were the first to come into contact with the peoples of the "Fertile Crescent". A great trade route from Mesopotamia to the Iranian plateau ran through heart of the region and contributed powerfully to the economic and cultural advance.[12] Proximity to Assyria naturally retarded the rise of political power of Media while the Medes were playing a great role in the affairs of "Fertile Crescent". The Kingdom of Persia was a vassal state of Media, southeast of Tigris and Euphrates Valley. The Persians had penetrated Elam and the surrounding territory; their migration probably was a direct result of the establishment of the Media Kingdom.[13] Under Teispes, the ruler of Anshan, material progress was made towards the unification of tribes. When Cyrus, the grandson of Teispes, became the King in 558 B.C., the Persians had been welded into a compact monarchy under the suzerainty of Anshan, although it was not until eight years later that he assumed the title of "King of Persia".[14]

Cyrus (558 B.C.-529 B.C.)

The rise of Cyrus created a new history of Persia in the Middle East. Earlier to this, these areas were dominated by Assyrian empire. So the fall of Assyrian empire gave the birth of Persian Empire in 6th century BC whose first and foremost ruler was Cyrus. He (Cyrus) extended his empire up to the Mediterranean and brought under her yokes the Asiatic Greeks and Phoenicians. But Greeks checked his further westward expansion. At that time there was a constant struggle among the powers like Etruscan, Carthaginian and the Greek.

In the modem western usage the term Persia is applied to the whole Iranian plateau stretching from the Caspian in the West to the Hindu Kush in the east and from the Persian Gulf in the South of Steppes of Turkestan, the region of Oxus and the Yaxartes in the North.[15]

Cyrus was the fourth king of the line of hereditary succession of Anshan. For the first time, he brought the various tribes under one umbrella. He at first became the King of Persia and then the King of Babylon. Three different titles used by the King Cyrus were - the King of Anshan, the King of Persia and the King of Babylon. He started to rule over Persia from 538 B.C. He attacked Astyages (550-49 B.C). He won over the area and finally married the princess of the ruler. Then he preceded the Median capital Ecbatana and conquered it. Then he overthrew the ruler of Lydia

(546 B.C.) who had occupied the west of Asia Minor. The Medians had occupied the east of Asia Minor. Then he proceeded and captured Babylon, which gave Cyrus a claim to the countries of the West to Phoenicia and Syria down to the borders of Egypt.[16]

Cambyses (529 B.C. - 522 B.C.)

During the reign of Cambyses, Persian rule over Egypt came to an end due to revolt. It took much time to Darius, to bring under control again. The history Cambyses is mainly based on the information provided by Herodotus and Greek sources.[17]

Darius (521 B.C. - 486 B.C.)

After Cambyses, Darius, a member of the Cadet branch of the Achaemenid house and a devoted adherent of Zoroastrianism, captured the throne. In the early part of reign he tried to put an end to the Scythian and Cimmerian by making an expedition across the Bosphorous and Thrace to the Danube. His empire comprised the area from Egypt and Aegean Sea to the banks of Indus and Jaxartes and from Persian Gulf to the Black Sea and Caspian. In 492B.C., he extended his occupation of Thrace and Macedonia and in 490B.C., after destroying Samos and receiving the submission of Cyclades, the Persian forces burned Eritrea and landed in the Bay of Marthathon, north of Athens.[18] But Athens, without the help of Spartans, succeeded in defeating the Persians and subsequently prevented the fleet from landing off Athens.

In 486B.C., Egypt revolted against excessive tribute and Darius was unable to check the revolt. Then his son Xerexes succeeded him.

Xerexes (486 B.C. - 479 B.C.)

After accession to the throne, he put down the revolt of Egypt and another in Babylonia and completed his father's preparations in the West. In the spring of 480 B.C., he made victorious march towards Thermopylae and invaded Africa. But then he suffered three continuous defeats, first on sea at Salamies, then on land at

Plateau in 479B.C. and thirdly in another sea battle at Mycale on the Asiatic coast.[19]

Artaxerexes-I (479 B.C. - 424 B.C.)

He immediately put down the Bactrian revolt supported by his brother and then he had to contend with Inaros of Egypt, who attempted, with Athenian aid, to liberate the country from Persian domination. The war lasted for 6 years and ended with reconquest of Egypt by Persia and the conclusion of treaty with Athens. The latter fixed the harbour of Phaselis as the limit for operations by the Greek and Persian fleets, on the West and East respective.[20]

Darius - II (423 B.C. - 404 B.C.)

He faced many revolts by satraps, the most serious being that of Pissuthenes in Lybia in 414B.C.. The king wanted two Greek coalitions, headed by Athens and Sparta, to wear one another out. But his satraps favoured first one city then the other and finally one placed under his son Cyrus the Younger. Meanwhile Egypt regained its liberty and kept it for sixty years.[21]

Artaxerexes - II (404 B.C. - 358 B.C.)

He started open rivalry with his brother Cyrus the Younger who fell at Cunaxa in 401 after waging a war on the king. He was then engaged in war with Spartax in Asia Minor from 401 B.C. to 394B.C. In this war, Sparta navy was destroyed at Cnidus and in the Corinthian war, which followed a Greek coalition, was organised against Sparta, permitting the revival of Athens under the leadership of Conon. But this did not prevent Spartans from achieving a revised political settlement under which they recognized Persian domination of Greek cities of Asia but secured Persian support for Spartan hegemony in Greece (386 B.C.).[22]

Artaxerexes - III (358 B.C. - 338 B.C.)

He ruthlessly suppressed the rebellions in the empire with the aid of Greek mercenaries. But his harsh treatment to the Asiatic Greeks began to attract the attention of Phillip - II of Macedonian whose expedition in 336 B.C. was designed to help them. The expedition ended in the same year when Phillip was assassinated, but a few months later Artaxerxes too was murdered and after a brief reign by his younger son Arses (who was quickly eliminated) the throne was passed to Darius - III.[23]

Darius -III (338B.C. - 330 B.C.)

Alexander the Great at Issus and Gaugamela defeated him, after the fall of Persepolis. He fled to the eastern Satrapies, where in 330 B.C. Bessus put him to death, satrap of Bacteria. His murder usurped the Persian throne under the name of Artaxerxes - IV, but Alexander, who entered Bacteria after his occupation of Hyrcania and Drangiana, brought him to book. The conqueror then took Sagdiana on his way to India (327 B.C.). By now all Persian possessions had passed to the Macedonian; he took over the rights of sovereignty and used the seals of the Kings he had put down.[24]

Assyria and Chaldea

Assur was located in on the northeast corner of the 'Fertile Crescent' on the east bank of the Tigris. It was on a plateau, bounded by mountains on the north and east, desert on the west and Akkad on the south. The position of the city on the Tigris was midway between the upper and lower Zab; both rivers facilitated expansion to the east. Little more than one hundred miles to the west, was the valley of Khabur, control of which subsequently proved vital to the economic interests. Powerful neighbours surrounded Assur. To the south, there was Kassites, who after 1800 B.C. conquered Babylon. To the northeast, was the Kingdom of Van (Urartu) to the west and northwest, were Aramaeans, Hittites and Mittani.[25] Assur continually had to fight these belligerent peoples, with the consequent development of her virility, discipline and military powers. Compared with Babylonia, Assyria was rich in natural resources. There were adequate supplies of building stone and minerals. The climate was temperate, the soil for the most part, fertile and arable without irrigation.[26]

With the accession of Tiglath-Pileser-III (745-727 B.C.) the empire became strong after a brief decline. After his accession to the throne Sarduris of Van was compelled to accept his suzerainty. After a brief reign of Shalmaneser V (727-22 B.C.) a usurper who assumed the name of Sargon-II (722-705 B.C.) was crowned as a result of rebellion. In the first year of Sargon's reign, rebellion in Palestine brought prompt reprisal with the conquest of Samaria (North-Palestine). But the main threat of action in Sargon's reign was the south Merodach-Baladan, ruler of Babylon, made a coalition with Elamites with the result that Assyrian commercial interests were hampered. The allies were defeated separately and Babylon came under direct Assyrian control.[27]

After Sargon, the powerful ruler in this line was Sennacherib IV (705-681 B.C.). He quelled the revolution in Babylon and finally annexed it. Tyre and Sydon were captured in addition with Jerusalem. But Jerusalem was escaped from the capture when Sennacherib's army left the siege. The reign of Sennacherib came to an end with his assassination by one of his sons. However Esarhaddon (681-668 B.C.) another son, ultimately captured the throne. Another coalition of Elamites and Chaldeans was suppressed by Essarhaddon. A hostile Syrian alliance, instigated by Egypt was formed under the leadership of Sidon,[28] but the military power of empire proved well able to crush the uprising. Upper Egypt was placed under native rulers who acknowledged the Assyrian suzerainty. Under Esarhaddon the territory reached at its peak.[29]

But under Assur-bani-Pal (668-626 B.C.) the empire fell into rapid decline. Egypt went out the control and other vassal states became powerful taking the opportunity of weakness of Assyria. After the death of Assurbanipal, a civil war in Assyria gave Nabopolassar, the governor of Babylon the opportunity to establish Chaldean supremacy in Babylonia (625 B.C.). Palestine and Syria revolted without reprisal.[30] Cyaxeres united the Medes and defeated the Assyrian forces along the upper Euphrates. In

614 B.C., a coalition of Medes and Chaldeans succeeded in capturing Assur.[31]

The Chaldean Empire (625B.C. - 539 B.C.)

With the internal weakness of Assyrian empire, the Chaldeans in conjunction with Medes, hastened to capitalise on this opportunity. Cyaxeres the King of Media attacked Asur, when the success of the movement seemed assured; Nabopolassar, and the Assyrian governor of Babylon in 626 B.C. won the independence of Chaldea. A joint expedition under Cyxeres and Nabopolassar, then marched against Nineveh and capitulated in 612 B.C. Nabopolessar was in a precarious position because Median allies turned against him and attempted to incorporate Chaldea to his empire. In other side the Assyrians supported by Egypt posed another challenge.[32]

In 610 B.C. Egyptians sent an army; they captured Carchemis and massacred the Babylonian citizens and Chaldean sympathisers. In face of this imminent danger, the Chaldean and Median alliance was revived. Nebuchadrezzar (son of Nabopolassar) of Chaddea, together with Median allies defeated the Egyptian army. Finally Syria and Palestine were annexed to Chaldean empire. Under the rule of Nebuchadrezzar (604-561B.C.) the revolt of Jadah was foiled and Jews were taken captive.[33]

After the death of Nebuchadrezzar (561 B.C.) the period of dissension started in Babylon. The energies of ruling class were sapped by luxury and debauch. When that last ruler Nabonidus withdrew from anti-Persian coalition formed under leadership of Croesus, Lydia was conquered by Cyrus, founder of Persian Empire (586-529 B.C.). Cyrus then conquered Akkad and began to attack Chaldea from Elam. Babylon was taken by Persians without a siege (539-538 B.C.). Finally the Persian Empire engulfed the whole Assyrian as well as Chaldean empire.[34]

Trade Routes

Various trade routes were opened for West Asia from the time immemorial. The different merchant communities have adopted different routes according to the suitability. Both Buddhist and Brahminical texts are replete with the references of sea borne trade of India. In addition with these sources, there are all sorts of evidences of literary, inscriptional and numismatic, both Indian and foreign. As a matter of fact, in various foreign works, there are abundant allusions of India's commerce, arts, and manufactures, indicating the glorious position she once occupied and for long maintained as the "Queen of Eastern Seas."[35]

From prehistoric times, the great trade routes have connected India with the West. Among these routes, the easiest and the oldest one was a Persian Gulf route, running from the mouth of the Indus to the Euphrates and at Euphrates, the roads branch off to Antioch and the Levantine ports.[36] There was the overland route from the Indian passes to Balkh, and from Balkh, either by river, down the Oxus to the Caspian, and from the Caspian to the Euxîne, or entirely by land, by the Caravan road and which skirts the Karmanian[37] desert to the north passes through the Caspian Gates. And this route reaches at Antioch by way of Hekatompylos and Ktesiphon. Finally there was a circuitous sea route, down the Persian and Arabian coasts to Aden up the Red Sea to Suez and from Suez to Egypt on the one hand and Tyre and Sidon on the other.[38]

The Persian Gulf trade was at first principally in the hands of Chaldeans, a troublesome nation that was always busy in piracy.[39] But Sennacherib exterminated them in 694 B.C. with the aid of a great fleet, which he built upon the Tigris. After breaking the nests of piracy, Sennacherib sent the pirates to dwell in Gerrha.[40] The trade of the Persian Gulf then fell into the hands of the ubiquitous Phoenicians, a colony of whom, according to Justin,[41] had settled in the Babylonian marshes, having been driven out of their own land by earthquakes. In the days of Strabo, there are more evidences about the presence of merchants at the mouth of Persian Gulf.[42]

Bahrain Island was the main centre where all the ships were carrying the water for their journey.[43] In comparison to Bahrain coast, Makran coast was inhospitable and there was nothing to offer the merchants. The immense trade with all nations carried on by Phoenicians may be estimated by studying the remarkable passage in which the prophet Ezekiel prophesises the overthrow of great city of Tyre in 573 B.C. by Nebuchadrezzr-II. "Tarshish was thy merchant by reason of multitude of thy riches; with silver, iron, tin and lead, they traded for thy wares... Clan also and Javan going to and fro, occupied in thy fairs: bright iron, cassia and calamus were in thy market... And in their wailing they shall take up a lamentation for thee, and lament over thee sayings "who is there like Tyre, like her that is brought to silence in the midst of the sea? When the wares went forth out of the seas, thou filldest many peoples; thou didnt enrich the kings of earth with multitude of thy riches and thy merchandise".[44] Herodotus refers to the Phoenician ships as "taking to long voyages, loading their ships with Assyrian and Egyptian wares".[45]

When Assyrian empire was overthrown (606 B.C.), Babylon took the place of Nineveh as the queen of western Asia. In the cities and crowded market places, the merchants of different countries were found.[46] Among them were Iranian traders, Jewish captives, and Phoenician merchants from distant Tarshish and Indians from the Punjab who came to sell their wares.[47] Babylon was the great resort of different races that were coming from different places for trade purposes. There are many stories in the Jataka about the Indian merchants' travel to Babylon. A Babylonian colony may have sprung up on the borders of India, for Strabo tells us that the followers of Alexander found at Taxila a marriage market conducted on his well known Babylonian principle.[48] The commercial intercourse between India and Semitic nations was mainly carried on by sea. The merchants traveling through Hindu Kush to Mediterranean parts were facing many wild tribes on their way. Again the journey through this mountain and deserts was a tedious task for the merchants. So the merchants usually preferred to the sea-routes. But it does not mean that the traders were not traveling through deserts.[49] No doubt, the caravans traveled from immemorial times to the great emporium of Bactria, where the roads from India, China and the West converged, there the cargos were shipped into rafts and floated down the Oxus the Caspian[50] and thence partly by land and partly by river to the Euxine.[51] Those who were traveling entirely by land, they followed the great road which still skirts the Karmanian Desert to the north, passes through Caspian Gates and crossing the Euphrates at Thapsacus, ends at Antioch and Levantine ports.[52]

Another important trade route between India and West Asia was that which ran from the north of the Red Sea to the India up to the Arabian coast.[53] This route carries the importance because it linked India not only to gold fields and the fabulously wealthy incense country of Southern Arabia and Somaliland, but to Egypt and Judaea. Through Judaea, Indian goods found another outlet by way of adjacent ports of their allies of Tyre and Sidon, to the Mediterranean.[54]

From time immemorial, the famous Egyptian traders were trading in the Red Sea by fetching the spices from the land of Punt and Arabia Felix.[55] Undoubtedly, the Indian goods were brought to Aden by the Arabian vessels, though it was clear that Egyptians were poor sailors. On the suggestion of Solomon, the Tyrian monarch prepared a fleet of "ship of Tarshish" at Ezion Geber. The "navy of Tarshish" made a voyage to the East, bringing back with them a vast quantity of gold and silver, ivory, apes, peacocks and plenty of almug trees and precious stones.[56] The port at which these goods were loaded is called Ophir. It is presumed that Ophir was the important port of India because India was rich in gold. Ophir may be Sophir, which is applied in Coptic in South India or Suppara[57] in Gujarat.

King Solomon tried to appropriate a share of this trade for the Jewish people by creating the facilities for the Eastern traders both on land and sea routes.[58] He built various resting places on the land route for the caravans in the cities of Tadmore (Palmyra), Baalbec (Heliopolis) and Hamaath (Epiphania).[59] And his foresight in protecting these caravan trade routes bore fruits in trading centres of Mesopotamia, viz. Babylon, Ctesiphon,

Seleucia and Ossis, which all flourished for a long time on the profits of the commerce with the East.[60]

Phoenicians were not so bad sailors. They were bold sailors as they were, ever accomplished the lengthy voyages from Suez to Indian port, particularly a South Indian port, in the primitive vessels then in use'.[61] Usually the sailors were traveling along the coast and the voyages would have to go right up the Arabian and Persian coasts, an enormously long way. It is much more probable that Ophir was an enterpot of Arabia where the boats and wares of different countries like India and Arabia was entering.[62] Basically the primitive trade was passed from tribe to tribe and port to port. Ophir was probably at the mouth of Persian Gulf, on the coast of Oman.[63] Hither came for export the gold from the rich fields of Southern Arabia, which has made Ophir famous. The death of Solomon, gave blow to the trade, the trade of Ezion Geber gradually declined with chequered fortunes of the Jewish nation.[64]

During the time of Buddha, there are many references about India's trade with Western Asia. Rhys Danids says, "Sea going merchants availing themselves of the monsoons were in the habit at the beginning of the 7th B.C. of trading from ports on the south west coast of India (Sovira at first, Supparaka and Bharukachha) to Babylon".[65] This evidence of Jataka and some of the Sanskrit law books leads to Jackson to conclude that the ships from Broach and Suppara traded with Babylon from 6th century B.C.[66]

The Supparaka Jataka[67] informs us that sea merchants once started from Bharukachcha and passed Khuramala, Nalamala, Valabhamukha, Agnimala, Dahimala and Nilakusamala. As these names are mentioned in the Gathas they are very old. Dr. Jaiswal has identified Khuramala with some ports on Persian Gulf situated in South-eastern Arabia. Agnimala according to him could be identified with the seacoast near Aden and some parts of Somaliland.[68] Dadhimala is the Red Sea and Nilakusamala is a part of Nubia situated in northeast coast of Africa. Nalamala is the canal joining the Red Sea and the Mediterranean and Valabhamukha is same part of the Mediterranean in which even today we find volcanoes.[69] If Jaiswal's identifications are correct then we will have to agree that Indian navigators were well acquainted with the sea route between Broach and the Mediterranean. But Greek and Latin sources point out that Indian sailors had no knowledge about this route.

The occupation of India by Achaemenids again opened the land routes to West Asia. The campaign of Cyrus and Darius-I were political in nature. The campaigns of Cyrus continued up to the river Jaxartes and of Darius-I to the Indus.[70] According to Pliny, however, Cyrus reached upto Kapisi and Herodouts is of the opinion that the campaigns of Darius reached upto the Indian Ocean.[71]

Darius at first decided to subdue the lower Indus and then reach the Arabian Sea. Probably with this intention he dispatched Skyalx to explore the lower Indus. His flotilla started from Multan.[72] A little below the city of the left bank of the Chenab, Darius' fleet was made ready which after sailing for two and half years reached Egypt. In the course of the voyage the fleet touched the Egyptian ports of the Red Sea thus ensuring the safety of the ports on the western Indian coast as well. With this conquest from the mouth of the Euphrates and Tigris upto the mouth of the Indus, Sind came under his control and the peace of the Indian Ocean was ensured.[73]

The invasion of Alexander brought a great change in the trade. After the conquest of Tyre by Alexander the Great and the foundation of Alexandria, the Egyptians came into the field of commerce and after the successive decline of the Jewish, Phoenicians and Persian powers in Western Asia, they retained the monopoly of the trade with Arabians for about 900 years.[74]

Export and Import of Goods

India, "the Queen of Eastern Seas" was famous for different goods that exported to different parts of world. The evidences, which are available, clearly show that in the pre-Mauryan phase, India had cultivated trade relations successively with Phoenicians, Jews, Assyrians, Greeks, Egyptians and Romans. A genial climate and a fertile soil coupled with industry and frugality of the Indian people, rendered them virtually independent of foreign nations in respect of their necessaries of life, while their secondary wants were few.[75] Therefore, export exceeded the import not only in quantity but also in price; and the balance of trade was in favour of India. There are various epigraphic, literal as well as archaeological sources available in this respect. On the basis of these sources the idea about the import and export of goods can be constructed.

The Jewish annals mention the names of various articles, which may be traced to Indian origin. Thus "ivory" is in the Herbrew text *Shen fiabbin* [76] elephant's teeth, a literal translation of the Sanskrit ibhadanta.[77]The word used for 'ape' is not the ordinary Hebrew one but *Koph* obviously the Sanskrit *Kapi.* "Peacocks" are *thuki-im* the Tamil *tokei.*[78] Tin, the late Sanskrit, *Kastira* may have come from Far East to Greece or vice-versa. India proper has no tin ore.[79] Ivory reached Greece at an early period from India. The 'ape' like the ivory of Solomon also found its way to Egypt, if the Egyptian *Kafu* like Hebrew *Koph* comes from *kapi.* Among the substances, which originally came from Dravidian ports, mention may be made of rice, which like ivory was originally brought to Europe by Arab traders.[80] The Tamil *arisi* became *aruz* in Arabian. Other articles of trade which reached Europe at various dates from Dravidian ports are aloes (tamil [aghit], Hebrew - [ahal]) Cinnamon (Tamil [Karappu], first mentioned by Ktesias); ginger (Tamil [pippali[) and the beryl-stone (Tamil and Sanskrit [Vaidury]).

Jataka stories inform us that various kinds of birds and beasts including the valuable Sind horses were exported to West-Asia. Among the animals monkey and among the bird's peacocks, parrots and crows were important.[81] India provided Europe with wool from the fleeces of the sheep bred on northwestern mountain ranges, famous in the days of Alexander the Great. Only, Chalcedony, lapis lazuli and jasper then esteemed as precious stones.[82] Other products were resinous gum, furs, asafetida and musk. The embroidered woolen fabrics and coloured carpets were highly prized in Babylon.[83] But the most valuable of the exports of India was silk, which under the Persian Empire, is said to have been exchanged by weight with gold. It was manufactured in India, as well as obtained for re-export from China. Next to silk in value were cotton clothes ranging from coarse canvas and calicoes to muslin of the finest texture. India also supplied foreign countries with oils, brassware, a liquid preparation of the sugarcane, salt, drugs, dyes and the aromatics while she had also a monopoly in the matter of the supply of pepper, cinnamon, and other edible spices which were in great demand throughout Europe.[84]

Again the Indian teak was found in the ruins of Ur. It is assumed that this wood must have been sent by sea from the ports of Malabar Coast, for it was only there that teak grew near enough to the sea, to be exported with profit in those early times.[85] Again muslin was the most favourite item of Babylonians, which must have been brought by sea from India. The Indian beam of Cedar is found in the palace of Nebuchadnezzar at Birs Nirmud.[86] Again two rough logs of Indian wood are found in the Temple of Moon God at Ur, which was also built by Nebuchadnezzar.

The principal commodities imported from India were gold, precious stones, ivory etc. Further, according to Wilkinson,[87] the presence of indigo, tamarind wood and other Indian products have been detected in the tombs of Egypt and Lassen has also pointed out that the Egyptians dyed cloth with indigo and wrapped their mummies in Indian muslin.[88]

In comparison with export, import was quite less. Through the ages, India had occupied a unique position in the commercial world as the main supplier of the world's luxuries. As a consequence, she enjoyed the balance of trade clearly in her favour. A balance that could only be settled by the export of treasure from European and West Asian countries that were commercially indebted to her.[89] India desired nothing in exchange of vast number of goods except some precious metals. Thus she has been for many centuries the final depository of a large proportion of metallic wealth of the world.[90] India imported mainly tin, lead, glass, amber, steel for arms, coral and to small extent medicinal drugs from Europe and Western Asia. From Arabia, India was indebted for frankincense, which was used in temples.[91] There were some goods, which were imported from West Asian countries. But the goods, which were exported, had outnumbered the goods, which were imported. A great question disturbs the scholars that how the countries of West were repaying cost of goods, which were exported from India. Some of the hoards of foreign coins, which are found in different parts of India, are indicating that probably they were paying for the extra goods in cash. But this view does not provide the satisfactory answer to this question because what was the use of these coins in India is another puzzling question. But the need of metals by Indians was satisfied in some extent by these coins. No conclusion can be drawn on this fact unless and until further proofs are not coming in this way.

Political Contacts and Administrative Impacts

India's relation with Iranians is very old. It is generally presumed that the Aryans and Early Iranians were two branches of a single stem. After the migration of Aryans or Indo-Iranians to India, the old cultural link between the two lands severed. The two people turned their backs upon each other and developed their distinctive civilization apparently without least mutual influence. The geographical barriers created a chasm in the relations between the two lands. But in 611 century B.C. the political scenario changed a lot and helped the Iranians to establish their old contacts. In the first half of this period, the Uttarapatha beyond the Madhyadesha, like the rest of India, was paralleled into a number of small states, the most important of which were Kamboja, Gandhara, and Madra.[92] These small states were not only wealthy but also disunited which attracted the attention of foreign invaders in order to satiate their desire to amass the untold wealth of India. Taking the opportunity of this fragmented politics, the Achamenian monarch swayed their influence.[93]

Kurush or Cyrus (558-530 B.C.) the founder of Persian Empire led an expedition through Gedrosia to India.[94] But the exact limit of his territory in India, conquered and annexed by him during this campaign is difficult to determine. We have two opposite versions about the extent of empire of Cyrus in India.

Herodotus,[95] Ctesias and Xenphon, the three classical writers point out that Cyrus conquered parts of India. According to Herodotus, Cyrus conquered the borderlands between India and Iran comprising Seistan, Sattagyidia and Gandhara. Ctesias has suggested that the Indians fought on behalf of the Debrikes against Cyrus. An Indian fighter inflicted a wound on Cyrus, which caused his death. These Debrikes were probably some frontier tribes of India.[96] According to Xenophon, Cyrus brought under his rule Bactrians and Indians and that he extended his sway from Syria up to the Indian Ocean (Erythrean Sea). Xenophon narrates a story that some Indian kings sent an embassy to Cyrus to pay him tribute. On the basis of these evidences it is supposed that Cyrus had conquered Gandhara, which was part of India.[97]

But the statements of Nearchus and Megasthenes go against the above evidences. Nearchus, a Greek writer of Alexander's time has rejected the possibility of Cyrus's advance in India. He has narrated a story heard from the people of Baluchistan that Cyrus made an attempt to invade India through Baluchistan and suffered a great loss of his army and escaped with seven men only.[98] Megasthenes has remarked that, "the Indians had never engaged in foreign warfare, nor had they ever been invaded and conquered by any foreign power except Heracles and Dionysus and lately the Macedonians". He has pointed out that the Persian hired mercenary troops from India called Hy drakes.

Probably Nearchus and Megasthenes were misguided and thought river Indus as the western boundary of India and the land lying the west of the Indus as outside of India.[99] As Cyrus conquered the western part of India, which was part of India, Megasthenes held the view that foreigners never attacked India. That Cyrus conquered the land to the West of Indus is attested by other Greek writers. Pliny states that Cyrus conquered Kapisa in the Ghorband valley. Arrian states that Indians living between Kabul and Indus were subjected to the Assyrians, Medes and to the Persian under Cyrus and paid tributes imposed upon them.[100] However, it is reasonable to conclude that Cyrus definitely conquered Afghanistan and Baluchistan i.e. Hindukush and the Kabul valley. Whether he conquered territories upto the Indus, it is not definitely known.

During the reign of Darius-I (522-486 B.C.) the Persians made some real advance in India. The Bahistan inscription mentions that Gandhara was the part of Darius-I Empire.

Inscription-VII (Thus) Saith Darius the King: these are the provinces which are subject unto me and by the grace of Auramazda became King of them: Persia, Susiana, Babylonia, Assyria, Arabia, Egypt, the (Islands) of the Sea, Sparda, lonia (Media) Armenia, Cappadocia, Parthia, Drangiana, Aria, Chorasmia, Bactria, Sogdina, Gandara, Scythia, Sattagydia, Arachosia and Maka; twenty three lands in all.[101]

This is further confirmed by the Susa Palace Inscription of Darius, which mentions that teak was brought from Gadara (Gandhara) for the construction of the palace of the Emperor.[102]

The extent of the empire of Darius in India was not merely confined to Gandhara but extended further towards the Indus is well attested by the Naksh-i-Rustam and the Persepolis inscriptions. In these inscriptions Gandhara and Sindhu or Hindu (Punjab)[103] are mentioned as the provinces of Darius' empire. The Hamdan Gold and Silver Tablet Inscription also mention Sindhu as a province of the empire of Darius.[104]

Like all other foreigners, Darius was also motivated by the wealth of India, which he came to know from the different sources.[105] He probably, like Alexander, advanced up to India from Baktra and reaching the river Indus at the town of Kaspapyrus, frontier city of Gandhara, he sent an expedition under a Greek mercenary, Skylax of Karyanda, to explore the river down to its mouth.[106] Presumably, Skyalx had ordered to find his way to the Red Sea and not to return by the shorter Persian Gulf Route, with which the Persians were probably well acquainted. He completed his adventurous voyage in two and half years' duration to reach at Arsinol, the modem Suez already used by the Egyptians for the trade with the East.[107] The time he took, from that one may infer that Skylax probably enquiring his way from port to port. He traced his route along the old trade route to Ophir, and from Ophir to Aden along the Arabian coast. Skylax has double distinction of having been the first Greek to visit India and to make Red Sea voyage. The latter feat was not repeated till the days of Eudoxus, three centuries later.[108] Unfortunately the work of Skylax is lost but some parts of original text have been found in the work of Herodotus.[109]

Darius annexed northwestern part of Indus Valley and made it twentieth satrapy of Persian Empire. But some scholars opine that the part of India was not conquered by him but he had inherited from his father Cyrus. Whatever may be the fact, Indian Territory was the part of his empire. The Indians were paying 360 talents of gold dust as tribute. This gold dust was probably collected from the gold mines of Dardistan.[110]

The Persian Empire reached at its furthest limit under Darius. Darius earned the fresh laurels in India in addition what he had inherited from his predecessor. The extent of Indian conquests of Darius can't be determined. It is however, reasonably held that Darius undoubtedly conquered some territories in Punjab lying to the East of Indus. That the Persian Empire did not extend beyond this limit is inferred from the silence of Herodotus. The explicit statement of Herodotus that Darius never conquered the country south of Indus and the desert of Sind and Rajputna[111] also confirms this.

Xerxes (486-465 B.C.) came to the throne as the successor of Darius-I and maintained his hold over Indian provinces. But he failed to make any forward movement in India due to the commitments in Greece. Herodotus[112] states that Xerxes requisitioned large number of troops including infantry and cavalry from India for invasion of Greece. They were denoted by two terms, "Gandarians and Indians".[113] The Gandarians, according to Herodotus were bearing boars of reed and short spears and the Indians as being clad in cotton garments and bearing can bows with arrows tipped with iron.[114] Among the interesting relics of Persian dominion in India, mention is sometimes made of "Taxila inscription in Aramaic characters of the fourth and fifth century B.C.[115] The Persians are attributed to the introduction of Khorosti alphabet, "The Persepolitan capital" and the words like "dipti (rescript)' and 'nipista (written)' occurring in the inscription of Ashoka.[116] Persian influence has also been traced in the Preamble of Ashokan edicts.

The defeat of Xerxes in Greece initiated the process of decline of Persian power in India. But Artaxerxes Mnemon (418-398 B.C.) had a tiger and two swords of Indian steel sent to him from India, according to the Greek physician Ctesias who was the resident in the Persian court at Susa.[117]

However, the Achaeminian (Persian) rule over India continued upto 330 B.C. In that year Darius-III, the last Achaemenian rulers summoned Indian troops to fight against Alexander, the Great, at Gaugamela and Arbela. The Indians in addition with Bactrians, Sagdarians had come to the aid of Darius-Ill, all were under the command of Bessus, the viceroy of land of Bactria.[118] Barsaents, the viceroy of Arachoitia, led the Arachoitians and the men who were called mountaineer Indians. There were few elephants about fifteen in number belonging to the Indians who lived this side of Indus.[119] But the hold of Achaemenians over India at that time was very feeble and the defeat of Persians by the hands of Alexander brought the chapter of Indo-Persian relations to the point of end.[120]

R.C. Majumdar holds a different view about the continuation of Persian rule in north-western India during Darius-Ill. According to him, after the rule of Xerxes, the Persian domination over India weakened which gave an opportunity to raise the heroes like Porus and heroic tribes like Asmakas whom Alexander faced during his invasion. The Indian army employed by Darius-Ill at Arbela might have been the mercenary troops.

Results of Persian Domination over India

The impacts of Persian dominion over India are mostly indirect and did not last for long time. It was an episode in Indian history, a triumph without result. It inspired the rulers of India, particularly in Magadha, to set up vast empires in imitation of Leviathan Empire of Persia.

The invasion of Alexander was the byproduct of Persian domination over India. Alexander followed the route, which was largely used by Persians. After the invasion of Alexander, the relation between Persia and India continued in an unabated zeal. Persia served as the high way of contact between India and Greece. Indian scholars visited Greece though Persia and some Indian philosophers debated with Socrates.

Again the exploration of Persian navigator Skylax opened better trade routes of communication between India and western Asia. Ashokan scripts like Kharosti was derived from the Persian script Aramaic and Persian alphabet like Yavanani entered into the family of Indian language.[121]

The excavation of Achaemenid town at Taxila gives some interesting facts about Kharosti script. There was an Aramaic inscription, which has been examined by Herzfeld who read it as "Priyadarshan"[122] which is identifying the Mauryan ruler Ashok. John Marshall observes, "The discovery of this inscriptions is of special interest in connection with the origin of the Kharosti alphabet, since it confirms the view that the Kharosti was derived at Taxila (which was the chief city of Kharosti language prevalent area) from Aramaic, the latter having been introduced into the North-West of India by the Achaemenids after the conquest of the country about 500 B.C.".[123]

There is a great debate over the question that whether Kharosti was originated in India or was originally the script of Kashgar.[124] After the discovery of Kharosti documents in Central Asia, it may be taken as finally settled. None of these documents are earlier than Christian era, while on the other hand, the epigraphs of Ashoka in northwestern India are all written in Kharosti script.

According to Buhler, the Kharosti language came to India by the Persian officials in satraps. It became wide prevalent in India when Indian officials, village headmen and heads of town maintained their records in Kharosti script.[125] At first the Indian probably used Aramaic characters, just as in later times they used the Arabic writing for a number of their dialects, and they introduced in course of time the modifications observable in the Kharosti alphabet. This supposition of Buhler was strengthened by the fact that the vowel system and the compound consonants in Kharosi point to the fact that they were elaborated with the help of Brahmi, which was the original script of Indians.[126] It prevailed in most part of the country while Kharosti was used only in the region which once had passed under the foreign rule.[127]

The Persian coins like Daric and Shekels influenced the Indian coinage.[128] Persian influence on Mauryan dynasty was felt largely. The Mauryan palace at Pataliputra and Ashokan pillars were influenced by Persian architecture.[129] The Mauryas even borrowed some court manners and hair washing ceremony from the Persians.[130] Early Buddhism influenced the philosophical movements in Persia like Manichacism. Later on Zoroastrianism of Persia made its impact on Mahayana Buddhism.[131]

Alexander's Invasion of India

Alexander resolved to launch the invasion of India after inflicting the first blow on Emperor Darius-Ill of Persia. The approximate cause of Indian campaign of Alexander may be varied. India's vast wealth and prosperity was the chief factor of his invasion. Again he felt it necessary to conquer the remaining parts of the Persian Empire in order to give the real meaning to his adopted title, "The Great King of Persia".[132] His expansionist zeal was further awakened when an embassy from the King of Taxila met him at Sagdiana. This is the first recorded instance of the Indian seeking foreign aid against fellow Indians.[133] But Dr. Smith has suggested that Alexander wanted to surpass the heroism shown by the mythical heroes like Heracles and others.[134]

In the spring of 327 B.C., when the snows of Hindukush melted away, Alexander crossed the mountain with 30,000 men.[135] He divided his army into two parts. A part of the army proceeded under Hephaestion and Perdiccas and marched along the southern bank of Kabul valley with a view to reach the Indus. The second part of the army was laid by Alexander himself was to move along the valley in the north of the Kabul river. On their way they subjugated many tribes who opposed them. One tribe, Massagans, who inflicted a serious wound on Alexander, which nearly cost his life. Finally the mighty army of Alexander inflicted a severe blow on Massagans and mercilessly butchered 7000 mercenaries. Diodorus and Plutarch have condemned Alexander for his cruelty.[136] But V. Smith has justified the massacre on the ground of military expediency.[137]

Alexander crossed the river Indus, in the spring of 326 B.C. Ambhi, the ruler of Taxila greeted him and offered his homage as an overlord and presented rich tributes. Alexander sent an envoy from Taxila to Elder Porus or Paurav whose kingdom was situated in between Jhelam and Chenab, asking for his submission. But Porus gave a defiant reply and prepared for the battle. Mr. Bevan suggested that Paurav did not fight for India's honour, solidarity and Indian nationalism.[138] He is correct in some extent because the concept of nationalism was rare among the ancient rulers and almost all rulers were fighting for protection of their own kingdom. But Porus' desire to face the death of honour instead of surrendering like cowards to the foreign rulers, is indicative of his nationalist fervour, typical to the age in which he lived.

Porus accepted the defeat because his army could not stand against vast well-equipped army of Alexander. After that, Alexander had a sweeping march up to Beas.[139] The war weary soldiers of Alexander refused to proceed after Beas. In that situation, Alexander had no way out excepting to return. On his way of return journey, he subdued some tribes. At Patala, Alexander divided his army into three sections for homeward journey. One section marched through Archosia (Kandahar) and Drangiana (Seistan); Alexander himself marched at the head of second section through Gedrosia (Baluchistan) and the third part led by Nearchus sailed through Persian Gulf.[140] The Macedonian army returned to Persia in 324 B.C. While Alexander was encamping at Babylon, he was attacked with fever and died in 323

B.C.

Impact of Alexander's Invasion

Alexander's adventure to include India in his principalities was a part of his much-cherished ambition of World Empire. Some of the scholars are fascinated by the splendour of Alexander's name and the so-called vision of "Hellenizing the East" Mr. V. Smith has estimated the military success of Alexander in India with remark, "The triumphant progress of Alexander from Himalayas to the sea demonstrated the weakness of greatest Asiatic armies when confronted the European skill and discipline.[141] Prof. Bury has explained the noble intentions of Alexander in India as follows. "The advance to the Indus was no mere wanton aggression. The solid interests of commerce underlay the ambition of Macedonian conqueror".[142] Though commercial interest was one among the prime motives of Alexander, he could not take concrete initiatives in this direction. He could not live long to fructify his ambitions.[143] But his contribution to the commercial linkages between India and West was no less praiseworthy. He built a harbour at Patala, where Indus splits into two branches. It remained as an important trade centre of western trade and was the principal harbour in northwestern India until Barygaza rivaled its claims. Phillip, the satrap of Parthia, was put in charge of the new provinces with the orders to push on the development of colonies and the completion of naval docks and other commercial undertakings with all speed.[144] On reaching the mouth of the river Indus, Alexander determined to build a dock at the end of eastern arm as he found there an excellent natural harbour forming a lake like basin.[145]

Alexander set up the trading depots at various places on the way of his long and arduous journey. Bukephala and Nikaea were built on the bank of Hydaspes; Alexandria on Indus was the important spot where Akesines joins the main stream.[146] Alexandria in Indus became an important port through which Indian traders carried out their trade to the West.[147] It survived till the overthrow of Macedonian power in the Punjab, for many years and became famous under Bactrian king as a great Graceo-Buddhist centre. "Alasanda of Yonas" is mentioned in the Mahavamsa, as the capital of "yona country" and 30,000 monks are said to have come from this place to the dedication festival of the great tope of Ruanvelli in 137 B.C.[148] We have curiously enough, in the name of this town, the only mention in Indian literature of the name of the great Macedonian conqueror.[149]

Alexander, during his preparation of return journey, came to know from Indians that there was a fair sea-route to Mesopotamia. Admiral Nearehus was given orders by Alexander to sail from the mouth of the Indus to the Euphrates.[150] The Admiral acquired flotilla of riverboats, some of which were 30 oared built in the Punjab by a tribe known as Ksatri (Xathori)[151] to make a sea-voyage of nearly 1500 miles. The fleet set sail along the coast of Persian Gulf and despite the gales of rough sea, reached Ormuz, which is a testimony to the hardy structure of Indian built boats of those days. Bulland comments that, "From a maritime stand point its (the sea voyage of Nearchus) special interest lies in the proof that even twenty three centuries before our times, the sea men of the East were already quite familiar with the navigation of Indian Ocean between India and Persia, and aware that at the proper season of the year a west bound coasting voyage between the countries was safe and feasible even for river craft".[152]

The exploration of Indus-Valley was the beginning of the new chapter of India-West relations. We can't gauge what might have been the result, if Alexander was alive for a long time to carry out his schemes. Would the Indus valley have become the centre of Hellenistic culture, as Egypt and Syria became, where the civilization of the East and West blended to form a new product? The question never got a satisfied answer due to the immature death of Alexander.[153] The voyages and expeditions of Alexander in the northwest opened up new lines of communication between India and west and added to the store of geographical knowledge and trade. Just like Columbus. Alexander did not bring India into the map of the world; he opened four distinct trade routes, which helped the traders in later dates. He discovered the route via, the land route through Kabul, Mullah pass in the Baluchistan, and through Gedrosia (Makran) and the maritime route through the Persian Gulf.[154]

Culturally, India was greatly influenced by coming in contacts with Macedonians. Alexander broke the wall of separation between the East and West and established the direct contact between the Indian and Mediterranean civilizations. This contact did not cease with the decay of Alexander's empire. All subsequent contacts between India and Greece are the legacies of Alexander's campaign.[155] Alexander's invasion opened the door of cultural contacts between India and Greece. India received from Greece the lessons of astronomy, Gandhara Art and the art of coinage. The Aethian type of 'owl' coins and silver drachms are impacts of this contact. Whether Mauryan art and architecture was influenced by Greek style of art and architecture is difficult to determine. India, on other hand influenced Greece with her philosophy and religion.

Some of the scholars view the invasion of Alexander was culturally barren because India was not Hellenized and she continued to live her life of splendid isolation and soon forgot the story of Macedonian deluge. Again they point out that Alexander's invasion was so superficial that there is no faintest allusion to his deeds in the works of Hindu, Buddhists and Jainas also.[156] Probably these scholars have not paid adequate attention to the indirect impacts in the sphere of art, architecture, education etc. that became prominent in the age of Mauryas.

Commercial and Cultural Contracts

The period between the Rig Vedic Age and the rise of Mauryan Empire has been often labelled as the, "Dark Age" of Indian history. Because during this time there is great scarcity of materials to reconstruct the history in details, the meager archaeological evidence available in foreign sources, especially West Asia points to the limited amount of cultural and commercial intercourse between India and her western neighbours.[157] It is from Sixth century B.C, onwards, that we reach on firmer grounds as far as socio-political economic history of India both in internal and external contexts, is concerned. The Jatakas as well as Buddhist sources provide knowledge and relations with other countries especially about Egypt and Mesopotamia. Alexander's invasion is a well-documented event of world history, besides being a turning point of history. He was accompanied and followed by a number of Greek historians and their writings directly provide us the valuable in formations for the history of this period.[158]

Egypt

In one of the Egyptian inscription, it is clearly mentioned that the goods like ebony, ivory and Abyssinians and Somali traders supply cotton goods.[159] It is usually expected that the traders of Abyssinia and Somali lands received ebony from India, where alone this wood was found during this period.[160] Elephant hunters of Abyssinia and Somali lands used axes, Adzes and swords of Indian manufactures.[161] Indian traders used to sail straight to Abyssinia and with their frequent visits to the region they became quite familiar with the various parts of Nile.[162] According to Wilkinson, indigo, tamarind, wood and other Indian products have been found in the Egyptian tombs.[163] It has also been pointed out that Egyptians dyed cloth in indigo and wrapped their mummies with Indian muslin.[164]

Considering the perfection, which Egyptians attained in the science of embalmment at such an early age and the use of Indian muslin for the purpose, one can safely say that the two countries had close commercial contacts during those days.

Judaea

The Hebrew King, Solomon, took several steps for the development of maritime activities. To make Jerusalem as magnificent as the capitals of his neighbours, he needed gold, silver and rare type of wood in sufficient quantities to beautify the city. So he asked his ally Hiram of Tyre to lend some of his skilled seamen to build a fleet for use of eastern waters. The part of Eziongeber, modern Akaba, at the northern extremity of the right arm of the Red Sea became their headquarters and soon they crossed the straits of Beb-el-Mandeb and reached to the port of Ophir, their final destination. From Ophir they returned with four hundred and twenty talents of gold as well as sandalwood, ivory, apes and peacocks. The voyage took three years.[165] In the light of this description the part of Ophir has to be located some where on western Indian coast.[166] The export of vast quantities of gold from it suggests its identification with the "Barabaricom" of Greek traders, which stood at the mouth of Indus.[167] Another point, indirectly in favour of this identification may be the recovery of significant amount of gold jewellery from Indus-Valley sites in early times, i.e. 3rd and 2nd millennium B.C.

Again most interesting fact is that some of Hebrew items bore close resemblance with Indian names of goods. For ape, the Hebrew word *Koph* is identical with Sanskrit words *Kapi.* On the other hand peacocks seems to have been imported into these ancient lands from the south Indian ports, as the Hebrew word *fhuki* for peacock seems to have been derived from the Tamil *tokei.*[168] The Hebrew word *(shen bobbin)* for ivory, also appears to be a translation of Sanskrit ibha danta , e.g. elephant's teeth.[169]

Besides above-mentioned terms, many other words also point to India's influence on Hebrews. Hebrew *almug* is probably a variation of the Sanskrit *Valgu,*[170] Hebrew *sadin,* Arabic Batin[171] and Greek *sindon,* all seem to be derived from *Sindhu,* which stood for Indian cotton cloth. Hebrew *Karpas* and Greek *Karpuss* are also derived from Sanskrit *Karpasa* (Cotton).[172]

About the land routes of India and Judaea, there is little information about this. The land route journey was difficult and dangerous due to the presence of wild beasts and wild tribes also. In any case, the route must have been passed in the Caspian and north of Carmanian desert to Buikh, where the roads running to China and India converged.[173]

Assyria

Representatives of Indian elephants, apes and Bactrian camels can be noticed on the obelisk of Shalmanesar-III (859 B.C.) an Assyrian King.[174] These animals were likely to be imported from India by over land route[175] passing through Makran. This archaeological evidence supports the export of Indian animals to Assyria, particularly elephants and apes.

Including all these animals, birds too reached in Assyria. There is evidence that a peacock was among the wonderful birds, received as a tribute by Tiglath Pilaser-III (744-727 B.C.).[176] During the reign of the same king certain other Indian articles were also exported from India to Assyria. Tribute paid to this king from Chaldean State of Bit-Yakin, included mostly Indian articles - precious stones, pearls, timber, stripped clothing and spices of different kinds. During this period, the parts of Persian Gulf were the thriving centres of commerce.[177]

In foreign countries, the Indian cotton was highly praised. One interesting fact is that, Sennacherib; a king of Assyria was responsible for the introduction of cotton plant in Assyria. He was very fond of Indian cotton. He had a fleet built on the Persian Gulf by Phoenicians carpenters and he is reported to have sailed against the Babylonian King Merodach Baladan who fled to Magitu on the coast of Elam. The very cause of conflict was the trade with India. One can easily assume the importance of trade out of this conflict.

The articles, which were imported from India, were mainly cotton, rice and peacocks.[178] The fact that the word 'Sindhu' which is taken to mean cotton, is written on tablets found in the library of Ashur banipal,[179] an Assyrian king (668-627 B.C.), goes to confirm the export of cotton from India. It is reported that this king is known to have sent for Indian plants, including the 'wool bearing trees' of India. Such evidence proves the antiquity of cotton trade between India and Assyria.

The above-mentioned details indicate that West Asia had commercial contacts with India and Indian articles were highly liked by the people. But out of this it is very difficult to determine the exact nature and quantum of trade. Sometimes it appears that the relations though started with commerce, it spread to other areas.

When the commercial intercourse developed, the contacts were established in other spheres also. According to some scholars the Brahmi script, which can be traced back to the Phoenician alphabets, which are said to have reached India through Mesopotamia.[180] This, however, is a controversial issue and nothing can be said with certainty either in favour or against the contention; some scholars opine about the indigenous origin of Brahmi script, which is equally acceptable.

Iran

Relations between India and Iran were not confined to political only but to other spheres like commercial, economic and cultural also. From the time immemorial, both the countries had started their relations. The Iranian influence on the economic field is clearly visible. Persian coins were in circulation in the region of Sind and Punjab.[181] The Danes (Persian gold coins) are rare in India but 'sigloi' or 'shekels' silver coins have been discovered in large number.[182] Some of the 'sigloi' discovered, bear peculiar countermarks on both sides.[183] According to some numismatic sources, historians[184] point out that they resemble the counter marks of indigenous Punch-marked coins. Some marks of these coins are similar to Brahmi and Kharoshi letters.[185] Scholars like Rapson thinks that both the types of these coins were made in India and were continuing side by side.[186]

Two types of 'daric' coins are noticeable. Type I datable to 5th and 4th century B.C. on the obverse, the figure of King holding a spear and stringed bow and wearing kidaris and kandhys; and an irregular oblong incuse on reverse. It has some resemblance with gold coins of Darius-1.[187]

Type - II assigned to a later date, seems to be a copy of Darius - III's coin. It is double daric. On the obverse, there is the depiction of the Achaemenid king as an archer, half kneeling to the right. There are Greek letters and a symbol in front and an inscription behind and beneath the figure of the king.[188] On the reverse side occur "wavy bands", irregular in use, with the conventional pattern formed a curved line in relief.[189] Type-11 consists of Greek monogram or Greek letters.[190] It seems that Alexander issued them after the defeat of Achaemenids.

Whether these coins came to India in commercial intercourse or were struck here for purpose of trade is not clear. Foreign invasions, to some extent, are responsible for the introduction of the coins. Whatever the reasons behind the introduction of coins, it obviously became helpful for the growth of trade and commerce. There are some direct evidences, which substantiate the facts of trade. The records of Curtius, Diodorus and Arrian refer to the articles that Alexander presented as gifts to the king of Taxila. Along with several articles of gold and silver, many Babylonian and Persian pieces of embroidery find mention in the lists of the gifts.[191] Nearchus, an admiral of Alexander's navy, described a secured port with the name of Alexander's haven, where he stayed for twenty-four days at the time of Greek invasion.[192] This shows that the harbour existed before the arrival of Greeks and the Iranians must have developed it for trade and other purposes.

Arrian informs us that when Nearchus made departure for home by sea, he got an Indian guide in Gedrosia.[193] The guide had a very good knowledge about sea routes up to Ormuz. From this fact, it can easily be inferred that Indian vessels were sailing along the coast of Gedrosia to Arabia and the Persian Gulf. Maritime trade witnessed a marked development after the Persian conquest. It is interesting to note that a Hindu woman, called Busasa, had a lodge under police supervision at Kish for travelers and merchants.[194]

Silk and ivory were exported from India to the Persian empire in exchange of gold.[195] Some inscriptions on clay tablets and on stone slabs recovered from the palace of Darius-I in Susa confirms the export of ivory from India.[196] Some scholars have given the credit of introducing iron working in the Indian region of Achamenid Empire to the Persians, although recent archaeological discoveries don't support this contention.[197] These evidences provide light about the close commercial contacts between India and Iran.

It was a result of the Achaemenid conquest that a new industry of blanket making developed in Indian borderland.[198] Kamboja was one of the border land of Indian Territory, which was inhabited by mainly Iranians. In Mahabharat, it is clearly mentioned that, " *the Kambojas they enjoy blankets (Kamhala) or beautiful things"*'. The blankets manufactured by the people of Kamboj were largely used in Rajasuya sacrifice.[199] The Kamboja King presented to Yudishitra[200] many of best kinds of skin, woollen blankets made of the fur of animals living in jungles in the earth and also of cats, all inlaid with threads of gold. This blanket trade, which flourished in Kamboja, was a result of Achamenid occupation of India.

According to some scholars the practice of exposing the dead to the birds prey, common in Taxila,[201]which was introduced in India by Magians after the Achaemenid conquest of India. The Mahasilava Jataka and Siksamuccaya bear clear references to it: There are various theories regarding the origin of these Magians tribal people. Thus Dr. Vidyabhushana observes: "It appears me very probable that while about 515 B.C., Darius the king of Persia, sent an expedition to India, some of his Persian subjects in Nisibis (off Herat) immigrated to India and having found Punjab over-populated by orthodox Brahmanas, came down as far as Magadha (Bihar) which was at that time largely inhabited by Vratyas or outcaste people.[202] This theory has been severely criticised by the later scholars, and indeed there is absolutely no evidence that the Persians in the Achaemenid days advanced as far as Eastern India. The presence of custom of exposing the dead to birds of prey however requires explanation. The Apasthamba Dharmasastra refers to the customs of burials and exposure of the dead on a raised platform.[203] On the basis of this, Dubreil claims that this system of exposure of dead bodies to animals has existed among the Aryans in their early home in Central Asia.

The colonialisation of Alexander created a fusion of Persian with Hellenistic Ideas, which took place in Bactria and the neighbouring countries. This hybrid culture was introduced in

India by Alexander's invasion.[204] And it continued to flourish as a result of peaceful commercial intercourse between the Mauryan Empire and Western Asia or as a result of subsequent invasions of the Bactrian Greeks, Scythians, Parthians and Kushanas, all of who must have been imbued to a greater or lesser degree with the Graeco-Persian culture. Hence, it will be wrong to assume that all Persian elements in Indian culture found their way into India at that time when the Persian Empire extended over North-West of India.[205]

Babylonia

The evidences of commercial contacts and communications between India and Babylon go back to Harappan period.[206] But very little information of this relation is available in the post Harappan period. But Skylax's exploration of India and discovery of a new route proved very useful in furthering the trade and cultural contacts between India and Babylonia.[207]

In 606 B.C., Nebuchadnezzar conquered Assyria and Babylon became one of the most prominent cities of Western Asia. Merchants from different countries, especially from Egypt, Palestine, Phoenicia and India, assembled here and used the markets of the city as their meeting place.[208] Indian merchants had a colony there, which continued to exist in the later period also.[209] The presence of Indian merchants at this place is proved by the reference to them in the tablets bearing the business records of the great farm of Murashu and Sons at Nippur.[210] It appears that probably in their turn, the Babylonian merchants also built an establishment in India at the frontier town of Taxila.[211] According to Strabo, the followers of Alexander saw a marriage market at Taxila, arranged in well-known Babylonian style.[212]

Information about India-Babylonian contacts is largely found in Buddhist literature. The well-known Baveru Jataka[213] indicates regular commerce and continuous navigation between these two countries through the Persian Gulf. According to the story told in it,[214] some Indian merchants went to Babylon[215] through sea for the sale of crows and peacocks. It appears that in this period

Indians were the first rate expert mariners. It has been pertinently suggested that the age of commercial intercourse might be earlier than the date of Jatakas, as the folk tales on which these stories are based, were of much earlier date.[216] According to a scholar, peacock became symbol of commercial and cultural contacts between the two countries.[217] Probably export of this bird began after exploration of the Indus by Scylax.[218]

Precious stones, dogs[219] (Indian hound) and wood were main articles of export to Babylon. The records of Herodotus[220] also confirm the export of Indian animals; a Persian governor of Babylon had large number of big Indian hounds. The discovery of Indian cedar in the palace of Nebuchadnezzar at Birs Nirmud[221] and of two rough logs of Indian teak in the second story of the temple moon at Mughur[222] (of Chaldeas) rebuilt by Nebuchadnezzr and Nabonidus, bear ample testimony of this fact.

Cultural influence is closely related to the commercial contacts. A similar story of Judgement of Solomon King of Judae[223] is found in Mahosadha Jatak. According to Rawlinson probably it came to India along with the Babylonians at the time of captivity (597-538 B.C.). It has been suggested that in the field of astronomy, the idea of designating the days of the week after the name of sun, moon and five planets originally belonged to Babylon and possibly from there it came to India. It has been pointed out that relic worship and stupa architecture are not of Indian origin and may have been derived from Babylonian tradition of urn[224] burials. Urn burials were, however, in vogue, in India, in the Harappan and post-Harappan cultures.

It is thus clear from the facts that the contacts between India and Babylonia had been established from Harappan period. But it continued to flourish in different periods although there are many missing links.

Greek Empire

After conquest of some parts of western Asia, the Greek hero, Alexander marched into India. His conquest of Indian territories was another point of culmination of India-West Asian relations.

The voyage of Skylax, a Greek sea captain of Caryanda, whom Persian king Darius-I sent out in the latter part of Sixth century B.C. to explore the Indus, helped in bringing the Indians and Greeks together in that period.[225] It is said that he had found his way from the city of Kaspapyrus in the Paktiyakan district, sailed down the stream to the sea and after the voyage of thirty months, reached the lower Kabul valley. His journey might have taken him through a part of Kashmir and the bulk of Indus-Countries.[226] The fact that Alexander found several settlements of the Greeks in the Trans-Indus and Afghanistan areas during the course of his invasion[227] is a further evidence of such contacts. The people of Nysa, reported of themselves to the Greek King, as Greeks.[228] The Persian King Xerexes also found an Ionian Greek colony between the boundaries of Balkh and Samarkand.[229] In Ktesias's Indica (400 B.C.) a Dravidian word *Karpion* can be noticed from Cinnamon.[230] According to Dr. Caldwell, it can be identified with Tamil and Malayalam word *Karppu* or *Karuppa* similar to Sanskrit *Karpura.*[231] The Greeks also borrowed some other Tamil words. These are following: Greek *oryza* from Tamil *arts,* Greek *ziggiberos* from Tamil *injiver,* Greek *peperi* from Tamil *Pipali* etc.[232] This philological evidence goes to show that Greek knew of some South-Indian articles, which they obtained from India through commercial intercourse. Alexandria was then the famous centre of international trade and cosmopolitan civilization of that time. Here converged the trade routes from Ethiopia, Arabia, India and Egypt.[233] The Greeks were fond of Indian merchandise-rice, peacocks and sandalwood; are reported by Sophocles (495-405 B.C.). These articles were probably exported to Greece directly from India.[234] The peacock was an important item of export. It appears that peacock had reached the Greek market by about the 5th century B.C. and became popular in the time of *Pericles,* when the birds were seen at many public exhibitions.[235]

Some of the Greek coins, which are found in India, testify the commercial intercourse between the two countries. Two silver coins, bearing the name of Alexander and one silver coin of Phillip Arrhideace have been found in the excavations at Bhir

Mound in Taxila.[236] On the obverse of first two coins is a carving of Alexander's head wearing the lion skin and on the reverse there is Zeus seated on a throne with the eagle on his right hand and the sceptre in the left. According to Marshal, they can be dated to 3rd or 4th century B.C. This is the first and unique recorded find of Greek coins in India. Marshal holds very strongly that they were brought to India from outside.[237] A few unique silver decadrachms, issued by Alexander, found at sites outside India, bear on the obverse a device of an elephant with two riders followed by a warrior on a prancing horse and an reverse a standing figure of Alexander, shown as God Zeus.[238] According to some numismatics, the obverse device represents Alexander's battle with Porus, although some scholars do not accept this view.[239]

Indian Kings also copied Greek styles of coins. The coin of Sophytes (Saubhuti) who were ruling in the Punjab at the close of 4th century B.C. is purely Greek in style. The regular intercourse had its impact on Indian culture and Hellenic influence is noticeable in several spheres.[240]

Some legends, ideas and philosophical concepts are common to Greece and India. We are not sure in which country they originated. Sometimes it is argued that both the countries independently developed it though it seems similar. It may be a matter of coincidence.

The Mahasodhak Jatak[241] bears close similarity with the story related to the judgment of Solomon. Another famous story of Hippokleides, who was careless about his wife at the time of dancing, seems to be similar to the Jatak story of the silly young peacocks who danced so indecently that he shocked the father of golden goose and lost his wealthy bride.[242] The story of the wife of Intaphernes[243] who pleaded for her brother's life saying that she could get another son or husband but not another brother, finds its parallel in the Uchchanga Jataka.[244]

In the sphere philosophical thoughts, Indians may have influenced the Western philosophical thought to some extent.

According to Garbe, the theory of Greek philosopher Thales (6th century B.C.) that everything comes out from water, and that of Anaximander that the first thing is not water but infinite atmosphere or air which is the root of the universe, these elements are similarly found in Vedic texts also. Probably the Greek philosophers learnt these things from Persia, where they had come for a mission of pilgrimage for philosophical studies.[245] The theory propounded by Zenophanes (c.575 B.C.) father of Eleatic school that the God and the Universe both are one, eternal and unchangeable is more akin to the spirit of the Indian pantheism than the Hellenic spirit.[246] Furthermore, William Jones has shown that the Sankhya System and Pythagorean Philosophy (550 B.C.) have some similar features.[247] Similarly, the belief in the transmigration of soul from one body to another in the Pythagorean philosophy is supposed to be Indian origin based on the philosophy of Brahmanas and Upanishadas.[248] Some scholars believe that Indian philosophical system went to the foreign countries through the Hellenistic system.[249]

There are other philosophical systems of West, which also bear close similarity to Indian philosophy. The views of Heraclitus (500 B.C.) that, "all bodies are the transformation of fire and everything that exists is derived from it and strives to return to it" are similar to the thought of Chandogya Upanishad.[250] Garbe compares it with the Sankhya theory of innumerable annihilations and reformations of the Universe.[251] The philosophy of Empedocles (450 B.C.), which describes about eternity in destructibility is borrowed from the Indian philosophy. Belief in the transmigration of souls and in the development of material world out of the primeval matter, which is governed by three virtues - lightness, activity and heaviness, is quite similar to three Gunas -Sattva, Rajas and Tamas of Sankhya Philosophy.

Sometimes this is believed that these philosophers were migrating to different countries. During their journey they were teaching their philosophy and learning the philosophy of other countries. There is an interesting story, about Indian philosopher who found his way to Athens and held an interview with Socrates

(469-399 B.C.).[252] When Socrates told that his philosophy consisted of an enquiry into human life, the Indian philosopher smiled and told, that no one can understand the human affairs unless he had no knowledge of divine.[253]

This clearly establishes the fact that there was some sort of interactions between the two countries. Probably the Greek philosophy was more influenced by the ancient Indian philosophy. Plato (427-347 B.C.) the disciple of Socrates was also impressed by Indian philosophy. He paid visit to different countries of the world including Persia. Some scholars believe that he had come to India for some time. His theories of the bondage of soul to matter and its liberation therefrom, his doctrine of reincarnation, seem to be distinctly Sankhyan.[254] According to Hopkins, Plato derived the Sankhyan thoughts from the Pythagoras. His smile of the Charioteer and the horses recalls the smile of Kathopanishad, "of the body with a car, the soul with a charioteer, the senses with the horses and the mind with the ruins".[255] Unwrick says that Plato's conception for his republics is probably an echo of Indian ideas and his division of ideal polity as Guardians, Auxiliaries and Craftsmen, is similar to the Hindu caste system,[256] Brahmanas, Kshatriyas, Vaisyas. The smile of the cave, referred to in the 7th book of the Republic, recalls the Vedantic doctrine of Maya or illusion.[257]

The legend, that Universe was created from the body of Zeus, after he had swallowed Phanes, the offspring of the great 'world egg' is almost similar to the story of the coming into being of "Supreme-soul by thought of the golden egg" (Brahmanda) was mentioned in the tenth book of Manu.[258] Max Mueller points out the amazing similarity between the language of Plato and Upanishads.[259] Rawlinson believes it as a accidental. But the possibility of influence of Indian philosophy on Plato cannot be denied in total.

Indian logic was also influenced by the Greek system of logic. The definition of the most important logical terms and the explanation of various structures seem to have been derived from the prior Analytics of Aristotle.[260] (384-322 B.C.). It is usually believed that the logic started in India by Akshapada, whom was a monk residing near Broach of Kathiwar. Probably he learnt this system from any person or traders coming from Alexandria, a trade centre had close connection with Broach. At Alexandria, the Greek philosophical works were preserved in library through the efforts of Callimachaus.[261]

It is clearly visible that Indian religion had left indelible impacts on the religion of Greek. The Greek Gods like-Zeus, Minerva, and Helios can be identified with Indian Gods - Indra, Ushas, Savitar.[262] Buddhism also has something common with Orphism in Greece.[263] Both the sects lived in monastic communities, abstained from taking life or eating meat and believed in the doctrine of Metempsychosis.[264]

The exchange of idea was not confined to the sphere of religion and philosophy; it was extended to other spheres like mining, armies also. It is generally inferred that the Indians learnt the system of mining from the Greeks.[265] The word *surangi* in Sanskrit, meaning mine, seems cognate with word *'syrinx'* which is the Greek word for mine.[266] The idea of palisade may have been introduced through the Indians enlisted in the Greek armies.[267] In the field of medicine also there was some exchange of ideas also. Greek physical conception of the wind was influenced by the Indian nervous activity. It has been claimed that in 4th century B.C. "Hippocratic treaties of the winds" was influenced by the Indian conception, which was already in vogue in about 8th C.B.C.[268]

From this, one can clearly presume that Indians and Greeks had close connection not only in the matters of trade but also in other spheres of culture, philosophy, logic, medicine etc. Alexander's invasion accentuated the process of intermingling. Religion, literature, coinage were the fields where the exchange is clearly perceptible. The quest of knowledge had dragged the Greek philosophers to Indian soil to unravel the Indian philosophy in front of the world.

The traders were going through either by land routes or sea routes. The traders had different kinds of experiences in different routes. Again they were taking some precautionary measures to avoid the difficulties in the journey. Both the routes were not free from troubles.

Caravan Traders

In spite of many difficulties in traveling there is hardly any doubt that the masters of caravan increasingly carried the internal and external trade of India. Though the basic motive of these traders was to earn the money through the commercial activities, they were interested sometimes to carry the culture to the distant land. It is usually believed that the trade during the ancient India was peaceful and free of troubles. But the fact is that the traders were facing a lot of difficulties in their way of journey. Like today, even in those days the robbers and thieves were posing great danger to the trading activities.[269] Again some tribes in the jungles were disturbing the traders. Forests were infested with wild beasts and caravans often missed the right direction and proceeded in a wrong direction. In these types of journey, the leader of caravan play a leading role by taking the right decision by his intelligence and experience and keeps a proper control over all the members of his group.[270] He usually took care of arrangement of food and proper distribution. Again in the time of danger he never lost the equanimity of the mind. It is mentioned in Jataka[271] that when a caravan entered into a forest, then the master of Caravan issued an order to his followers that without his permission they should not eat strange leaves, fruits and flowers. Once his followers fell ill by eating the forbidden articles but the master of the caravan cured them by administering emetics.

The traders were taking care of various things like the possibility of roads being ruined, water would become scarce, and there would be no food and grass for bullock and availability of fresh vegetables. Water scarcities were the very common problem and for that reason the caravan leader kept a proper control over water by issuing the order.[272] Due to the scarcity of water, the group of traders perished in the desert. Journey during the daytime in the deserts was very difficult due to scorching heat. And, therefore, the caravan carried with it water, oil, rice and travelled during the night. In the morning the travellers arranged their wagons in circle and covered them with an awning. After finishing their breakfast they rested for the whole day in the shade. After the sunset, taking their dinner they pushed on their wagons and resumed their march. Their travel in the deserts was like sailing in the ocean. A guide (*Sthalaniyamaka)* with the help of stars guided the caravan.[273] When they crossed the desert they throw the water *and* wood, which bore a lot of burden. The guide seated on the leading wagon and marking the movements of stars guided the caravan.[274]

In spite of so many difficulties the traders continued their journey. Sometimes they were assisted by armed men to protect them from the dangers of robbers and man- haunting tribes and wild animals. In these types of journey, the caravan leader's experience, presence of mind, his knowledge about geography and astronomy, gave them success.

Sea Merchants

In Jataka stories many sea voyages are mentioned which point to the difficulties of Indian sailors. The Baveru Jataka (Jataka 339) informs us that some merchants of Varanasi taking the direction finding birds with themselves when they set out on a sea voyage to Babylonia. This voyage was performed through the Arabia Sea and Persian Gulf. The Supparaka Jataka (463) tells us that the brave sailors of Ancient India passed through Khuramala (the Persian Gulf) the Agnimala (Red Sea), Dadhimala Nilakusamala, Nalamala and Balabhamukha (the Mediterranean Sea). However history informs us that before the Christian era the Indian navigation did not proceed beyond Bab-el-Mandeb. Taking this into account, it is usually believed that Arab merchants to Egypt carried out the Indian goods and then it was passed into other countries. But some scholars don't believe in this principle.

In Ancient India, sea travellers had to face many difficulties and dangers and those who returned home safely, were considered lucky. In such conditions, the near and dear ones of the traders often dissuaded them to carry out such a long journey. But unlike the medieval sailors, the ṣailors of Ancient India were brave and adventurous. At one place it is said that when a wealthy merchant of Varanasi built a ship and decided to take a sea voyage, his mother tried her best to dissuade him, but as he was determined to sail, he left his mother weeping and boarded the ship.[275]

In Ancient India, the wooden ships were drowned by the whirlpools. Their greatest weakness was their very simple construction. Unlike the Arab merchants and sailors, India merchants were unable to built the boats and ships which could stand against the whirlpool and winds in the mid- sea. Usually the ships, which were made of timbers, are unable to withstand the pressure of water. The water seeped through the joints of timber and sinks the whole ship.[276] When the ship began sinking the merchants prayed to their gods to save them from the calamity.[277]. When they saw their prayer did not bear fruits, they left the wrecked ships. But before abandoning the ships the voyagers filled themselves with ghee and sugar which could sustain them for long-time. It is mentioned in Sunkha Jatak that on the seventh day of Sunkha's voyage, the ships developed the leaks and the sailors were unable to bale the water out. Fearing for their lives, they became boisterous but Sankha, keeping calm took a servant with him and oiling his body and partaking a meal of ghee and sugar climbed the mast and plunged into the sea and floated for seven days.[278]

The Jataka further informs us that the ships were made of timber planks (daruphalakani). They sailed with favourable wind (erakvyayutta).[279] We get further information about the construction of the ships. Besides its outer framework it was provided with three mast (kupa), rigging (Yottaran) sails (sittam), planks (padarani) and oars (lankharoh).[280] The helmsman controlled the movement of the ship with the help of steering wheel.[281] The navigators were tracing the route by closely viewing the position of stars. Sometimes people who had much more experience about navigation assisted them.

Like the ancient Phoenicians and Babylonians, the Indian sailors also used direction-finding birds for locating the seashore. These direction-finding birds were released from the ships. In Keraddhasutta of Dighanikaya, in the words of Buddha, "In very ancient times the sea going merchants took the direction finding birds on their ships which were released when required. They flew on all directions and alighted when they saw solid grounds. But if no such ground was seen they returned to the same ship.[282] There are also references about the direction finding birds in Baveru Jatak.[283] According to this Jatak, the Babylonians had no knowledge of such birds and, therefore they bought it from an Indian merchant, but the Babylonian literature is explicit on the point that the Babylonians knew about the direction finding birds from the hoary past. It is mentioned in the story of Gilgamesh that the ship of Utanipishtam reached the Nistir Mountain and then settled down. At first he released a pigeon, and afterwards a sparrow to find the shore. In the end a crow was released and when it did not return then it was decided that the seashore was very near.[284]

Some strange customs were prevalent in the journey. When the ship was in trouble then the reason for that is assigned to the presence of some unfortunate voyagers.[285] His name was found out by casting the lot. There is very little material in Buddhist literature, which tells us about the programme of entertainment of voyagers in the ship. Music was the common mode of entertainment or amusement. One Jataka[286] tells us very interesting story about a musician in the ship who became responsible for the wreck of the ship. Because when he started to display the music, the ship was surrounded by big fishes and sea animals to hear the music and caused the wreckage of the ship.

There does not seem to have existed any agreement between the sea merchants except that they hired a ship in groups. It is mentioned in one of the Jatakas[287] that the two merchants had entered into a partnership for carrying the trade with five hundred wagons. In another Jataka,[288] partnership between several merchants is mentioned. The horse merchants from Uttarapatha also carried on their business in partnership. It was possible in a limited degree to prevent unhealthy competition and to realise proper prices.[289]

There was difference in the views of Buddhist and Brahmins about this international trade. The parochial viewpoint of Brahamanas was that the whole world was confined to the country between Vindhyas and Himalayas, in the South to the sea, in the west to the Indus and in the east Brahmaputra River. For the Brahmanic culture, Aryavarta was the centre of the Universe and those who are living outside were treated as hateful Mlechhas.[290] In the matters of food and drinks and in the marriage, the caste system held sway, and, therefore fearing contacts with foreigners sea voyage was forbidden, though it is open to question that in Ancient India how many people have followed the general ban.[291] The Buddhists, however, did not believe in the caste system and therefore, we get many accounts of sea voyage in the Buddhist literature which are almost absent in the Brahminical literature.[292]

The trade which continued for a long time was not due to get the goods of foreign countries and to sell the good of our own country in the lands of foreigners. The traders in Ancient India were not only merely mercenary traders but also ambassadors of Indian culture. Crossing the geographical boundaries they helped the human society to come closer.[293]

Herodotus' Account of India

Herodotus, whom Cicero dubbed the Father of History, was able to offer considerable information about the distant land of India. Herodotus was born at Haticamassus in Asia Minor and then dependent on Persians about the year of 484 B.C.[294] He was thus born as a Persian subject and was interested in the affairs of Persia and Egypt. He complied a history of Achaemenids and of Scythians, but as Keane has observed, "his knowledge of India was meagre and most vague."[295] Herodotus knew that India was one of the remotest provinces of the Persian Empire towards the East, but of its extent and exact position, he had not proper conception.[296]

Sources of Knowledge

An analysis of his account shows that his knowledge of India was derived from the following sources.

- The information that he was able to collect for himself in the course of his travel.
- The information supplied to him by the Persians.[297]
- The work left by Scylax of Caryanda.[298]
- The narrative of Hecatarus of Miletus.[299]

Hensdotus, as a traveler, travelled different parts of the world, though the dates of travelling are difficult to determine. He visited the Persian capital Susa and advanced as far as the land of Scythians in Central Asia.[300] So it may be presumed that in course of his travels, he might have gathered some information about India. But we don't know whether he did see the Achaemenid epigraphs. Macan thinks that, "The Achaemenid records which have within living memory greatly modified our knowledge of the rise and progress of Persian power were inaccessible to Herodotus, but his account of that empire and its organisation must go back, at second or third, to such documents and written records."[301]

The documents and written records of the Persians throwing light on India which may be divided into two groups, the Persian inscriptions and the Avesta. The references to India in the Achaemenid epigraphs have already been noted and it is clear from them that they show nowhere any knowledge of the interior of India. This closely agrees with the account of India as preserved in Avesta. The date of Avesta is highly controversial but most of the scholars agree to the point that Venandiad is the earliest part of work and may have been pre-Achaemenid period. There is the mention of sixteen countries, which were created by Ahura Mazda. One among them is Hapta Hindu or Sapta Sindhu, which is also occurring in Rig Veda.[302] Max Muller thinks that the expression of 'Sapta Sindhu' refers to the five streams of Punjab with Indus and Saraswati. While Ludwig. Lassen and Whitney hold that Kubha should be substituted for the last named river.[303]

Again in another statement of Velandid, it is clearly

mentioned that the religion of Ahura Mazda was introduced in the Sapta Sinhdu areas and the people of the region or at least a section of it, had Iranian blood in them.[304] This reminds us of the statement of Xerexes in his Persepolis epigraph that he suppressed the worship of the Daivas and introduced that of Ahura Mazda in its place,[305] while the traces of Iranian blood is found in the borderland of Indo-Iranian region. All the anthropologists again admit it.

The Work of Scylax

For his account, Herodotus utilized the work of Scylax of Caryanda.[306] Possibly, he was the first Greek historian to write anything about India (515BC). The work of Scylax is unfortunately lost which is preserved in the works of later writers partly in the form of references. In his History, Herodotus has preserved the following account of his.

A great part of Asia was explored under the direction of Darius. He being desirous to know in what part the Indus that produces crocodiles, discharges itself into the sea. Skylax set out from the city of Caspatyrus and the country of Pactyce, sailed down the river towards the east and then to the sea; then sailing on the sea westwards, they arrived in the thirteen months at the place where the King of Egypt dispatched the Phoenicians, whom I before mentioned to sail round Libya. After these persons had sailed round, Darius subdued the Indians and frequented the sea."[307]

The above account of Herodotus, in any case, shows that Scylax actually came to India and started his journey from "the city of Caspatyrus and the country of Pactyce. Sir Aurel Stein identified these places with north Afganistan and Kabul respectively. Majumdar, however, mentions that it appears from the account of Herodotus that the city of Caspatyrus in Pactyce was quite close to the lower Indus-valley bordering on the desert.

About Indians

Herodotus thought that Indians were the most remote nation

living in the east and beyond them was a desert. He was ignorant about the Ganges Valley and the Great Himalayan chains. He knew however, that 'there are many nations of Indians and they don't speak the same language as each other, some of them are nomads and others are not. These Indians wear a garment made of rushes, which, when they have cut the reed from the river and beaten it, they afterwards paint like a mat and wear it like a corselet.'[308]

Thus Herodotus knew that, "there are many nations of the Indians" and he enumerates some of them.

- Other Indians, living to the east are nomads and eat raw flesh; they are called Padaeans.
- Other Indians have the following different customs; they never kill anything that has life, nor sow anything....

It is generally presumed by historians that they were Buddhists or Jainas.

- Herodotus knows further of Indians who were inhabiting very far from the Persians, towards the south and were never subject to Darius.' From his description, as it is generally thought by some scholars that they were Dravidians.
- There are other Indians bordering on the city of Caspatyrus and the country of Pactyce, settled northward of India, whose mode of life resembles that of the Bactrians.

It gives an idea that Herodotus had knowledge about the different classes of Indian people who were living in different parts of Achaemenid Empire.[309]

Herodotus knew that Indians are by far the greatest multitude of all races of men whom we know but he had hardly any knowledge of the civilized Indians in Gangetic Valley. Again his reference about cannibals is no way related to Gonds who were cannibals.[310] His account of the Indians, who killed their own relatives on the approach of old age, seems to be a transference of Sogdian custom on Indian soil, for we learn it on the authority of Plutarch that Alexander taught the Sogdians not to kill their fathers. Strabo quotes Onesicritus to the effect that people of Bactria had reared dogs that were trained to eat the dying. When

Alexander conquered, Indian subcontinent, he stopped this practice.

Gold Digging Ants

Herodotus gives an interesting account of gold digging ants, which threw, up mounds of gold dust in the desert.[311] And out of this gold dust, Indians paid their tribute to the Great King Darius.[312] It was said this gold was guarded by gigantic ants but the Indians, mounted on swift she-camels, plundered the gold at mid-day when the ants were asleep in their holes.[313] These ants were smaller than dogs but larger than foxes and threw up the gold in excavating their burrows. Some of them were in the possession of Darius-I. Later writers talk of having seen their skin[314] or even their horns. The curious story arose from the Sankrit Paippilika ," ant-gold" a term applied to alluvial gold from its resemblance to the earth of ant-hills.[315] The gold was carried off from the miners of Dardistan who still keep fierce yellow mastiff to guard their houses. These mastiffs were the "ants" of the legend, the horns that Pliny asserts, were the horns of wild sheep, which mounted in the handles, are still used by the miners and farmers of Ladak as pickaxes.[316] The exorbitant demands of Persians exhausted the gold of Dardistan. For this reason, it is seldom mentioned in later literature. Many scholars accept this story as false because mines of metals like gold and silver were not known to exist in India. Scholars like Heeren and Lassen alludes doubtfully to Pliny's statement. They point out that it was presented wrongly because India's trade with gold producing countries likes Burma and Tibet, which was misconceived by the different authors.[317] No conclusion can be drawn on this fact and it awaits more evidences.

Indo-Achaemenid Empire

According to Herodotus, Darius conquered the region of Sind after the exploration of the river Indus by Scylax and his party. But it is partly true because after the conquest of India by Darius, Scylax traced the route. Again he had pointed out that Darius received 360 talents in gold dust as tribute of his Indian satrapy and this was the largest amount paid by any other province of the empire. Same scholars doubt about the truthfulness of this statement because the area conquered by Darius was arid region. Therefore, it seems utter impossibility to pay such a vast amount of revenue. But Smith thinks that owing to the changes in the course of rivers since ancient times, 'vast tracts in the Sind and the Punjab, now desolate, were then rich and prosperous.' Cousens contradicts this theory and points out that a great geological change seems to have hardly occurred to alter the character of the soil.

If it will be accepted that Arian is the party of Alexander, then he does not mention about the gold of India.'[318] The epigraph of Darius also mentions that though India was providing ivory and teak wood for the construction of Susa palace, the gold was procured from the satrapies of Sardis or Bactria. From this it is clearly evident that if the gold was abundant in India why Darius imported gold from Bactria, not from India.[319] No final conclusion is drawn on this statement.

Though the account of Herodotus provides a good knowledge about Indians, sometimes it drags into controversies. It is generally presumed that Herodotus' information is basically based on secondary sources.

Conclusion

History of West Asia is closely related with the history of India. The two regions had established their political and trade relations from the very beginning. Though it passed through many ups and downs in different periods, it continued without any break. From 6th century B.C., the trade with West Asia attained a new height due to political relations, which was established with the invasion of Cyrus. Politically the invasion of Cyrus was a triumph without results. But from the trade and cultural point of view it carries a great importance. Indian merchants carried their goods to different parts of Persian empires and through the channels of trade, wide relationship between India and Western

Asia was established. Again the exploration of Skylax, Persian navigator, opened better routes of communication between the two sub continents. In the sphere of culture, the impacts of Persians were widely felt in the Mauryan period. The Mauryan art and architecture, specially the pillars of Ashok, were influenced by the Greek and Persian styles. Ashokan scripts like Kharosti were undoubtedly derived from Persian script Armaic. Again Ashok's rock-inscriptions bears close resemblance to Darius' inscription. The possibility of Ashok's imitation to Darius' inscription can't be denied. Again Persian coinage, court styles had created impacts on Indians. It will be highly unworthy to say that Indians had no way influenced the Persians. Early Buddhism influenced the movements in Persia like Manichacism. Again the similarities between the stories of Jatak, and the judgement of Solomon and Babylonian mythology, clarify the suspense. But it is difficult to know who had influenced whom to what extent.

Alexander's invasion was another milestone in the path of this relation; it no way hampered the smooth progress of relations. His invasion of India was a wanton aggression, mayhem and bloody warfare in the chapter of Indian history. But his solid interests to establish a commercial intercourse are clearly visible. His immature death and breaking down of his vast empire gave a burial death to his long cherished ambitions. He broke the wall of separation between the East and West and the process of Hellenization started from this period. All subsequent contacts between India and Greece are the legacies of Alexander's campaign. In real sense, Alexander opened the floodgates of foreign invasions. He set up various trading centres, which helped the merchants to carry out their trade. Mauryan Empire, which rose from the ashes of Macedonian empire, helped the traders to carry out their peaceful, trade in a full swing and to bring the wealth and prosperity to India. The routes traced out by Alexander to India added further to the geographical knowledge of traders.

The trade between India and West Asia was basically indirect. The Indian traders were not carrying all the goods directly to western part of Asia. Sometimes the Arab traders and Jewish traders were carrying the goods from India. When Indian traders were carrying the goods, they were carrying up to the point of Alexandria and a little further to this point. Then other merchants carried these goods because Indian boats were not so much strong enough to travel long in the sea against the tides. But some of the evidences support the presence of Indian traders in West-Asian countries, whose number was quite low. Basically most of the trade was carried on indirectly.

On the basis of archaeological and literary sources, the names of the goods, which were exported as well as imported, have been identified. This points out that the balance of trade was in favour of India. Indian goods were highly acclaimed in Western countries and it drained the heavy amount of money from their treasure. It was a great concern for the rulers but they could not check the import of Indian goods. Nothing could be told about its prices but it can be presumed safely that the quality of the goods was undoubtedly high. That was the single most reason why these goods were praised in different parts of world.

Again the trade of recent days is totally different from those days. Now days, the goods, which cost more in one country, can be brought from other country if it is found cheaper. But in those days, the goods, which were unavailable in one country, could be imported from other country. This means that the non-availability of goods determine the list of imports. These countries rarely produced the Indian products, which were exported to other countries. Again if they were producing the same, it might not fulfill their demands. This was the fundamental law, which was determining the course of trade.

India is a vast country having large flora and fauna. The fertile soil of India was producing the agricultural products, which was enough to meet the demands of the people. In contrast, the West Asian territory was not fertile enough to meet the needs of their people. So the West Asian people were dependent on agricultural products of India. Again the small-scale industries and cottage industries under the system of guilds were producing the good quality of goods. And the people were trained sufficiently to produce the good things, which were liked by the people. Therefore, the woolen, silk and cotton garments were highly praised in foreign countries. The Indian people had few secondary wants. This was the reason for the balance of trade, which was in favour of India.

One question which always puzzles the scholars that if balance of trade was in favour of India then how the countries of West Asia were paying for the extra goods. Large quantity of foreign coins, which were excavated at different places, is the probable answer of this question. But another question arises that what was the use of these coins. Only one thing is clear that to some extent these coins were fulfilling the needs of metal of India. This question still awaits answer.

In the sphere of culture, the relations between India and West Asia carry special importance. Both regions were influenced by each other to a great extent. In the matter of architecture, the Mauryan palace, Ashokan pillars bear a close resemblance with Iranian style. Kharosti and Aramic scripts were introduced in India. Greek philosophy, religions are highly indebted to Indian counterparts but the Greek syllogism, medicine, mining technology created influence on India. Greek thinkers perhaps came to India to explore the ancient knowledge of India. Religion, literature, coinage, philosophy were the important areas where the considerable exchanges of ideas took place.

Trade was the only medium through which cultural migration took place. On the other hand, political domination also helped to some extent for this cultural transformation. When two ancient civilizations grew up in one continent it is obvious that the relationship would grow up between them, which happened in the case of India and West Asia. Again these two civilizations share their origin from one place, if Aryans had come from Europe. In this critical situation, the cultural mingling and transference were a common incidence.

The foregoing description makes it clear that India's relations in the matter of cultural, economic as well as political continued to be strengthened with West Asian countries with the passage of time. Such countries were Egypt, Judaea, Assyria, Iran, and Babylon etc. In these countries, new fields of mutual relationships were discovered in different spheres. The advanced techniques of sea-voyage and road journeys helped the people in this respect. The fact that man's quest for developing new relations knows no bound is attested by the above mentioned contacts which India developed with other countries during this period.

End Notes

---

[1] Asthana, S., *History and Archaeology of Indian Contracts with other Countries,* p 163.
[2] Ibid.
[3] Rao, S.R., Shipping in Ancient India, p. 8 8.
[4] Ibid.
[5] Mookherjee, R.K., *History of Indian Shipping,* p. 5 9.
[6] Ibid.
[7] Rawlinson, H.G., A Manual of Ancient History, p.23.
[8] Smith, C.E., and Moorehead, *A history of the Ancient World,* p. 1.
[9] Upadhyaya, B.C., *The Ancient World,* p.24.
[10] Rawlinson, H.G., *A Manual of Ancient History,* p.23.
[11] Sykes, P., *A History of Persia,* p. 119.
[12] Rawlinson, H.G., *A Manual of Ancient History,* p.77.
[13] Ibid. p.78.
[14] Ibid. p.79.
[15] *The Cambridge Ancient History,* vol. iv, p.4.
[16] Ibid. p.8.
[17] Smith , C.E., and Morehead, *A History of Ancient World,* p.80.
[18] Ibid. p.82.
[19] *The Cambridge Ancient History,* vol. IV, p.7.
[20] Ibid. p.8.
[21] Starr, P.,*A History of the Ancient World,* p. 124.
[22] Ibid. p.126.
[23] Toynbee, A.J., *A Study of History,* p. 146.
[24] *Cambridge, Ancient History,* vol.IV, p.9.
[25] Rawlinson, H.G., *Annual of Ancient History,* p.25.
[26] Ibid.,p.26.

[27] Smith, C.E., and Morehead, *A Short History of the Ancient World*, p.56.
[28] Ibid. p.57.
[29] Ibid. p.58.
[30] Smith, S., *Early History of Assyria*, p. 105.
[31] Ibid., p. 106.
[32] Smith and Morehead, *A Short History of the Ancient World*, p.71.
[33] Ibid., p.72.
[34] Rogers, R.W., *A History of Babylonia and Assyria*, p.59.
[35] Mookherjee, R.K., *History of Indian Shipping*, p.57.
[36] Rawlinson, H.G., *Intercourse between India and World*, p.l.
[37] Ibid.
[38] Ibid.
[39] Me. Crindle, *Ancient India*, p. 12.
[40] Ibid.
[41] Strabo, *Geography*, XVI, p. 5.
[42] Herodotus, VII p.89.
[43] Strabo, *Geography*, XVI. pp. 3-5.
[44] Rawlinson, H.G., op.cit, p.7.
[45] Herodotus, vol.IV, p.32.
[46] Smith, V.A., *Early History of India*, p.34.
[47] Ibid.
[48] Asthana, S., *History and Archaeology of Indian Contacts with other Countries*, p.138,
[49] Ibid., p. 139.
[50] Tarn, W.W., *Hellenistic Civilization*, p.243.
[51]Coomarswamy, A.K., *Arts and Crafts of India and Ceylon*, p.40.
[52] Strabo-II. p.15
[53] Ibid
[54] Rawlinson, H.G., op.cit., p. 10.
[55] Ibid. p. 10.
[56] Warmington, E.H., *The Commerce between the Roman Empire and India*, p.9.
[57]Banfey, *Indien*, p.90, quoted by Rawlinson, H.G., op.cit.,p.l 1.
[58] Mookherjee, R.K., *Indian Shipping*, p. 64.
[59]Ibid.
[60] Herodotus, vii, p. 65
[61]Mc. Crindle, *Ancient India*, p. 10
[62]Rawlinson, H.G., op.cit., p. 12.

---

[63]Ibid

[64]Das, D. R, *Economic History of Deccan,* p.237.

[65] Das. D.R., *Economic History of Deccan,* p.236.

[66]*Bombay City Gazetteer,* vol.11, p. 3. quoted by Mookherjee, R.K., *Indian Shipping,* p. 62 and Das, D.R., op.cit., p.236.

[67]*Jataka,* vol.4, pp. 138-142

[68] Chandra, Moti *Trade and Trade Routes in Ancient India,* p.63.

[69]Ibid.

[70] Rawlinson, H.G., op.cit., p.26.

[71] Ibid.

[72] Chandra, Moti, op.cit., p.49.

[73]Ibid.

[74]Ibid.

[75] Mookherjee, R.K., *Indian Shipping,* p.5

[76] Habbin is no doubt a corruption of ibha.

[77]Rawlinson, H.G., *The Commercial Intercourse between India and World,* p. 11

[78] Ibid.

[79]Ibid. p. 13.

[80] Asthana, S., *History and Archaeology of Indian Contracts with other Countries,* p. 162.

[81]Mookherjee, R.K., *Indian Shipping,* p. 5 8.

[82]Ibid.

[83]Rawlinson, H.G., op.cit., p.5

[84]Das, D.R., *Economic History of Deccan,* p.228.

[85] Watt, C.. *Commercial Products of India,* p.67.

[86] Ibid.

[87]Asthana S., op.cit.. p. 165.

[88] Ibid.

[89] Mookherjee, R.K., *Indian Shipping,* p. 5 8.

[90] Ibid.

[91] Jeamine Auboyer, *Daily Life in Ancient India,* p. 81.

[92] Raychoudhury, H.C., *Political History of Ancient India,* p.193.

[93] Ibid.

[94] Rawlinson, H.G., op.cit., p. 16.

[95] Herodotus-I, p. 190 quoted by S. Chattopadhyaya, *The Achaemenids and India,* p.55.

[96] Raychoudhury, H.C., *Political History of Ancient India,* p. 193. "Ibid.

[97] Ibid

[98] Jainazbhoy, R.A., *Origin and Spread of Ancient Civilization,* p. 115.
[99] William Jackson, *Cambridge History of India,* vol.1, p.297.
[100] Arrian, *Indica-I,* pp. 1-3.
[101] Tolman. J., *Sculpture and Inscriptions of Darius the Great on the Rock of Behistan in Persia,* p.4.
[102] Rawlinson, H.G., op.cit., p. 10.
[103]Raychoudhury, H.C., op.cit., p. 195.
[104] Raychoudhury, H.C., op.cit., p. 195
[105]Rawlinson, H.G., op.cit.,p.17.
[106] Ibid.
[107] Herodotus, IV.p.44.
[108] Rawlinson, H.G., op.cit., p. 18.
[109] Ibid.
[110]It is interesting to know that gold dust was available in the Upper Indus bed in these days. Herodotus also refers about "gold digging ants" in the region. Modern scholars have concluded that these so-called "gold digging ants" were Tibetan Mastiffs who grounded the gold rivers of Dardistan and are also mentioned in the Mahabharat, vide -Age of Imperial Unity, p.41.
[111]Smith, V.A., *Early History of India,* p.40 and H.C., Raychoudhury, op.cit., p. 192.
[112]Herodotus., vol.IV. p.185.
[113] Ibid.
[114] Ray Choudhury, H.C., *Political History of Ancient India,* p. 195.
[115] Ibid.
[116] *Epigraphica Indica,* vol.XIX, p.253.
[117]Jainazbhoy, R.A., *Origin and Spread of Ancient Civilization,* p. 117.
[118] Raychoudhury, H.C., op.cit., p. 196.
[119] Ibid.
[120] Ibid.
[121]. Raychoudhury, H.C., *Political History of Ancient India* p. 195.
[122] *Epigraphica Indica,* XIX, p.253.
[123] Marshall, J., *Guide to Taxila,* p.78.
[124] *Indian Antiquary,* 1905.
[125]Chattopadhyaya, S., *The Achaemenids and India,* p. 55.
[126] Ibid. p.56.
[127] Ibid. p.56.
[128] Ibid. p.59.

[129] Spooner, D.D., "The Zoroastrian Period of India History", *Journal of Royal Asiatic Society,* 1915.
[130]Ibid.
[131] Thapar, R., *A History of India, p.59.*
[132] Sastri, N.K., *Age of Nandas and Mauryas,* p.46.
[133]Ibid.
[134] Smith, V.A., *Early History of India,* p.52.
[135] Majumdar, R.C., *Age of Imperial Unity,* p.52.
[136] Mc. Crindle, *Invasion by Alexander,* p.306.
[137] Smith,V.A., *Early History of India,* p.59, Smith's arguments are highly subjective.
[138] Bevan, A., *Cambridge History of India,* vol.1, p.322.
[139] Majumdar, R.C., *Age of Imperial Unity,* p.54.
[140]Smith, V.A., *Early History of India,* p. 115.
[141] Smith, V.A., *Early History of India,* p. 117
[142] Burry, Bun *History of Greece,* p.56.
[143] Ibid.
[144]Arrian, *Expedition of Alexander, VI,* p. 15 quoted by G. Rawlinson, *Intercourse between India and Western World.*
[145] Ibid. (The course of the river was changing so rapidly that it is difficult to identify it. This is the part to which Nearchus gave the name of *Nausfathmos* Alexander's Haven. It may be port called by the strange name of Barbarikon in the Periplus.
[146] Cambridge *History,* vol.1, p.550.
[147]Ibid.
[148]*Mahavamsa,* (trans) Turnur, p. 110.
[149] Rawlinson, H.G., op.cit., p.35.
[150] Sridhar, K., *A maritime history of India,* p. 14.
[151]Ibid.
[152]Ballard, G.A., *Rulers of the Indian Ocean,* p.9.
[153] Wheeler, M., *Alexander the Great,* p. 136.
[154] Smith, V.A., *Oxford History,* ed. by Basham, L. p.65.
[155]Bevan, A., *Cambridge History of India,* p. 3 45.
[156] Smith, V.A., *Early History of India,* p. 117.
[157]Rao, S.R., *Shipping in Ancient India,* pp.88-90.
[158] Asthana, Shashi, *History and Archaeology of Indian Contacts with other Countries,* p.163.
[159] Ibid.

[160] Ayenger, S. K.,The Trade of India", *Indian Historical Quarterly-II,* p.3
[161] Ibid.p..9.
[162] Ibid.
[163]Mookherjee, R.K., *Indian Shipping,* p. 91. 64
[164] Asthana, S., *History and Archaeology of Indian contacts with other Countries,* p. 165.
[165] Ibid. p. 167.
[166] It has of course have been located variously in Arabia, Ceylone, the Malaya Peninsula and various parts of India.
[167] Ibid. p.218.
[168]Asthana, S., *History and Archaeology of Indian Contacts with other Countries,* p. 166.
[169] Ibid.
[170] Rawlinson, H.G., "Foreign Influences in the Civilization of Ancient India", *Journal of BombayBranch Royal Asiatic Society,* vol.23, p.218.
[171]. Ibid.
[172]Iyenger, S.K., op.cit., p.40
[173] Asthana, S., op.cit.,p.l67.
[174] Rawlinson, H.G., *Intercourse between Indian and Western World,* p.3.
[175] Ibid.
[176] Majumdar, R.C., *The Age of Imperial Unity,* p. 612.
[177] *Periplus,* pp. 123-160.
[178]Thompson, J., *A Dictionary of Assyrian Botany,* p. 106-107.
[179] Rawlinson, H.G., op.cit., p. 149.
[180] Asthana, S. op.cit., p. 168.
[181]Chakrovarty, R., 'The Persian and Greek Coins and their Imitations in Ancient India", vol. 10, pp.70-71.
[182] Ibid.
[183] Ibid.
[184] Chakrobarti, R., op.cit., pp.70-71.
[185] Asthana, S., op.cit., p. 171.
[186] Rapson, E.J., "Counter Marks on Early Persian and Indian Coins", *Journal of Royal Asiatic Society,* 1895, p.865.
[187] Chakrobarty, R., op.cit., pp.70-71.
[188] Ibid.
[189] Asthana, S., op.cit, p. 171.
[190]Ibid.

---

[191] Smith, V.A., *The Early History of India,* 4th ed. p.66.
[192] Chattopadhyaya, S., "Foreign Notices of Achaemenid India" Indian *Historical Quarterly,* vol.26, 1950. p. 102.
[193] Arrian, *Indica,* 22, p.27.
[194] Olmstead, A.T., *History of the Persian Empire,* p. 145.
[195] Mukherjee, R.K., *Indian Shipping,* p. 8 2.
[196] Asthana, S., op.cit., p. 172.
[197] Iron has been reported from some of the graves of the Swat Valley dated to 900 B.C. and also from neolithic-megalitic deposits of Hallow, Dist. Dharwar, Karnatak dated to1000-900 B.C.
[198] Chattopadhyaya, S., *The Achaemenids and India,* p.57.
[199] Ibid.
[200] *Mahabharat-II, p.5{3.*
[201] Smith, V.A., *Early History of India,* p. 135.
[202] *Indian Antiquary,* 1908,p.79.
[203]*Apasthamba Dhamrasastra-I. VI.*
[204] Chattopadhyaya, S., *The Achaemenids and India,* p.62.
[205] Marshall, J.,*A, Guide to Taxila,* p.24.
[206] Asthana, S., op.cit, p. 172.
[207] Chattopadhyaya, S., "Foreign Notices of Achaemenid India", Indian *Historical Quarterly,* vol.26, p.101. " 208 Rawlinson, H.G., *Intercourse between India and Western World,* p.7.
[208] Rawlinson,H.G.,*Intercourse between India and Western World,* p.7.
[209] lyenger, S. K., "The trade of India", *Indian Historical Quarterly,* vol,2, p.42.
[210] Asthana, S., op.cit., p. 173.
[211] Rawlinson, H.G., op.cit., p.7.
[212] Strabo-IV, p.62.
[213] Chattopadhyaya, S., op.cit, p. 102.
[214] Ibid
[215] Chandra, Moti, *Sartavaha,* p.59 though identification of Beveru with Babylon is not quite definite, yet the majority of Historians subscribe to this identification.
[216] Kennedy, J., "The early commerce of Babylon with India", *Journal of Royal Asiatic Society,* 1898, p.268, quoted by Asthana,S., op.cit, p. 173.
[217] Prakash, B., "Vyasa (A Study of lndo-Babylonian Cultural Contacts)"Journal of *BiharOrissa Research Society,* vol.37, 1951, p.35.
[218]Ibid.
[219]Herodotus-I, p.l92.

[220] Ibid.
[221] Asthana, S., op.cit, p. 174.
[222] Rawlinson, H.G., *Intercourse between India and World,* p.3.
[223] Rhys, D., *Buddhist Birth Stories.* vol.-I, p. 14. and Rawlinson, H.G., op.cit., p. 11.
[224] Ibid., p.222.
[225] Henodotus, IV, p.44.
[226] *Sastri, N.K., Age of Nandas and Mauryas,* p. 83.
[227] Rawlinson, H.G., *Intercourse between India and Western World,* p. 17.
[228] . Mc. Crindle, *The Invasion of India by Alexander the Great,* pp.78-79.
[229] Ibid
[230] Mc. Crindle, *Ancient India as Described by Ktesias and Arrian,* p.29.
[231] Caldwell, R., *Grammar of Dravidian Language,* p. 105
[232] lyenger,S.K., "The Trade of India",,*Indian Historical Quarterly,* vol.11, pp.42-43.
[233] *.bid*
[234] Asthana, S., op.cit., p. 180
[235] Ibid.
[236] Aathana,S., op.cit., p. 180.
[237] Jaiftazbhoy, R.A., *Origin and Spread of Ancient Civilisation,* p. 119
[238] Ibid.
[239] Asthana,S., op.cit, p. 181.
[240] Unvala, J.M., "Political and Cultural Relations between Iran and India", *Annals of Bhandarkar Oriental Research Institute,* vol.28, 1947,
[241] Rhyrs, Davids, *Buddhist Birth Stories,* vol.1, p. 14.
[242] Herodotus, VI, p. 110.
[243] Herodotus, III, p. 18.
[244] *Jataka-I,* no.67 quoted Asthana;S., op.cit.,p.l82.
[245] Mitra, S.K., *India's Cultural Empire and Her Future,* p. 13.
[246] Ibid., p. 14.
[247] Asthana,S., op.cit.,p.l82.
[248] Jairazbhoy, R.A., *Foreign Influences on Ancient India,* p. 82.; *Sastri, N.K., Age of Nandas and Mauryas, p.81.*
[249] Mitra, S.K., op.cit., p.l4.
[250] Ashtana, S., op.cit., p. 182.
[251] Ibid. p.13

[252] Asthana, S., op.cit., p. 183.
[253] Rawlinson, H.G. op.cit., p.53., Mitra, S.K., op.cit, p. 14, and *Cambridge History,* vol.VI, p.310.
[254] Mitra, S.K., op.cit., p.l5.
[255] Asthana, S., op.cit., p. 183.
[256] Unwrick, *The Message of Plato,* p. 29, and Rawlinson, H.G., *India,* p. 56.
[257]Mitra, S.K., op.cit.,p.l5
[258] Ibid.
[259] Ashtana, S., op.cit, p. 184.
[260] Vidya Bhusan, "Influence of Aristotle on the Development of the Syllogism in Indian Logic" *Journal of Royal Asiatic Society,* 1918, p.469-71.
[261] Ibid.
[262] Asthana,S., op.cit.,p.l84.
[263] Rawlinson, H.G., *India,* p. 5 5.
[264] *Arrian, Vi..,p7.*
[265]Winternitz, M., "Surang and the Kautilya Arthsastra", *Indian Historical Quarterly,* vol.1, p.429.
[266] Ibid.
[267] Jairazbhoy, R.A., op.cit., p.50.
[268] Ibid. p.79'.
[269] Chandra, Moti, op.cit., p.58.
[270] Ibid.
[271] *Jataka,* vol.2, p.269. quoted by Moti Chandra, op.cit.,p.59.
[272] Das, D.R., *Economic History of Deccan,* p.236.
[273] Ibid.
[274] Chandra, Moti,,op.cit, p.59.
[275] *Jataka,* vol.4, p.2 quoted by Rawlinson, H.G.,op.cit., p.28
[276] Chandra, Moti, op.cit, p.61.
[277] *Jataka,* vol.4, p.34.
[278] *Jataka,* vol.4, p.2.
[279] Chandra, Moti, op.cit,p.62.
[280] Ibid
[281] Mookherjee, R.K., *History of Indian Shipping,* p.61.
[282] Chandra , Moti, op.cit, p.62.
[283] Ibid.
[284] Delaporte, *Mesopotamia,* p.207.
[285] *jataka,*Vol.3 ,p.124

[286] *Jataka,* vol.3, p. 124, quoted by Moti Chandra, op.cit., p.63.
[287] Ibid.
[288] *Jataka,* vol.4, p.350.
[289] Ibid.
[290] Warrington, E. H., *The Commerce between the Roman Empire and India, p. 103.*
[291] Ibid.
[292] Chandra, Moti, op.cit., p. 60
[293] Ibid.
[294] Chattopadhyaya, S., *The Achaemenids and India,* p. 42.
[295] Ibid.
[296] Keane, P., *Evolution of Geography,* pp. 5-6.
[297] Herodotus explicitly refers to the Persians while giving his account of gold digging ants.
[298] Herodotus, IV, p. 44.
[299] Ibid., 36,
[300] Chattopadhyaya, S., op.cit, p.43.
[301] *Cambridge Ancient History,* V, p.416.
[302] Chattopadhyaya,S., *The Achaemenids and India,* p. 43
[303] Ibid.
[304] Ibid. p. 44
[305] Rawlinson, H.G., *Intercourse between India and Western World,* p-18.
[306] Ibid.
[307] Herodotus, IV, p. 44.
[308] Ibid. p.48.
[309] Asthana, S., op.cit. p. 49.
[310] Asthana, S., op.cit. p.51.
[311] Rawlinson, H.G., op.cit.p.23
[312]. Ibid.
[313] Pliny says they were of the colour of cats and the size of Egyptian wolves.
[314] Strabo, (XV. 1.44), Megasthenes, Schwanbeck and Marten report that the skins of those ants were imported from Tibet and central Asia. The famous statue of Anaitis at Baktra was "clothed in bearer-skins"
[315] Wilson, *Ariana Antiquary,* p. 135 and Mc. Crindle, *Ancient India,* pp. 44-51.
[316] *Indian Antiquary,* vol-XII, 1884, p,229.
[317] Ibid., p.230.

[318] Arrian, v.44.
[319] Asthana, S., op.cit., p.52.

3

Trade during the Mauryan Period

Introduction

The establishment of Nanda dynasty ushered an era of large empire and absorbed the petty states of Northern India. Northern India by virtüe of its fertile soil, favourable climate and its magnificent waterways must have from the beginning enjoyed exceptional opportunities provided by nature for economic prosperity. The strong administration of Nandas and Mauryas advanced the trade and industry more rapidly.[1] The commercial interests of Nandas in commercial development are perhaps indicated by their introduction of a new standard silver coins,[2] namely the punch marked coins.

The effects of Alexander's invasion did not affect adversely the economic condition of the territories subdued by his arms but his measure for laying the foundation of an extensive commerce between India and the Hellenistic World took root immediately. The conquest of Northwest India by Chandragupta Maurya and consequent victories over small principalities, gave a foundation of strong empire. For three generations the Mauryas ensured internal security and immunity from foreign aggressions. Ashoka's vigorous propaganda further paved the way for the spread of Indian culture to distant Hellenistic states. It is not unreasonable to suppose that these favourable conditions were attended with a phenomenal development of industry as well as inland & foreign trade of the empire under Maurya rule.[3]

His son maintained the wise policy of friendship with Hellenistic powers started by Chandragupta Maurya after the repulse of Seleucus and grandsons must have favoured the expansion of Indian trade with West Asia and Egypt.[4] The main commerce between the West Asia and India was borne partly by land routes (the northern one passing through Bactria and southern though Gedrosia and Carmania, Persia and Susiana) and partly by the sea routes (though Gerrha on the west cost) of the Persian Gulf.[5] Alexandria was the principal emporium of trade between India and the West.[6] But these routes were not free from piracy and some times the traders were taking the help of armed men in order to protect their goods.[7]

The trade during the Mauryan period had reached at a level of prosperity, which is witnessed from the systematic arrangement of Mauryan administration to regulate the trade. The active encouragement of commerce was contemplated as a duty of the state is illustrated by the measures included in Kautilya's scheme of state colonization of rural areas; they included working of mines and forests, the construction and security of trade routes and the foundation of market towns.[8] In order to facilitate the trade, the Arthasastra recommends the appointment the Superintendent of Shipping, Port Commissioner, Superintendent of Commerce, Superintendent of Tolls etc.[9]. They were entrusted with different duties to carry out the trade smoothly and stringent punishment was given to the people for the violation of trade rules and regulations. It is also assumed that the ship building industry was also controlled by the state, according to Megasthenes. These things point out the fact that there was a flourished trade during the Mauryan period.[10]

Among the products of export, the most important things were timber, bamboo, dyes, food grains; which were highly praised in West Asian countries.[11] A variety of livestock were exported from India were hunting dogs, elephants, peacocks, parrots, maina, pheasants and snakes.[12] The western people were so fond of Indian animals that they were paraded in royal procession.[13] Again spices, vegetable products, textiles were also exported to West Asian countries. The Indian list of imports was comparatively small against the list of exports. The goods of import were, fruits, wines, crude glass, asphalt and antimony etc. Therefore, it is presumed that the trade was in favour of India.[14]

In the sphere of cultural contacts, Mauryan period opened up a new chapter.[15] The art, architecture, sculpture, literature, all were influenced more or less by the contacts of West Asian countries. There are enough evidences, which supports the fact that Mauryan administration and ruling style of kings were under the due influence of western countries. On the basis of this cultural contact it may deduced that there must be a trade relation of West Asian countries with India.

The reconstruction of Indian maritime history of the period of our study is not an easy job because we have limited source materials, both literary and archaeological.[16] Large number of the literary sources of Ancient India is spiritual and religious in their contents. The important source materials of this period are Kautilya's Arthasastra and Megasthenes' Indica, in addition with Jatakas and other sources. The contents of Indica and Arthasastra throw more light on social, political and economic conditions of the people than the commercial contacts. But Jatakas, in this context provides valuable information about the trade routes, trading organization and trading activities.

Therefore, Jataka sources are referred at different places to provide authenticity to the information. Foreign sources like Strabo's Geography, Arrian's Indica and others are more helpful to establish a contact between India and West Asia. But the archaeological sources have some limitations with regards to the foreign trade through sea.[17] Ashokan inscriptions are not eloquent about this foreign trade except the rock Edict XIII, which gives the names of five contemporary Hellenistic monarchs.[18] The mention of these five Kings has its own historical interest.[19] The three major powers among there are, namely Antiochos of Syria, Alexander of Epirus and Ptolemy-II Philadelphus of Egypt. Antiochus-I, the son of Seleukus had relations with both Macedonians and Ptolemy.

Due to the matrimonial ties among them three different dynasties, the hostility between the major powers of Hellenistic wings came to low ebb.[20] The closeness of the Hopkines and Mauryas may have led to do with some trade relations. A version of the major Rock Edict of Ashoka has been found at Sopara, which identifies its importance as a great trading centre.[21] The location at Sopara may point to a direct route to Southern Arabia or the Southern end of the Red Sea. Given the Ptolemaic interest in trade with East and establishing the ports of Lyos Hormus and Berenike in third C.B.C. such a possibility cann't be discounted the motive behind the attack of Ptolemy Philadelophos on the Nabateans was to capture the Wabatean trade.[22] The maritime links between the west coast of India and Red Sea might have been limited to the Southern Nabatean ports but extended North towards Gaza and Egypt under Ptolemies. If the ports of Southern Arabia had direct contacts with Sopara there would have been an interest on the part of Ptolemy to control these ports.[23]

On the basis of mere mention of names of the Hellenistic rulers in Rock Edicts, it would be imprudent to think that we had good commercial contacts with themselves but the possibility of trade can't be condoned. Again the excavation reports from different places like Pataliputra, Mathura and other places are indicating that there was a good cultural contact, which also in a round way establishes the fact that the trade relation was there in between these lands. The first authentic proof of Indian influence in the Mediterin region is revealed by the excavation at Memphis dating back to 200 B.C. where an Indian figurine of an Aryan woman has been unearthed, reveals the proof of Indian influence in the Mediterranean region[24]. The help of assumptions and presumptions, an effort has been made to present a clear picture.

Trade Routes

It is necessary to deal with topography of the region before going into the details of trade routes of West Asia with India. Persia which extended along the coast of Gulf and Assyria was contiguous to Persia and Susiana viz. Babylonia and a large tract of the country around[25]. Strabo describes Syria bound on the east by Euphrates, on the south by Arabia Felix and Egypt on the west[26]. Next he mentions Judaea, the 'Persian Gulf and Arabia inhabited by Nabataeans whose capital was Petra and also by Sabaeans whose metropolis was Mariaba viz. Saba.[27] According to Pliny;" Syria as once the greatest lands and distinguished by many names" occupying the coast of Phoenisian sea.[28] Then

Seleucus Nikator founded came Mesopotamia, which was at the confluence of Tigris. The banks of Euphrates were occupied by, "Nomad of Arabia" as far as the deserts of Syria from which it turned to south, leaving the solitary deserts of Palmyra.[29]

When India became a part of Achemenid Empire, India's isolation was broken and she had the chance to come into closer contact with the western world.[30] Again Alexander wished to improve and cheapen the means of communication by sea and thereby united the richest and most prominent parts of his empire, India, Balylon & Egypt.[31] He sent Nearchus to explore the Persian Gulf and sea route from India to Balylone with an eye to secure the channel of trade between India and Mesopotamia.[32] He intended to explore the south Arabian coast to connect India with Egypt. He had set up most of the colonies with an eye on economic value, which emerged as the great commercial centre of trade in the later phase.[33]

The route from Taxila to Bactria crossed the river Indus at Udabhanda[34] and proceeded towards Varsapura near Shahabazgarhi. From there the route passing through Hoti Mardan reached Pushkalavati. Then the route entering through the Khyber Pass entered into the region of Kapis. There were three routes across Hindukush into Bactria.[35] Once an Indian trader had reached Bactria, he had a direct route before him for the West Asian markets through Seleucia and Babylon. Seleucia and Babylon, for long served as emporiums of Indian goods. Another route, which passed through Khawak pass and Bamyan, was very suitable for trade and transport between Kapisa and Bactria.[36] The third route, which was diverted from Bamiyan and passed through Robat, Dandan, Shikan and Karakotal and then proceeding along the river Derra Yousuf, it went to Bactria from some place near Mazar-I-Sarif.[37]

Bactria was an important place for the trade between India and West Asia. Numismatic evidence suggests that the scale and volume of trade at Bactria was quite high.[38] As a junction of land routes, it controlled Oxus trade with India and exercised a commanding position in the Indo-Syrian trade.[39] The relations between India and Syria, in economic as well as cultural sphere were quite intimate and Asoka sent his philanthropical mission to Amtiyoka[40] (Antiochus II Theos) the king of Syria. The industrial development of Syria was primarily based on the supplies of Indian raw materials. It had many prosperous industrial centres such as Antioch, Palmyra and Damascus. Antioch was a significant city, second only to Alexandria in political importance and none in wealth.[41] There were several routes between Seleucia and Antioch but the normal one crossed the river Euphrate. Ashoka had relations with the neighbouring kings of Egypt, Magas, king of Macedonia and Alexander who ruled either Epirus, or Corinth.[42] To most of these places the routes went from Antioch, either through Asia Minor or along the cost of Mediterranean touching the famous markets of Sidon, Tyre, and Gaza to Alexandria.[43]

King Ptolemy Philadelphus who had commercial intercourse with Ashoka had founded the city of Alexandria, which became the principal emporium of trade between India and West. The coastal voyage from Indian ports such as Tamralipti, Barygaza, Patala etc. to Alexanderia was very tedious and fraught with recurrent danger of piracy.[44] According to E.H. Warmington, the routes lay from Arabian Euadaemon following round all the gulf coasted along Arabia and then along Assiatic coast of Carminia and Gedrosia to the India and then Southward.[45] Again the traders started from Arabia Eudaemon or from Cane, from there they went directly to Patala. The traders who were not desiring to go to Indus directly sailed from Arabia or from Cane proceeded to Sigerus or Melizigara some where near Bombay[46]. Because Barygaza was suitable place for this trade.[47] Those who were intending to go direct to Tamil land after leaving Ocelis, of Arabia. Eudaemon, Cane or Cape of Gurdafui in July[48] and they go across the Malabar marts .[49]

Traders usually preferred the sea routes. It was not only convenient to carry goods with less transportation cost but also time saving. The Arthasastra in one section compares the relative importance of the land route and sea route.[50] Quoting the ancient authorities Kautilya observes that according to them, the sea and river routes were more profitable than the land routes, because the cost of water transport was cheaper than the land routes. But Kautilya was not ready to accept this theory. According to him, the sea routes were full of dangers like attack of pirates, hurricane, storm etc. While pointing out the dangers of sea route Kautilya observes that open sea routes were more difficult than the coastal sea routes because on coastal routes there were ports where the goods were sold and bought easily. In the same way, the river route in comparison with sea routes was much easier. If any difficulty arose, it could easily be manipulated.[51] According to Moti Chandra, Kautilya,was an orthodox Brahmin and that was the reason why Kautilya did not prefer the sea voyage".[52] But the concept of Moti Chandra is however may not be acceptable in this context because Kautilya has pointed out the inherent difficulties of the traders while they were traveling through the sea routes. Again Buddhist texts also refer about shipwrecks and sea dangers. The ships during this period were not strong enough to withstand the hurricanes in the mid sea and other natural calamities.[53]

Exports and Imports during the Mauryan Period

Exports: Mauryan period does not provide much evidence about the goods of export and import. Scanty evidence provided by Kautilya's Arthasastra, Megsthene's Indica and Jataka stories, are not sufficient enough to bring a clear picture of goods of export and import. The chief exports from India were ivory, tortoise shells, pearls, pigments and dyes (especially indigo), rice, various medicinal substances, cotton and silk fabric.[54] Timber was greatly demanded in West Asian countries and Indian timber was found in the temple of Ur also proves[55] the fact. Kautilya refers, among others, to the following kinds of strong timber (Saradaruvarga) viz. Sala (teak-Taelona Grandis) Simsupa (black wood-Salbergia Sissue)[56] and 16 kinds of sandal trees.[57] Another celebrated Indian timber was ebony (Diospyrus) mentioned by Megasthenes.[58] About this, Herodotus had also mentioned that the Indians and Ethiopians brought the logs of ebony among other gifts to the Persian King Darius I as tribute.[59] As such ebony tribute was continuing from the days of Herodotus; it may be justly inferred that Indian ebony was exported from India to Persia from 6thC C.B.C. to 3rd C.B.C. Megasthenes who had noted that ebony grew in the land of Prassi[60] viz. Pracyas or the Esterners, implying that ebony must have been cultivated in the Eastern part of India during that period.

Again the Indian bamboo, which highly praised by Pliny,[61] also finds mention in the Arthasastra. Kautilya mentions 8 kinds of bamboos, which he calls by general name of Venu. Utaia, Cimiya, Cava,Vamsa, Satina. Kanaka and Bhalluka.[62] Pliny, comparing the virtues of Indian reed admits that advantages possessed by India reeds however possessed by most of the approved kinds of bamboos found in Crete, although those of India are preferred.[63] This statement implies that the Indian bamboo must have been definitely exported to West Asian ports.The question of preferring the Indian bamboo to those from Crete or from Italy itself could hardly have arisen.[64]

During the days of Mauryas the goods, which were exported from India the most prominent were Indian copal, indigo and lac. It is very clear that various kinds of dyes must have been prepared in India from very early times. From the Jatakas, we come to know that yellow dye was prepared from the sunflower (Kusumbha)[65] which grown in the king's conservatories.[66] Kautilya mentions, this flower along with certain other flowers, which were used for dying purposes.[67] Another ingredient, which Kautilya calls *Varnadhatu* employed for colouring purposes, was the lac or *lakasa*, which seems to have been well known to him.[68]

The Periplus reveals that "coloured lac" was exported from northwestern India to the east African ports, Adulius and Egypt.[69] Apart from its use as a dye, lac appears to have been used to paint the lips and the feet in specific lines. It seems to have been used to colour the tips of the fingers, the palms of the hands and soles of the feet. It was also used to colour the leather, wool and silk etc.[70]

Another dye exported from India was the purple, which in its own right became celebrated among the Persians. The Indian purple at that time had to face the commercial competitions with other varieties; from the Caucasus (Hindu Kush) and Phoenicia. The Persians used the purple dye for their tunics, which several Greek writers had observed.[71] Alexander found a "multitude of purple fishers came to him from Phoenicia.[72] This gives an indication that at that time Phoenicians also traded in dyes. Neither Hehrodotus, nor Strabo, nor Pliny refers to Indian dyes. Strabo's reference from Megasthenes to Indian dyes and Pliny's mention of the indicum are understood as allusion.

It should not be interpreted that there was no historical evidence of dyes. Megasthenes saw how Indians had arrayed "themselves in garments dyed of bright colours" and he also noted that dressing in "grey-coloured clothes" among them was also a custom.[73] Various colours like the yellow, blue, golden and saffron dyes are mentioned in the Jatakas.[74] Kautilya also knew the saffron flower.[75] The Cyrens came to the Mauryan Empire and probably came to know about the dyes. Cyrene was renowned for the production of a special herb, the silphium plant, used in a variety of ways and exported to various parts of the then known world which could have included India.

About the export of food grains, Kautilya refers to the purchase, sale, barter and manufacture of grains through state agency, their storage and use in periods of scarcity. But we hardly find any specific reference to the export of these commodities. Although it would not unreasonable if we presume that during the period of Mauryas, the food grains were exported to Egypt from Barygaza (Broach) by ships, "the food products were – wheat, rice, clarified butter and sea same oil" and other goods.[76] Kautilya also refers about these products and he clearly notes the oil seeds from which the edible oils were extract for consumable purposes.[77]

A variety of livestocks were exported from India including a number of Indian animals and birds. The animals were Indian hunting dogs, elephants and peacocks were undoubtedly most celebrated. Tropical beasts like tiger, bull, cattle and birds like parrot, maina, pheasant and even snakes were also exported.[78]

Peacock was highly praised in western society, which is clearly evident from the Book of Kings (6th C.B.C.).[79] The export of Indian peacocks can be traced with greater certainly from the Baveru Jataka, The Indian peacock also reached Greece in 5th century B.C. and this must have been through commercial contacts with Persia. During Pericles (498-429 B.C.) Pyrilampes, his friend and his son had a famous zoo in which the peacock was exhibited to the public.[80]Still, when Alexander saw it in India, according to Allien, he was "struck with astonishment and so charmed with its beauty that he threatened the severest penalties against any one who would kill a peacock.[81] The Indian peacock lastly reached in Rome as a commercial commodity in 1st C.B.C.[82] Aufidius Lucro (a glutton) and a maternal grand farther of the Empress Livia, in 61 B.C. ,was the first Roman who taught the Romans the art of flattening peacocks. He had made it a business to sell his flattened peacocks and from the source of the profit he acquired an income of 60, 000 sesterces (about 12, 770 francs). Thus the peacock, which, in the early centuries before Christ, had been exported to Rome only by first century B.C. and positively by 61 B.C.,it became an article of commerce.[83] Among the other birds that were exported to West Asian countries were parrot, black grouse, guinea hens and pheasants.[84]

In addition to the birds, the animals were also exported to Rome and other West Asian countries. In the grand procession organized by Antiocuhus – IV (215-163 B.C.) it is known certainly that some Indian animals were seen in the capital at Antioch. In a representation of the return of "Dionysius from India", it was shown as Dionysius measuring eighteen feet reclining upon an elephant's back, clad in a purple coat and wearing a gold – would lace and his feet shod with shoes fastened by gold straps. The elephant had trappings of gold and round its head was, "an ivory crown in gold". Many interesting objects among which were, "an ivory crown in gold", followed the cart. The cart was followed by many interesting objects among which were "twenty six Indian oxen entirely white" a chariot drawn by elephants and there were also Indian women in that precession, the elephants too must have been from India itself.[85] The tiger was another animal exported from India to West Asian countries. The Greeks were well aware of Indian wild beasts like tigers.

Strabo relates how, according Megasthenes, "the largest tigers were found in the western part of India, almost twice the size of lion and of such strength that a tame one led by four persons, seized a mule by its hind leg, over powered it and dragged it to him.[86] This indicates that Indian tiger must have been exported to Rome. Again the Indian elephants were not only exported to Asyria but also to Egypt during the Ptolemies. In the battle of Raphia, between Ptolemy and Antiochus (217 B.C) the Indian elephants had participated.[87] In Italy, the Indian elephants were sent for the first time in the war with kings Pyrrhus in the year 281 B.C. these elephants were called Lucian oxen because they were seen for the first time in Luciania.[88] The first harnessed elephants seen in Rome were in triumph of Pompeius Magus over Africa (65 B.C.) when they drew his chariot. The Hellenistic Kings required the Indian elephants to fight against enemies. Seleucus received 500 elephants as a part of his treaty with Chandragupta.[89] The elephants were prized commodity is indicated by their use in the war field fought by Pyres of Epirus against the Romans in Southern Italy.[90] The Plolemies were also have been anxious to import Indian elephants into Egypt, even though they had access to African elephants because it was widely believed that Indian elephants were stronger and tougher and therefore superior in battle particularly those from Taprobane or Sri Lanka.[91] The description left by Arrian of the grand procession in honour of Plolemy Philadelphus ,in 270 B.C. mentions Indian women sitting in carts and elephants from India.[92]

Another most important item, which was exported to Assyria and Egypt, was ivory. From ivory the Assyrians manufactured luxurious couches. This can be seen from the *Book of the Prophet Ezekeil* (Sixth century B.C.) where in Tyrus (Tyre) in thus addressed; "The Company of the Ashurites have made by benches of ivory".[93] This ivory was probably exported from India, which continued up to the days of Kautilya. He has provided certain directives how to cut the tusk of the elephants. According to him, the elephants were bred in the countries like, Kalinga (Southern Orissa), Anga (South-East Bengal), Karusa (Shahabad district of Bihar), Vidisa (Besnagar).[94] Kautilya's reference about the tusk of elephants and the centers of highbred elephants indicates that the trade of ivory was also in the same pace during the Mauryan period. In the later phase, Pliny also refers about the export of the Indian ivory to Western countries. In addition with these things, the Indian hunting dogs were probably exported to Rome because there are enough evidence about this in Pre-Mauryan and Post Mauryan period. Darius had granted his Assyrian governor[95] revenue free villages for the purpose of maintaining numerous Indian hunting dogs. These hunting dogs were very favourite items of import of Assyria, Persia and Greece.[96]

India was another country where spices were also cultivated and .exported to foreign countries like Assyria Egypt, Rome etc. Their commercial prospects and possibilities can be seen from the observations of Kautilya who refers to many of them in the preparations of strong liquors, which were also patronized by foreigners.[97] He calls them by the general name of *jatisambhara* or *bijottara*.[98] In the preparation of wines medaka and prasanna the ingredients are *lodhra* (symplocos Racemosa) *tejovati* (Piper chaba), elavaluka (Solanum Melongena), *daruharida* (Amonumxanthorrhizon) a species of turmeric, black and long pepper which were added as the requisite species or *sambhara*.[99] He cites several other types of spices used to make the drink pleasant. It is quite possible that the foreigners, who frequented Indian markets during the 4th B.C. as specially mentioned by Kautilya, must have also included the Arabs from south Arabia who had practically monopolized the trade in spices, carrying them to various countries like Phoenicia, Israel and Egypt.[100] When the control of the seas passed on to the Romans it is not surprising that the Romans in their turn became the carriers of the spice trade in the various markets of their age.[101] Indian spices continued to be exported to Egypt during the reign of Antiochus IV Epiphanes (C215-163 B.C.). Along with Indian oxen, Indian women, elephants, thrones of ivory and "eight hundred cart loads of spices were in the procession".[102] This could not have been from any other country except India, which was so largely represented, in that grand procession. This export trade continued for one century after the death of Kautilya.[103]

Among other food products exported from from India, were possibly the palm wine, castor and sugarcane. Kautilya's reference about the family of *sveta-sura*[104] who were specially the manufacturer of this kind of sura in allusion to coconut, palm juice. Kautilya also refers to the production of sugar from sugarcane. About the food products and vegetable products during the Mauryan period, Kautilya and Megasthenes do not provide much ideas.

The pepper was exported to western countries in ancient times is definite but when this export trade began it is difficult to know. There are various controversial versions about it, of courses some scholars give a greater antiquity to this trade by advancing the view that the Indian pepper packed in small packets found in its way to Greece as early as fifth century B.C.[105] It was used there as a medicinal drug. But certain other authorities do not confirm this view of ancient foreign trade in pepper. For example we find no mention of it in the Papyri and from this it may be deduced that it was definitely not exported to Egypt on any scale in Third or Second century BC. Tarn on other hand assigns a rather later beginning to this trade by asserting that, "the export of pepper from India on any scale certainly began in the period of Greek rule.[106] A further support to the verdict of Tarn is provided by the fact that plenty of pepper was found in the house of an Althenian tyrant, Aristion (88B.C.). So to be on the safe side we may conclude that export of pepper from India very probably began about C100 B.C. but definitely not later).[107] As early as 4th Century B.C., the Egyptians brought back cinnamon believing it to be a product of Southern Arabia where as it came from India.[108]

Now we may see how far textiles of India were exported to foreign countries. If we look into the Book of Ezekiel (6th CBC) we find that Syrian merchants traded, in the fairs of Tyre

(Phoenicia), with embroidery work and precious stones like emeralds and purple. It is also seen on the authority of Chinese texts that Syria had commercial relations with India and Parthia from the first centuryB.C. and it imported the Medicinal plants during Ashoka.There must have been such relations between India and Syria not only in the third CBC but also during Kautilya in 4th CBC.[109] It may be assumed that the trade on textiles was continuing from early times but accidentally it was not referred in Ezkiel. But hardly it can be explained why and how the Syrian merchants were able to procure the embroidered work and the linen of finer variety because we don't have enough evidences about this.[110]

The goods, which were exported from India to West Asian country, were mainly perishable. Therefore, except literary evidences, there are a few such archaeological evidences about the trading goods. Again during the Mauryan period, the Arthasastra of Kautilya and India of Megasthenes are main sources of our information from Indian side which don't throw much light on the trade relations. Therefore most of the items, which are included in the list of export, are mainly based on assumption. The goods, which were exported during the Pre-Mauryan period as well as Post Mauryan period, can be; included in the list of export items during the Mauryan period.

Imports: It is already seen that Asoka sent his famous mission to certain countries so that, wherever, medicinal herbs, needed for men and animals were found, they had been caused to be imported and planted. Ashoka had sent his missions to Syria, Egypt, Macedonia and Cyranaica.[111] There is no such direct evidence that Ashoka had brought different medicinal herbs from different countries. Therefore, we have to rely on the literary accounts of foreign authors about the different herbs which were famous in different countries. On the basis of this we can presume that Ashoka might have brought these products from different countries. In Syria, according to Pliny, were found certain plants, which were beneficial for medicinal purpose. One of them was pistachio which was taken with food or drink against the bite of snake.[112] The pistachio which had been found in Syria, Damascus, Mesopotamia, is now cultivated in Punjab and North Western Himalayan region. Again Syria was also known from certain types of figs, which was known as carie.[113] It was called 'anjira' in Sanskrit and it destroys warts. It has since been cultivated in Rajputna, Madhya pradesh and Bihar. Other medicinal herbs which were famous in Syria were, Myxaplums, storax, Imphacium and Oenanthe. Some of these like storax and Oenanthe were particularly beneficial in curing running sores on all parts of the body, both in human beings as well as animals.[114] From Egypt came the Cypros (Cyprus) zizyphus,. adioposis, figs (ficus), the sarcocolla, all of which were utilized in a variety of ways in view of their healing properties.[115]

Though they were claimed to have proved beneficial chiefly in treating the ailments of human beings, some of them appear to have been capable of effecting cures in cases of animals also. This was specially in case in regard to laspertium or silphium, a product of Cyrene which was highly useful not only for human beings but also in effecting cures of various distempers of cattle, which was also found as a palatable food.[116] It was one of the most celebrated medicines of the ages. Probably, all such plants and roots were started to be imported during the reign of Chandragupta Maurya and not necessarily it started during the reign of Ashoka.

Among the consumer goods, which were imported to India, were fruits like grapes, figs, dates, and beverages and wines.[117] Onescritus has referred to Indians in market places, probably of Taxila, "carrying figs or bunches of grapes".[118] Grapes were certainly no novelty in India, for Kautilya clearly refers to lands frequently overflown by water as suitable for cultivation of long pepper, grapes and sugarcane. He also refers to the countries of origin of grapes as Kapisayana (Kafirstan).[119] It represents Kandahar region. But according to Pliny, the grapes were widely grown in the areas like Italy, Egypt Syria, Persia and Kandahar also. The grapes from these countries couldn't be imported because it is difficult to preserve in the long journey, but the juice of grapes wine can be imported from these lands.

The import of foreign wines and liquors from early times into India can be traced from Kautilya's Arthasastra, it refers to foreign customers in liquor shops lying with their beautiful mistresses in intoxication.[120] That such a liquor must have been sold as one of the kinds of beverages in the liquor traffic. It can be seen in the directive that the Superintendent of liquor had to fix the amount of compensation determining the daily sales of liquor and the difference between the royal and public measure.[121] We have no means of ascertaining, whether during Kautilya, there were imports of foreign wines other than those he has specifically mentioned.[122] It is also referred by Megasthenes and he points out that the elephants were provided black wine in order to cure certain diseases.[123] But it can't be said with certainly that these wines were brought from foreign countries. In the post Mauryan period, there are enough evidences about the import of wine from Greek, Arab and Italy.[124] In Vedic period the soma was the intoxicating drink, which was prepared by Indians indigenously.[125] So about the wine in the Mauryan period nothing could be said with authenticity.

Among other products which were imported into India were, asphalt, glass, antimony etc. though Kautilya refers about the presence of these products in India, he did not clarify whether these things were imported into India or not. Pliny refers about asphalt, which was exported from Babylon, Syria, to Rome.[126] Surprisingly Strobo, Pliny, do not refer about its export to India. But in view of its commercial and medicinal use for man and beast, its import into India may well be taken. [127] Asphalt was certainly known in India in 4th CBC for Kautilya calls silajatu or bitumen. He tells us that it had a piercing smell and bitter taste. But he does not refer whether this was produced in India or not. Therefore, about asphalt, nothing can be said with guarantee but the probability of its importan into India was there.

Here is enough evidence that the rude glass was imported into India in first century A.D.[128] but it must not be inferred that glass was not known in India earlier. Kautilya,(during 321 – 296 B.C).

refers about three types of ornamental works made up with gold and glass.[129] Again he points out that the merchants dealing with glass were bound to pay the tax. So it is conceivable that either glass was manufactured in India or it was brought from outside. But the probability of from outside is more because Pliny refers, in 1st CAD, it was imported from Rome.

About antimony, there is also no clear-cut proof of its import. The Periplus is our best authority for inferring that antimony was imported into India in 1st CAD.[130] Kautilya mentions it is an ore, which exists in combination with lead or silver. Again it was also used for medicinal purposes like beautifying the eyebrows, dilating the eyes, healing burns. Taking these things into consideration it may be presumed that antimony might be imported into India during the Mauryan period.

The goods, which were imported during the Mauryan period, are not mentioned in literary sources clearly. Again archaeological excavations do not outline the commodities of import because most of the goods were perishable. Kautilya and Megasthenes don't give a very good idea about the imported items. Kautilya's reference about various goods in the Mauryan period gives a way to presume many things without any authenticity. Therefore, to get a list of items of import as well as export during the Mauyran period is undoubtedly difficult and controversial.

Barter and Exchange in the 4th Century B.C.

Though there are enough evidences about the currency system during the Mauryan period, the barter system was also prevalent. But Kautilya strongly condemned the barter as one of the causes contributing towards the depletion of public treasury. In the view of Kautilya some factors which were responsible for the growth of the economy were: public prosperity (pracarasamriddhih) rewards for good conduct (Cari tranugrahah) capture of thieves (coranigrahah) dispensing with the services of too many viz. retrenchment of surplus staff, abundance of harvest, prosperity of commerce, and income in gold as against these the factors which tended to deplete a public treasury, were barter, loan, fabrication of accounts and defalcation.[131]

Kautilya defined barter (parivartana) by stating that it was an act of exchanging government articles for similar goods of others.[132] Thus commodities of same type must have been manufactured through the state as well as private agencies and both of these varieties were available in the open market for sale or for other commercial purpose like exchange with other countries in the shape of barter. He amplifies this operation further by stating that such an offence was explained by enjoyment.[133]

All type of barters was not considered illegal. The barters like, the commodities of greater value could be bartered for those of smaller value and vice verse. What was of lesser value that could be interchanged for some thing of greater value and in such deals prices could be raised or lowered, were considered illegal.[134] Severe penalties were prescribed for offenders for enjoying gems, the death sentences, for enjoying valuable articles, the middle most punishment viz. 200 to 500 panas fine and for enjoying articles of inferior value, a fine equal to their value, were imposed.[135]

Kautilya had noted the utility of the barter in the sphere of foreign trade.[136] He distinguished between the kings (state) merchandise of local manufacture, which was centralized and imported goods, which were to be distributed in several markets for sale. In sale of such goods no discriminations would be made towards any goods but such merchandise of the king was to be sold in the foreign countries on a barter basis. The Superintendent of Commerce after scrutinizing and ascertaining the values of local produce as compared with that of foreign goods which could be obtained in barter had to find out whether there was any money left as margin of profit after deducting the different taxes.[137] From the above regulations it may be seen that the Superintendent of Commerce, after comparing the local products with foreign products obtainable in barter and meeting all the incidental charges, had to determine whether such a transaction yielded any margin of profit or not. If no such profit was realized first by the sale of king's own local produce, he had to examine the question whether such merchandise could profitably be bartered for the other products. Here it is important to note that such transactions had to be made only if they were expected to be profitable and not otherwise.[138]

In spite of the existence of currency, Jataka provides many stories related to barter. In Vessantara Jataka, a Brahman who had given a loan of 500 Kahapanas to a Brahmin family but the Brahimin family could not repay the money and in exchange he gave his daughter to the lender.[139] Rhys Davids contended that in the Jatakas,barter "emerges in certain contingencies" and was not normal.[140] In the Jatakas, we find that barter, which was certainly not exceptional, depended on the circumstances of each case. If a person wanted a particular article and if he had not cash at the moment or was to able to procure it for effecting an immediate exchange, he offered another commodity which he considered equivalent in value to the goods he required. If the seller was satisfied with the article offered, the exchange was effected. With the presence of money economy, barter indicates towards exceptional situations.[141] Again it became effective when the prices of two commodities, which were to be exchanged, became equal.[142]

India's Important Markets

The important ports of India from where the Indian traders were carrying the goods were Barbaricum, Baryaza, Suppara, Muzris, and Patala etc. Bararicum had been identified with "Alexander's heaven".[143] Kautilya mentions of two varieties of coral, which were available in Bararicum.[144] Tara speaks of pepper trade, pepper being exported from India in large scale in this period of Greek rule. Indian vessels used to ply first coasting along Gedrosia to Arabia and then to Persian Gulf.[145] The Arabs had then a monopoly in trade in Indian spices and they sold the Indian spice with their own spice in the western world. When the Greek Eduoxus of Cyzicus first sailed from Egypt to India in 120 B.C., he returned with in the ships loaded with spices and precious stones.[146] Plutarch says that in 88 B.C. Ariston of Athenes had amassed large quantities of pepper in his house and this fixes the beginning of substantial export of Indian pepper not later than 100 B.C.[147]

According to Strabo, "Pataliputra was one of the finest & best organized markets in India in 4th B.C. Patala had no doubt a market of considerable importance but as a commercial centre it was not mentioned. [148] The next important town was Baryagaza, which was mentioned as the chief distributing centre of western India. It is however, interesting to note that Barygaza became more important than Barbaricum in the beginning of Christian era.[149] Pushkalavati was the first important station of Royal Road of Mauryas. Its importance in the first century A.D. does not seem to have faded. It was the enter pot for spikenard, costs and bdellium. After Barygaza, according to the Periplus, the most important port was Supara.[150] The name of Suppara is founding one of the edicts of Ashoka. Horse dealing was an important trade of this locality. These were most important trade centers in India.

India's Overseas and International Markets

With regard to India's over seas and external exchanges, it is difficult to obtain any satisfactory details of international markets. India's commercial interaction had spread to the regions like Assyria, Egypt, Israel, Syria, Parthia and Persia etc. The Phonicians had their chief markets at Sidon and Tyre whose kings had commercial relations with Persian Kings.[151] The Babylonian principal mart was at Babylon, the Egyptian at Memphis[152] and Avaris, the Judaean at Jerusalem, Caesaria and Ezion Gebir but a few particulars about them are available to us. The Greek market at Alexander in Egypt was a storehouse of "The superfluities of native products" which were distributed though every quarter of world.[153] Its greatest advantage according to Strabo, arose from its being the only place in Egypt, situated by nature for communication with the sea by its excellent harbour. Therefore, Alexandria seems to have remained the most important market of the world.[154] It was connected with all other marts namely the

Bolbitine, Sebbenytic, Phanitic, Tanitic and Pelusiae by the canals.[155] Of the Seleucid (Syrian markets) the most important was Antioch, during 174-172 B.C, it was famous for gold smith and silver smith's workshop.[156] The market at Palmyra was connected with India and formed a link with Arabia and Persia. The goods, which were bought from Persia, Arabia and Indian commodities, were disposed to the Romans[157]from here.

After its destruction, Batra became the intermediary of Indian trade with Persian Gulf. In Parthian the central market was Hecatampylos, which derived its name from the fact that it was the "meeting place of all roads leading to the surrounding districts.[158] From Strabo, we learn that Erotosthenes whom he followed the trade route from Caspian sea to Hecatampylos, thence to Alexandria, Prophthasia, Arachotus until the traders came to Ortospanal (Kabul) and thence to India. Hecatampylos was the meeting place of nations where according Curtius and Diodorus, Alexander halted for a long time but curiously enough Arrian does not refer to this halt.[159]

West Asian markets were the most attractive places of Indian goods. The luxury goods of India and the east were sold in the special markets like Campus Martins round the Saepta Julia and the Portus Argonauutrum.[160] The trade between India and Egypt was mainly carried from Egyptian sides from the ports of Red sea or Mediterranean Sea.[161] The Arabs brought goods from the caravans of Indian and the Egyptians brought them from the Arabs. One day, a startling news was received that a strong Indian man who had sailed straight from India and had lost his shipmates (200 B.C.) was found in a boat on the Red sea coast. Eudoxus of Cyricus in Asia Minor persuaded Eueregetes to give him the command of a vessel from the voyage of discovery with the guidance of this Indian. He reached India by sea and brought back a cargo of spices and precious stones. In the same way the Geek sailors of Eueregetes made a settlement in the Island of Socotra in the Indian Ocean and there met the trading vessels from India and Ceylon.[162]

Guilds

The Mauryan empire, a vast and fairly well knit empire, had developed an efficient system of administration. The long distance highways, constructed and maintained largely by the state, facilitated greater mobility of the people and easy transportation of goods from one region to another.[163] The Mauryan state regulated trade and commerce and brought under its monopoly the mineral resources of the land and controlled to quite some extent the economic activities of production and distribution. Megasthenes had recorded that in the municipal administration of Mauryas, one committee was dealing with management and control of industries.[164] The Arthasastra fixes rates of profits on indigenous and foreign goods, meticulously.It also mentions the lists of dutiable articles and prescribes punishment for violation of rules including artisans, default in delivery of goods in time.[165] It was the duty of govt. officials to keep all the records regarding traders[166] and crafts and related transactions and conventions of the guilds.[167] In addition to taxes in cash, the artisans many of whom must have been members of the guilds also paid taxes in the form of labour.[168] Though state had some stringent restrictions on the guilds it had given some concessions and facilities.[169] Separate areas were provided by the state to the guilds to run their trade and crafts.[170] The guilds could make deposits with competent agencies, which they got back in time of financial stress and they also advanced loans to merchants.[171] The revenue was usually collected in cash and in kind as per the evidence of Arthasastra, and paid the salaries of the employees ranging from 60 to 48,000 panas. It indicates that the greater circulation of money was favourable for trade and commerce.[172]

When Mauryan Empire extended its territory, a number of tribal republics lost their ancestral economic activities. Some of them formed the economic organizations like guilds for their livelihood. Kautilya refers to the Kshatriya Srenis of Kamboja and Saurastra earning livelihood by Varta (agriculture and trade) and the Sastras.[173] As he was a strong protagonist of centralized state, he never liked the activities of guilds, which were behaving like a state within a state.[174] Therefore, he followed the policy of divide and rule and promoted the quarrels among different guilds. There are qualms in the use of unscrupulous means for undermining the authority of the heads of guilds.[175] He distrusted the artisans whom he referred as "thorns".[176] However it is true that despite of step motherly treatment of Kautilya, a large number of guilds were involved in trading activities.[177]

In Kautilya's scheme of town planning (to which he devotes a whole chapter in the Arthasastra), proper care was taken to allot quarters and streets to different craftsmen.[178] Merchants, trading in scents, garlands, grains and liquids etc. were to settle in eastern quarters of a town; traders in cooked rice, liquor and flesh etc. in the southern quarters, artisans manufacturing wrested threads, cotton threads, bamboo mats, skins, amours, weapons and gloves as well as the people sudra caste in the western quarters, and smiths workers in precious stones and Brahmans in northern quarters.[179] It clearly states that within a town, separate areas were earmarked for the people following different trades and the scheme of placing differs from each other in different times and also in different places; it is known from that of Arthasastra.[180]

Sometimes other artisans and handicraftsmen were residing in guilds. Therefore, Kautilya enjoins, "Artisans and other handicraftsmen may on their own responsibility, allow other merchants to own their profession. Similarly merchants may, on their own responsibility, allow other merchants to reside where they themselves carry on their mercantile work"...[181] The localization of industries and trade in different streets within the city was convenient to different parties and the consumers for making purchases and to the govt. for regulating state laws related to craftsmen and collection of state taxes.[182] Again it was quite convenient for the people living in one area to discuss and debate on any new ideas related to invention and improvement in the machinery.

Guilds, not only provided training to the workers and work to the workmen but also some social status to the workers of the guild.[183] Again the guilds ensured the supply of sufficient good quality new materials and finished products and located markets for their sale. They provided a modicum of safety to the members of guild and also to merchandise. They employed armed guards for the safety of goods carried by the caravans in their long journey against the attacks for wild tribes, robbers plunderers, marauders and wild animals.[184]

It is clear from the Arthasastra that the guilds made use of some agency for making their deposits and could get them back when needed. The term *adesa* occurring in this context in the Arthasastra probably means "a letter of credit" which was some what like a modern bill of exchange, an order to a third person to pay up a sum of money on behalf of the sender of the order.[185] A passage in this work deals with *upanidhi* (deposits) of guilds runs thus.

"Those who can be expected to retrieve in misery, who can give instructions to artisans, who can be trusted with deposit, who can be relied upon by guilds of artisans many receive the deposits of guilds. The guilds (sreni) shall receive their deposits back in time of distress.[186]

A Machievelian plan was devised by Kautilya to use the guilds to the advantages of the state. In order to resort the ruse, the kings spies disguised as merchants were to borrow from guilds, gold, bar gold, and coined gold for various kinds of merchandise to be procured from abroad and thereafter get themselves robbed of them.[187] However it is clear that guilds were providing money as loans for trade. But there is no evidence in the Arthasastra, of guilds providing credit and banking facilities to the public general.[188] But once the guild had entered the field of credit and banking services, it howsoever limited way, it did not take long for them to provide such facilities to the general public as well.

Ship Building and Administrative Organization of Mauryas

The shipbuilding industry was a flourishing industry during the Mauryan period because the trade and commerce received a boost. The river as well as ocean routes were used for trade and commerce in addition with movement of people from one place to another. When Alexander was preparing to cross the rive Indus, he made a flotilla of boats with the help of Indians.[189] For the purpose of famous voyage of Nearchus[190] down the rivers and to the Persian Gulf, all available country boats were impressed for the services and a stupendous fleet was formed numbering, according to Arrian,[191] about 800 vessels, according to Curtius and Didorus about 1000 vessels but according to the more reliable estimate of Ptolemy, nearly 2000 which accommodated 8000 troops several thousands horses and vast quantity of supplies.[192] It indicates that the Indians had the capability to build so large vessels entirely by Indian woods. But this view was contradicted by some scholars like Vincent Smith and Robertson.[193] According to them as Arraian informs that "Alexander, in the country of Assconi and before he reached Indus, had already built the vessels which he sent down the Koppenes to Taxila."[194] And later on he used this flotilla, which was suspected that it was the creation of Indians. Robertson also expressed the same opinion.

According to him, "that a fleet so numerous, it appears at first sight incredible. But as the Punjab country was full of navigable rivers on which all the intercourse among the natives was carried on, it abounded with vessels. Probably, these fleets came to the hands of Alexander after his conquest of Punjab so that it might easily he collected that number."[195] But Arrain makes a clear mention of the construction of dockyards and the supply of transport vessels of thirty oars by tribal people called Xanthori.[196]

All these things clearly indicate that a regular and flourishing industry of shipbuilding was there in the Mauryan Empire. So far, the Yuktikalpataru is the only work available, which deals with the technical details of shipbuilding.[197] It is not an authority of ship building technology. According to Megasthenes[198] this industry was however in the hands of state and it was a Government monopoly. There was a special class to ship builders among the artisans and they were salaried public servants and were not permitted to work for any private person. About shipping and navigation of this period, Pliny[199] gives a very interesting account. According to him "The ships are built with prows at each end." He also indicates the tonnage of these ancient vessels, which is said to be 3000 amphorae, the amphora being regarded as weighing about a fortieth of a ton.[200]

The advancement of ship building industries probably compelled the Mauryan ruler, Chandragupta, to create a special organization named as board of Admiralty.[201] The head of the organization was called as the Navadhyaksha or the Superintendent of Ships.[202] It was his duty to deal with all matters relating to navigation in ocean as well as in rivers and lakes. He was like a modern day Port commissioner and his duty was to see all the dues of his port were paid and not one evaded.[203] Besides seeing to the realization and collection of all proper taxes and dues, the Superintendent of Ships was also entrusted with the duty of enforcing many humane harbour regulations. Thus whenever any weather beaten tempest tossed ships arrived at the port, his first duty was to lend her the protecting hand of a father.[204] It was also his power that he could exempt toll of any ship laden with merchandise that was damaged or spoiled by water. Sometimes he might impose half of the due toll and then allow sailing. Again whenever a ship laden with merchandise found drowned owing to want of hands or on account of ill repair, it was the duty of Superintendent of Ships to make goods to the loss of merchandise in part or full, as the case might be because presumably the loss was due to not to any fault of the merchants but to defect to state vessels and therefore, state must provide goods from state funds.[205]

To ensure safety of traders, the superintendent of ship sometimes took preventive measures during the period from the 7th day of Ashadha till the month of Kartika i.e. when the rivers were swollen owing to the rains, the crossing of rivers by state or licensed ferries was strictly enforced.[206] Again in those large rivers which could not be forded during the winter and summer seasons, the Superintendent of ships had to see that large and perfectly safe vessels were launched and manned with all necessary officers and hands viz. a captain, a steers man and a number of servants who would hold the oars, ropes and bale out water.[207] Small boats were launched only in small rives that overflowed during rainy seasons. Some strict regulations were enforced to ensure safety to river crossing .Fording or crossing of rivers without permission was prohibited in order to ensure that no traitor or enemy could escape.[208] The time and even the place for fording and crossing rivers were definitely fixed so that person fording or crossing rivers outside the proper place and in unusual times was punished.[209] Exemptions to these stringent rules were however, allowed to lax in the interest of trade and public good. Brahmanas, ascetics, children,royal messengers and pregnant women were provided free passes to cross rivers by the Superintendent. There was also another regulation permitting foreign merchants who had often been visiting the country, as also freely in port towns.[210] Finally it was the responsibility of the Superintendent of ships to punish all violations of harbour regulations and miscreants those were dangerous to public peace.[211]

The Mauryas had created a large number of departments to control the trading activities. The king had the sole right to impose various types of taxes from time to time.[212] The village on sea shores, on the banks of rivers or lakes had to pay regularly a fixed amount of tax.[213] To get the fishing license, the fishermen were paying one sixth of their haul as fees. The merchants were paying the customary tax levied in port towns. State boats were also let out to those who wanted to use them for pearl fishery or fishing for conch shells and they had to pay the required amount of hire[214] but they were also free to use their own boats. The taxes were payable to the Port Commissioner. There were various sorts of ferry fees, which are also very interesting and equally indicative of a brisk trade and a throbbing commercial life.[215] A man with minor quadruped carrying some load had to pay a ferry fee of one *masha*. A person who is carrying a load of cow or horse had to pay two *mashas,* load of a small cart- six *mashas* for a cart of medium size and that was drawn by bulls- seven *mashas* .[216] These conveyances and beasts of burden as well as loads of merchandise were subject to ferry fees.[217]

There was a Superintendent of Commerce whose primary duty was to ascertain demand or absence of demands. Again it was his duty to check the rise and fall of prices of different commodities coming through either of land or water routes.[218] He centralized the locally manufactured merchandise forming the part of monopoly of the king. It was also his duty to distribute the imported merchandise in several markets for sale. He was also entrusted with the responsibility to encourage the trade by giving various concessions to merchants and mariners. He usually showed the favour to mariners. The foreign merchants[219] were provided special facilities that they were exempted from being sued for debts.[220] This officer had to be particularly clever, for he had to look after the sale of foreign merchandise in the following manner:

"Having ascertained the value of local produces as compared with that of foreign produce that can be obtained by barter, the Superintendent will find out whether there is any margin left for profit after meeting the payments (to the foreign king) such as toll, road cess, conveyance cess, tax payable at military stations, ferry charges, subsistence to the merchant and his followers and the portion of merchandise payable to the foreign king. If no profit could be realized by selling local produce in foreign countries, he had to consider whether any local produce could be profitable bartered for any foreign produce. Then he might send one quarter of his valuable merchandise through safe roads to different markets on land or he might take his merchandise to other countries through rivers."[221]

There was the Superintendent of Tolls, whose duty was to erect near the large gate of the city a tollhouse with a flag, facing either, the north or the south. When merchants reached at the tollgate their goods were sealed properly. Strict rules and regulations regarding imported and exported merchandise were practiced.[222] There were three kinds of merchandise viz. External, (arriving from the country) internal (manufactured inside forts) and foreign (imported from foreign countries). Seal marks had to be used by all and those who failed, had to pay twice the amount of toll. Attempts were made to prevent counterfeit seals.[223] Undue at tempts to increase the prices of commodities were checked. Commodities had to be precisely weighed, measured or numbered, Commodities for presentation or sacrificed performance or gifts were let off without toll. The Arthasastra expects the panyadhyaksha to chose between a wide distribution (*viksepa*) and a single channel centralized distribution (*Sanksepa*) policy depending on the conditions of glut or scarcity of exchangeable commodities. It was the duty of Panyadhyaksha to strike a balance between the economic interests of the producer and those of the consumer by directly intervening in transactions.[224] One of duties is also to arrange the sale of royal item (*rajapanya*) produced in royal farms (*sita*). Though Kautilya had a very distrust attitude towards merchants, he seems to have promoted the foreign trade. Imported goods are liberally encouraged literally with favourable invitation *(parallumejam parya mancegrahea vahayet*).[225] Moreover, certain fiscal remissions granted to the merchants who were coming from abroad. The same spirit is displayed when the text recommends (IV-2.28-30) 10% profit for the foreign commodities and only 5% for the indigenous commodities perhaps the most interesting concession granted to the foreign merchants is that he should not be sued in a court of law for dispute in money maters (*anabliyogas earthesvagatunan)*

According to Kautiya, it was the duty of Panyadhyaksha to explore the profit potentials from both export and import trade. If in any case, no profit is earned out of this trade, he should assess the possibilities of economic advantages of barter trade. Kautilya advises the Panyadhyaksha to go wherever there is profit and to avoid a situatuion of no profit. [226]

The interest of Mauryas on sea born trade is difficult to define. The appointment of Navadhyaksha, Panyadhyaksha and Shulkadhyaksha etc. and the interest of the stats the to control the ship building activity clearly defines the interest of Mauryas to take the advantage out of inland and foreign trade. Again the edits of Ashoka, which are found in places like Sopara in Konkan, in

Girnar, in Kathiawad and Dhauli and Jaugada in Orissa, which are situated on or near the sea coast. And all these facts points out to the interest of Mauryas in sea trade[227].

The officers who were in charge of boundaries were helping the superintendent of tolls regarding imported commodities. This envisages that the Mauryan rulers were careful about the import but there is no such record about the export, which was discouraged.[228]

Megasthenes, speaking on the administration of public affairs refers to the second Board, which attended to the entertainment of foreigners.[229] "To these they assign lodging and keep watch over their modes of life by means. They escort them on the way when they move to their country or in the event of their death, forward their property to their relatives. They take care of them when they were sick and if they die bury them.[230] According to Smith "the existence of these conclusively prove that Mauryan Empire in 3rd C.B.C. was in constant intercourse with foreign states and that large number of strangers visited the capitals for business purposes.[231] And it was for this purpose the "Private ships," which were bound for the country of an enemy as well as those violated the custom and the rules forced in port, were to be destroyed.[232] Arrians testimony points out that "ship builders" and sailors employed in navigation" enjoyed special privileges is an excellent testimony to the attention paid to commerce in those days.[233] Dr. Seal acclaim, "one broad historical generalization stands out clearly and convincingly for which all histories of world culture will do well to take note, viz. the central position of India in the Orient world well nigh two thousand years not merely in a social, a moral, a spiritual or an artistic reference but also an equally in respect of colonizing and maritime activity and of commercial and manufacturing interests.[234]

Brief and tantalizing references regarding the duties of various officers under imperial Mauryas gives a thorough idea that there were various industries and trades which were organized by the state, which enjoyed monopolies in many of them and also foreign commerce was duly encouraged. Much care had been taken to prevent the smuggling and spies were appointed to check it.[235] They had particular instructions regarding foreign merchandise of superior or inferior quality arriving by land or water and to ascertain the amount of toll, road cess, conveyance cess, ferry-fare and one sixth portion (paid or payable by the merchants) the charges incurred by them for their own subsistence and for the accommodation of their merchandise in the warehouse.[236]

Due importance was to trade and commerce by Mauryan rulers. Kautilya said, "Prosperity of commerce led to financial prosperity".[237] To maintain the trade and commerce smoothly, the Mauryan kings paid importance to the construction of roads for traffic both by land and water[238]. Eratosthenes (275-194 B.C.) a junior contemporary of Ashoka, was aware of a royal road which connected West Asia with Pataliputra.[239] Arrian too speaks of such road. Attention may also be given to the observation of Megasthenes that the officers in charge of countryside (*agoranomoi*) were entrusted, among other things the construction of roads and with the setting up of pillars after every ten stadia (1 stadium = 606 ¾ feet) to show the roads and distance.[240] This account of Megasthenes is strikingly confirmed by the evidence of royal road *(Karapathi)* in Laghman area in Afghanistan.[241] Two Aramaic edicts of Ashoka from Langman, which speak of the royal road, also contain some information about the distance of several places from Laghman.[242]This was the duty of Superintendent of Tolls to make goods whatever merchants in his journey lost. And he carefully examines the foreign commodities as to their superior or inferior quality.[243] Foreign merchants often visited the ports of India with the help of local merchants.[244]

The rules, regulations and departments to organize the trade which were created by Chandragupta Maurya, probably remained in force under Ashoka also. It may be assumed that Ashoka made very effort to advance the trade. In the words of V.A. Smith, "when we remember Ashoka's relation with Ceylon and even more distant powers, we may credit him with a sea going fleet as well as an army"[245] and perhaps we would not be going far if we say that the religious missions to Syria, Egypt, Cyrene, Macedonia and Epirus also led to the establishment of commercial relations.[246]

A story in the monumental work called, "Bodhisattva Vadana Kalpalata" by the Kasmirian Kshemendra of 10th century A.D. indicates the progress of foreign intercourse and naval activity of India during the days of Chandragupta, which also continued in the days of Ashoka. Once Ashoka was seated on the throne in the city of Pataliputra, while holding his court, did some India merchants who traded approach one day to the distant islands. They informed him of their losses and complete ruin brought about by sea pirates called Nagas (Probably Chinese who were worshippers of Dragon) who destroyed all their ships and plundered their treasures. They said that if the emperor was disposed to be indifferent to them, they would to be forced to take to other ways of earning of their livelihood. But the imperial exchequer in that case was liable to be emptied owing to the absence of sea voyages. Then the story goes on to relate, how Ashoka, after bestowing some thoughts on the sea faring Nagas, he was persuaded by a Buddhist priest to issue a sort of edict (which we may call Ashoka's Marine Edict). It was only when Ashoka become a devout Buddhist that he was able to make the Nagas respect his edict and give up all their booty, which was afterwards distributed among the merchants robbed.

These evidences point out that there was a flourishing foreign trade during the Mauryan period. Therefore, Mauryan had created so many departments to take care of trade and had framed so many regulations to carry out trade smoothly. Both inland and external trade were given due importance.

Cultural Contacts

The cultural contacts, which were continuing from pre-Mauryan periods, got a boost during the Mauryan period. The exchange of embassies and smooth flow of trade strengthened the cultural relations. Again Ashoka's missionary zeal to propagate Dhamma, expanded the cultural relations further.[247] The caravans from India included mercenaries to protect against piracy, priests to propitiate the gods for safe journey and astrologers to guide the caravans. These people became helpful to spread he knowledge in foreign lands.[248] From the very beginning India was famous as a repository of knowledge which attracted many scholars to India. These people also became agent for the spread of Indian culture in distant lands.

Therefore, the Mauryan period is marked as the new chapter in India's relations with other countries.[249] Four major tools brought about the directional changes in this relationship: exchange of embassies, the outgoing missionaries, the enterprising traders, devout pilgrims and casual travelers. Mauryas not only established a vast empire bordering the Persian Empire but also maintained peace and tranquility throughout the empire.[250] Due to this conducive atmosphere, the trade and cultural transmigration continued smoothly. India's cultural contacts with different West Asian countries were not uniform. While some countries were influenced more by Indian and other had influenced India more. Again the lack of proper evidences keeps us always in dark about the proper cultural contacts.

Egypt

India's contact with Egypt during the third and second millennium B.C. was indirect and limited. We have very little evidences of intercourse between the two regions in post chalcolithic and pre-Mauryan period (i.e. between late second millennium B.C. and the late 1st millennium B.C). But the emergence of Mauryan Empire brought a drastic change of these relations in sixth and fifth century B.C. The northwestern part of India came in contact with Egypt, although indirectly, as both regions formed the part of the great Persian Empire.[251] However, different historical evidences point out the existence of political relations as well as diplomatic relations between the two countries during Mauryan period.[252] According to Pliny[253] Dionysius, an ambassador from Egyptian King Philadelphus (Ptolemy II 258 B.C.)[254] visited the Mauryan court. The identification of King

Philadelphus as Ptolemy Philadelphus of Egypt is accepted by all historians.[255]However, the name of the India King who had received the ambassador is not mentioned. So there is controversy regarding the identity of Mauryan King.[256] The Same Egyptian king had also sent an embassy to Rome in the year 273 B.C. So it is expected that he might have sent embassy to India at the same time and Bindusra was the ruler of Mauryan India. The intention behind the mission is not known properly but it is presumed that it marked the beginning of diplomatic relationship between India and Egypt in the historical period.[257]

Ashoka further extended the relations between India and West Asia. Though he was motivated by missionary spirit of Buddhism, it fostered the diplomatic contacts.[258] Ashoka's Rock Edict XIII reveals the expansion of his missionary activities in Syria, Egypt, Macedonia, Cyrene and Epirus.[259] These missions helped to spread Dhamma but with the exchange of missions, a regular intercourse developed two regions of the ancient world.[260]

Athanaeus had given an interesting fact about this that the presence of Indian women, Indian hunting dogs, Indian Cows, and Camels in the royal procession of Ptolemy Philadephuys of Egypt[261]. The source categorically informs us about a saloon lined with Indian stone in the yacht of Ptolemy II Philopator.[262] At Memphis, these excavators have found female figurines in terracotta[263] (2nd century B.C.) whose facial features and dress and completely Indian. Wheel is a known motif in India and it was quietly popular in Egypt.[264] This creates a lot of controversies about the origin of wheel. The representations of wheels between animals on the abacus of Ashoka pillar at Sarnath recalls the sun emblem of Egyptian Obesilks at Alexandria.[265] But according to Davar, it was an Iranian symbol.[266] Since both the countries were using the symbols randomly, so it is difficult to determine which country at first originated this. But it seems that India is the first country where it first originated and this spread to Egypt.[267] Because it was continuing in India through ages and Egypt borrowed by symbol from India. In this context, another piece of evidence is equally worthy. On the desert route to the Red Sea a temple has been recently discovered at Redesiya.[268] It was dedicated by an Indian to the Greek God Pan. This points out that a close intercourse between Indians and Geeks living in Egypt.

Some Greek historian point out that Indian articles, especially ivory, shells, pearls nard, clothing pigments, malabathroom and rare woods quite popular in Egypt and these were imported from India.[269] Alexandria, the city founded by Alexander on Isthmus, was a great centre of trade between India and West.[270] From Alexandria the traders followed by the route which passed through the old Suez Canal and along the Makara coast, finally reached the western shores of India.[271] Strabo informs us about the arrival of a few traders in India from Egypt.[272] The establishment of seaports normally Bernice and Myos Hormos on the Egyptian coast was aimed at facilitating the trade with India.[273]

According to Rostovezeff,[274] the financial and economic organizations of Ptolemaic Egypt bear close similarity to the organizations under Chandragupta Maurya and his successors. For instances, the organization of state monopolies in oil and salt and mining as well as what may perhaps be called "state socialism" under the rule of enlightened monarch", were common to both Mauryan Indian and Ptolemaic, Egypt.[275] The main points of similarity between the Kautilyan and Greek civil institution are (I) contract of mines (2) The designation and functions of financial directors (3) Indian land organization and Ptolemaic Agrarian system (4) Complete control of govt. in certain articles of trade. (5) The Organization of salt trade.

Again there are some close similarities between the Egyptian and Indian astronomical theories.[276] These relations might have been established due to close commercial intercourse between two lands.

The above-mentioned evidences though don't provide a clear picture of indo-Egyptian trade; it proves the close commercial contacts beyond doubt. The exchange of embassies, the participation of Indian men and women in the royal procession, are sufficient enough to conclude that India had close commercial contacts with Egypt in the Mauryan period.

Iran

A part of India was brought to Iranian rule by the Aechaemenian invasion. Bu the invasion of Alexander, could not give an opportunity for the Iranians to leave any permanent impact on Indian administration.[277] But the rise of Mauryan empire in third century B.C. extending its border upto Iran, the Indio-Iranian contact became wide ranging. The main features of the contact may be seen in the following sphere like, art architecture, town, planning, court life, administration, script, edicts and numismatics and customs and manners.

There is a long controversy among the scholars about the stone use in art and architecture of India. For the first time, Mauryans employed stone for their art architecture. Some scholars point out that it was borrowed from Iranians because these types of art and crafts on stone had been long used in Iran.[278] In the Pre-Mauryan phase, the long use of wooden structures in house as well as palaces clearly proves this fact. Again the capitals of Ashokan pillars, which bears close resemblance to Iranian examples. Scholars are again facing the same problem identifying the origin of these types of architecture. But Barbar cave excavated and embellished under the patronage of Ashoka do exhibit a purely Indian tradition of working on stone.[279] Mauryan art and architecture bears a close similarity with Iranian counter part and creates confusion among the scholars to trace out the origin of these styles. There are however two theories running side by side; one is indigenous style of architecture developed and matured in India. Second is that it was borrowed from Iranian and other West Asian sources. Though it is difficult to determine the exact amount of Iranian contribution to the development of Mauyran art and architecture, the possibility of Iranian influence on Indian art and architecture can't be ruled out.[280]

Meghasthenes, the Greek ambassador at the court of Chandragupta Maurya has spoken highly on the Grank Trunk Roads (Royal Road) connecting Pataliputra, the Mauyran capital town in Bihar, with great cities of northwestern India.[281] He gives a vivid description of the roads. It creates an impression that Megasthenes was acquainted with these types of road before coming to India. Probably Iranian roads and Indian roads in Mauryan Empire were similar in some way, which attracted the attention of Megasthenes.[282] It may be viewed in other way also that probably Megasthenes became astonished by seeing such wide Grand Trunk Roads of India. This was the reason why he described a lot about the roads of India.

The town planning of Magadha had equally impressed Mehasthenes. He compares it with the town planning of Susa and Ecobatana of Iran. He also tells that Pataliputra was far more beautiful than these two cites.[283] It is very difficult to say how far the town planning of Pataliputra was influenced by the Iranian pattern of town planning. Archaeological excavation at Pataliputra[284] has yielded the great pillared hall in the palace complex which as some scholars hold was planned or Iranian pattern. But this view was not accepted by V.S. Agarawala.[285] The rest of town was not planned on the grid pattern of Iran style. However, Spooner,[286] and Wheeler[287] mention that square pillared hall of Mauryan palace was designed on the pattern of Achaemenid Hall of Hundred Columns, built by Darius Hystaspes at Perspepolis. Wadell[288] the excavator of Pataliputra, points out that the ground floor of the palace was made on the model of Persepolis. But this view is unacceptable for Chanada.[289] Some of the Greek writers, however, praise the Mauryan place which was much superior than the place of Susa and Ecbatana in their views. But Ray[290] finds indigenous style of Mauryan place. According to him, Darius, himself, in his foundation characters of building at Susa and Persepolis, has imported skilled Indian workman. Again the polished character of stone pillars is very old than Iranian counterpart. Further excavations and research may clarify this controversy.

Ashokan monolithic columns characterized by a unique luster. Some scholars believe that Ashoka had followed the Persian examples.[291] Similarly, according to them the capitals on these colomns do show unmistakable evidence of Persian traits viz. Bell shaped top, the seated lions on the famous capital at Saranath and Lauriya Nandangarh. But some scholars don't accept this theory and opine the indigenous origin of these creations.[292] It is very difficult to determine the country that had influenced other in this style of architecture.

It is again a moot point that the style of Indian rock-cut caves had also been traced to Persian rock-cut tombs of Darius and others located at Persepolis and Naksh-I – Rustan.[293] But according to Buddhist sources the First Budhist council was held a Sataparni cave,[294] which is oldest cave. on the basis of this Indian cave structure can be traced back from 5th century B.C.[295] however, it is said that Sataparni cave has not been identified yet.

The resemblance of Ashokan Rock Inscription and Darius' Edict, compels to believe that Ashoka could have influenced by the Achaeminid model of inscriptions.[296] The Aramaic script of the Iranian empire and the Kharosti script (which was derived from the former) used widely in northwestern India, central Asia and other regions. The scripts were prevalent in India side by side during this period. Again the Aramaic inscription has been found at Sirkap.[297] It indicates that the Iranian influence in the region since it presupposes the existence of some people in the city who knew this script.[298]

Goyal[299] has summarized the main characteristic of Asokan and Achaemenid edicts. Obviously they are similar and Asokan edicts are believed to be originated from Achaemenid edicts. This clearly establishes the fact that there was close commercial contact between Indian and Persian world. The similarities have been compared in this way. (1) The opening formula of Asokan edicts is same as that of Achaemenids. (2) Ashoka had used their term lipi in his Brahmi inscription of dipi in the khorosti edicts which was certainly taken from the Iranian inscriptions.[300] Here it is interesting to note that the terms lipi and Lipikara were known to Panini, who lived in an area which was or had been under the Iranian hegemony but do not occur any where in the Buddhist record. In the Shashbazgarhi edict, Ashoka used the principals of likhita, lekhita and lekhapita which are supposedly derived from the ancient Persian nipish to write (3) the kharosti script which was prevalent in north-west India even in Pre-Asokan period,[301] and lastly (4) many of the scribes like Ghapada employed by Ashoka to engrave his records were the person who hailed from the north western region.[302]

We see much common customs were prevalent in both India and Iran. The Arthasastra[303] informs us that the shaving of hair was a common kind of punishment in India and a similar practice was also found in Iran too.[304] Another custom which was also common in both Indian and Iran – the hair washing ceremony of the king on his birth day.[305]

Indians borrowed the measure of money, a talent from Iran.[306] According to Rawlinson, the Mauryas did not have regular coinage of their own. So the Persian coins were in free circulation in their domination.[307] Some recent excavations provide fact that at several sites the coins were minted in the period, earlier than Mauryas, going back to fifth century B.C.[308] But in Mauryan period, the minting of coins was more or less influenced by Persian coinage. The Persian sigloi most have been the legal tender in the Persian satrapies in India.[309]

Persian influence may also be seen on the system of administration, court manners and etiquette etc.[310] just like the Persian style of Satrapies, the Mauryan governors bore the title "satrap".[311] It may be assumed that under the Achaemenid rule the local people were following this system. When Mauryas came to power, they did not attempt to ban this system and they also followed this. Though it is controversial , Yavanraja- Taushapa who was the governor of western part of India under Ashoka, was accepted by most of the historians as Iranian.[312] It clearly proves that the foreigners were occupying high posts in Ancient India without any discrimination.[313] The Mauryan emperors, as recorded by Megasthenes, held the court like Persian kings.[314] There was tradition of taking out royal procession on festivals.[315] They were arranged in the following manner-first there were elephants decorated with gold and silver ornaments, after them cam e four horsed chariots and yoked oxen. Then followed the attendants, wearing a holiday dress, and holding in their hands golden cups, goblets, boards etc. whether it was a copy of similar royal procession of Persia or was a local innovation, can't be said for certain. But it is possible that while on one hand Chandragupta followed an Iranian practice, the Iranian themselves added colour and grandeur to their own royal procession by adding the most majestic animals of the world including the elephants especially from India.[316]

About the origin of Mauryas, Dr. D.B. Sporner opines that Mauryas belong to an Iranian house of the famous city of 'Merce'.[317] But this view of Spooner is not accepted by most of the historians. Again curiously enough he traces the origin of Chanakya, the prime Minister of Chandragupta from Iranian tribes on the ground that Chanakya was great astronomer and Iran and not India, was leading in oriental astronomy. Detailed study have clearly shown that firstly the Indian school of astronomy was very different from Iranian school and secondly Chanakya is more known for his book on polity and administration than for the knowledge of astronomy.[318]

Iran and India were very close not only from commercial but also from cultural exchange point of view. India is greatly indebted to Iran for its cultural transformation by coming in contact with Iranian culture. The two cultures exchanged the ideas, values, life styles and other and enriched each other. Though it is very difficult to determine the cultural exchange in terms of quantity, the impacts of different cultures are clearly visible.

Hellenistic World

The invasion of Alexander, brought India very close to Greek world. After Alexander, the Indian territories were under the charge of Selecus, who was defeated by Chandragupta Maurya.[319] Selecus ceded four Greek provinces to Chandragupta, named as Paropamisadae (Kabul) Aria (Heart) Arachosio (Kandahar) and Gedrosla (Baluchistan) and received five hundred elephants as gift from Chandragupta.[320] This was followed by a matrimonial alliance,[321] the exact nature of which is not known. Meghasthenses[322] was deputed by Seleucus to the court of Chandragupta. From Althenaeus; we know that the Indian king (Chandragupta Maurya) sent some precious gifts including some Indian drugs, to the Greek satrap.[323]

During the period of Bindusara, the relation between the two countries became deeper. According to Strabo,[324] Antiochus Soter (281-260 B.C.) a Seleucid king sent Diamachus as envoy to the court of Bindusara. Athenaeus (3rd C.A.D.) says that this second Mauryan King asked Antiochus I to send him wine, dried figs and Greek philosopher, but received wine and figs only, as it was considered an insult for the Seleucid house to send a philosopher to a foreign country.[325]

Epigraphical evidence on the proximity of the Greeks to the Mauryan Empire is available from the Greek inscriptions issued by Asoka and found in the environs of Kandahar in southern Afghanistan. A recently discovered pre-Asokan Greek inscription of the early third century B.C. has added to our knowledge of Kandahar as a Greek settlement.[326] In the course of excavation a stone threshold turned out to be the base of a status inscribed with two elegiac couplets referring to a new statue. Paleographically the inscription, though badly worn, is similar to the Hellenistic Greek of the Asokan inscriptions from Kandahar. The inscription refers to a sacred precinct and to the son of Aristonax. It has been argued that this and other evidence points to Kandahar having been a regular Greek settlement along the lines of other major centres such as Ai-Khanum on the Oxus. Some scholars have identified Kandahar with Alexandria in Arachosia. This may well be so given the strategic location of Kandahar as the meeting poinjt of routes going to Heart, Kabul and Seistan and linked with India via the Gomal and Bolan passes. There is also evidence to suggest that the site of Shahr-I-Kohna, which later developed into Kandahar, was earlier an Achaemenid fortress. That Asoka issued edicts in Greek and Aramaic in this area is therefore not surprising.

Similarly in the Aramaic version at Kandahar and in other Aramaic inscriptions, Dhamma has been translated by modern scholars as Truth and as "the conduct of the good". The latter phrase is suggestive of Zoroastrianism in which a contrast is drawn between the conduct of good and evil. An intriguing statement in the Aramaic version reads: "and there is no judgment for all pious men". This has been interpreted in the context of Rock Edict Four, i.e., the officers of the law who have the power to judge. However, it may be suggested that in the same way as the Greek translation draws on terms familiar to Greek philosophy such as eusebeia and diatribe, the Aramaic translation uses terms derived from Zoroastrian thought. Perhaps the Judgement in this case referred not to officers but to the Zoroastrian belief in judgments after death. This concept being unfamiliar to Greek thought was not used in the Greek version. What the king might have been saying in effect was that those who observe the Dhamma or the conduct of the good would be regarded as pious and therefore exempt from judgments after death. Such an interpretation would in principle be perfectly logical. The Aramaic inscription was intended for those familiar with pre-Hellenistic ideas and practices and its appeal was to the Iranians settled in the region. Asoka's familiarity with Zoroastrianism probably derived from his period as viceroy at Taxila before he became king. That he had this degree of sensitivity to the religious beliefs of those within his empire enhances one's assessment of him as administrator. There is also no mention of Brahmanas and Sramanas in this inscription presumably because, as he states in his Thirteenth Rock Edict, these two categories are absent in the land of the Yonas.[327] The above reading would further endorse the suggestion of the significance of a considerable number of Iranian population in the northwest of India.

Conclusion

The period of India's history, during the days of Mauryas, witnessed the economic development largely due to flourished trade and economic development largely due to flourished trade and commerce. From the Arthasastra, Megasthenes Account and Jatakas, we learn that Mauryas had developed a well built administrative structure to carry out trading activities smoothly. The strong and centralized Govt. created a new sense of security, which acted as a stimulus to production and exchange. The appointment of officers like, Superintendent of ships, Superintendent of commerce, Superintendent of Tolls, and others, clearly indicates that the Mauryan rulers were taking proper care of trade and commerce. Again the Mauryas had created a separate department to take care of foreigners. The violations of trade regulations were punished with an iron hand and the difficulties of traders were paid utmost care. The monumental work of Kehsemendra clearly points out the fact that Mauryan rulers were taking utmost care of the difficulties of traders. The financial prosperity of Mauryan dynasty was mainly built on the prosperity of commerce. Though there are activities between India and West Asia had reached at its epoch, the possibility of a well-developed commerce between the two subcontinents can be corroborated on the facts like, cultural similarity, administrative organizations, the emperor's interest in trade, and a few archaeological facts.

In the sphere of cultural contacts, the Mauryan period opened a new chapter in India's relations with West Asian countries. The directional change of relationships were mainly brought by exchange of embassies, the enterprising traders, the missionary zeal, and devout pilgrims, travelers etc. the cultural impacts of West Asian countries on India and Vice-Versa are visible on many aspects like architecture, sculpture, art, literature, day to day life, royal ceremonies and others. But it has created the controversy among the scholars to decide which cultural practice was borrowed and which one was indigenous. But the cultural impacts of West Asian Countries on India can be perceived on many spheres which cultural contacts between two subcontinents can't be thought without having a good commercial relation. Therefore, a flourished cultural contact is again indicating that there must be developed commercial relations.

The real difficulty arises for a scholar to prepare a list of commodities of export and import between these lands. Because most of the goods of trade were perishable which leaves not trace in archaeological excavations. Therefore, scholars mainly take the help of literary evidences whose authenticity is not the beyond of doubt. Usually the literary works of Ancient India were much more influenced by spiritual and religious ideas, keeping these mundane things like trade and commerce in the backseat. But Kautilya's Arthasastra, Meghasthene's Indica and Jatak stories throw some light on the trading activities, which are not sufficient enough to build the whole story. Foreign sources like Pliny's Natural History, Strabo's Geography, Arrian's Indica and others are more helpful in this regard. They give an idea about India's trading activities with foreign countries during this period, which are no free from errors. The limited archaeological excavations at Pataliputra, Mathura, Memphis and others; gives more idea about cultural contacts than the trading activities. Ashoka's Rock edicts, except a few names of West Asian rulers, don't provide valuable information about the trade. Hence, keeping things in the mind, scholars, sometimes construct the fact taking the help of assumption and presumption, which are not new to history.

The products, which were exported by India to West Asian countries were mainly, food products, textiles, copal, indigo, lac, animal stock etc. Again the goods, which imported by India were mainly figs, beverages, wine, glass, metal etc. But the imported goods were less in comparison to export which symbolizes that the trade was in favour of India; and it confuses that how the foreign countries were paying for the extra amount. The answer for this question is really difficult. Some scholars opine that the western countries were paying the balance in the form of coins, which are founding different places, while others are in opinion that was not favorable to India because India was importing the gods of equal value.

When Megasthenes came to India, he became wonderstruck by seeing the richness of India's natural resources. The network of roads and waterways were well developed which facilitated the trading activity. Mention may be made, the industries like textile, carpentry, stone cutting and mining, pottery were in a flourished condition. Guilds played a major role in this trading activity, they not only supplied good quality of goods which were highly praised in western society but also controlled the price by producing the huge quantity to goods. Sometimes these guilds acted as banking organizations and helped the traders for their transaction of money. The role of guilds in this commercial interaction was immense helpful.

The social conditions and attitude of canon laws were not so much favourable for the development of trade. The trading activity, which was especially confined among the Vaisyas, was not accepted as a very good job and highly respected. Again the intelligentsia mass like Brahmanas; and Hinduism were not giving much respect this job because there was a fear of losing caste. Earning money and achieving prosperity by this trading activity was equally reprehensible in Hindu religion because this money was considered as black money. Therefore the trade activity in Ancient India was not to much socially approved and it was not open to the every class of the society. So the surplus wealth of the people of the other castes excepting, Vaisyas, was spent for luxury, amusement and other unproductive purposes. These types of socials restrictions were impediments on the path of trade.

In this connection, the royal support was very much essential to continue and further the trading activities. Fortunately, the Mauryan rulers provided their extensive support to traders as well as trading activities. State itself was also involved in this trade. Some of the industries were also under state supervision like boat building, stone cutting, brick making and others. With the active support of state, the trading activities under the Mauryas reached in a thriving stage.

Under the Mauryas, the commercial interaction between India and West Asian Countries was undoubtedly in a flourished state. The geographical position of India, its fertile soil, suitable climate and strong, centralized Govt. of Maurya; provided a conducive climate for trade. The goods, which were produced in India, was highly needed by West Asian Countries because their unfavorable climate and infertile land was insufficient to cater the needs of the people. Again the luxurious items, created by artisans, were highly praised in foreign soil. The principle of demand and supply became the major determinant of this trade. Finally the trade, which was continuing from the Vedic period, under active the support of Mauryas, it witnessed its prosperous phase. It's multifaceted impacts were felt on culture, art, architecture and day to day to life which was not previously felt in such a large extent.

End Notes

---

[1] Sastri, Nilakantha, *Age of the Naadas & Mauryas*, p. 260
[2] Ibid
[3] Rawlinson, H.G., *Intercourse between India and the Western World*, p. 88.
[4] Sastri, K.A.N., op.cit, p. 273.
[5] Ibid
[6] Chakrabarty, Haripada, *Trade and Commerce in Ancient India*, p. 4.
[7]Chandra, Moti, *Trade and Trade Routes in Ancient India*, p. 84.
[8] Sastri, Nilakantha, op.cit., p. 276.
[9]Chakrabarti, Ranabir, *Trade in Early India,* pp.54-56.
[10] Rawlinson, H.G. *The Intercourse between India and the Western World*, p. 41.
[11]Mc.Crinddle, *Ancient India as Described in Classical Literature*, p. 131.
[12]Saletore, R.N., *Early Indian Economic History*, p. 204.
[13] Ibid.
[14] Rawlinson, H.G. op.cit, p. 43.
[15] Asthana, Shashi, *History and Archaeology of India*, p. 45.
[16] Swamy, L.N., *A Maritime Contacts of Western India*, p.39
[17] Sastri, K.A.N., *Age of Nandas and Mauryas*, p.20.
[18] Thapar, Romila, *Ashoka and the Decline of Mauryas*, pp.40-41
[19] Thapar, Romila, "Epigraphic Evidence and some Indo-Hellenistic Contacts during the Mauryan period", in I.K. Maity and Upendra Thakur (eds), *Indological Studies*, pp. 15-19.
[20] Ibid.
[21]Rostovzeff, M., *The Social and Economic History of the Hellenistic World*, p.267.

---

[22]. Thapar, Romila, "Epigraphic Evidence and some Indo-Hellenistic Contacts during the Mauryan period", in I.K. Maity and Upendra Thakur (eds), *Indological Studies*, pp. 15-19.

[23] Shreedharan, K., *A maritime History of India.* p. 17

[24] Shrivastav, Balaram, *Trade and Commerce in Ancient India,* p. 95

[25] Ibid, p. 95

[26] Strabo, *Geography,* Bk-xvi, chapt-I, p.142

[27] Strabo, *Geography,* Bk-xvi, chapt-I, p.142.

[28] Ibid, p. 143.

[29] Cunningham, A., *Geography*, p. 49.

[30] Mc.Crindle *As India Described in Classical Literature*, 160-62, quoted from Saletore, R.N., *Early Indian Economic History*, p. 362.

[31] Cf. Breasted, P., *A History of Egypt,* p.36.

[32] Chakraborty, Haripada, *Trade & Commerce in Ancient India,* p.1.

[33] Ibid, p.3.

[34] Saletore, R.N. op.cit., p.366.

[35] Srivastav, Balaram, op.cit, p. 94.

[36] Ibid.

[37] Majumdar, *R.C ., Corporate Life in Ancient India*, p. 36.

[38] Srivastav, Balaram, op.cit, p. 97.

[39] Ibid.

[40] Rostovzeff, M., *Social & Economic History of the Hellenistic Empire*. pp.545-54.

[41] Ibid.

[42] Ray Chaudhury, H.C., *Political History of India*, p. 331, R.E. XIII of Ashoka.

[43]Charles worth, M.P., *Trade Routes & Commerce with Roman Empire*, p. 146.

[44] Srivastav, Balaram, op.cit. p. 99. Ibid.

[45] Ibid.

[46] Buch, M.A.,op.cit, p.234.

[47] Srivastav, Balaram, op.cit, p.103.

[48] Warmington, E.H., *Commerce Between Roman Empire & India*, pp 44-45.

[49] Kangle, R.P., *Arthasastra*, Kautilya, p.415.

[50] Ibid.

[51] Chandra,Moti, *Trade and Trade Routes in Ancient India*, p.78.

[52]Swamy, L.N., *Maritime Contacts of Ancient India,* p.54.

[53]Mc. Crindle, *Ancient India as Described in Classical Literature*. p. 111.
[54] Warmington, E.H.,op.cit. p.45.
[55] Srivastav, Balaram, op.cit, p. 105.
[56] Sastri ,Nilakantha, *Advanced History of India,* p.122.
[57] Cahudhury, H.P. op.cit, p.247.
[58] Kautilya, *Arthasastra*, BK II, chap-XVIII, p. 140.
[59] Ibid, p 100.
[60] Mc. Crindle, *Ancient India as Described by Megasthenes & Arrian*, Frag-XIII, p.56
[61] Herodotus, *Persian Wars*, BK-III, ch-97, p. 205.
[62] Pliny, *Natural History,* III, BK-XVI, ch-65, pp 404-5.
[63] Saletore, R.N. *Early Indian economic History*, p 191.
[64] Ibid.
[65] Ibid.
[66] *The Jatak II*, No.172, p. 66.
[67]Shamasastry, R., *Arthasastra,* p.46.
[68] Shamasastry, R., *Arthasastra,* p.46.
[69] Ibid, p.48.
[70] Saletore, R.N., op.cit., p. 193.
[71] Chakrabarty, H.P., op.cit, p. 241.
[72] Herodotus, *Persian Wars*, 5th BK III, ch-22, p.174.
[73] Ibid.
[74] Saletore, R.N. op.cit., p. 199.
[75] *The Jataka, III*, No. 138, p. 297.
[76] Srivastav, Balaram, op.cit., p. 241.
[77] Pliny, *Natural History, III*, BK XV, ch. 7, p. 289.
[78] Shamasastry,R., op.cit, p. 49.
[79] Saletore, R.N., op.cit., p. 202.
[80] Rawlinson,H.G., *Phonenicial*, p. 69.
[81] Prakash, Buddha, *India and the World*, p.234
[82] Mc. Crindle, *Ancient India as Described in Classical Literature*, p. 131.
[83] Ibid.
[84] Saletore, R.N., op.cit., p. 204.
[85] Saletore, B.A., *India's Diplomatic Relations with the West*, p. 222.
[86] Saletore, R.N., op.cit., p. 206.
[87] Strabo, *Geography*, *III*, BK XV, ch.37, p 97.

[88] Thapar, Romila, "Epigraphic Evidence and Some Indo-Hellenistic Contacts During the Mauryan period", S.K. Maity and U. Thakur (eds.), *Indological Studies*, pp.15-19.
[89] Scullard, H.H., *The Elephants in the Greek and Roman World*, p.37.
[90] Maity, S.K. and T. Thakur, (ed.), *Indological Studies*, pp.15-19.
[91] Ibid.
[92] Rawlinson, H.G., op.cit, p.121.
[93] Pliny, *Natural History, III*, BK-VIII, ch-6, pp. 251-52.
[94] Breastfed, P., *A History of Egypt*, p. 280
[95] Saletore, R.N. op.cit, p. 210.
[96] Kennedy,J.F., "The Early Commerce of Babylon with India", *Journal of Royal Asiatic Society 1898*, p. 259.
[97] Ibid
[98] Srivastav, Balaram, op.cit, p. 68
[99] Ibid.
[100] Samasastry,R., op.cit, p. 125
[101] Ibid
[102] Chakrabarty, Haripada, *Trade and commerce in Ancient India*, p 215
[103] Polybius, *Histories*, VI, BK-XXX, ch-III, p. 145
[104] Ibid
[105] Kautilya, *Arthasastra*, BK-II, ch-XXV, P. 136
[106] Watt,G., *Commercial products of India*, p. 891
[107] VanBeek, G.W., "Frankincnces and Myrrh in Ancient South Arabia", *Journal of American Oriental Society*, July – September 1958, pp.141-52.
[108] Tarn, W.W., *Greeks in Bactria and India*, p. 370-71
[109] Agrawal R.S. *Trade centres & routes in Northern India, Delhi 1982*, pp 122-123
[110] Mc. Crindle, *Ancient India as described by Megasthenes & Arrian*, p. 55
[111] Ibid
[112] Levin Bongard ,G.M., *Mauryan India*, p. 46
[113] Saletore, R.N., op.cit, p. 130 (It is mentioned in Girnar Edict of Ashoka)
[114] Ibid
[115] Ibid
[116] Warmington, E.H., op.cit, p132
[117] Saletore, R.N., op.cit, p 140

[118] Warmington, E.H., *The commerce between India and Western Countries*, p. 164
[119] Kautilya, *Arthasastra*, BK-II, ch XXIV, p. 129
[120] Samasastry,R.,(trans) *Arthasastra*, p. 112
[121] Bongard, Levin, *G.M.* ,*Mauryan India*, Bangalore 1985, p. 159
[122] Periplus (49) p. 42
[123] Chakrabarty, H.P., op.cit, p. 265
[124] Ibid
[125] Pliny, *Natural History*. IV, p. 112
[126] Saletore, R.N., op.cit, p. 158
[127] Ibid, p. 154
[128] Loane,R., *Industry and commerce of the city of Rome*. p. 48
[129] Chakrabarty, H.P. op.cit, p. 262
[130] *Arthasastra*, Kautilya, BK-II, ch-viii, p. 65
[131] Ibid
[132] Saletore, R.N., op.cit, p.640
[133] Ibid
[134] *Epigraphica Indica*, XVIII, 1.4, p. 390
[135] Ibid
[136] Chakrabarty, Haripada, op.cit., p. 64
[137] Saletore, R.N. op.cit., p. 133
[138] *Indian Antiquary*, Vol-IXX, no. 170, p.161
[139] *Epigraphica Indica*, no. XVIII, PP 232-236
[140] Saletore, R.N. op.cit., p. 641
[141] Ibid
[142] Chakrabarty, Haripada, op.cit., p. 88
[143] Ibid, p. 89
[144] Arrian, *Indica*, p. 21
[145] Strabo, II, p.98
[146] Chakrabarty, Haripada, op.cit., p.90
[147] Saletore, R.N.op.cit., pp. 413-14
[148]Ibid
[149] Saletore, R.N. op.cit. p. 416
[150] Chakrabarty, H.P. op.cit., p. 100
[151] Appian,J., *Roman History, the civil war*, BK-II, p. 407
[152] Strabo, *Geography*-III, BK XVII, ch. I (16) p. 237
[153] Ibid
[154] Saletore, R.N., op.cit., p.431
[155] Buch, M.A., op.Cit., p.223

[156] Mc. Crindle, *AICL*, p. 214
[157] Bunbury, H., *Ancient Geography*, I, p. 424
[158] Saletore, R.N., op. Cit., p. 432
[159] Ibid
[160] Buch, M.A. *Economic life in Ancient India*, p. 223
[161] Ibid, p.234
[162] Thaplyal, Kiran, *Guilds in Ancient India*, p. 27
[163] Mc. Crindle, Megasthenes *and Arrian*, pp –86-87
[164] *Arthasastra*, II p. 22, Kangle, p. 53
[165] Ibid
[166] Majumdar, A.K., *A concise history of Ancient India*, p. 349
[167] Adhya, G.L., *Early Indian Economics*, p. 82
[168] Thaplyal, Kiran, op.cit., p. 27
[169] Ibid
[170] *Arthasastra*, II, 4
[171] *Arthasastra*, VII, p. 1
[172] Thaplyal, Kiran.,op.cit., p. 28
[173] Ibid
[174] *Arthasastra of Kautilya*, Shamasastry, R., p. 18
[175] Thaplyal,Kiran, cp.cit., 28
[176] Adhya, G.L., op.cit, p. 138
[177] Shamasastry,R.,(trans). *Arthasastra*, p. 53
[178] Ibid
[179] *Arthasastra*, II, 36, Shamasastry ,R., (trans) p. 162
[180]Shamasastry, R., (trans) *Arthasastra*, p. 162
[181] Thaplyal, KK.,op.cit, p.60
[182] Coomarswamy, A.K., *Indian craftsman*, p.59
[183] Ibid
[184] Das, S.K. *The Economic History of Ancient India*, p.174
[185] Shamasastry,R., (trans) *Arthasastra*, p. 227
[186] Thaplyal, KK. op. cit., P. 89
[187] Ibid
[188] Smith, V.A., *Early History of India*, p. 55
[189] Mookherjee, R.K., *A History of Indian Shipping*, p. 70
[190] Smith, V.A., op.cit., p. 87
[191] Mookherjee, R.K., op.cit. p. 70
[192] Ibid, p. 71
[193] Smith, V.A., *Commerce of Ancients*, Vol. I, p. 12
[194] Robertson,R., *Disquisition Concerning Ancient India*, p. 196

[195] Cirtius, IX, p. 9, quoted from R.K. Mookherjee, *A history of Indian Shipping*, p. 73

[196] Swami, L.N., *Maritime contacts of Ancient India,* p.52.

[197]Strabo, XV, p. 46

[198] Mc. Crindle, *Ancient India*, p. 55

[199] Pliny, VI, 22, with regard to equivalent of amphora and the tonnage of these ancient vessels, Mc. Crindle, says, " the amount of cargo carried by ships was generally computed by the talent or amphorae, each of which weighed about a fortieth of a ton. The largest ship was of 10,0000 talents or 250 tons. The talent and anaphora each represented a cubic feet of water and as the Greeks or Romans food measured about 97 of English feet, the talent and amphora each weighted very nearly, 57 lbs. See Torry's *Ancient ships*, p. 25 and R. K. Mookherjee's "*A History of Indian shipping*" p.72

[200] Smith, V.A., *Early History of India*, p. 124

[201] *Arthasastra*, BK-II, ch-xviii, quoted from R.K. Mookherjee, *A history of Indian shipping*, p. 73

[202] Asthana, Shashi, *History and Archaeology of India's contact with other countries*, p. 189

[203] Mookherjee, R.K. op.cit., p. 75

[204] Majumdar, R.C., *Corporate life in Ancient India*, p. 62

[205] Sastri, K.A.N. op.cit, p. 227

[206] Ibid, p. 227.

[207] Mookherjee, R.K. op.cit, p. 76

[208] Ibid, p. 77.

[209] Samaddar, J.N., *Lecturers on Economic Conditions of Ancient India*, p. 118

[210] Mookherjee, R.K. op.cit. p. 76.

[211] Sastri, K.A.N., op.cit, p. 275.

[212] Mookherjee, R.K. op.cit., p. 174.

[213] Kangle, R.P., *The Kautilya Arthasastra*, p. 97.

[214] Sastri, K.A.N., op.cit., p. 276

[215] Mookherjee, R.K. op.cit., p. 75

[216] Subba Rao, N.S., *Economic and Political Condition in Ancient India*, p. 85

[217]Kangle, R.P., op.cit, p. 259

[218] Ibid, p. 260

[219] Samaddar, J.N.,op.cit, p. 114

[220] Ibid, p. 115

[221] Sastri, K.A.N., op.cit, p. 276
[222] Ibid, p. 276
[223] Chakrabarti, Ranabir, *Trade in Early India,* pp.54-56.
[224] Ibid.
[225] Ibid
[226] Kautilya, *Arthasastra* (edited and translated) by R.P. Kangle,op.cit. p.16 . The functions of Panyadhyaksha figures in chapter 2 p.16
[227] Chakrabarti, Ranabir, op.cit, pp54-56.
[228] Sammaddar, J.N.,op.cit, p. 116
[229] Ibid
[230] Kolta, N.S. *India as described by Megasthenes*, p. 109
[231] Smith, V.A., *Early History of India*, p. 127.
[232] Sammaddar, J.N.,op.cit, p. 128.
[233] Mc. Crindle, *Ancient India as described by Megasthenes and Arrian*, , p. 211.
[234]Introduction to Dr. Mukherjee's, *History of Indian Shipping and Maritime activity*
[235] Sasti, K.A.N. op.cit. p.273
[236] Shammaddar, J.N. op.cit, p. 122
[237] Ibid, p.126.
[238] Gopal, M.H., *Mauryan Public Finance,* p.69
[239] Chakrabarti, Ranabir, op.cit., pp.56-58.
[240] Ibid.
[241] Chakrabarti, Ranabir, *Trade and traders in early Indian Society,* p.48.
[242]Mukherjee, B.N., *Aramaic Edicts*, pp.9-22.
[243] Ibid.
[244] Shammaddar, J.N. Op.cit, p. 127.
[245] Smith, V.A., *Early History of India*, p. 125.
[246] Ibid.
[247] Saletore, B.A.,*India's Diplomatic relations with the West*, p. 156.
[248]Ibid.
[249] Asthana, Shashi, op.cit, p. 188.
[250] Ibid.
[251] Charlesworth, M.P., *Trade Routes and commerce of the Roman Empire*, p. 54.
[252] Ibid., p. 56.
[253] Asthana, Sashi,op.cit, p. 188

[254] The identification of King Philadelphus as Ptolemy Philadelphus of Egypt is accepted by all the historians. Cf Smith,V.A.,*The Early history of India*, p. 156, Sastri,K.A.N., *Age of Nandas and Mauryas*, p. 168.
[255] Sastri, Nilakantha, *The Age of Nandas and Mauryas*, p.168.
[256] Smith,V.A., thinks that the ruler was either Bindusara or Ashoka (*The early history of India*, p. 156) Saletore,R.N., however identifies him with Bindusara (*India's Diplomatic relations with west*, p. 136.)
[257] Asthana,Sashi, op.cit, p. 189.
[258] Jairazbhoy, R.A.,*Origin and Spread of Ancient civilization*, p. 123.
[259] Bhandarkar, R.G.,*Asoka*, p. 58.
[260] Sastri,K.A.N.,., op.cit. p. 167.
[261] Rawlinson,H.G., *Intercourse between India and the Western world*, p. 93-94.
[262] Ibid.
[263] Asthana,Sashi, op.cit, p. 189.
[264] Coomarswamy,A.K., *History of Indian and Indonesian Art*, p. 17.
[265] Jairazbhoy,R.A., op.cit, p. 57.
[266] Davar,F.C., *India and Iran through ages*, p. 54-55.

[267] Jairazbhoy,R.A., op.cit., 63. Both the inferences are doubtful and the device could very well be indigenous, An attempt has been made to trace Budhist influence on revolving wheels of Egyptian temples referred to by Henron of *Alexandira* (Asthana,Sashi op.cit., p. 189). The depiction of wheel with Trident on a Ptolimic gravestone has been found in Egypt. It might suggest Indian influence (Singhal,D.P., *Indian and world civilization*, p. 75).
[268]Charles worth,M.P., *Trade routes and commerce of the Roman Empire*, p. 59.
[269] Mukherjee, *The culture and Art of India*, p. 101.
[270] Mc, Crindle, *Ancient India its invasion by Alexander*, p. 27.
[271] Elphinstone,R.and Cowell,A., *Ancient India*, p. 136.
[272] Strabo-IV, quoted from Asthan,Sashi op.cit., p. 190.
[273] Singhal, op.cit., p. 75.
[274] Rostovzeff, *Cambridge Ancient History*, VII, p. 154.
[275] Ibid.
[276] Saletore,B.A., *Indian's Diplomatic Relations with west*, p. 160.
[277] Asthana,Sashi op.cit, p. 191.
[278] Ibid.

[279] Rawlinson,H.G., "Foreign Influence in the Civilization of Ancient India" *Journal of Bombay Branch Royal Asiatic society*, vol. 23, p. 228.
[280] Ray, N.R.,*Mauryan and Sunga Art* p. 44.
[281] Ghosh,A., *The city in Early Historical India*, pp. 67-70.
[282] Pliny, *Natural History*.VI, p. 21.
[283] Rawlinson, H.,G., op.cit, pp. 29-43, "Foreign influence in the civilization of Ancient India" *JBBRAS*, vol. 23, p. 228.
[284] McCrindle, op.cit, Fragment XXVI, pp. 67-68.
[285] Agrawal, *Indan Art*, pp. 104-108.
[286] Spooner, D.D.,"Mr Tatan Tata's excavation at Pataliputra" *Archaeological Survey of India: Annual Report*, 1912-13, pp. 56-67.
[287] Wheeler,R.E.M., "Iran and Indian in pre-Islamic Times", *Ancient India*, no. 4, p. 96.
[288] Unvala,J.M.,"Political and cultural relations between Iran and India" *ABORL*, vol. 28, p. 176; Jairazbhoy,R.A., op.cit, p. 55.
[289] Chanda,R.P., "The Beginning of Art in Eastern India," *MASI*, no. 30, p. 12.
[290] Ray,N.R.,*Maurya and Sunga* Art., p. 48.
[291] Altekar,S., "Origin and Early History of Coinage in Ancient India" *JNSI*, vol. XV, pt-I, 1953.
[292] Agrawal,R.S., *Indan Art*, pp. 104-108..
[293] Bapat, P.V.,(ed.)*2500 years of Buddhism*, p. 32.
[294] Ibid.
[295] Thapar,Romila, *Ashoka and Decline of the Mauryas*, p. 127.
[296] Sircar,D.C., *Select Inscriptions*, p. 811.
[297] *Epigraphica Indica*, vol. XIX, p. 251.
[298] Ibid.
[299] Goyal, S.R., In a privately circulated paper, quoted in Asthan,Sashi op.cit, p. 200.
[300] Ibid.
[301] Wheeler, R.E.M.,*Early India and Pakistan*, p. 173.
[302] Rawlinson,H.G., *Intercourse between India and Western World*, p. 29.
[303] *Arthasastra*, IV. 9.
[304] Smith,V.A., *Early History of India*, p. 137.
[305] Herodotus, IX, 110, Strabo, XV, I, 69.
[306] Ray,N.R., *Numismatic Notes and Monographs*, 8.
[307] Rawlinson,H.G., *Intercourse between India and Western World*, p. 29.

[308] Pusalker,A.D., Cultural interrelations between India and outsides world" *Cultural Heritage of India* vol. I, 1958, p. 157.
[309] Muller, *Ancient Sanskrit Literature*, p. 501.
[310] Ibid.
[311] Mc. Crindle, op.cit, p. 71-73.
[312] Strabo, XV, I, 69, see the Account of the Antioctus, Epiphanes and Ptolemy Philadelphus in Athanaen, IV, 45.
[313] Selecus got 500 elephant from Chandragupta Maurya as a part of treaty between them and Antigonus got several of them at a later period.
[314] Spooner,D.D., "The Zoroastrain period of Indian History" *JRAS*. 1915, pp. 416-417.
[315] Bose, Sen, Subbarappa, *A concise History of Science in Indian*, p. 60.
[316] Ibid.
[317] Spooner,D.D., "The Zoroastrain period of Indian History" *JRAS*. 1915, pp. 416-417.
[318] Asthana,Sashi, op.cit, p. 202.
[319] Mc, Crindle, *The Invasion of Indian by Alexander the Great*, pp. 404-5. We did not know the exact nature of alliance.Perhaps Seleuius married his daughter by Megasthenes and Arian, p. 132.
[320] Alhaenaeus, I. 32 quoted by Mc. Crindle, *The invasion of India by Alexander the Great*, p. 405
[321] Ibid
[322] Ibid
[323] Asthana, op.cit, p. 202
[324] Rawlinson,H.G., *Intercourse between India and the western world*, 1916, p. 39.
[325] P.M. Fraser, "The Son of Aristonax at Kandahar", *Afghan Studies*, 1979, 2, pp.9-21.
[326] Thapar, Romila, "Epigraphic Evidence and some Indo-Hellenistic Contacts during the Mauryan Period", in S.K. Maity and Upendra Thakur (ed.), *Indological Studies*. pp.15-19.
[327] Ibid

4

Trade during the Post-Mauryan Period

Introduction

India's contact with the West is as old as the beginning of Indus Valley civilization.[1] This contact continued even after the downfall of the Mauryan Empire in spite of subsequent political anarchy caused by the onrush of the Greeks, Parthians, Sakas and Kushanas. The establishment of Satavahan power in the Deccan in first century B.C. and of the Kushana Empire in north India in first century A.D. gave fresh impetus to the growth of India's economic and cultural contacts with West Asia, a large part of which was either within the Roman empire or under its sphere of influence. The establishment of the Roman Empire and the increasing prosperity of the Roman nobility created a heavy demand for India's luxury goods and gave a further fillip to Indo-Roman trade connections in the early centuries of Christian era.

Rome enriched herself by the spoils and tributes from so many foreign lands and had acquired a taste for luxuries of every kind. The capital of the greatest empire ever established in Europe was filled with people who had inherited the great wealth and whose sole occupation was enjoyment of these riches. The retiring generals found their villas dull, rustic, and old fashion made and all the more unbearable because they had brought back with them masses of coinage, bullion and slaves. They had developed expensive tastes whilst staying in other continents and now they had means to indulge those tastes at home. They did so with feverish haste and great display. Oysters were brought all the way from Spain or Britain and wild blasts were imported from the farthest corners of Egypt to be featured in games. Common men always emulate the fashion determined by the elite.[2]

Of all goods in particular flavour with luxury living Romans, Indian products were most popular. To meet the demands, new and greater efforts were made to increase trade with India and this was accomplished to a degree, which would appear astonishing even today. The Romans' demand of Asian luxuries was unprecedented. Chinese silks, Indian pearls, jewels, fine muslin, drugs, specie, condiments, incense, ghee, ivory, dyes, cosmetics, oils and perfumes all fetched high prices.[3] It appears that towards the end of the first century the greatly prized Chinese silk as well as furs were being shipped from Indian ports to the western countries because the land routes were blocked by Parthians and sea route gained much popularity. In return western merchants carried tin and lead to India, minerals which India herself did not possess, as well as wine, coral and glass - a widely exported Roman products, especially coloured glass - brightly coloured grifles and gold and silver coins. Special presents were carried for kings including maidens for harems. However, the principal means of exchange between India and Rome was gold. Therefore, Pliny bewailed the enormous drain on Rome's resources created by the demand for eastern luxuries. There was not a year in which India did not take at least 150 million sesterces from Rome[4] in equal amount going to Arabia and China. Great quantities of Roman coins found in South India where jewels and spices were sold. Pliny also tells us that Indian wares cost a hundred times more in Roman markets than the Indian markets.[5] Later, Vespasian's policy, in 69-79, of cutting down extravagant expenditure may have made some differences in the import of luxury goods from India but there is no concrete evidence of this.

The trade between Europe and Asia was so brisk that, despite the hostility of Parthia towards Rome and their periodic clashes and the increasing popularity of the Red Sea route; the Persian Gulf route nevertheless carried a flourishing trade and a land borne trade also grew considerably. This trade led to rise of great cities along the routes and new ports on the coasts. Petra the town of Nabataeans and Palmyra which commanded the Caravan rôutes to Asia, served as terminal points for the maritime trade of the Red Sea and the Indian Ocean Gerrha, Ommana, Spasini were all large mercantile towns to which Indian vessels regularly brought cargoes of timber, black wood, and ebony whilst Arabia sent the frankincense, the spices of Cana.

Trade inevitably led to some tourism, especially to Roman and the Indian settlement in their respective areas of influence. There was a Yavana colony at the mouth of Kaveri river and foreign population were known to have existed in Madurai district.[6] Mercenary Roman soldiers were attending the Indian princes, are mentioned in Tamil literature. Romans had close commercial contacts with Tamils in India especially for its cloth, dyes, pearls etc. Hence it is not surprising that the Tamil poems sing of Yavana ships bringing wine and other wares to the ports.[7] A late map shows a temple of Augustus at Muziris on the West coast of India, which would indicate that there must have been a large Roman settlement to erect the temple honouring their deified emperor. According to Morteem Wheeler, "the temple of Augustus" at Muziris indicates an "official arm" long enough to reach at the Malabar Coast".[8] Dyon Chrysostom, the Greek rhetorician and sophist, who lived in the reign of Trajan (98-117) mentions that the population of cosmopolitan Alexandria included many Indians who had come there to trade.[9] About the Indian traders, Pausians also refer that Indian traders brought the marvelous creatures like the parrots.[10]

The trade between India and Rome brought immense prosperity to India though Indian merchants who acted as middlemen in this trade. It also seemed that the Roman state also directly did not participate in this trade but it was not averse to collecting substantial taxes, on the cargo.[11] It also considered the enterprise important enough to protect the routes from the Red Sea ports to Alexandria with forts, garrision, with military camps and to establish watering places along the routes.[12] These facilities were double useful since the routes also gave access to profitable mining activities in the region.

Trade between India and Rome continued to thrive steadily during the second and third century A.D. But with the rise of great Gupta Empire, the heart of the Indian empire moved inland towards central India and a splendid cultural renaissance set in with a distinctive Indian character. This however, interrupted the continuous flow of trade between India and Rome. The emergence of the Sassanian Empire in 227 also checked direct communication between the two nations. But the contact continued through Alexandria to which Indian flocked in increasing numbers until the fall of Roman Empire in the fifth century and the consequent decline of Alexandira. In the later phase, the Indian trade was diverted towards Southeast Asia. Rome's apetitie for luxuries was so huge that India could not satisfy it.[13] India's supply of precious stones, ivory and spices had begun to run out. Consequently, the Indian traders began searching eastwards for fresh suppliers of stones, ivory and spices which had begun to run out. They imported the goods from South-East Asia to cater the increasing demands of Roman people. This contact of Indians with Southeast Asian people later bloomed into an exceptionally fruitful cultural intercourse. With the decline of Roman Empire, the Roman demands ceased and the enterpot trade of India collapsed.[14]

Presence of Kushan Empire in the political scenario of ancient India brought a sea change in the Indo-Roman trade. The vast Kushan Empire, which included Afghanistan, Bacteria and much of Central Asia, comprised a variety of nationalities- Indo-Greeks, Parthians, Scythians, Iranians, Chinese and others. This role of Kushanas in providing a meeting ground for the great civilizations of the time and disseminating Buddhism to Central Asia and beyond has been extremely important for the advancement of trade.[15] The cosmopolitan nature of Kushan Empire is aptly illustrated by their coins, many of which carry a Persian title for the King in Greek letters and the effigy of the kings in Turkish dress. The Kushan kings were in close with the West Asian and Roman emperors. The political ambitions of the Romans to expand into India also brought them nearer to Kushan frontiers. The Kushanas, it is suggested, also imported a large number of Greek sculptors from Asia Minor who settled in Punjab and were associated with the Gandhara School of art.[16] The cultural contacts between India and Rome were also felt on the sphere of astronomy, mathematics, art, architecture and sculpture, coin system and others. The exchange of envoys also strengthened the political contacts, which consequently helped the growth of trade. The impacts of Rome on the living style, language and culture of Indian people is clearly perceptible.

Having a vast empire, the Roman Empire enclosed an uninterrupted area around the Mediterranean Sea. The northern frontier was bordered by Hardian's wall between England and Scotland and the rivers Rhine and Danube on the continent. The eastern border ran across the territories of Modern Turkey, Iraq, Syria, Lebanon, Jordan and Israel. The provinces of the African continent were relatively small with the exception of Egypt.[17] This vast empire of Rome opened the ample opportunity to trade with different countries in different directions in order to meet the needs of the people. On the one hand Rome, which was solely dependent on agriculture, had risen after centuries of triumph to be the mistress of a vast empire of the people with whom and through whom she conducted all her commerce.[18]

Again the establishment of comparative peace by the Roman Empire, which showed the ways for new explorations and developments. The geographical importance of Arabia, the Asia Minor and the north-eastern Africa serving as a chain for joining west and Western Asia and became the focal point of attraction. Roman merchants in Western Asia strengthened their business, with ample financial resources, thus consolidated their influence.[19] But one most strange thing in this trade was, Indian merchants seldom met their Roman counterparts. The very reason was that the intermediaries of Indo-Roman trade were the Alexandrian Greeks, Syrian, Jews, Armenians, Arabs, Axumitis and the Parthians controlling the Somali land and the land route leading to the East.[20]

India's contact with Rome, not only brought the financial prosperity but also the cultural which is clearly felt in art, architecture, language, coins, and on the living patterns of the people.[21] Almost all classical authors of Imperial Rome talk a volumnious trade and brisk commercial intercourse of Rome with

India. They also supply us the information's of trade articles and mode of exchange as well as the flow of Roman gold coins to India. In this context, Pliny complains about the drainage of wealth is which substantiated by the excavations of as many as 68 hoards of coins in India. However, it may be noted that the Roman coins were employed not as currency but as bullion in India.[22] This heavy flow of Roman coins in India had one significant impact was that the mutilation of the gold coinage by the Kushanas and the Imperial Guptas.

About the various aspects of Indo-Roman trade, the foreign sources like The Periplus of the Erythrean Sea, Strabo's Geography, Pliny's Natural History, Arrian's Indika provides a good account to construct the history of this trade. But one major constraint in this way was the trustworthiness of these sources is questioned. In this connection, the excavations at different places like Arikamedu, Baroda, Maheswar, Navadatoli, Nasik, Paithan, Tagara, Broach, Kalyana, Soppara, Dwaraka, Yelleswaram etc. has enhanced our sphere of knowledge. The findings of these places corroborate the facts left by the foreign literary sources as well as Indian sources also. The reports of excavations of different places, which throw some light on Indo-Roman trade, are inserted in this work to enrich the existing knowledge and to create a separate identity from the existing works. In this effort the classical Latin and Greek sources are also used in addition to the excavation reports of Berenike, Pompei and other places of Western world. By doing so we have tried not only to fill up the gap in the existed studies on the subject but also examine the interaction between Indian and the Western world at economic as well as social and cultural levels.

Forest Produce

India was famous for the timber from antiquity. Kautilya refers to various types of strong timbers and 16 kinds of sandal trees.[23] Among the various types of timbers, the ebony, teak wood, black wood sandal wood etc. were important. There are enough evidences of trade of these goods.

It appears as an article of trade of Tyre, referred to in Ezekiel[24]. Where we see trade in ebony between India and Persia before the Christian era. In his book, Warmington, notes that the export from India of ebony and other woods was very old[25]. Indian ships carried it coasting along. Gedrozia and the Arabs monopolised the trade in species and fragrant woods to feed the Roman markets.[26] Theophrastues[27] is the first to mention the ebony tree of India and to make distinction between the two kinds of ebony, a rare and nobler one and a common variety of inferior wood, according to Periplus[28], the large ships were built with ebony and other woods from Barygaza. Pliny says,[29] that ebony came to Rome from India and was much in demand there, since the victories of Pompey the Great in Asia, was exhibited it at Rome." Again he points out that the second type of ebony grows as a shurb like the Cytisus, and is spread over the whole of India.[30] Solinus[31] notes that ebony was solely sent from India and images of Indian gods were sometimes carved from this wood and similarly on drinking cups.

The Indian ebony was known in Greece where too it must have been imported from India is borne out by the reference from Virgil.[32] After the fall of Greece and rise of Rome, the exports of Indian ebony continued. Pliny observed that it was laid before Nero (A.D. 54-68) and it indicates that this tree was very uncommon in the country.[33]

Use of ebony

Indian ebony, which was certainly known in Rome where it must have been imported and of this there can't be no doubt. Pliny, citing Fabianus, declared that ebony would give flame although it burnt with a very agreeable small. There were two kinds of ebony; the rarest was the best and produced from a tree singularly free from knots. The wood was black shining and pleasing to the eye. [34] The other kind of ebony was produced of a shurb resembling the Cytisus, "found scattered over the whole of India".[35] Though it was unknown to Pliny which type of ebony he refers, he was clear about this that the first variety of ebony was coming from India.

Ebony was largely used for the purpose of ornament as well as medicine. According to Pliny, "the dust of ebony was a sovereign remedy for the disease of the eyes, and the pulps of its wood, receded upon a whet-stone moistened with resin wine"[36] dispelled all films, which impede the sight. The root too applied with water, was capable of curing white specks in the eyes and with addition of the roots of dranculus in equal proportions and also with only, could cure cough. According to Muslim medical opinion in India, it is considered as an astringent, a Henuant and lithontriptic. The gum obtained from ebony tree has been used as a remedy for removing obstruction from any cause in the vision.[37]

Ebony was largely cultivated in Malabar (Kerala) Coromandel, Orissa and North Kanara and from the Himalayas, Khasi Hills and from Bengal especially in Sylhet, Tiperrah, north Bengal and Bihar.[38]

Teak Wood

Another timber exported along with ebony in 1st century A.d. from Barygaza (Broach) to the Persian Gulf port of Apologus and Ommana was teak wood, exported 'regularly' in large vessels.[39] This statement clearly refers that in broach the teak wood was grown extensively. It has also cultivated in Bengal, Assam and Sikkim and throughout northwestern India as far as Shaharanpur. It has also been developed in western India between the Narmada and Mahanadi rivers although it has been found in Maharastra and Travancore.[40] It is also found in Orissa although it can hardly be compared with the teak from Burma.[41] Teak forests of Malabar, Travancore, and Gujarat and the Malaya Peninsula were best suited for building purpose.[42]

According to Theophrastos,[43] ships of this wood of India were seen in the Persian Gulf. The town of Siraf on the Persian Gulf was entirely built of this wood and in 1811 Teak was found in the walls of Persian palace near Baghdad pillaged in the 7th CBC.[44] Hence we may assume that teak was exported to Persia. Again

Periplus[45] mentions that in teak and Blackwood and for shipbuilding.[46] From Arthasastra, it can be assumed that the teak wood was an important item of lucrative business in India in third century A.D.[47]

Blackwood

It is one of hard woods of Punjab and of western India. For its durability it was, as now, highly appreciated for agricultural implements, carriage frames, wheels, boat building, furniture and woodcarving.[48] Along with teak wood, ebony, logs of Black wood also were sent from Barygaza to the Persian ports.[49] Mandagora and Calliena gained importance in this trade later on as reported by Cosmos.[50] It is strange that with Strabo nor Pliny even casually refer to either the teak or the black wood imports from India.

In first century A.D. the Periplus has recorded that in the reign of the elder *Saranganes* (Saraganus – probably Satakarni – I) Kalyana had become "a lawful market town" of Sisam wood.[51] Most of the Sisam trade was conducted through Kalyan. Persia was the main country to which most of the Sisam woods were imported. After Persia the next country, to which exports from Kalyan, included the Sisam wood was Homerite region, which roughly corresponds to South Arabia.[52]

In these circumstances it may be inferred that Sisam wood from Kalyana received there from the forests of western India in general, probably reached, if the same routes continued to exist from first to second centuries, Cyeneum in Eastern Sudan, and Auxum, the capital of Abyssynia. From these markets or from Persia it must have reached the markets of Rome in the wake of other exports from India throughout this period.

Sandal Wood

Most probably sandalwood was exported from India much earlier than ebony, teak wood and black wood. From the *Book of Kings*[53] we learn that in view of Tyrean monarch, Hiram's admission of Solomon, the king of Judah, in participation of formers western traffic. Solomon with his own ships, aided by shipwrights from Tyre, sailed to Ophir (Sindh-Sauvira region) and thence brought back to his own country among other commodities, "plenty of almug trees and precious stones"[54]. It is written in the King of Books that King Solomon used the almug wood (from Ophier) for decoration in the house of the lord and in the royal palace and for harps and lyres for musicians.[55] Some scholars question whether almug is really sandalwood. Forty years ago P. Joseph wrote that sandalwood could not be used for musical instruments.[56]

In 6th CBC there are enough evidences about the export of sandalwood from India. In first century A.D. from Periplus, we find that along with teak, black and ebony woods, sandalwood was also exported from Barygaza (Broach) to the Persian Gulf, ports of Ommana. The Silapapadigaram speaks of Puhar and its streets were full of silks, corals, sandals and myrrh.[57] Hence we may assume that sandal wood[58] was exported from the port about the 3rd century A.D. Sandal wood, teak, ebony, eaglewood most of which grew in the hilly forest tracts of Coimbatore, Salem, Malabar and Karnatak.[59]Laufer remarks that, "it is more probable that the sandal wood used in western Asia came from India.[60] According to Watt, "the sandal wood of Mysore and Coorg has not only been known from the most ancient times but has ranked as the finest qualities for centuries.[61] S.N. Majumdar thanks that is was sandal wood it was imported through Barbarcum in South India was also exporting the sandal wood to West Asian countries. From these various accounts it can be safely assumed that the sandalwood was a commodity of great demand in West sian countries for a long time. North India as well as South India were calering the needs of western people.[62]

Use: According to Kautilya, it (sandal wood) was adhesive to the skia, retentive of colour, tolerant to heat.[63] It's medicinal utilities were quite well known in ancient Hindu material medical. An emulsion made of ground sandalwood is used as a cooling application to skin in erysipelas, prurigo and sideman. Its paste was applied to local inflammations.[64] It is also useful for hemicrania, skin diseases, to allay itching and an approdisiae.[65]

Charak speaks of sandal as the best of all, which act as poultices and which eradicate bad smell and cure all cases of burns.[66]

Region of Sandal: Sandal grows naturally in the drier parts of Mysore, Coimbatore, Salem districts, Madurai in the south, while in Maharstra it can be seen at Kolhapur. It is also found in Poona, Bombay, Gujarat & some parts of North India.

Bamboo

When Chan Kien in 128 B.C. reached Ta-hia (Bactria) he was surprised to see walking sticks made from bamboo[67]. Hirth takes it to be a finished product of bamboo imported in a larger quantity.[68] On enquiry the people of Tahia that they had brought them from India reported Chan Kien. Laufer speaks of the ancient trade route running from Sec. Wan through Yunnam to N.E. India Whence the square bamboo in the shape of walking canes was forwarded to Bactria in the 2nd CBC.[69]

Pliny says that, "the peoples of the East employ reeds in making war . . . The reeds of India are placed highest of all. . . . The Indian bamboo are of a size of a tree, as we see in the case of the specimens frequently found in our temples. The bamboo grows especially on the banks of the river of Chennab.[70] Thus, we have little doubt of the abundance of bamboo in Ancient India of the highest quality and its export to Rome for use in the making of temple.

Use: Apart from common use, the bamboo in India is basically used for house building, swords, bows, arrows, and obstruction purpose in canal. From medicinal point of view, bamboo is useful for cooling. But Pliny does not mention that bamboo in Rome was used for arrow and bow as in the case of India. From Pliny it is clear that Indian bamboo was the most preferred one in Rome.[71] The evidence of Pliny (A.D. 23-79) who published his Natural History in the year circa 75 A.D. does not find any corroboration in the Periplus, ascribed to about 60 A.D. as one of the exports from India. But these lacunae need not necessarily be considered that on this account Pliny's statement should be discredited.

Region Bamboo: Usually bamboo is not confined in particular part of India. In almost all forest of India, bamboo is found According to Pliny[72], that the bamboo, which was found in the temples, was usually found on the bank of Chenab. In tropical and extra tropical forests, the bamboo has been found largely. But in temperate zone, bamboo looks like shurbs.

Consumer Goods

In the Mauryan period, about the export of food grains to West Asian Countries, there is no clear-cut evidence. Kautilya, though give emphasis on agriculture does not refer about the export of food grains. It is only in the first century A.D. that we find definite proof that among food grains were exported to Egypt from Barygaza (Broach) by ship, "the products of their own places – Wheat, rice, clarified butter and seasame oil[73] and other goods". Their goods were not only consumed in Egypt but also re-exported from there to other towns and places like Taba, Pano (Raas Bina) and Opone.

The Periplus records that rice is exported from Ariaca and Barygaza to Opone and other ports of east Africa.[74] According to Kalidasa, Magadha and the low laying plains of Vanga and of the Southern plateau produced sufficient paddy. According to Varahamihir, India was producing different sorts of paddies in different parts[75]. These evidences points out that there was a large scale cultivation of rice and it may be presumed that India might be exporting the rice to other countries. South India and Western Coast of India was famous for the rice cultivation and Periplus gives the clues that rice along with other commodities were exported to African countries.[76] Just like rice, wheat was also exported to different parts of the world, evidenced by Periplus[77]. Wheat was chiefly grown in the Northern and Central India and was exported from these regions though the port of Barygaza especially in the first century A.D. Yuanchwang refers to the plenty of wheat cultivation in Ahichhatra and Sindh.[78]

Strabo mentions sugar, Indian honey, procured from trees without the help of bees.[79] Charak and Sushruta mention the medicinal qualities of sugar in detail. The Periplus[80] mentions honey, called Sacchari, exported to Africa and from Barygaza ships to the markets of east Africa sent it. Milindapanha[81] also indicates the existence of sugar industry in its period. The Silappadhikaram[82] refers to the maidens of Puhar pounding "pearls using sweet sugar cane as their pestles" Hence, we may suppose sugarcane was exported from Barygaza as also from Puhar and Ganga. Rostovzeff says, "the production of honey was limited in Western countries and and no attempt was made there in Hellensitic and Roman times to learn more of it or to acclimatise any of sugar yielding plants in the Greeco-Roman but perhaps in the Hettenistic age.[83] This clearly establishes the fact that sugar was an item of export to Roman world from Hellenistic times, Kalidasa and Fahien also mention about the sugar cultivation.

These were some food products, which were exported to Rome as well as West Asian countries.

Exports: Various kinds of dyes, which were exported by India, were copal, indigo and lac. It is evident that from a very early time India was famous for the production of various types of dyes. From Jatakas we know that a yellow dye was prepared from Karnikara flower[84] and a saffron dye from safflower (Kusumbha), which were grown in the king's conservatories[85] Kautily refers about various types of dyes.

Indian Copal

According to Periplus in first century A.D. Indian copal was exported from Africa[86] covering roughly north western India, viz. modern Cutch, Kathiwad, and Gujarat to Malao an important town in the Arabian gulf. Apart from this type of copal, other varieties of copal were also exported from India. Yule identified the coneamum with the Indian copal, the Malabar tallow or white dammar, a gum exuded from *Vateria Indica* order *Diptero carpeoe.* According to Watt, it is a large green of forests at the foot of Western Ghats from Kanara to Travancore and surviving upto 4000 ft. above sea level.[87] Usually this gum or resin like copal was and has been used chiefly for making varnishes.[88] Therefore, the Indian copal must have been exported through Gujarat areas to the Arabian ports like Malao & others in the first century A.D.[89] What was the use of these commodities in the western land, it is very difficult to presume. But keeping the efficacy for varnishing purposes it maybe asserted that it must have been the primary object of export from India to western lands.

Another product, which Kautilya largely refers in his Arthasastra, was lac[90] which was employed for the purpose of colouring. The Periplus reveals that "coloured lac" was exported from Arica or roughly north-western India to the East African ports, Adulis Avalites and Arabian ports in the first century A.D.[91] Whether this export of lac continued after 1st C.A.D. is very difficult to ascertain but keeping the utility of lac in view it can be assumed that this trade might have continued.

From Periplus it would appear as if lac was grown somewhere in northwestern India though he clearly does not mention about the area of cultivation. According to Saletore, R.N., the lac must have obtained from Northwestern provinces and especially from Gorhwal forests in Sindh, it was also expected to be found in Oudh and Punjab[92]. The vast forests of Burma were capable of producing an almost unlimited quantity of lac. Again this lac was produced in abundant quantity from the jungles of Birbhum (Bengal) and in Assam and Orissa.

The use of lac was multiple. It was not only used for dyes but also used to colour the tips of fingers, palms of the hands and soles of the feet. It was also employed as a varnish. Excepting to colour the textile, it was used for colouring the leather, wool and silk. Kalidasa mentions about the lac juice, which was used for coluring the tips of fingers.[93] Bane (7th C.A.D) also refers about the utility of lac-juice.[94] This was also employed for medicinal purposes. A decoration of lac-juice has been used incase of enlargement of liver, in complaints of dropsy, liver & ulecers. Taking the uses of the lac into consideration it can be safely presumed that the women in Arab haerems to colour the different parts of body must have favoured this lac. Perhaps it must have played the important role to colour the leather, woolen goods in the Arabian region except silk because silk was dyed in India and re-exported to the Arabian regions.

Indigo

It was another dying ingredient, which was exported from India. Pliny refers it as indicum[95] which according to him was "a substance imported from India "but its composition was unknown to him. The export of this product was probably made in the beginning of 1st C.A.D. Pliny observes that it was, "not long since indicum began to be imported.[96] He further states that this product of India when powdered was black in appearance but when diluted in water, it yielded, "a marvellous combination of purple and caerulium".[97] Staining pigeons' dung with genuine indium of else by colouring Selenusian earth or anularian chalk with wood also adulterated this dye.[98]

Indigo was used to alleviate cold shiverings and diffluxions inaddition with as a dye. It is also acted as dessicative on sores.[99] Pliny's reference about indigo as attramentum, it has been suggested rightly that he alludes to the real indigo.[100] It was again beneficial in epilepsy, nervous disorders, bronchites, as an ointment to cure sores and largely employed as a test regent.[101] Considering the multiple benefits of indigo, India was cultivating this crop largely for the export purpose.[102] Its medicinal use in the foreign lands can't be said with authenticity but its use as a dying agent is undoubtedly clear. Although Periplus does not mention indigo as one of the exports from India,[103] we know certainly from Pliny that it was exported from India to Rome where it was used not only as a dye but also as a medicine. There is no reference of indigo in Bible but it appears in the Talmud.[104] Rabbies threatened punishment for the professional dyers in Talumdic times who made the substitution.[105] Rathanvel reported that the Egyptians as early as 18th CBC used Indian indigo.[106] Archaeologists of Israel have found the signs of dying facilities dating from 8th CBC and an indigo dyed cloth has been found in 2nd CBC.[107]

Indigo was probably first cultivated in South India especially in Carnatics. As it was exported to Rome apparently from Southern and Western parts of India such a suggestion appears plausible but some epigraphic evidences point that indigo was largely cultivated in Bengal in 6th CAD.[108]

Purple

Purple was another article of dyeing, which was celebrated among the Persians. At that time Indian purple was facing competition from Phoenician purple. Several Greek writers had observed that the Persians used the purple dye for their tunics.[109] The Persians valued their scarlet robes so much so that they offered them as presents to the kings; the manufacture of purple continued down to first century A.D. has been borne out by Strabo and Pliny. Strabo had observed that a great number of dyeing works at Tyre had rendered the city unpleasant as a place of residence.[110] But the main wealth of Tyre city was the superior skill of dying industries. These industries are continuing to work in cities still now. During Pliny (23-79 A.D.) the fame of the Phoenicia was confined to the production of the murex and purple.[111] About Indian purple, Herodotus, Pliny and Strabo don't mention. But from Meghasthenis's account it is clear that Indian purple was no less bad. Etesias (415 B.C.) mentioned in clear terms, "Their (India) dye stuffs are superior to those used by the Persians",[112] Actians also refers about the Indian purple in the 2nd century A.D.[113]

Indian purple, which was produced from vegetables, was mainly used for the purpose of dyeing. According to Ctesias, the purple grown at the banks of Ganga was not inferior to Greek counterpart.[114] Probably under Nero, the Tyrian dye trade was practically liquidated but the use of purple continued under Ortho (69 A.D.) and Domitian (81-96 A.D.). So the Romans must have imported dyes probably from India for Aelian even a century later, refers to the superiority of Indian purple which must have been well known at that time.

India was also exporting various livestocks like, the bull, cattle, birds like the parrot, maina, pheasant and even snakes. Among others, the Indian hunting dogs, the elephants and the peacocks were no doubt most celebrated.[115]

Peacock

One of the most important items in the export of livestocks was peacock, which appears to have travelled to the kingdom of Solomon (South Arabia). About this there are much evidences in the Book of Kings in the Baveru Jataka; and it indicates that the trade of peacocks was also continuing like earlier in the post Mauryan period. Pliny mentions that it continued to attract the attention of Roman people in the first century A.D.[116] He gives a detailed description about the peacocks. According to him by the first century A.D. the Roman people were quite familiar with the Indian peacocks.[117] The peacocks might have been exported to West Asian countries in addition to Rome because in Pre-Mauryan period and in Mauryan period these peacocks were exported to West Asian countries. In the Post Mauryan period, there are so such evidences to point out that it was an item of export to West Asia .

Besides peacocks, Romans liked parrot and they call it by the name of Sittaces. Allien relates how it could become, "as talkative as children and speak with a human voice" if taught to speak like them. The bright plumaged birds had equally attracted the attention of Greeks and Romans.[118] Strabo says that, according to Clitarchus, in India four wheeled Indian carriages, bearing trees with large leaves from which were suspended in cages different kinds of tamed birds, were solemnly driven[119] in procession. Again, among the presents by the Indian Ambassador from Azes-I at touch to the Roman emperor Augustus was a patridge "larger than a vulture."[120] Among the Roman Caesars, birds like the peacock, bright plumaged birds become popular. Caius Caligula (A.D. 37-41) on each particular day of the month offered as sacrifice, flamingoes, peacocks, black grouse, guinea hens and pheasants.[121] In view of the Indo-Parthian trade connections and the commercial relations between Rome and India, birds like the flamingo from the Rann of Cutch where they still abound and the pheasant and peacock from the other parts of India might also have been taken for feasts.[122] In the routine procession of the Roman emperor Tibericus in A.D. 21, among other wild animals, were, "multitude of birds of variegated plummage and fine song."[123] These could only have taken from India about which birds, Pliny almost during this period (A.D. 23-79) Strabo (23 B.C.-19 A.D.) and Aeliar in the middle of second century A.D. had written with much enthusiasm.

Export of Animals

There are enough evidences about the export of animals from India to West Asian countries. As it has already been observed earlier that the Indian animals were to be seen in the capital of Antiochus Iv Epiphanes at Antioch Again in the retinue of the Roman emperor, Tiberius in A.D. 21, besides a host of attendants, there were animals such as buffaloes, leopards and tamed lions[124] together with bright plumaged birds. It is usually believed that the lion and elephants were exported from India as well as from Africa to Rome. During the reign of Augustus (63 B.C. – 14 A.D.) the animals from India invariably found in Rome. It was maina on the parts of Roman people to maintain wild animals, especially which were largely exported from India. Caligula (A.D. 37-41) who succeeded Tiberius (A.D. 14-37) also collected wild animals for his shows and it was difficult for butchers to feed the wild animals and therefore, these animals were served with criminals as their food. Sometimes the man from decent families was also thrown to these wild beasts.[125]

Among the wild beasts, which were exported from India, were the tigers, elephants, hunting dogs and others. The Greeks were well aware of Indian wild beasts like tigers. The Indian elephants were very much popular among the Assyrians and Egyptians also. These elephants were marching with the army in the battlefield and they were creating terror in the hearts of the enemies.[126] African elephants were also used for the same purpose but there was great difference between these two varieties of elephants. Pliny observed in first century A.D., how the African elephants fought shy of the Indian, which was much bigger and much powerful than the African.[127] But Cosmas in 545 A.D. however and probably from hearsay noted that the Indian elephants were "not furnished with great tusks like those in Ethiopia". Unless the Indian elephants were not exported from India to the Egyptian Kingdom of the Ptolemies, its presence in the armies as a fighting unit can't be explained. The presence of Indian elephants in Italy is widely corroborated from different sources. Claudius (A.D. 41-54) made the Senate decree, an elephant drawn carriage for his grandmother Livia's image to match Augustus's ritual procession and around the circus. Pliny gives a detailed account about the Indian as well as African elephants and ivory which were famous in the western land.[128] The elephants in Rome were employed for gladiatorial combats. At the conclusion of gladiatorial combats, which the gladiators performed, the last exploit was fighting with elephants single-handed.[129]

The elephants were landed at Puteoli, now Puzuolo, on the coast of Campania and also at Alexandria over which the Romans had a firm hold over a century. Such exports of elephants from India continued till the fall of Roman Empire. The export of ivory to Assyria and Egypt is also symbolically presenting the fact that the Indian elephants and ivory were very much popular among the West Asian people. There can be no doubt about the export of Indian ivory to Rome where, as Pliny recorded the ivory tusks could be "constantly seen in the temples, like the bamboo.[130] With the Caesars, the import of ivory continued. Nero, the ruler of this dynasty, rebuilt what he called the Golden House whose dining room had a ceiting of fretted ivory, the panels of which would slide back and let a rain of flowers of perfume from hidden sprinklers showers upon the guests.[131] Ivory was largely used for the purpose of chairs, jewellery, interior decoration, chariots and toys. The elephants were bred in the regions like Kalinga (south Orissa), Anga (East Bengal) Karusa (Shahabad district of

Malawa), and Saurastra. The elephants of this region were exported to different parts of West Asia as well as Rome.

Export of Skin

Among the skins imported into India were the Serican types, which seem to have come from Serica, located in the north west China and Chineese Turkestan. Periplus reveals that from Barbaricum the skin were exported among other goods, this Serican goods in the first instance to the Arabian and Persian ports and then ultimately to Rome. Where as Pliny has noticed earlier, refers to their tissue and their dyes.[132] These skin products might have imported from Serican lands and then it was exported to western countries where its demand was high. Kautilya mentions about the varieties of skins which were procured from Himalayan lands. Among other products, perhaps the heavy woolen coats, woolen clothes were obtained from Kaveripattinam, Chera kingdom in South India.

Hunting Dogs

Next to the elephants, the Indian animals, which were very much popular among the western people, were the hunting dogs, internationally famous. Though there is no such direct evidence about the export of Indian dogs to West Asian countries, the sculptures depicting Ashurbanipal's offering a sacrifice after a bull hunts. And the hunting dog usually did such type of bull hunts. Therefore it is expected that the hunting dogs were exports from India, which is further proved by the statements of Darius, when he ordered some villages of India to rear dogs and in exchange they were exempted from taxes.[133] These early evidences points out that the hunting dogs which were the favourite items of the western people, must have been same in the post Mauryan period and the Indian dogs might be expected to be exported from India. Indian dogs, which were introduced in Western land, were valued high due to size.

Another living animals, which we can name as brought from India, are snakes. Indian Cobra-de-Capello, known to the Greeks and Romans as "aspis" and other members of this order. There are clear records that the serpents were exported from India, Ceylon, Burma, Nicobars, and Malaya.[134] An Indian embassy which came to Augustus, presented a small python and other snakes and Augustus exhibited in the comitum comities one fifty cubits feet long, while Strabo saw in Egypt a serpent nine feet long brought from India.[135] These examples show that snake was also a favourite item of export to the European countries.

With great certainty we can speak that the Musk Dear which produced the famous odour whichwais very highly valued in the East, must had been imported to west through Persia or from the Indus or from the Broach before the time of Cosmas. It was established in trade during the Arabian epoch.[136] The musk is known today in three kinds, the most valued coming from China, a less valued from Assam or Nepal or the least valued from the Central Asia. So it may be presumed that Indians might meet the demand of Roman people for the musk dear to some extent.

Among the animal products, the mention may be made about the hides, teeth and horns of rhinoceros. Pliny says that the lycium was sent by the Indians in the skins of rhinoceroses and the camels but the more important were the horns out of which Romans made oil flasks, called gutti and the vessels made out of the horns of Indian rhinoceroses and the so called "Unicorns" have always been esteemed for their supposed medical properties and for the alleged property of rendering harmless any poison drunk out of them.

A Roman medicine was prepared out of the flesh of lizards. These lizards were usually available on Egypt, Red Sea coasts, Arabia and India. Of these Arabian and larger Indian lizards were said to be land crocodiles, were sent to Roman Empire salted.[137] This must mean that Romans imported an Indian and Arabian preparation of the flesh of typical skins (genus-scincus), which range from Northern Aftica through Arabia and Persia to Sind, yielding medicine and food today. The other products, which were in great demand in western Asian society, were tortoise shells, pearl, conch shells silk goods, lac etc. Tortoise shells, especially of Hawk Bill Turtle, which was found in Indian waters, was also in great demand.[138] In the west, it was put to various uses but it was sought above all by wealthy Romans to provide a veneer for their rich furniture, in particular for decorating bedsteads of solid ivory; western people did not eat the flesh in ancient times. Usually the shells of tortoise were sent from Malaya Peninsula by the way of Muziris and Neleynda and reached to the Greeks at the marts of Damirice.

Pearl was the major item of trade between India and West Asia and it was also the favourite item of ladies. No greater praise could have been bestowed on pearls than these words of Pliny who stated at first rank then and the very highest position among all valuables belongs the pearl.[139] In ancient times as now there are no fisheries of the true pearl in European waters, all references to British pearls, for example indicating merely pearls from the river Mussel, turned to the Far East just as is the case today, the Romans could obtain inferior pearls in the Red sea and the pearls of very best quality from the Persian Gulf (Bahrein Islands) but their most abundant supplies came from India.[140] Before the exports of Indian pearls to Rome, at first it was exported to Greece, which is clearly evident from the observations of Pliny.[141] Arrian in the middle of second century A.D. observed that according to Nearchus in 325 B.C. along the coast of Persia at a place called Ilas; near an island called acaicandrus pearls were caught, "as in the Indian sea".[142] The allusions may be drawn to island of Bahrain but what is interesting is that Nearchus was certainly aware of pearl fishing in the Indian Ocean at that period. Another astounding observation made by Arrian about the pearls is that among the other pearls Indian pearl was "Worth thrice of its weight in refined gold[143].

Pearls appear to have been exported form Persian Gulf, India and Ceylone. During Augustus, the export of pearls and precious stones from the East especially from India through Alexandria must have not only continued but have been considerably increased. After his Alexandrian triumph when he returned to Rome, with the treasures of Ptolemocs, he made lavish gifts, for instance in a single donation to capitoline, Jupiter gave 16,000 pounds of gold besides pearls and precious stones worth 500000 gold pieces.[144] This is not strange because the Egyptian pearls were also highly paid in contrast with Indian pearls. Cleopatra is said to have possessed two pearls respectively from India and Egypt. Various references about the pearls clarify the fact that the West Asian and Roman people largely imported the pearls from India in addition with other countries like Egypt. Not only the Buddhist and Indian literature but also the Greek and Roman writers from Megasthenas onwards, the Periplus and Pliny observed that the pearl fisheries were centred at Kolkai in the Pandyan kindom, controlled from Modura. The Periplus also tells us that pearl fisheries extending from Kanya Kumari to Kolkhoi or Colchi where actually the pearlfishing was carried out.[145] From Pliny's statement it is clearly established that the Indian Ocean was supplying the pearls to Rome. He adds about the Indian pearls that it resembled in tint the scales of mirror stones and exceeded all other in size. It is no wonder that next to diamonds the Romans valued the pearls of India and Arabia.[146] In Rome, pearls come to be considered, "an everlasting piece of property" passing from father to son like heirlooms and were offered for public sale like landed estates.

Pearl was also very popular in India from the days of Kautilya. Silapadikaram (5th C.A.D) refers about the pearls that Tirumalavan was given by the king of great Vacciranadu whose sway extended "as far as the roaring sea in the east", a pearl canopy as tribute. A woman's breast was decked with pearl strings. The city of Puhar is described as a place where the surging ocean like dealer exchanged lustrous pearls for wreaths of flowers.[147]" The political disturbance in Rome probably checked in third century A.D. the export of pearls from India to Rome. But the popularity of pearls in India continued unabated. Fahien (399-414 A.D.) refers about the pearls, which were available in the treasuries of Ceylonese Buddhists. According to him, Ceylon was also a great centre of pearls. In India especially south India was famous for pearls. According to Pliny, the Korkai, Agaru,

Kaveripatttinam were the main places where the large scale trading of pearls was taking place. At the same time the large quantities of inferior pearls were brought from the Persian Gulf of Barygaza to find a market there.

Spice

Spice in general may be said to include pepper, clove, mace and such aromatic and pungent substances. From the very early times its export from India is corroborated by different sources. Bible provides the ample evidences about this trade. The kingdom of Sheba (South Arabic) was an emporium of spices from where the spice was sent to Jerusalem, Phoenicia and Egypt. We are further told that the Arabs from south Arabia also seems to have taken the spice to Egypt with its routes, which appears to have existed from ancient times. In Egypt, the need of spice was high because inorder to preserve the dead body they were using the spice in large scale. Though most of the West Asian countries were demanding the spice, it is not clear how far India had fulfilled their needs. Arabs had kept the trade contacts with India from the Mauryan period to secure the spice from India.[148] Again Indians must have been the commercial contacts with Greeks and Romans. One prickly shurb which is found in both Arab and India, named as liana and the knowledge about this plant in Arab indicates that there must had been a commercial contacts between the two lands. Again in Arabia, says Pliny, the olive tree distilled a sort of tear from which Indians made a medicament known by the Greeks as enhaemon which in Greek means "blood stopping" and which was called in Italy as "*de lecie*".[149] These statements can be implied to mean that Arabs must have been in contact with India, if this had not been the case, could never have prepared the medicament, which was also known, to the Greeks. So on the basis of these evidences it may be concluded that the spice trade was a flourishing trade between India and West Asian countries.

Among the spices, which India was expected to export to West Asian countries were, pepper, cloves, bdellium, myrrh, spikenard, macir, ammomum, cinnabar or calamus, lycium, costus, cardamon, sweet calamus, saffron and malabathrum. It is quite possible that Arabs from South Arabia who had practically monopolised the trade in spices, carrying them to various countries like Phoenicia, Israel, Egypt and Italy etc[150].

Export of Pepper

Early in the imperial era, pepper (Tamil-Pipali) became a staple article of Rome's sea trade with India. But Pliny admits that he is unable to state definitely at what period the use of unguents found its way to Rome. An edict of Antiochus which prohibits the sale of enotics (enotica) gives an idea that, until that date, the trade in exotics must have been current in Rome. Probably the trade in spice started in Rome, after the conquest of Asia Minor, Syria and Egypt by Rome. Frequent reference about the pepper by the Augustan writers, which firmly establishes that pepper, was staple article of sea trade and almost removed it from the class of luxuries by reducing the prices considerably.[151] The spice came from Malabar, Travancore and consisted chiefly of the common Black pepper, which was exported, in most quantities from Muziris and Nelecynda, being brought down from Neleyanda to Bacare in large boats.[152] Tamil literature tells, how the Greeks carried away large sacks of pepper giving apparently gold in exchange and Roman money was deliberately imported into Muziris and Neleynda.[153] So profitable was the trade of pepper was that this item was called "Black gold", the pepper being exchanged for gold.[154] According to Pliny it was the cheapest pepper.[155] Possibly the pepper was also used as a ballast on the journey back.[156]

In South India, the Cholas, Cheras and Pandyas fought among themselves to control the pepper trade. But Cheras have final monopoly over this trade.[157] The ports of Muziris and Nelcynda owed much of their prosperity to pepper trade.[158] It is possible that Tondi was also involved in a small way in this trade though the Ponnai river whose tributaries would have brought down the pepper from the Malabar hills.

Due to its Indian origin, the Indian word for pepper is pervasive in the world. It is obvious that the He brew word for pepper is derived from the Sanskrit word pippali, which however refers to long pepper.[159] There are references about the two types of pepper. One is black and another is white. The black pepper was the favourite item of western people. Originally it was obtained through the Phoenicians and Carthaginians (as Persians, Syrians and Lybians) the spice was brought by the Romans directly from south Malabar. Periplus indicates that the foreign merchants sent large ships to the market towns of the kingdoms of Ceraputra (Kerala) and Pandya viz, Nelcynda, Muziris, Tyndis etc.[160] Again Periplus states that Broach and Ujjaini in North India were also exporting the pepper. The Egyptian traders were also carrying large amount of pepper from India. Long pepper another variety of pepper, exported from Barygaza and was chiefly used for medicine purpose. It was more expensive than ordinary kind and it was available in Ceylon, Malaya and India also.

Pepper became the part of everyday life of Roman people since its chief use was a culinary spice.[161] Again pepper find its presence in the every recipe, was more important than the salt and sugar. But besides this, the pepper was used in all kinds of medicines and drugs. Its use as medicine dates back from the time of Hippocrates to whom it was the "Indian remedy".[162] Therefore, the need for Indian pepper in Roman market grew in such a proportion that various attempts were made in Italy to substitute pepper with mustard and junipers berries.[163] Again the cultivation of pepper in Italy also did not provide the expected result and this was the main reason of import of vast quantity of pepper by Romans.

The export of pepper continued till the fall of Roman Empire. There is epigraphic evidence that to prove that the vast quantities of pepper were stored in ware houses.[164] Again the continuity of pepper trade can be assured on the basis of availability of Roman coins but these evidences are mere supporting evidences. Again Pliny observed that, "so large quantity of perfumes was burnt by Nero" during the obsequies of his wife, "Poppaea".[165] Unless their imports had been on a very large scale, such egregious waste of these precious substances could hardly have been possible. These are things, which indicate the huge trade of pepper between, the west and east.

Cloves

One of the spices, which were exported from India to West Asia and Rome in the first century A.D., was clove (lavanga) about which Pliny does not mention much. But he refers about the caryophyllon,[166] which he apparently confused with cloves; according to him "had a considerable resemblance to pepper," but was more brittle and longer. He was evidently aware of the clove oil and its medicinal value but he was not certain whether it was imported from India or not. Since these armoatics did not come within the notice of the author of the periplus and even when it occurs in a version of Digest List, clove is one of the nards, there was no great demand of this.[167] But in the later phase, means in the period of Rome's decline and of the Early Byzantine Empire, references about the cloves are found. Cloves formed the part of rent paid by Egyptian estates to churches in Rome during the fourth century A.D. and Cosmas shows that in 6th century this aromatic was well known to come from India by way of Ceylone to the marts of west coast of India.[168]

Spikenard

It was another important item, which was exported to Rome in first century A.D. From Periplus we find this commodity through the port of Barygaza was exported to Alexandira and thence to Rome. The Periplus reveals the regions where it was cultivated, alluding to the north thus: "though this same region and from the upper country is brought the spikenard and that comes through Poclais (Pushkalovati) Caspapyrene and Paropanisae (Hindu Kush) and Cabolithic (Kabul). After its collection in these regions, it was sent to Barrygaza for exporting purposes through the city of Pushkalavati.[169]

Indian spikenard was famous in West Asian countries. The Syrian nard was held in high esteem in Rome. The references to Syrian nard, according to Dioscurias, only meant that such nard, as was cultivated in certain mountains of India, which looked towards Syria,[170] obviously north-western mountain regions already referred to. There was another type of Indian nard which according to Pliny, was grown on the banks of the Ganges called Ozaentis (perhaps Ujjain) emitting, a fetid odour and condemned as useless. This was apparently the Gangetic nard of the Periplus, which was so useless as Pliny made it out to be, would hardly have been re-exported from Muziris to foreign countries like Alexandria and thence to Rome.[171]

Nard was also profusely found in the Chera Kingdom.[172] It w as used to extract an oil, a fragrant one, for cosmetic purposes.[173] It was known to Pliny and Periplus as the sweet smelling oil of the Nard – the word probably derived from Narantam in Tamil.[174] According to Miller and others, the spikenard grows in the Himalaya and is shipped to Malabar.[175] Its oil was also used in temple.[176]

About the prices of Spikenard, Pliny states that the larger leaves were worth denarii or a pound, smaller leaves sixty, the smallest seventy five. He also states that the genuine spikenard oil contains costus, omomum, and other elements besides Indian nard but adulteration and therefore variations in prices were very frequent.[177] The use of spikenard is multifarious such as: the root considered bitter tonic, stimulant, antiseptic and has been employed for the treatment of epilepsy, hysteria, convulsive affections, palpitations of the heart and intestinal colic.

Costus

Another important product exported from Barygaza to Alexandria and thence to Rome was the costus. According to Pliny, the root of the costus had a burning taste and a most exquisite odour. Again he mentions that this costus was cultivated in India at Patala, situated at the very mouth of Indus.[178] The real costus was and is still largely found at Kashmir but it was later cultivated in Arabia, Syria, Tibet, China etc. [179]

Bdelliem

It was also another armoatic product, which was exported through Barygaza in the first century A.D. to Alexandria and thence to Rome. This aromatic, which was so esteemed, was cultivated not only in Bacteria, Media, and Babylonia and also in India and Arabia. In India, bdellium was mainly cultivated in the region between the Hindu Kush and Indian Ocean. And it was transported to the West through the Persian Gulf ports as well as by the overland route to Babylonia[180]. The price of bdellium in its pure state in Rome was 3 denarii per pound.[181] Its gum resin is an astrigent, antiseptic, expectorant, aphrosidiaiac and good for enriching the blood. Medicinally it was so useful that it was exported to Rome from the very early age. It is also mentioned in Bible.[182] It is a gum or resin of a tree and was used for perfume and incense.[183] Pliny referred to it saying it came from India overland via the famous trading centre Nabatean, Petra.[184]

Cardamum

Cardamum was another export product from India, again is not mentioned in the Periplus as one of the commodities sent out from the country. It was one of the exports of India in the first century A.D. can be seen from the Pliny who has observed that it was found in Arabia and India.[185] It was rightly pointed out that cardamum was exclusively found in India. Cardamum was produced in Coromondal coast, Malabar, Travancore and especially in the high lands of Madurai, Trinnevelly and Dindigul.[186] However, strangely, there is hardly any direct reference to Cardamom in Tamil sources although it is well known to classical accounts.[187] The sea route from West coast of India to the Persian Gulf usually brought it.[188] It must be noticed that Pliny says that the plants lost its strength when it was grown anywhere outside India.[189] Perhaps the plant was considered perishable if brought by the sea and so came by the land routes only, or it may be that the Arabians kept the sea traffic in their hands for Pliny's cardamum is Arabian and Median. That the spice came by the sea is proved by the inclusion in the Digest List.[190] Acording to Strabo, the Cinnamum reached the Mediterranean from the countries no nearer than Burma, Ceylone and India. Then Arab traders were working as Middlemen to transport these things to Rome and Eastern Africa. By this they were earning much money. The people of Egypt and Syria were also getting this Cinnamum from the Arabians.[191] Like all other products its medicinal value was immense. It was used in the preparation of the Mendesian unguents. Its seeds have been found useful for neuralgia, gonorhhoea, an antidote to scorpion bite and snake venom. The oil from its seed has been applied to the eye leads to allay inflammation.

Aloe

Aloe was another gum resin, which was exported from the country. Although Periplus does not mention the export of any aloes from India still we know from the testimony of Pliny that the most esteemed aloes were those impored to Rome, in the first century A.D., from India.[192] Pliny also noted that the aloe was also grown in the Asiatic provinces. Instead of being used as aromatic, it was also used as purgative for all diseases of eye. The Herbrew name for an aloe seems to be derived from Old Tamil.[193] Miller says that the word for aloe in Sangam literature is naraiakil "As the K" of akil is soft, the Prakrit it makes the transition from Sanskrit *agaru* to the Hebrew *ahaloth* and the Greek *agalochon* the more intelligible.[194]

Safforn

One of the important exports from India must have been Saffron, which according to the Periplus was exported through Barygaza to Muza (Mocha)[195]. There was an active trade between Muza and Barygaza is clearly revealed in the Periplus which has recorded that the whole of Mocha, crowded with Arab shipowners and sea-faring men, was busy with the affairs of commerce for they carried on, "a trade with the far side coast and with Barygaza, sending their own ships there".[196] Among the imports into Maza the Periplus refers to saffron and so it may be concluded that saffron was exported from Barygaza to Muza in the first century A.D. But Pliny's silence about this creates the problem to draw the conclusion. The locality of its origin may have been Kashmir where, as Kalhana recorded, it was available among the commodities, which even in heaven would have been difficult to obtain.[197] It was used as perfume and medicine also. In the sphere of Ayurvedic medicine it has been famous as a stomachic and anti-spasmodic and stimulant and an aphrodisiac. It is considered a sovereign remedy.[198] It must have been very popular in Rome, as Pliny reveals it was stewn in the halls, theatres and courts.[199] Saffron was also used as colouring and flavouring agent. Among other products, which were exported to West Asian, countries as well as Rome were cloves, spikenard, costus, myrrh, mastich, macir, amomum, cinnabar and musk etc. These products were carrying less importance because of other low demand but they were the part of the trade. These products were not only famous for its food value but also for its medicinal value. Just like other products, these products had been exported from different parts of India to Rome and other West Asian countries.

Export of Vegetable Products

Among the vegetables products exported from India, the most important were palm wine, castor and sugarcane. Stratro mentions about this date palm: as the reeds, which yielded honey although there were no bees but whose fruit cater caused intoxication. But Pliny clearly states the date palm fruit was employed for the purpose of making wine 'by the Parthians as well as Indians and indeed throughout the entire East".[200] From Pliny's reference it is not quite clear whether or not the palm wine was actually exported to India but his statement regarding its use throughout the East suggests that it might have been exported as it actually was not only during his time but also even later.

Castor

It was exported to West during Pliny which can hardly be doubted for he refers to castor plant as the fruit of the cicus which was grown in Egypt "in great abundance". There were different names of this product among the European countries. Periplus does not also mention the name of Indian castor incidentally. But huge production of castor in India gives a hope that castor might have been exported from India which is not clarified yet. It was very useful for disorders of the joints, all kinds of indurations, affections of the uterus and ears also.[201] The light produced by the oil was very dim due to its thickness. Its leaves were applied with vinegar for ersypelas and especially when freshly gathered, utilized for diseases of mamillae and defluxions[202] with so many uses its export can well be appreciated.

Cane sugar

Sugar from India must have been exported from an early period. Referring to Arabia, which is also stated to have yielded sugar, probably date palm sugar, Pliny comments, "but that of India is the most esteemed". The export of cane sugar can be substantiated from the Periplus, which clearly states that ships, "customarily fitted out from Ariaca (north west coast of India, especially the region round the Gulf of Cambay, modern Kutch and Gujarat) and Barygaza (Broach) to go to Egypt carried besides other goods, "honey from the reeds called Sacchari".[203] Scoff observed that "this was the first mention, in the history of European world, of sugar as an article of commerce"[204] This is not strictly correct for the sacchari of the Periplus is evidently identifical with the saccharon of Pliny (23-79A.D) who refers to the imports in Rome of sugar not only from Arabia but also from India which he specifically mentions as the better variety. From this it is clearly established that the cane sugar was an important commodity of export of Rome that time. The Roman knowledge about the Indian sugar was that it was an art by which the juice was extracted from the plant but it was never used for sweetening the table foods.[205] Sugar was largely used for the medicinal purpose by the Romans instead of sweetening purpose; for this they were using the honey.

Metals, Minerals and Precious Stones

Now the question arises about the export of metals, minerals and stones, which played an important role in the export trade of India. Among the metals, the anticipated metal of export was silver, copper, iron and steel. About the export of gold there is no such authentic evidence. In regards to minerals, we may cite glass and sand in particular. In the matter of precious stones, the list of goods of export was quite lengthy which include beryls, carnelians, lapis-lazuli (saphire) amethysts, agates, onyxes, diamonds, and transparent stones of several kinds, corals and pearls. The women usually used these precious stones for ornamental purpose while some of the stones had medicinal use also. In contrast, the metals were used in fashioning of implements and accoutrements of war; while other metals were used in fashioning articles of daily use and ornaments.

Gold

Gold was not regular article of trade but Pliny clearly states that gold from the Ganges reached the empire[206] and implies the some of the famous "ant-Gold" of the miners of Dardistan and Tibet whose pick-axes seem to have been a curiosity at Erythroe[207]. Biblical sources as well as the Book of Kings point out that the gold was brought from Ophir. But it is very difficult for scholars to point out the place Ophir. Quite possibly India is not the land of Ophir while some scholars view India as the land of Ophir because India was paying the gold as tribute to the King Darius-I. If the annual tribute from the days of Darius-I (521-485 B.C) to the defeat of Darius-III on 1st of October 331 BC at Arbela by Alexander of Macedor, was at the rate of 360 talents, the flow of gold from India to Persia for 191 years would come to 72000 talents of gold, which is indeed an extremely large quantity to be dispatched out of any country. With the death of Alexander the Great, this flow seems to have been temporarily arrested but whether it was revived subsequently it is difficult to state for lack of adequate evidence. This position continued in the later phase also. In the first century A.D., according to the Periplus, gold does not appear to have been largely exported from India. Scoff suggested that this was probably an allusion to the gold mines of Chhotangpur plateau, located from 75 to 150 miles west of the mouth of the Ganges.[208] This is plausible though not certain because the Periplus itself is vague on this point.

Silver

Like gold, in the first century A.D., silver was not apparently exported from India and even later. Pliny narrates that after the conquest of Asia, probably including Asia Minor and Syria[209] , first silver was introduced into Italy. Lucis and Scipio in his triumphal procession in the year 565 from the foundation of the city of Rome, carried 4500 pounds of chased silver with 500 pounds weight of gold vessels.[210] About the origin of this silver there is no clear-cut mention of this. Mention may be made of Chronicle, which states, that along with 3000 talents of gold of Ophir, 7000 talents of silver were exported to the kingdom of Solomon.[211] This, again, does not clarify the statement whether gold was brought from Ophir or anywhere. Therefore, the possibility of supply of silver from India lies with further evidence; but now nothing can be said with authenticity.

Copper

This metal was required in India for coinage and inscriptioins of Ancient India were sometimes, inscribed on copper plates. According to Periplus, "the copper was regularly sent from Barygaza loaded in large vessels to Ommana and Apologos in the Persian Gulf which was perhaps the surplus European metal exported to Malabar and Barygaza and thence reshipped by Indians to the Persian Gulf probably when Romans and Parthians were at war.[212] Pliny also mentions that the iron, copper, arsenic, red lead as products of Carmania shipped to the Persian Gulf and Red Sea ports for marketing.[213] In Schoff's view, this copper was brought from Omanna including European copper from Canna.[214] This view does not contain much water because in India, the large amount of production of coins in copper and some copper inscriptions point out the fact that the availability of copper in India was large.

Iron and Steel

Indian steel and iron was exported from India to Egypt in the first century A.D. The Periplus tells us that "from the district of Ariaca (north-west coast of India) across the sea" were imported Indian iron and steel.[215] The iron and steel imported into these regions must have been used for manufacturing instruments for hunting these animals. The Periplus again tells us that the iron was "made into spears and used against the elephants and other wild beasts".[216] Fine swords made of Indian iron were famous since the time of Ctesias. Again some foreigners noticed the use of implements made of iron. Whether iron or steel were exported from India after first century, it is difficult to state for lack of adequate evidences.

Minerals

Among the minerals, exported from India, there was a kind of sand, which was used for polishing the marble. In Rome, after making the blocks of marble, they were cut into pieces by the use of this sand, which was pressed upon a very fine cleft in the store as it moved to and for. For this purpose two kinds of sand were imported to Rome, one was from Ethiopia and other from India. According to Pliny, "this Indian sand was held in the next highest esteem after the Ethiopian sand which was a softer nature and better adapted for dividing the marble without leaving any freshness on its surface whereas the Indian sand "did not leave so smooth a face on it".[217] Still for polishing marble, Pliny recommends the Indian sand, which was named as Male. This male type sand might have exported from the west coaster Malenad.

Crystals

About crystals Pliny refers that, "the East too sends us crystal, there being none preferred to the produce of India". He incidentally adds that certain Greek writers had mentioned a crystal vessel from India, which held four sestarii.[218] The Greeks and Romans used it for ring stores, hand balls, burning lenses and so on but wealthy Romans of the empire used crystal above all as drinking cups, particularly for cool or iced drinks. These vessels are frequently associated with wealth luxury and extravagance. Pliny gives examples of these large cups and bowls, some of them from India and of high prices and foolish whims connected with the possession of them.[219] Most of these things came ready made from India but sometimes they were made on the way in Alexandria.

When Pliny speaks of the unequalled excellence of Indian rock crystal glass, he does not refer about Chinese but he refers about rock glass made in Ceylon.[220] The Greeks knew well that the Indians could stain rock crystals into the colours of real precious stones and Pliny refuses to give information about the extant on the subject. The Indians still make their imitations. [221]

Precious Stones

The business of precious stones between Inda and West Asia is quite old. Tyre was the important centre of trade in West Asia for these types of precious stones like sardious, topaz, diamond, beryl, onyx, jasper, saffire, emarald etc. The trade between Tyre and Syria is mentioned in the Book of Ezkiel (6th century B.C.)[222] The trade on stones between Syria and India may not be earlier than the days of Ezkiel. The trade of Tyre with Arabia, Judah, Assyria and Palestine area is clearly mentioned in this book. Probably Pliny is the only author of ancient times who had clearly recorded the glories of Indian gems and had furnished adequate evidence of their export from India to foreign countries including Rome. The precious stones of India so impressed the Romans that in the Pliny's words "Indeed the stones of India, it is said, quite dim the sight by their brilliancy".[223] About the precious stones

Strabo mentions. "India produced precious stones such as crystals, carbuncles and all kinds of pearls.[224]

Pliny also points the Indian stones like the crystal, quarts, beryl, opal, sardonyx, onyx, carbuncle, amethyst and seven varieties of topaz.[225] Milinda Panha also mentions of sapphire, gem, cat's eye, flax gem, sun and moon crystal, topaz ruby etc.[226]

Beryl

The emerald and beryl were very highly prized by the Romans. The beryl was the only precious stone, which was preferred to wear without the addition of gold. Pliny and Ptolemy point out that the beryl was found in Coimbatore (Tamilnadu), Padiyur, Chera territories etc.[227] But the Pandya areas were not famous for these stones. Of the large quantities of Roman coins found in the Coimbatore district Where the splendid six sided beryl prisms are found which may be given in exchange.[228] For berly mines, Padiyur in Coimbatore district was famous for this.[229] Excavations in coimbatore region have brought to light six sided beryl prism who has been interpreted as evidence of exchange of beryl for Roman coins.[230] The stones were often polished in the original shape and worn by the ladies as cylindri in their ears. About the t.ade of beryl, the evidence of Josephus Flavious (A.D. 37-107) is important. According to this India was exporting beryl stones to Judaea prior to 1st century A.D. There can be no doubt that the beryl was exported from India to Rome, as Pliny clearly stated that the paedeors (lovely youth) Which was one of the precious stones "of the finest quality" Came from India where, as noted earlier, it was known as the "sangenon" On the basis of these evidences it can be presumed that the beryl stone was the important item of trade between India and West Asia.

Carnelien

Another important product, exported from India, was the carnelian, which is clearly mentioned in Periplus in the first century.[231] It seems that these carnelion were brought from Pratisthan and Ujjaini to Barygaza for export purpose not only

Rome but also Arabia and other regions of West Asia were also importing this carnelien.[232] There are enough evidences, which point out that the carneliens were found in Arabia as well as the vicinity of Leucas and in Egypt also.[233] But on the basis of availability of carnelian on these lands it can't be predicted that these carnelians were brought from India. On the testimony of Periplus it may be concluded that possibility of Indian carneliane on these lands is more like all other exports from India, the carneliane along with other precious stones must have been first shipped to Alexandria and thence to Rome.

According to Pliny, there were three varieties of carnelian (sarda) stone; the red type, the pionia, and another class beneath which they placed a base of silver or leaf of gold. The Indian carnelian according to Pliny was transparent while those of Arabia were more opaque.[234] India has always been the most plentiful source of the finest red sard which comes chiefly from the Decan trades especially with agates from Ratnapur near Broach in Rajpipla where are sard or sardonyx mountains of the Greek.[235] Burma and Japan also produced the carnelian in great extent. Romans obtained their ready-made carnelian goods from India but sometimes they were manufactured on the way in Alexandria. With the discovery of Monsoons the trade in carnelian agate was increased vastly, especially when men like Nero set an example.

Lapis lazuli

From the very early times this lapis lazuli stones were exported from India. But Warmington strangely refutes this view, according to him; these stones were brought from Persia. Tibet and China through India to Europe[236]. Kautilya refers about the rarieties of lapis lazuli but his reference does not indicate that these stones were available in India in large scale.

This lapis lazuli, according to Pliny, was refalgent with the spots like gold. He also stones that it had other varieties with an azure and sometimes though rarely, purple hues with the best kind come from Media. In no case, according to him, was this stone diaphanous and it was not suited for engraving purposes when it was intersected with hard particles of crystalline nature.[237]

Good Child says that it has been known from very remote times being much used by the Egyptians and to lesser extant by the Assyriaas, Epiphanius, Bishop of Salamis says that the Tables of Law given by Moses were inseribed on lapislazuli. Beekmann says that the lapislazuli came from. Bokhara and it was sent thence to India and from India to Europe.[238] Laufer also states that the stones came from the mines of Badakshan[239]. This is very likely that lapis lazuli was imported from Persia, Badakshan and China to India for reshipment via-Barbarism to Egypt and Rome. S.N. Majumdar thinks that lapislazuli was obtained in the vaidurya mountain, most probably a part of Satpura range, mentioned in the Mahabharat.[240] The evidences of lapislazuli was also found in Mrichhakatikam, works of Kalidasa and Yuanchwang also refers about these[241]. This wide ranging evidences clear the fact that the lapis lazuli was widely available in India.

Agate

Pliny and Periplus both refer about the agate which were available in India. Pliny relates how Indian agate possessed the properties of similar stones found in Sicily and Crete.[242] The Periplus records, how the Indian agate was exported from Barygaza to Egypt and Arabia. It also states that the agate was brought down to Barygaza from Ujjaini and Paithan along with the Carnelian.[243] Pliny and Philostratus, draw the special attention to the Indian agates which were large in size and there is extant a large antique agate worked as a leopard's head.[244] According to Warmington "Romans obtained their best and largest pieces from India.[245] Besides being used in jewellery, the largest and finest onyxes from India were used by the Romans from making cups, toilet articles, statuttes and other things. A local industry of agate had been found in the neighbour hood of Rajpipla.[246] Agate was abundantly available in the Deccan, Rajmahal traps of Bengal, Jubbulpore; the finest agate was coming from Ratanpur where these were cut, polished and sold largely in Cambay. However the excavation at different parts of South India, except Kodumanal, have yielded the limited numbers of chalcedony, agate, carnelian and others semi precious stones with pearls are least represented in archaeology.[247]

Amethyst

Among Indian precious stones, observed Pliny, the very first rank belongs to the amethystos of India, for they had the very richest shades of purples[248]. The amethyst was also found in that part of Arabia, adjoining Syria, known as Petra. India was producing five kinds of amethysts :- purple, imitated by the purple dyers, inferior sapphire coloured (called socondion by the Indians)two kinds very pale and another wine red.[249] The Romans obtained the Ceylonesee pebbles in Tamil ports, probably through a secret trade, which was unknown to Pliny.[250]

Diamonds

The Periplus states that they (Greeco-Romans) send large ships to the market towns (Muziris and Nelcynda) from which "are exported great quantities of transparent stones of all kinds, diamonds and sapphires.[251] Pliny describes the Indian diamonds as "Adoms" found out in a stratum of gold but in a substance of a kindred nature to crystal.[252] He includes under Adome, other substances such as quartz, iron-ore, emery etc but he also says that diamond possessed the greatest value. Ptolemy also mentions that, "diamond is found in great abundance in the country of the sabrai towards the greatest value. Ptolemy[253] also mentions that diamond is found in great abundance in the country of the Sabrai towards the Ganga River". He also refers to the town of "Kosa where are diamonds" which belonged "to the country along the eastern bank of Narmadas. So it is not unlikely that the diamond of Narmada and Ganga Valley was exported viz; Barygaza and Ganges respectively in the 2nd Century A.D.

Both Kautilya and Pliny refer about the six kinds of diamonds. The Junagarh Inscription of Rudradaman of 150 A.D.

also refers to diamond[254] (Kanaka-rajate-vajra) Watt says that "India was the first and for a long period the only source of diamonds known to the European nations."[255] To the proof of Pliny's diamond, in the British museum there is an antique diamond set of several rings and one gold seal in the British Museum. All these sources point out that India was the sole source of diamonds. Diamonds were probably used by the Indians as amulets.[256]

According to Periplus, the Cottonara District and Malabar areas were famous for the production of diamonds. As for its size, Pliny observed, it was as large sometimes as a hazel nut. [257]

Coral

Among the precious stones, coral was one of the important item which had a remotest past from a commercial angle. The Periplus says that the coral was exported from Barbaricum, Barygaza, Muziris and Nelcynda in India and also to the Arabian port cane. In India, it was probably reshipped to West Asian countries.[258] But Pliny gives a different version that coral or corals were native of India and Syrene.[259] He observed that Indians valued the coral as much as the Romans. The prices of pearls and corels were determined by the fashions of each country. So it is clear that the corals were exported from India to Rome and other West Asian countries otherwise Pliny might not have gathered so much informations about this coral. Pliny says that the Indian pearl was a highly prized by a Roman lady as a bead of coral by an Indian man and coral was held by the Brahmanas to be sacred amulet besides an attractive adornment.[260] It is possible that Greek merchants exchanged their coral at the Indian marts for which the pearls were brought upto the coasts from the Gulf of Manaar for that purpose. At that time, the Kaveripattanam in the Chola kingdom was also famous for corals. Similarly a poet who visited Uraiyur, the ancient Chola capital, speaks of coral and pearl together.

After the fall of Roman empire, the export of coral seems to have been diverted to the Byzantine Empire and also to Syria which was actively involved in the trade with India, carried large amount of corals in the first centuries of Christian era and it was presented for the sale in the fairs of Tyre.[261] Century's later coral was in much demand in the times of Marco Polo, of Vasco-da-Gama and of Tavernier and it was undoubtedly of immense value to the Romans in their trade with India and China.

Pearls

Parl was another important item of export from early times. No greater praise could have been bestowed on the pearls than these words of Pliny who stated, "the first rank then and the very highest position among all valuables, belongs to the pearl.[262]" We have enough evidences, which point out that the pearls were exported to Rome and to other countries. These pearls were at first exported to Rome and then it was transferred to Greeks. Pliny observed "Even to this day the Indian traders who bring us their wares, eagerly buy up their pearls and carry it away to foreign markets, while it is more eagerly brought up by the wealthy Romans to day, as it was wont to be done by the wealthy Greeks long ago."[263] From this statement it may be seen that Indian, not any other like Arabians, Persians, Syrians merchants sailed to Rome where they sold their pearls to the rich Romans who brought them eagerly just as the ancient Greeks had purchased such pearls from Indians. In an astounding observation of Pearl he state, the pearl was, "worth thrice its weight in refined gold.[264] Probably he was mentioning about some special pearls otherwise this statement is not correct for all types of pearls.

Pearls appear to have been exported to Rome from the Persian Gulf, India and Ceylon. It is said that the fresh water pearls seem to have prompted Julius Ceaser's (81-44 B.C) invasion of Britain. During Augustus the export of pearls and precious stones from the East and especially India through Alexandria must have not only continued but considerably increased. When Aguustus returned after the victory over Alexandria, he distributed the large amount of gold pieces in addition to pearls. It is not strange at all because the pearls, which were highly liked by the Egyptian people, might have come to the hand of Augustus.

Foreign writer like Strabo and Pliny were specific in their locations of the areas in India. Stabo refers to Sora (Chola), which he calls Perimuda, inhabited by fish eaters who fished out pearls.[265] This city has also been referred to by Aelian and Pliny and identified with Simyulla (Chaul), which Pliny declared to be the most productive of pearls along with the island of Ceylon. But, Chaul at no period of Indian history was under the rule of Cholas although it was famous port for a considerable time and Mc. Crindle rightly pointed out that Aelians Perimuda must be located more south in the southern portion of Coromondala. [266]

The pearl continued to be popular in India from the days of Kautilya (4th century B.C.). The city of Puhar (Kaveripattanam) is described as a place where the surging ocean like a dealer exchanged lustrous pearls for the wreaths of flowers.[267] South Indian pearls were rated among the best and highly valued in the ancient world,[268] as borne out by Greek, Tamil and Sanskrit sources. They reached in a considerable quantity to Malabar ports of Muziris and Nelcynda from where they were exported to Rome.[269] The Political disturbance in Rome probably checked the out flow of pearls but it never diminished the interests of Indian people.

Glass

There is not enough evidences about the origin of glass in India. The origin of glass has been attributed by an accidental contact of nitre with sand, to the Phoenicians but the story has been discredited.[270] Kautilya's reference about the glass and its style of manufacturing points out that glass was produced in India from 4th C.B.C According to Pliny, "Glass was exported from India.[271] Pliny refers that the glass of India was made of broken crystals and therefore its value was high. Alexandria, Tyre and Cidon were famous for their works in glass, which spread all over the empire and very far beyond.[272] It may be expected that the crude glass be exported from Alexandria to Barygaza, Nelcynda and Muziris, doubtless for making mirrors. Besides that vessels of glass were also imported into Barbaricum Moreover, much Greek glass reached in China as shown by Chinese annals which record glass of several different colours received as present from the west by the emperor Tsaou-tsaou, in the beginning of third century A.D.. In India, few glass objects of first centuries of Christian era have been found in Manikyala in Punjab were probably made from the crude glass imported from the west, while the fragments found at Bahmanabad in the Indus region are, "hardly distinguishable from the Roman glass of the imperial period."[273]

In different parts of India, the glass objects of Roman origin have been found. Paithan, the capital of Satavahan Kings, has produced various types of glass beads and rim of cobalt blue vessels described as "fashioned by curling the ends of requisite shape by tooling.[274] At Ter, a large number of glass beads were discovered as well as two rims of glass cups and a rare solid base. Glass beads and apparently the glass vessels have been excavated at Nevasa.[275] Glass beads also reached at the urban centers of Chola Kingdom where the excavations have brought to light enormous quantities of raw glass and finished glass objects. Similarly some of the raw glass unloaded in Pandyan ports of Nclcynda and Bakare. In South-eastern India, the fragments of Mediterraneean amphorae are largely found at Vasavsamudram.[276] The bulk of glass from Arikamedu consists of beads and remains of bead making.[277] A few glass vessels have been reported from Ter, Taxila, Dharanikota, Karwan, and Ujjaini.[278]

Textiles

India was famous for the production of cloth, which is clearly evident from the reference of Kautilya. Kautilya prescribed that those who manufactured fibrous clothes rainments, silk cloths, and cotton fabrics were to be rewarded with presents suches sceats, garlands, and with other prizes by the Superintendent of Weaving.[279] [280]From the Periplus we learn that through the market-port of Barygaza (Broach) which was fed by the market products of Ujjain and Pushkalavati, especially the cotton goods besides other goods. From the Ganges, implying the Gangetic regions where exported, great qualities of silk and other goods. About the export of silk, nothing is certain. Whether the Roman people used the Chineese silk only or they liked Indian made silk. As the Periplus states the export of silks and other goods must and can only be taken to have been of Indian and not foreign origin.[281]

There were two types of textile exports, besides silks, cotton and linens from India, we have seen that India exported cotton textiles to Rome from very ancient times. Before the discovery of monsoon the quantity of exported cotton cloth was limited but after the discovery, the demand of cotton goods grew tremendously. Indian muslin was very famous in Rome.[282] According to the Periplus, the best muslin was known as monache, sagmatogene and molchine were ordinary kind of rough cotton cloth. Textile material in some quantity came from Ujjaini and Tagara to Broach which exported them to Arabia and Egypt. The Argaritic muslin of Trichinopoly was very popular. Sri Lanka and Masulipattanam also manufactured good muslin but the best muslin came from Varanasi or Dacca. In the variegated textiles from Memphis and Panopolies the influence of Indian pattern is apparent.[283] . It is interesting that although 'Argaritic' muslin (from Uraiyur) were in demand in the Roman world, Tamilakam imported Kalagam and Kalingam from Kalinga in addition to a thin cloth variety from Egypt.[284] The Tamil sources mention about the varieties of cotton clothes produced from Uraiyur. The Silapapdikaram refers about 32 varieties of cotton cloth.[285]

Woolen Banket Export

Kautilya mentions about the varieties of blanket, which were produced in India from the wool of sheeps and hairs of wild animals. Such blankets were coloured, some plain and others of a specialized type, which must have been of superior variety. From the port of Barygaza in the first century A.D. mention, may be made of cloaks, blankets, sashes of different colours, which were exported, to Muza.[286] The Periplus does not reveal the areas from which these goods were collected. It may be presumed that these goods might have been collected from the wool producing countries like those of northwestern and Himalayan region. It is apprehended that these goods were produced locally and were brought to ports for export purposes.

Silk trade

Silk was mainly imported from China by the west. It was largely used during the regin of Augustus but the fashion was condemned as effeminate so that early in the reign of Tiberius, the Roman Senate enacted the law "that man should not defile himself by wearing the garments of silk.[287] The cost was enormously high and from Aurelian we learn that silk was worth its weight in gold. Pliny and other moralists resented at the use of their luxury.

Rome imported the Chinese silk by the silk routes, passing through Iran. In the time of Periplus, Barbaricum, the ports of Sindh also exported silk goods to Rome. But more costly textiles reached Broach from Balakh, Muziris and Nelcynda and other markets on Kerala coast received their silk goods from the mouth of Ganga passing the eastern seacoast. In these way the Chineese silk either came by the sea routes or reached the Bay of Bengal from Yunnam, Assam and then along the Brahmaputra River, or it was exported by Singan-fu-Lan-chow, Lhasa and Chumbey valley to Sikkim and finally reached in Bangal.[288] The discovery of silk in the tombs in Southern Russia indicate the use of Oxus route while the same sort of silk discovered from Panopalis in Egypt, indicate the use of sea route as well.[289]

The antiquity of silk industry in India is uncertain but the weight evidence seem to tbe infoavour of importation from China by way of Brahmaputra valley, i.e., Assam, Bengal route early in the Christian era. Kautilya refers about the cinapatta variety of silk cloth. The Arthasastra (II, 11, 114) also refers to silk from Cina-Cinabhumijah but actual specimens are difficult to recover in archaeological excavations. A piece of silk found in a relic casket in Nagara is dated to early centuries AD.[290] Though this underlines the importance of silk in Buddhist ritual, there is not information on the origin of the silk.[291] There is also a fragment of Han silk in the tombs of Palmyra.[292] Kalidasa and Manu aslo refers about the silk but they don't clarify whether these were imported or originally manufactured in India. We have to accept that these silk clothes were imported from China, unless and until further evidence regarding the origin of Indian silk is not coming forth. Silk entered the internal circuit of exchange through gifts by the rulers to panars (Bards) as was a luxury item of the ruling and urban elites attire.[293]

Though India had imported silk from China, yet the Periplus shows that the silk-yarn was exported from Barbaricum, probably in exchange of frankincense, Indian muslins and mallow cloth were brought down from Ozene to Barygaza.[294] The statement of Periplus may not be correct because the Chineese goods, which had fed the markets of west, passed through India to reimport to the western countries, especially Rome. The fight between the Parthians and Romans were mainly due to grab the route of silk, which was very much profitable.[295] The merchants also used sea route, which was passed through the harbours of India such as Barygaza, Nelcynda and Kaveripattanam.

Imports

After mentioning the list of goods of export it is now the time to deal with the names of goods of export, which has long implications on the economy of different countries. For the list of imported goods we have to rely on the same sources which had provided the idea about the list of export. Here one major advantage is that the archaeological evidence occupies the central stage to throw light on different goods of import. The favourable items of India which were imported from western lands were mainly aromatics, medicinal plants, roots, metals, minerals, mineral, byproducts precious stones, live stocks, skins and hides consumable commodities like wines and dates.

According to Herodotus, "the Arabs procured the frankincense by means of the gum, storax which the Greeks obtained from the Phoenicians.[296] "He also provides the information that the serpents and nothing guarded these incense-bearing trees in Arabia but the smoke of storax would drive them away from the trees. It may be a fiction but it procides a good idea about the frankincense. In Pliny's days, the frankincense, after being collected was carried on camels back to Sabota (Sabatha) a town belonging to Trogodyte on the Red Sea[297] where a single gate was open to pass these goods. It was a capital offence to deviate the goods from high way. The frankincense was very much costly during the days of Pliny and it was sold during Pliny at six denarii, the second rate at five denarii and the third rate at three denarii. The process of adulteration was taking place in Rome but it was easily identifiable. [298]

A good account about frankincense was left in Periplus about its production and transport in 2nd C.A.D. According to Periplus, "it is shipped from Mosyllum and from Malao"[299]. It gives us the following record of the frankincense country with cana as its market town. "All the frankincense produced in the country is brought by camels to that place to be stored and to Cana and this place has a trade also with.... ..Barygaza and Scythia and Ommana and the neighboring coast of Persia.[300] The Ships those were carrying these goods to the port of Barygaza were returning with cloth wheat, sesame, oil in exchange of frankincense.[301] The Periplus mentions Barbarism as the only mart where frankincense was imported, most probably by the some ships, the goods like silkyarn, cloths were brought from India.[302] Both Arabian and Roman subjects would naturally bring the incense which would ultimately reach to Chinese by whom it was highly prized, and in return the silk yarn was sent by cChina to the mouth of Indus which ultimately reached Arabia and Syria.[303]

Pliny says "The chief products of Arabia then are frankincense and myrrh. There is no country in the world that produces frankincense except Arabia.[304] But Periplus and Strabo point about the Sabota land where from these frankincense was procured. This land is usually expected to be flanked by the Arabian sea in the west, the Persian Gulf in the east, the Indian

Ocean in the south. On this description it is very difficult to locate the state.

The Sachalitic or Sabaean types of frankincense were certainly imported into India. Periplus gives the idea of export of frankincese to Syria and Egypt by Arabia. Herodotus bears the testimony to this effect that when he states that the Arabs paid the yearly tribute of 1,000 talents of frankincense to the kings of Persia.[305]

According to Periplus frankincense, like storax was transported by the Arabs to Egypt, viz. Alexandria, which must have proved to be a convenient port to sail to India.[306] The Arab ships which lay anchored at Barbaricum brought among their cargoes, frankincense which along with their other goods was carried upto the metropolis, by the river, probably the Indus.[307] The other ports of India with which the Arabs were carrying the trade of frankincense were Barygaza (Broach) and the city of Ozene (Ujjaini).

It can be inferred, therefore, that from the Barbaricum the region of Sind, from Barygaza (Broach) the whole Gujarat and from Ujjaini which was in those days a great market for various kinds of goods, the whole of the Middle country (Madhya Desa) must have been served with the supply of frankincense.

The frankincense was quite popular in India for its medicinal purposes. It is used as an antidote to hemlock.[308] It has an external application in carbuncles, blind boils and gangrenous sores and also acts as an internal agent in case of gonorrhoea. According to Pliny the best frankincense is recognised by its whiteness, size, rittleness and ready inflammability.[309]

Storax

Another important item, which was imported to India, was storax. The Periplus[310] speaks of the import of storax from Egypt to Cana, which was commercially connected with Barygaza and Scythia. It also records its import at Barbarycum and at Barygaza. It was usually exported from Egypt and from the Chineese records it is known that it was brought from Syria also.[311] In 97 A.D Kan

Ying reported to the Chinese that the Syrians after extracting the finest quality of storax from the odoriferous plants sold the residue to the foreign people. It passed through many hands before reaching in China and by this process it lost its fragrance. Busically the cheap varieties were sent to the people of India while the kings were supplied with the best quality of storax.

According to Pliny the trace of storax bore the same name and had a strong resemblace to the quince. Its tear has a harsh taste with a pleasant smell and its reed was filled with juice. The worst quality was of a type, which crumbled like bran and was covered all over with a whitish mould. The Periplus[312] mentions of two types of ointment imported at Barygaza one the most ordinary "not very costly not much" and the other, "the choicest ointment brought for the king." The first type included that storax about which the Chineese people complained. The price of the best quality of storax was 17 denarii per pound. Compared with the price of the best type of frankincense, the finest kind of storax, on the authority of Pliny, was nearly thrice expensive. Its leaves have been used as a cure for stones in the kidney and bladder.[313]

Though once it was imported into India from Syria, it was later cultivated in India where it has been found in the sub tropical western Himalayas from Chamba to Kumaon at the heights varying from 2,500 feet to 5,500 feet.[314]

Sweet Clover *(Trifolium Melilotus, order – Leguminosae)*

Another important item of imports into India was the sweet clover of which Watt has distinguished three kinds. One of these types was the straw berry headed clover and the second variety was red or broad leaved clover.

It is only from Periplus that we learn the sweet clover was certainly imported into India in the first century A.D. This account reveals us that the sweet clover was imported into the market town of Barygaza (Broach) and thence from Ujjaini According to Schoff this sweet clover was probably intended for the manufacture of chaplets for reexport to Rome[315]. This suggestion was perhaps made on the statement of Pliny who observed that "in later times the rose chaplet has been adopted and luxury arose at last to such a pitch that a chaplet was held in no esteem at all if it did not consist entirely of leaves sewn together with the needls. More recently again they have been imported from India or from nations beyond the countries of India".[316] From this statement one can conjure that Pliny was not sure of the locality. But with much more certainty it can be presumed that the sweet clover was imported into India in first century A.D.

So we may infer that the sweet clover (sliphium) was grown in Media and Bactria. But Pliny tells us the best kind of melilote was found in Italy especially in Camponia, in Greece at Cape Sunium and next to that in Chalcidice and Crete.[317]

Again it may be gauged that the sweet clover was imported into India from Bactria rather than Media. The proximity of Bactria to India is a potent factor for its export because sweet clover was the perishable goods. On the same ground the validity of fact of import from the lands like Rome and Greece are also refuted.

The silphium was used not only as a fodder for horses in Media but its juice was utilized as a medicine. This juice which was extracted from the plants could be kept for certain period though it is not specified. According to Strabo this plant promoted the digestion of raw meat of beasts of burden which Alexander's forces had to consume for lack of fire wood and also of food itself.[318]

Balsam (*Skt-Rasagandhi)(Myrrh) commiphora Opobalsammum*)

It was imported into India including other commodities. It was consisted of four varieties viz. Mukul, muyrrhl (rasgandhi) agaloch, opabalsammum etc. In the book of Ezkiel we find myrrh (Jaudea) and Israel (Palestine) exported it to tyre along with other goods and from there the Phoenicians must have exported to other countries including India.[319]

The plant was mainly used for the preparation of one kind of unguents or ointments. From the early times this ointment was manufactured in India having a good fragrance. It is also said that the servants assisted by the ambassodars were using these ointments which might be costly. The plant of Balsam is not visible in India today which indicates that these plants were brought from the foreign lands to prepare this ointment.

About the origin of plants we may ascertain where these types of trees were cultivated. Josephus Flavius (AD 37-107) reveals where exactly the balsam was cultivated. "This (Jericho) "he says" the most fertile district of Judaea, nourishes the palmtree as well as the balsam tree, the stems of which being cut with sharp stones, is received at the incisions, in drops like tears[320]. As a consequence of the intrigues of the Cleopatra of Egypt with Mark Antony, king Hberod with Judaea was forced by the Antony to cede to her the entire coast of Palestine, which Antony had granted to her as personal property. This region included the city of Jericho on the Jordon with its surrounding plantations containing the most valuable plants, the balsam bushes[321]. This indicates the importance of balsam tree.

The balsam was mainly used for the preparations of unguen s ointments and balms and it seems to have had a many medicinal properties. Strabo mentions that it was an excellent .nedy for headache, incipient, suffusion of the eyes and the dimness of the sight.[322] Therefore the price of these goods were high because it was not available except the afore mentioned regions.

The balasam was first grown in Syria, next in Judaea and then in Egypt. In view of the close connection between India and Alexandria, it is usually expected that these goods night have exported from the port of Alexandria. From Periplus we learn the selected myrrh" was exported from Muza (Mocha).[323] As the Periplus has borne out almost all the imports into the Indian waters and ports on the east and west coasts proceeded from that ports, it would not be erronous if we assume that this ralsom was exported to India from Muza Via Alexandria.

Myrrh was adulterated with pieces of mastich and gum. It was also drugged with the juice of wild cucumber in order to produce certain bitterness and with litharge for increasing its weight. But the cleverest method of adulterating myrrh seems to have been by mixing it with Indian myrrh, which in words of Pliny was, "a substance that gathered from a certainly prickly shrub. Which grew in India.[324] The price of myrrh varied according to the number of purchaser and also depended on its variety. Myrrh sold at prices varying from there to 40 denorii for pound.

Cinnamon (*Skt. Gudatvak, Hindi-Dalcina, Cinnamomum Zeylanium Beeyn F1*)

From the very remote period the cinnamon was a product of import. But its import in the 1st C.A.D. cann't be doubted as we can see from the Periplus. It informs us that from the Avalites, Malao and Arsinoe , it was imported into India and other ports en-route to India, "the harder cinnamon".[325] According to Pliny, cinnamon was exported from Arabia and Ethiopia. He states that the right of regulating the sale of cinnamon was a royal monopoly of the king of the Gebanitae who could open the market for the sale by public proclamation.[326] The observation of Watt points out that the Arabia and Ethiopia produced cinnamon, spikenard and other spices. [327]

About the varieties of cinnamon, Pliny held that the thinnest parts in the sticks, for about a plam in the length, were looked upon as producing the finest cinnamon. The part that came after, though not quite so long was the next best and so on. The worst of all was that surviving nearest the roots as it had the least bark, which was the most, esteemed.[328] But some other writers prefer to divide the cinnamon into two varieties, the white and the black. The black cinnamon was the favourte item.

Cinnamon was imported into India for medicinal aromatic, stimulative and carminative purposes. It has been used in flatulence, flatulent Cotic, spasmodic affections of the bowels, atonic diarrhoea and gastric irritation. It has also been supposed to act as a stimulant of the uterine muscular fibre and hence employed in menorrhagia and in tedious labour depending upon insufficiency of the uteric contractions. Due to these variety uses the cinnamon was imported into India.

Consumer Goods

Figs and Dates: From the Periplus, it is known that the market towns of Ommana, Apollogus and Cana despatched every year to Barygaza (Broach) wine and a great quantity of dates and figs.[329] This statement may be taken to mean that in the first century A.D. the dates in large quantities were imorted to Broach. Although Periplus indicates that the imports of dates came to India from the ports of Persian Gulf but it does not mention particularly the names of ports. But the evidences of trade of dates are found in early times, which present the fact that the best kind of dates came from Thebais in Egypt, Judnea in addition to other kinds of dates.[330] So on the basis of these points one may easily conjure that the dates were an important item of between India and West Asia.

Which were the regions from where India imported dates? The Periplus does not provide any conclusive idea about the original place of dates. As the Arab, Cryte, Judaea and Syria were the lands of dates and a flourished trade between these lands with India was continuing, therefore it is quite worthy to predict that these items were brought from these lands.

Beverages-Wines or Liquors

The foreign wines and liquors were the products of import from early times as Kautilya refers the foreign customers in liquor ships. But in 1st C.A.D. we can say positively the wines imported into India. The Periplus reveals that the port of Barygaza (Broach)" received wines of which "Italian was preferred also Laodicean and Arabian".[331] The South Indian ports were largely receiving the foreign wines though not much and these were market ports of Muziris, Tyndis, Nelcynda in the kingdom of Kerala. The use of wine became extravagant in the Pandyan and Chola courts.[332] Roman wine was popular with Tamils who were familiar with its quantity and fragrance.[333] In the *Purannuru*, a poet lauds a about the Roman wine which very much cool and fragrant.[334] The amphorae sherds have been found from the exactions at Arikamedu, Vasavasamudram, and Karaikkadu.[335]

Though India was producing the wine from the Vedic period when some were the intoxicating drinks, wine was also imported from west.[336] Wine making began in Asia Minor and Syria from very early times. Wine of the Damascus valley was an important article of export in the period of Ezekiel.[337] Strabo speaks of Greek wines of the Aegean islands and the Asiatic coasts near Ephesus to be the best of all. Wine was also made at Loadicea on the Syrian coast near Atioch. Strabo speaks of its richness and its export to Alexandria.[338] Laufer, says that the grape wine[339] belongs to the ancient cultivated plants of West Asia and Egypt.

According to Periplus, "the country around Muza produces a great deal of wine.[340] Probably it was grape wine. The Periplus also speaks of "wine and great quantity of dates"[341] exported from Ommana and Apologus to Barygaza. In Iran, the viticulture was in a state of flourishing condition. According to Posidanius grape wine was made in Damascus, Syria and from wines planted by the Perisans.

The yavanas also carried wine with themselves; it was referred in the Tamil poem where Nakkira exhorts a Pandya prince to drink in peace the cool and fragrant wine.[342]

About the different qualities of wines in Europe, Pliny gives a detail account and mentions that, "the wine made from date plams… is used by the Parthians and Indians and by the whole of the east.[343]

The concept of grape wine was not borrowed from the west solely because Kalidasa in his Raghuvamsha mentions about this means that it was also produced in India.

The Arab wine sent to India[344] was probably so called because it must have come either from Arab ports or from Arab merchants or from both. Egypt, Babylonia, Judaea, Cyprus, Syria, Seleucia were the main centres of date production and it may be expected that these regions were providing date wine to East countries including India. It may be suggested that Arab traders were mainly exporting this wine to east. It is to this wine Herodotus refers when he observes that the plam cultivated in Bablon, supplied its citizens with, "bread, wine and honey". "It need not be understood that the Arab wine was solely the date wine, though primarily it was so because Syria also produced the vine which yielded the grape wine which was exported to India from Laodicea. Schoff's suggestion that the grape wine from Yemen might have been included in the Arab wines.[345] Supplied to India plausible though it requires further corroboration. It may be remembered that the Egyptians brewed the barely wine[346] which might also have been exported to India.

So, the wine was the favourite items of Indians, which was imported from the west. Though there are enough evidences to point out fact that from the early period India was producing the some; out of a plant juice to which was intoxicating; the foreign wine was highly appreciated by the Indians.

Metals and Mineral Products

Among the various metals, the metals as copper, tin, lead, iron, gold & silver coins were mainly imported into India.

Copper

From Periplus it is known to us that in the first century A.D. the copper was shipped from the port of Bernice to the Indian ports of Barygaza, Meiziris, Nelcynda, Tendys etc.[347] There must be a special variety of copper which was sent from Barygaza to the ports of Oman and Apologus.[348] According to E.H. Warmington at the time of war between Rome and Parthia, there was the scarcity of copper and that was the reason why Indian exported copper though it was dependent on the copper of west.[349]

According to Periplus the import of copper was from Egypt, for it tells us: "These are imported into the place (Sabbatha) from Egypt.....and most of its spurious; and copper and tin and coral and storax and other things such as go to Muza."[350] The main source of the European copper was the island of Sypruss, Soli, Curion of which the Roman government had complete control. The copper transported to India, could hardly have come from Italy or Germany. But it is more likely that it was shipped from the Carmania in first century A.D. from there the copper must have been transported to the Persian Gulf and Red sea ports of onward transshipments to India.

In India, copper was mainly used for the coins making purposes. Copper was also used as an alloy in the manufacture of silver coins as also for making utensils.

Tin and Lead

The periplus again reveals us that in the first century A.D., the tin and lead were imported into India. It first mentions that it was imported into Muza and then into the Indian ports of Barygaza, Ujjaini and Nelcynda.[351] According to Pliny, "India had neither brass nor lead and exchanged the precious stones and pearls for them.[352] He was probably misguided or he has ignorance. Because Vajaseyani Samhita refers to *tin(trapu)* and lead *(Sisa)*- Kautilya's Arthasastra mentions about the officers like superintendents of metals and mint were also dealing with the metals like copper, tin, lead and brass.[353] It indicates that India had the tin and lead but it might not be sufficient enough to meet the needs of Indian people for which they felt the need of import of these metals from western lands.

The importance of tin as an imported article to India is hinted by the fact that the Sanskrit word "Kshatira" is borrowed from the Greek word, "Kasseteros". Marshall says that the Indo-Parthians at Taxila...would have little difficulty in importing copper & tin from the west or obtaining it more immediately from Kashmir and Afghanistan part of which they annexed to their dominion in the 1st century A.D."[354]

These metals were largely used for coins during the first few centuries of Christian era. However, Romans used lead largely for manufacturing water pipes and soldered these with an alloy of lead and tin.[355] Pliny looks lead and tin as the varieties of the same species. He uses the term 'minimum' in its modern sense of red lead.[356]

The Periplus speaks of import of gold from Ommana and Apologus to Barygaza. It records further that the silver and gold plate were imported into Barbaricum and "Silver and gold"[357] coins were imported at Barygaza. The Romans obtained their gold in great extent from Transylvania, which was still a gold field.[358] It may not be unlikely that the gold of Egypt and Asia Minor might have crept into India through Ommana and Apologus, the intermediate ports of transshipment in the period of Rome's trade with ancient India, as indicated in the Periplus.

Again the Periplus reveals us that the gold and silver coins were imported into India through the port of Barygaza. This import of coins was the result of favourable trade of India with Western countries. The profit in exchanging Roman currency for Indian, must have been due to the superiority of Roman gold and silver, as the first century was the hey-day of Roman empire, when the currency had not suffered any deterioration as it did later on.[359] Into the South Indian ports "a great quantity of coins" was imported in the first century A.D. the trend of flow of gold and silver coins also continued in 2nd and 3rd century A.D. as Silappadikaram[360] speaks of sale of gold in Madura and Puhar.

Not only the gold coins but also jewellery was an important item of import. Works of gold jewellery were discovered in treasure-hoards of Taxila, which Marhsall thinks, were buried in haste beneath the floors of houses under the menace of Kushan invasion. Some pieces of gold jewellery bear a very striking resemblance with the contemporary art of south Russia and furnish interesting evidence of trade relations between India and Black sea region in the Saka-Parthian period.[361] In the Kushan period the supply of gold was supplemented by imports from the Near East by way of Persian Gulf. According to Tarn,[362] The Kushan Kings imported gold coins from the Western World". Marshall has also noticed that " an ingot of gold found in the Saka-Parthian city of Sirkap" bears a significant resemblance to the ingots which were traded in the Roman world.[363] The archaeologists spade has unearthed at Bhita, one gold ring, one hollow gold bead, two miniature gold beads tied together, one wheel of gold and also a disc of gold engraved with a human face; is expected to have the resemblance with the Roman jewellery.[364]

There are two main concentrations of Roman coins in Peninsular India, the Coimbatore district of Tamilnandu and along the Krishna river of Andhra Pradesh.[365] The coins mainly comprise the coins of Julio Claudian period. The distribution of Roman coins in various parts of India is indicating the degree of monetization in different regions of country. Thus under Kushanas and Satavahanas, the north and Deccan had a complex currency system and as a result any Roman coins imported were exchanged at same profit against local currency.[366]

The influx of large amount of gold coins and gold jewellery is indicative of favourable trade of Indian with Western Countries. The Kushan emperors used the Roman bullion as their coins but most of the times they modelled their coins according to Roman coins after melting their bullion.

Minerals

We shall now deal with minerals like salt, asphaltus and glass. About the import of salt there is no such strong evidence. But, according to Kautilya; there were two varieties of salt. One was indigenous and other was imported.[367] The opinion of Sama Shastri is that this imported metal was probably very costly and in view of high costs, comparatively fewer persons used it. Gerrhae (identified by Ajasson with Heart and the Dijihoun) an Arabian city, Pliny tells us, had ramparts and houses constructed with the blocks of salt, soldered together by being moistened with water.[368] Another rich region of salt were Bactria, Crete, Egypt, Babylonia and Germany. So it may be expected that the salt might have been imported into India from Bactria, Egypt and Arabia where the salt was available in two forms, sea salt and rock salt. The Egyptian salt though acrid, calorific and bad for stomach, acted also as sudorific and was taken with wine and water, served as a purgative.[369] Therefore it may be accepted that if there was any kind of imported salt was used in India, it must be brought from these countries, which were rich in salt. And India's continued trade relations with the countries like Arabia, Egypt, Crete make the possibility deep-rooted.

Glass

Another important mineral imported was glass of which there seems to have existed certain varieties like ordinary, flint, murrhine. In 1st C.A.D. there can be no doubt that the varieties of glass were imported into different ports not only of Arabia but also of India. The variety of glass was imported into the ports of Muza.[370] The Periplus records the import of "Vessels of glass' at Barbaricum and of crude glass at Barygaza.[371] However, Rostovzeff says that glass was extensively used in Egypt and Phoenicia".[372] Into South Indian ports of Nelcynda, Muziris, Tyndis and Bacare were imported only crude glass.

We know from Pliny[373] that the glass making was originated in Phoenicia and the sand of river Belus was long used for the industry. During his time the white sand at the Mouth of the river Volturnus was much used far glass making. According to Warmington, "Alexandria, Tyre, Sidon were famous for their works in glass which spread all over Roman empire and very for beyond. Alexandria is also noted to have become prominent in certain branches of glass making"[374] about in 1st century B.C. and probably continued in the two succeeding centuries. The credit of discovery of glass blowing may go to Syrian glass workers who appear to have moved to Italy in 1st century A.D. and in the course of the century Italy probably became one of the chief glass producing areas of the empire. We may expect that India might have imported glassware from Italy, Syria and Egypt in the period of our enquiry.

Marshall[375] opine that, " all glass vessels found at Taxila are of foreign origin and nearly date from 1st century A.D. The best preserved are small flasks of sea or jade green glass identical with those which are common throughout the Roman empire during the early centuries of Christian era. However, M. Hackin provides an interesting fact from his recent excavation at Begram where he found the rich collection of glass ware, almost all of which was imported from Syrian or other factories round of the coasts of Mediterranean. The land routes of Middle East might have imported the glass vessel of Taxila and also by the sea route through the ports of western India mentioned in the Periplus.

Mineral By-products

Asphalt: One of the mineral by product which was also imported into India was asphalt. Though there are no enough evidences about its, import, its utility for different work, especially for the construction works, points out the possibility of import. From Strabo we learn that the liquid asphaltus, called naptha, was found in Susiana and the dry kind, which could be solidified, was available in Babylonia. He again pointed out that other types of asphalts were also found in Babylonia.[376] But according to Pliny, "a type of asphalt which was found on the earth in the Vicinity of Sidon was in the famous Maritime city of Syria". Another kind of liquid bitumen, resembling oil, found in a spring at Agrigentium in Sicily, the waters of which was tainted by it.[377]

Asphalt was exported from Babylonia, Syria, Sicily and Judaea to Rome or else. Pliny gives the idea about the varieties of esphalt and its different uses but about its import into India, he is silent. But it is surprising that neither Strato, nor Pliny nor the Periplus nor even Comas refer at any time to its export to India but in view of its various commercial and medicinal uses for men and beasts its import into India may be well taken as not improbable. Its great utility for building of ships may have been one of its great attractions.

About its utility, Strabo, has pointed that the liquid asphalt was used for smearing boats woven with reeds which became thereafter firmly compacted.[378] According to Pliny in its liquid form it was used as the substitute as oil for burning lamps and also for the cure of itch or scabies in breasts of burden. It was also employed for coating the inside of copper vessel rendering it fire proof. It was adopted as a substitute for lime and walls of Babylone was cemented with it. From Medicinal point of view, the Babylonian bitumen is said to have been very efficacious in curing cataract, albugo, leprosy, lichens, and prurugenous affections and used as bandolines for the eye lashes which were refractory and impede eyesight. It was applied topically with nitre, served as curative for toothache and taken internally with wine, alleviated the chronic cough and difficult respirations. It could detect any tendency to fits of epilepsy.[379] Taking its multifarious medicinal qualities into account it may be expected that it was imported into India because Ashoka had taken special care to bring the various medicinal plants into India.

Antimony

We have evidence with regard to the import of antimony into India. The Periplus is our best authority for inferring that the antimony was imported into India in the first century A.D. It was transported not only to Ujjaini but also to southern market towns of Nelcynda, Muziris and Bacare.[380]

Schoff observed that the stimmi (antimony) came from Eastern Arabia and Carmania.[381]Pliny however tells that as antimony was a siliver ore, it came from Spain to Italy and from Italy it might have been exported to India.[382]

Antimony was mainly used as a medicine for eyes. Hence, it was called by the most of the people as "*platyopthalmon*" or eye dilating and used extensively in calliblepheric preparations of women for beautifying their eyebrows. It acted as a check on the fluxes of eyes and their ulcerations, was employed as a powder with powdered frankincense and gum, considered useful in arresting discharges of the blood from the brain, sprinkled in the form of powder and found extremely efficacious in curing fresh wounds and dog bites. It was helpful in healing burns.

Orpiment *(Skt-Manassila)*

It was another mineral product, which was imported into India in the first century A.D. From Periplus again we know that along with antimony, orpiment was also imported into the south Indian ports of Nelcynda, Mluziris and Becare.[383]

According to Pliny,[384] orpiment was a mineral drug, dug from the surface of the earth in Syria and was much used by the painters. It had just the colour of gold but was brittle like the mirror stone. Ball remarks that, " the United Kingdom, Austria, China, Turkey in Asia contribute to the supply of arsenic, orpiment and realgar".[385] Hence we may also expect that China and Turkey were also exporting orpiment to India.

Orpiment was used as one of the constituents for making gunpowder in ancient India. It was also used to prepare the paper, which was not ravaged by the insects.[386] About its medicinal properties, Pliny refers; it was most remarkable for its antiseptic properties. Applied with vinegar, it was considered to cure alopecia and employed as an ingredient in ophthalmic preparations. It was applied with honey for cleansing the faces and believed to make voice clearer. If it would be taken with food and turpentine, it was reckoned as a pleasant medicine for cough and asthma. It was a detergent, astringent and corrosive.[387]

Precious stones

The precious stones which the mines of earth and of the ocean yielded, which have happily been defined by *Kautilya (manidhatuh)*. These stones were very hard and of little colour. Generally the correct shells, diamonds, precious stones, pearls, corals were imported into India from the ancient times. The other sub classifications of these precious stones were via; topazes, emeralds and tortoise shells etc.

The Topaz

According to Periplus[388], the topazes were shipped to Barbaricum from Ommanitic and Parsidae regions. Strabo and Pliny[389] both furnish some details regarding the precise regions where the real topaz was procured. Strabo mentioned that it was found in the islands of *Ophiodes (Zamargat)* in Arabia where the kings of Egypt appointed a guard to protect the locality where the topaz was available. So it is expected that the topaz. Of Arabia was imported into India. There were two kinds of topaz stones, the yellow and the genuine topaz stones and both were imported into India. According to the Periplus that the topaz stones were imported into India through Red Sea. From the Ommanitic and Parsidae regions the topaz stones came to the ports of Barbricum through Indus and to Barygaza (Broach) in the northern India and the southern ports like Bacare, Nelcyanda, Tyndis and Muziris in the first century.[390]

Pliny[391] considered the topaz the largest of all precious stones and the only one that among all these of high value. The popularity of topaz can be assumed to much earlier times and associated with the country of Ethiopia where it recorded to have been known. In the "Book of Job" we hear of the topaz of Ethiopia referring to wisdom. "The topaz of Ethiopia shall not be equal of him". [392] The importance of topaz can be alluded from this.

Pearls

From Periplus again we find that in about 60 A.D. through the markets of Ommana and cane, the pearls of Persian Gulf was readily sold in the Indian markets. From there, "many pearls but inferior to those of India" was sent to the port of Barygaza (Broach)[393] from where they must have been found their way into several markets of north as well as south India. Whereas the Periplus admits that the Bahrain pearls were inferior to those of India, Schoff has contended that the former though more yellow than those of the Straits of Mannar commanded a sale in India because their lustre kept better particularly in the tropics.[394] According to Pliny those pearls, found in the vicinity of the Arabia and Persian Gulf which forms the part of Red Sea, were "mostly highly valued' because there were a much clearer water than the Indian pearl which resembling in tint the scales of mirror stone,[395] exceeded all other kinds of pearls in size and became the greatest favourite in Rome.

Corals

Pliny[396] remarks that the corals were highly priced in India as pearls were at Rome. The Gauls ornamented their swords, shields; helmets with corals until the beginning of Roman trade in corals with India.[397] Pliny gives an interesting fact that the large-scale exports of corals created a shortage in the place of production. The main centre of coral production was Mediterranean Sea. There were black corals in the Red Sea and along the Arabian coast but they were not so much prized. Corals of Rome were interchanged with the pearls of India.

According to Periplus, "the red corals reached at Barbaricum, Barygaza and at Muziris and Nelcynda."[398] It mentions its import from the further west into cara whence it was reshipped to India in Arab or Hindu bottoms.[399] Tauffer says that "Persian corals have found their way all over Asia... and the coral encountered by the Chinese in Kipin may also have been from Persian origin. Red coral from the Western Mediterranean and Red Sea was on of the major items shipped to the East from the time of Periplus.[400] Coral beads have been found in a stupa of Mirpur Khas, a site on the Indus in Sindh in early Christian era[401] and in many stupas of Dharmarajika monastery in Taxila.[402]

The Manimekalai describes the whole streets of Puhar as, 'full of silks, corals etc."[403] Uraiyur is also praised for corals in the Tamil poem. Hence we may expect that the corals were imported in 2nd and 3rd century A.D. According to Kautilya,[404] there were two types of corals such as 'Alakandaka and Vaivarnaka" the two varieties of corals which is possessed of ruby like colour. The commentator notes that the first type is obtained in the mouth of river Barbara and the second type is received near the island of Yavanas. Hence it may be presumed that Kautilya hinted towards the export of corals in India from the Mediterranean world.[405]

The price of the corals can be assessed from the comments of Sukra,[406] belonging to later period. He says that the corals weighing one tola deserve the half price of the gold of the same weight. Watt[407] says that in addition to being used for adornment ornamental corals have been used as Hindu medicine from very ancient times and are mentioned by Susruta. Indian soothe-sayers and divines looked on the coral as an amulet endowed with sacred properties and a sure preventive of all dangers. Hence Indians valued it as an ornament as well as an object of devotion.[408] Its medicinal property was that powdered coral was considered an excellent remedy for patients who brought up or spat blood, calcined coral was used as an ingredient in composition for the eyes, being productive of certain astringent and cooling properties. It was also supposed to rebuild flesh in cavities left by the ulcers and to efface scars on the skin.[409]

Among the other product, which was imported into India, were the skin of rhinoceros, ivory and horses. The Periplus informs us that in the first century from the Ptolemais of the Hunts, not only ivory but also the rhinoceros' horn were imported into India. About the ivory, the scholars refute the claim of Periplus[410] on the ground that India was the main center of ivory trade and it was supplying the ivory to the western loads. Therefore the import of ivory into India remains inconclusive unless further evidence substantiates the facts. The horn of elephants was also used for making handles of swords and different kinds of armour.

Horses

The importance of horse from West Asian countries was increased insanely during the medieval period in comparison to ancient times. Horses have been imported in to India from Kamboja, Sind, Bactria, Persia, and Syria from the first century A.D. if not much earlier. Surprisingly, Periplus does not refer the import of horse from Persia, but it mentions the import of horses from Arabia.[411] It relates how the merchants from Arabia presented to the king and the chief of Muza (Mocha) horses and mules.[412] Therefore the import of horses from the alien lands like Persia and Syria can't be denied but they might have been arrived in India by and land routes instead of sea routes. To the Pandyan coast came horses and other precious things, which are presumably exchanged for gems.[413] Horses for breeding of which southern climate was not conducive, have always been imported into South India mainly from Arab countries. Pattinpallai and maduraikknchi make a reference of the import of horses to the South Indian Kingdoms.[414] References of horses as gifts are fewer that other items perhaps due to the military importance to the rulers.[415]

Trade in horses seems to have been an important factor in the commercial life of South India in 1st C.A.D. [416] Horses of Parthia are said to have been imported at Puhar from "distant lands beyond the seas." [417] The horses are primarily imported for military purposes. The regular training of horses was its preparation for war. When the horses were incapacitated owing to old age, disease or hardships of war, were declared unfit for the war and existed only to consume food in the interest of citizens and country people, then they were allowed to breed.[418]

Slaves

Before going into the deep of import of slaves from western countries to India, we should analyse the slave trade situation in the western world. "Besides the sale of slaves which took place as a result of the capture of cities or other military operation, there was a systematic slave trade in Greece, Syria, Pontus, Lydia, Gallatia and others. Egypt and Ethiopia also furnished a certain number and Italy a few. Of foreigners, the Asiatics bore the greatest value but the Greeks were highest of all in esteem and they were much sought for foreign sale. Greece proper and Ionia supplied the pretty Eastern princes with courtesans and female musicians and dancers. Athens was an important slave market. ..... but the principal marts were those of Cyprus, Samos, Ephesus and Chios."[419]

Probably India took the advantage of the existing slave trade of western markets. Various kinds of slaves were imported into India in the first century A.D. From the Periplus we find that through the Arabian Gulf ports like Ocelis, Muza and Malao, slaves were exported to India.[420] But whether they were only men or women it is not clear. Eudoxos[421] (at the end of 2nd C.B.C.) who wanted to discover the Cape route to India, whished to bring some young singing and flute girls to India for her princess (Poseidonides).

In a legend about St. Thomas, we hear of an Indian king who made a Jewish slave girl to play on her flute and entertain his guest.[422]

Another conclusive evidence in this regard is the unique specimen of the slave "Agesilas". Who was the architect of Kanishka's stupa near Taxila who made his relic casket. Tarn notes that the casket, ", may have been anything from a skilled Greek slave imported from the west to a subject of Kanishka.[423]

In another evidence, the Tamil poem speaks of "dumb mlechhas clad in complete armour" who acted as guards to Tamil kings and who were most possibly the yavana slaves imported from the west.[424] The Silapapadikaram says that it was impressed by the stern discipline of the Yavana soldiers employed by the Tamil Kings[425] as the guards of fortress gates. They were also permanently settled as guards of palaces and royal camps. There were also settlement of Yavanas in important trading and commercial centers like Puhar and Muziris.[426] They were most likely Romans, which are indirectly attested by the Roman pottery, and other associate finds in excavation.[427]

So it is the fact that in the first century A.D. the slaves were imported into India from the ports of Ocelis, Muza, Malao and Opone. And the slave trade during this period was mainly in the hands of Arabs who were the slave drivers of the day. But it is very difficult to determine that wherefrom they procured these slaves. Presumably they had brought from Syria, Persia and Mediterranean areas. Whether the slave markets of Greece, North-Western Assyria and Phrygia still continued to supply slaves to the Arab traders, it is difficult to because for we have no definite proof to draw the conclusion.

These were the goods, which were directly imported from Western Asia and Roman world to cater the needs of Indian people, but the number of items of import was small in comparison with the number of goods, which were exported. Therefore it may be concluded that the trade was in favour of India, which is clearly expressed by Pliny. Pliny bluntly called them a "drain" on his country and he was not alone in raising his voice against the outflow of Roman wealth. "In one year" he said "does India drain us of no less than 550 million sesterces (£ 22,000,000) giving back our own wares which are sold among us fully 100 times of their prime cost.".[428] Again he remarked. "At the very lowest computation India, the Seres and the Arabian Peninsula withdraw from our empire 100 million of sesterces every year so dearly do we pay for our luxury and our women."[429] Pliny was not the only author who had raised the voice but the other authors like Tacitus, Dion Chryosostom also gave the similar views of the drain of wealth. The emperor Tiberius in A.D. 22, also protested against the fruitless expenditure. "The very existence of Rome" he told, the senate once, "is daily at the mercy of concretion waves and storms and unless master, slaves and estates have the resources of the provinces as their mainstay, our shrubberies, forsooth and our country houses will have to support us. The neglect of them will be the utter ruin of the state. The cure of the evils must be sought in our own hearts."[430]

From these statements it is clearly established that the drain of wealth was a great headache to the Roman historians as well as the rulers. The large amount of inflow of gold from the west was mainly used as the coins or for the ornamental purposes. The imports, which the Roman empire received for the extra ordinary amount, were not commensurate with the expenditure incurred in procuring them; for they were mere "baubles" fit only to satisfy the vanity of senseless women and the thoughtless wealthy.[431] The unquenchin thirst of Roman people for the Indian goods like spices, precious stones and aromatics created a favourable condition for the Indian traders. The traders of Indian peninsula earned much more profit out of this trade.

About the favourable conditions of trade in India has raised the serious questions among the historians. It has been contended that Pliny was alluding to only such traffic maintained along the northern route via. Caspian and Black Sea and that he omits the cost of pearl trade.[432] Warmington also suspected about the validity of Pliny's comment. He points out the fact that, Pliny was probably misguided because he did not take the cost of carriage, price of Indian goods, heavy charges demanded at the various points of routes into account before his computation.[433] However Pliny's comments may be hyperbole.[434] There is little evidence that the Romans actually brought many of the items they desired from the East. Again they used the system of barter and exchange to get the goods of East.[435] This being the case, there naturally would be little or no indication that the Romans were pre occupied with concept of balance of trade deficit or surplus s as we are today.

The Romans were paying a heavy price for Indian goods. There are various reasons, which are responsible for the rise of cost of Indian goods is the Roman markets. The first and foremost reason must have been the insistent and unceasing demand for constant supply of these Indian products. Secondly the intermediaries, atleast in the cases of commodities, not transported by the Romans or through Roman agencies, like the Arabs, Parthian, Jews, Indo-Greeks, Syrians, Phoenicians and Persians, must have played their parts in raising the total costs of commodities like aromatics, spices or precious stones which Rome had ultimately to pay. Thirdly, the distance through the land and sea routes, which were invariably so lengthy, arduous and expensive, must have contributed in so small measure in enhancing the total costs of every article. Fourthly, the Roman people had not developed the price controlling mechanism to check the inflation of the prices of the imports from India or any eastern countries and the traders of Rome used every device within their power to raise prices, citing various excuses in support of such manipulations. Finally the Indian goods were not exported to Rome only the goods were reaching at Persia, Arab, Ethiopia and Egypt and therefore, the comments of Pliny about the drain of wealth by India holds no ground. The commodities, which commanded such high and fantastic prices, were mostly luxurious goods for which natural fancy prices had to be paid and they hardly remained steady or uniform. The prices of single good like myrobalanum was two denarii per pound while the costs of unguents ranged from 35 to 400 denarii per pound depending on the qualities and places of origin. In view of the steady and encouraging demand for such goods and the willingness of Romans to pay for them, the supply continued to meet the demand until Rome collapsed and its demand with it.

The trade was favourable to India, such fact is endorsed by numismatic and archaeological data. The presence, though sporadic, of the coins of the Roman republic may suggest earlier coins could have been circulating even at a later period in the Southern India when the trade considerably increased.[436] The high value of Roman coins, the aurii and denarii of Augustus and Tiberius in particular, occur in hoards, found in South India and coincide with the period of Roman demands for oriental luxuries and with the complaints about the paucity of such coins in the empire.[437] In Second Century AD the number of hoards increased, as do the numbers of aurii in Kerala and Andhra Pradesh with many imitations.[438]

About the various hoards of coins in different parts of India, raises various questions about the idea behind this. It has been said that they were treated as bullion or used as jewellery or ornament as also was the case of some local coins.[439]

Sometimes these types of coin hoardings were regarded as status symbol. Again it may be presumed that the coins were hoarded as protection of money for the safe passage of goods. There for the coins played the dual role as high value currency in trading markets but as prestige items in the hinterlands of markets.[440]

Trade Routes

The trade routes between India and western world considerably increased in the first two centuries of Christian era. The establishment of comparative peace by the Roman Empire became a potent cause for new explorations and developments of trade. The geographical importance of Arabia, the Asia Minor and Northeastern Africa serving as a chain for joining the west and western Asia came into focus is this period. The Roman merchants in Western Asia strengthened their business with ample financial resources thus consolidating their influence.[441] But one of the strange things is that Indian merchants seldom met with the Roman merchants because the intermediaries of this trade were Alexandrian Greeks, Syrian Jews, Arabs, Axumites and the Parthians.[442] These people were not under the Roman subjects anyway and hence they wanted the trade between India and the west should not be carried directly but through them, their geographical position being midway between India and western world.[443] The entire traffic between east and west was controlled by them with a view to conceal the actual sources of treasures of India and China from the Greeks and Romans; with an eye to gain more profit by acting as middlemen.

Rome and India were brought closer together through the Persia Gulf and the Red sea. According to Prof. Maiuri, the Indian ivory might have reached the shore of Campania by this route.[444] He discovered, in 1938, an ivory statuette, identified with Lakshmi, at Pompeii, which he took to be purely an work of Indian art of C.97 A.D.(see figure-6) Inscription along the route record the coming and going of merchants and one dating to 2nd CBC refers specifically to the person having recently returned from India.[445] Kingdom of Indian sub-continent may well have drawn a re venue from the trade but here again there is little evidence of direct state controlled participation. The Tamil and Prakrit sources frequently mention about the Yavanas who have been identified with those came with Roman trade from the Egypt and eastern Mediterranean.[446]

The Roman Empire was established in Asia Minor, Syria and Egypt but Arabia was not under its control and the tribes of Caucasus did not care for its orders.

When Augustus rose to the imperial power in 27 B.C. and established his vast empire including various races of the west,[447] the middle East and the North-East Africa hence Rome became ripe and ready for further developments in the intercourse of men and she backed her merchants with capital who pushed themselves with fresh enthusiasm into the East both by land and water.

Rome had two ports, Ostia and Peuteoli. Ostia was harbour less and more dangerous one for the sitting up of the Tiber "which was fed by numerous streams". Strabo however says that "the good supply of tenders make it possible to sail away quickly before they touched the river or else, after being partly relieved of their cargoes, they sail into the Tiber and run inland as far as Rome."[448] Hence Puteoli was better used as a safer harbour where 'the greatest merchant ships could moor with safety"[449] and it was an important centre for transshipment to different provinces of Italy and it was ever filled with ships plying with Alexandria and Syria.

Rome and India were brought closer together through the Persian Gulf and Red sea. The Red sea is within the nearest distances from the Mediterranean Sea through the Heroopolite gulf. Most of the middlemen mentioned above, were living in this region, side by side of the Red sea and Persian Gulf.[450] All the routes from India and China to Rome converged at the strip of land formed by Asia Minor, Palestine, Arabia and also by Egypt. Usually the merchants from east and west exchanged their products here.

According to Warmington, there were three routes from Puteoli to the Middle East. First it was 'from Brundisium across the Adriatic, along with Egnatia and across to Belhynia or Traos, whence great routes to the Far East could be reached at Sardis, Tarsos, Antioch and other centers.[451] The second route was "from Italy to Ephesos by the way of Corinth and Athens or round the Peloponnese to Asia Minor and Syria – a route used in Summer by the sightseers and traders with Greece." The third one was the direct route" from Rome to Puteoli to Alexandria' the center of transshipment of Indian wares from the Red Sea and even from Antioch. This route was specially used from May to September.[452]

In our enquiry of trade routes to Egypt, we will find the hinterland of Alexandria. The city of Alexandria was founded at the mouth of river of Nile by Ptolemy Philadelphos to serve the Egyptian merchants who had already established an indirect trade with India. About this harbour, Strabo gives a very good comment. According to him. "As far the great harbour, in addition to its being beautifully enclosed both by embankment and by nature, it is not only so deep close to the shore that the largest ship can be moored at the steps but also is cut up into several harbours."[453]

One merchant who starts his journey from Alexandria to India, he usually goes through two different routes. One route was passing by the Red sea and the other route was avoiding this route as far as practicable. The Red Sea with its treacherous Hiroopolite gulf proved very dangerous to storms and pirates. Hence the merchants preferred the route by Nile. They navigated in this river southwards for about 11 days in fair weather upto the horseshoe bend of the river. Two main important stations on the bank of Nile were Canepolis (Kenah) and Coptos (Keft), from which the roads struck out towards the Red Sea. One road connected Canepolis with Myos Harmos and another Coptos with Bernice. But according to Strabo,[454] "Myos Harmos was more important as a naval station" but Pliny[455] mentioned that this was "deep inland on the recess of the gulf' with its better landing places proved to be far superior. Both the ports were simultaneously used; Bernice as a center of unloading and Myos Hormos as a good natural harbour for vessels, filled with trees and guinea fowls.

There was a network of roads across the desert between the Nile and the Red Sea. The Canepolis-Myos Hormous route branched off at Aras towards Philoteras on the Red Sea just south of Myos Hormos. Another route branched off from the Coptos-Bernice road at Phoenician leading to Leucos Limen, standing further south of Philoteras. Besides these a track from Rhodesiya on the Nile joined the Coptos- Bernice road at Phoenician and another from Ombos was found joining that route at Apollonos (Wadi Gemal). Nubia south of Egypt was beyond the Roman influence with Meroe as its important centre from which also another route ran towards Ptolemais, standing further south of Bernice.[456]

The routes were well maintained and the Romans kept them intact. The Romans left them unpaved for camels and maintained the Ptolemaic division of the main roads into stages with fortified supply stations cisterns and armed guards. The roads were well equipped with large caravansaries and hotels for travelers. According to Periplus, Mussel harbour and Bernice were harbours of Egypt. But the Ptolemais had no harbour and was reached by only small boats and below it was Adults a port established by law.

The choice of routes was mainly depending on one's taste and proximity of one's habitation. The sea route was more risky due to bad weathers and the fear of pirates. Ptolemy-II first cleared the deep Canals and added locks to prevent flooding from the Fed Sea and founded Arsinoe or cleopatris. Augustus repaired it afresh. But the south wind and shoals were much distressing to the travelers.[457] Pliny[458] notes that the three land routes from the Egyptian sea-one from Pelusium across the sands following the line of reeds, the second route beginning two miles beyond Mt. Cassias and after 60 miles, rejoined the roads of Pelusium; and the third one starting from Gerrum, called the Agipsum route; all those routes led to Arsinoe. The sea route from Arsinoe to the strait of Babel Mandeb was again connected with sidetracks upto Aela and Leuce come on the east coast. A road joined Aela and Petra and that route through Petra passed to Persian Gulf.

The Roman merchants usually preferred the Red Sea route instead of land routes to India. One of the major reason of this was the main rivals of Roman merchants who were staying in the midway of the land route and the Scythians also had settled throughout the Central Asia Again the land routes were time taking due to its enormous length and expensive also. Hence Augustus looks all steps to make the Red Sea Journey more convenient and profitable. He made all sorts of arrangements for collection of taxes.

The people of Arabs took the advantage in the commerce mainly due to their geographical position. The Arabs mainly supplied the Indian goods to Egyptians who in turn supplied it to Romans.[459] The Sabeans and the Gerraheans of the Persian Gulf prospered as traders and the chief intermediaries for a long time between the east and west. They used both the sea route and land route for commercial purposes. Strabo following Artemidorous, notes that "the masses of the country of the Sabaeans traffic in aromatic...From their trafficking both the Sabaeons and the Gerrhaeans have become the richest of all; they have a vast equipment of gold and silver articles viz., couches, bowls etc. and costly houses."[460] They kept the Indians away from the Red sea and kept secret from the Greeks about the use of monsoons. The Arabs of Suez and the North- Western part of Arabia who served as an intermediary between the India and Rome and exerted a great influence down the Red Sea coast upto the Leucecome and also upto the Euphrates along the borders of Syria and Arabia. But the Nabateans occupies the most enviable position and could easily prosper by bitumen trade with the Egyptian, by the Caravans trade with the Persian Gulf. According to Rostovzeff, the Nabateans adopted the measures to safeguard the caravan routes to Babylonia. He says that "the native Arabs, reinforced by the Nabatanen colonies protected the Caravans and secured their water supply" as evidenced by a Nabatean inscription, found between Dumatha and Forat.[461] It was the centre of many routes, the first leading to Leuce Come via-Aela, receiving the wares to be diverted to Rhinocula of Egypt and to Gaza on the Mediterranean sea; the second connecting it with Bostra, Damascus, Palmyra and other important centres of Syria and the third one leading across Sinai to Arsinoe; besides the greater road from Petra to Gerrah and through the Northern deserts to Farath and Charax. Roads ran also from Petra to South Arabia, one via-Leuce to Arabia Eudemen and to Hadramaut by coastline. Both Indian and Chinese goods were carried through these routes.

Pliny[462] gives an interesting fact about the different stages of routes connecting Arabia with India. In the first two stages, Pliny shows, the shipping along the coast of Arabia, Persia and Carmania with Barbaricrem and Patala as the terminus. Barygaza and Sigerus rose to importance in the period of 3rd stage i.e. beginning about 70-50 B.C., according to Tarn, when the direct voyage between the Arabian coast and the Barygaza, cutting out

Demetrius-Patala was introduced.[463] In the period of 4th stage ie; after C. 50 B.c. and in the first two centuries of the Christian era, ships went straight from Arabia Eudemen to Muziris and Nelcynda, ports of South India exchanging Roman coins for pepper and aromatics.[464]

A narrative of Pliny may be quoted here:

"There (at Susa) after months" voyaging they (Onesi, Critus and Nearchus) from Alexander, celebrating a festival; it was 7 months since he had left them at Patala. Such was the route follwed by the fleet of Alexander; but subsequently it was thought that the safest line is to start from Ras Fartak in Arabia with a west wind (Hippalus) and make for Patala, the distance being reckoned as 1,332 miles. The following period considered it a shorter and safer route to start from the same cape and steer for the Indian harbour of Sigerus (Jaigarh) and for a longtime this was the course followed, until a merchant discovered a shorter route and the desire for gain brought India nearer; indeed the voyage is made every year with the companies of archers on board because these seas used to be greatly infested with pirates."[465]

If we trace the routes which were connecting India and Iran; then we will find two main routes. One road which started from Babylon and Susa and another started from Ecbatana and met at Persepolis. From Rhagae, the road was diverted to a side track, south-east ward to Carmana. Gulaskird was the junction of the two routes, from Persepolis and from Carmana and from this place ran the main Persian road towards the Indus. From Persepolis ran another road through Carmana and Phra to Alexandropolis and Kabul, probably used by the Romans.[466] Alexander's return from the Indus through the Makran route proved disastrous and hence it earned an ill reputation. People preferred the coasting voyage to the Makran route. The merchants took to main silk route upto Merv and then to the Herat Kandahar route to India.

The Himalayas never obstructed the journey of merchants from east to west and vice-versa. Here were so many important passes used by the merchants and travelers from all ages. The

Khawak links Badakshan with Kabul, across the Hindukush range, the Irak pass links Balkh with Kabul across the Kohibala range and the Khyber; Kurram, Tochi, Gomal passes connect Afghanistan with India. Khyber Pass was the major traffic axis since the establishment of Peshawar as the metropolis in 2nd C.A.D.[467]

There were several routes, which were connecting India and the Caspian region via, Bactra. There was a route from Marchanda or from Bactria which crossed the Oxus and ran towards the Caspian sea and then either crossing or rounding it, proceeded to the Euxine sea and the Mediterranean Sea. According to Strabo "the river Oxus was so easily navigable that the Indian merchandise, packed over the mountains to it is easily brought down to the Hyrcanian sea and thence, on the rivers, to the successive regions beyond as far as Pontus".[468] He also says, "the upper Aorsi ruled over most of the Caspian coast and consequently they could import on Camels, the Indian and Babylonian merchandise, receiving it in their turn from the Armenians and Medes and also owing to their wealth, could wear golden ornaments."[469] It indicates that there was a large flow of merchandise from India or Babylonian region to the Caspian region. Pliny also points out this route of Commerce down to the Oxus and across the Caspian to the Cyros and says that the Indian goods were conveyed to Phasis in Colchis by this route.[470] But Strabo[471] speaks of the bad conditions of navigation is the Caspian Sea and also of the wild people of the Caspian area. Pliny also supports this view of Strabo. He hints at the dangers of navigation of the Caspian Sea, where the Indians were once victim to the storms and as a result the ship wrecked.[472] Most probably, some of the Indians became fugitive and came through Parthia and planted Colonies in Armenia between 130 B.C. and 300 A.D. The area of uncultured and wild tribes was almost free from the foreign yoke. The region including Bokhara, Khiva and Turkestan proper was always infested with robbers and inhabited by wild tribes known as Scythae. The Indians, Bactrians, Parthians and Scythians served as a middlemen upto the Caspian Sea. They landed over the goods to the Armenians and Caspian tribes, via, the Albanians, the Iberians, the Colchians. Wares also sent up the Araxes to Artaxata in Armenia and then distributed to all parts of Asia Minor. There was another land route passing along the north west coast of the Caspian Sea upto the north east of the Euxine, where the Siraces passed the goods from the hands of Aorsi over to the Greek cities.[473]

In Hellenistic Roman times, there were several trade routes connecting the Mediterranean world with the lands to the east.[474] The Northern Silk route led to China[475] and there were routes which combined maritime with overland caravan tracks: for example via: Petra-Capital of Arab kingdom of Nabatea[476] and Via-Palmyra, the Arab trading station in Syria. There were also routes, which connected Ptolemaic, Nabatean and Roman ports at the northern end Red Sea with maritime empire elsewhere in the Red Sea and Indian Ocean.[477]

The silk route ran from China to Mediterranean passing through India of the Kushanas and the Sassanian territory who played an important role in the trade of Asia Sassanians took the profit by controlling this trade route. Contact between the Mediterranean, Iran, India and China led to the repeated exchange of ideas, techniques and decorative motifs.[478] From Loyang, the eastern terminus of Silk road, the road went to Sepeucia or Ctesiphon from where it forked on outside the Antioch and on other to Petra via Persian Gulf. But the Chinese chronicles points out that a route proceeds to Seleucia from south regions of Petra. This of course does not exclude the route of Antioch.[479] The true western terminus of Silk Road was Seleucia where the western silk merchants had their head quarters.

The Silk route roughly covered an area of approximately four thousand three hundred and fifty miles from its eastern terminus to Seleucia. From Seleucia it went to Lopnor and the other toward the Bay of Bengal passing through Sikkim but the main road moving from Lopnor ultimately reached Kashgar. Moving further west, the branch of road could reach Bactra or Balkh also as it was considered as one of the main trading centre. Silk route connected China with India, central Aśia, Parthia and Rome. It bifurcated itself from the main to Ujjain in central India and from there it joined the ancient international port of Barygaza on western coast.[480]

The Silk Road was secured and existed for a long time due to the foundations of four powerful and prosperous empires during the opening centuries. The Kushanas acted as intermediary between the Roman and Chinese empires. The rivalry took place among the empires to get the control over road, which provided them immense economic benefits. Probably Kushanas had a good understanding with Chinese rulers. Therefore, Panchao had sent an embassy to Rome who passed through Kushana Empire. The Kushana Empire also advanced economic interest due to its advantageous position on the Silk route.

These were the routes, which were largely used by the traders for trade between India and western Asia; especially to Caspian region.

About the Indo-Babylonian roads, Strabo gives a detailed account. Strabo has observed that a road from Babylonia at Susa by Persepolis to the middle of Kerman (Carmania).[481] This road never carries to Seistan and probably therefore most of the caravan trade from India by southern route through Seistan did not, in Hellenistic times, go overland to Babylonia by Perspepolis but came to the sea at the Gulf of Ormuz again as in the middle ages.[482] Form this statement it would appear that the Upper Aorsi, tribes transported on camels, namely by roads alone, the commodities of India and Babylonia, after receiving them from the Armenians and the Medes or the Persians. This journey was not entirely on the load routes; sometimes they were crossing the rivers. Strabo elaborates the actual road through which the traders passed from India towards westward destinations. "The road" he notes "for merchants from Syria to Seleucia and Babylon lies through the country of the Arabian Scenitae, now called Malli[483] (Probably an interpolation) and through the desert belonging to their country. After crossing the river (Euphrates) the road lies through the desert country on the borders of Babylonia to Scenae, a considerable city, situated on the banks of canals.

From Strabo's account we may infer that there certainly existed a road from Caspian gates to Alexandria in heart. It coursed through Bactria, over the mountain passes to Ortospana (Bal Hissar of Kabul) down southwards, reached Propthasia (Farah) until it came to the borders of India and the banks of Indus. This statement of Strabo not necessarily indicates that the Indian merchants had no share in this trade excepting Persian and Syrian traders.

The Persian High way, which was the greatest advantage for the traders of Persia, was undoubtedly helpful to the merchants of India also. It was not only promoting the commerce between the west and East but also transporting vast quantity of military equipments of Persian Empire. This road was presumed to represent the Upper road from Sardir to the Valley of Tigris and to converge in a great measure into one of the great lines of the Roman Road.[484] From a commercial angle it can be viewed that this Persian Highway was the main routes through which Indian Merchants were carrying their goods to the Persian empire.

Sea Routes

The merchants were also using the sea routes though the pirates endangered these routes. Again the unruly behaviour of monsoon increased the losses of wealth and manpower of the merchants. The merchants preferred this route still because the cost of transport was comparatively less than the land routes. Usually in the months of Asadha (June-July) to Karttika[485] (September),.the merchants were starting their journey when the Monsoon was favourable to them. These merchants were taking the help of some trained birds to discover the lands in the near-by-regions. About the time of journey, Periplus furnishes a good account. The periplus tells us that the voyages were undertaken from Egypt to North-Africa port towns and thence to India " about the month of July".[486] The voyage was made by stages, as they had to depend on the winds chiefly. It relates, how the merchants in their ships from Opone came to Muza (Mochha) by stages and the voyage to that place was made "about the month of September, but there is nothing to prevent it from being earlier".[487] So there is no doubt that the voyages from Egypt to India were made in the first century A.D. only in or about the month of July. The very basic reason for setting out from Egypt in July was to take the advantage of the Etesian South-West winds. The periplus explains it thus, " For at the same time when us with the Etesian winds are blowing on the shores of India, the wind set in from the ocean and the South- West wind is called Hippalus, in the name of him who discovered the passage across"[488] Although the observation of Hipplaus might have been a discovery to the west in general, it was certainly known very well in India, centuries earlier or else, there could hardly have been any voyage or trade between India or west during this periods or prior to this.[489] Pliny also furnishes the same account of Periplus.

About the return journey we may calculate the time taken by a ship to reach Mluziris from Ocelis as 40 days and if the ship left Egypt or the port of Alexandria in or about the month of July then, at the end of the month they must have arrived at Ocelis and at the end of the August or the first week of September reached Muziris.[490] In all probability, the ships must have weighed anchor at Muziris for the whole month of September and then set to sail. The Periplus vaguely relates " reasonably they put to sea about the month of September".[491]

But Pliny who predicts the time of return was December did not corroborate this fact. Therefore, both the account, on the matter of return journey, was not sure and they probably gave this idea on the basis of hearsay. The gradual emergence of Red Seas as the main artery of Roman maritime trade to the east dislodged the pre-eminence of the Arab Persian Gulf.[492] The Red Sea Route avoided the hostile Parthians closer to the Persian Gulf, required negotiations with t6he more malleable Arab traders and brought the west coast of India into quicker contact. In order to protect themselves, the traders took the help of board of archers in the Gulf Sea Routs.[493] Cargo arriving at the port of Red Sea was transported overland to coptos and from there taken down the Nile to Alexanria. Such transportation was familiar to the Egyptian administration and economy since grain had been regularly transported down the Nile from the Upper Egypt to Alexandria under Ptolemies.[494] The small-scale canal transportation was in Egyptian hands but the Greeks from Alexandria controlled the large-scale grain business on the Nile.[495] The Laventines also participated in this trade.[496]

About the sea-borne trade between India and Egypt, Strato[497] informs us that Egypt under the Ptolemies had not developed a sea –borne trade with Indians, whereas Periplus[498] states that the Egyptian ships came only as far as Arabia Eudaemon (Aden) because in the early days of the city when the voyage was not yet made from India to Egypt and when they did not dare to sail from Egypt to the ports across the ocean, but all came together at this place. It received the cargoes from both countries as Alexandria now receives (77A.D.) both from Egypt and abroad.[499] But the Romans faced many hazards on the land routes to India for which they were compelled to open the sea routes instead of many difficulties. They persevered hard for this purpose and employed all resources and energy at their command.[500]

About depicting the physical features of Egypt, Herodotus[501] gives a detailed account from which one could trace out the possibilities of sea-route between Indian and Egypt. In Arabia, he observed, not far from Egypt, there was a very long and narrow gulf running up from the Indian Ocean. According to Diadorus,[502] a canal which was actually excavated during 285-245 B.C. connecting the region of Nile with Arabian gulf, had mainly facilitated the Indo-Egyptian trade. The ports like Captos, Myos Harmos, Arsinoe is 247 B.C. mainly helped to further the bilateral trade. From this date it may be said the commencement of regular trade between India and Egypt appeared and all vessels sailing from the Indian ports on the eastern and western coasts, sailed first into the Red Sea from the Indian Ocean until they reached the great international port of Alexandria which was practically the clearing house of commerce between the East and West.

Herodotus,[503] about Indo-Phoenician trade, makes a clear-cut mention. Referring to Arabia, which he called the last portion of inhabited lands towards the south and was the only country, which produced frankincense myrrh, cassia, cinnamon and laudanum, noted that Arabs were not getting any of these expecting myrrh without trouble. He again points out that the Greek's procured frankincense from the Phoenicians who were not only familiar with the sea- route from the Indian ocean via the Persian Gulf but also with the route to the Mediterranean and thence to Hallas. The Phoenicians were well acquainted with the route from the Indian Ocean, from the Persian Gulf or the Red Sea into the Mediterranean.[504]

In the age of Augustus, the Roman merchants from Seleucia reached at Ctrsiphon, then passing Assynia and Kurdistan, they reached at media. From there, reaching at Behistan, they took up the route of Caspian Sea near Teheran. From here the route passing Haectompylos, near Jirm approached Teheran.[505]

Myos Harmos was an important station of trade and commerce activities after Alexandria. From Myos Hromos camels took the goods to Coptos[506], which was another important centre. Coptos is situated on the right bank of river Nile and its modern name is Keft. From Coptos the goods were carried down to the Nile and then to Alexandria, the biggest and most important port of Egypt.

It is generally observed that many Arabain and Egyptian ships were entering into Indian Ocean but there is little evidence of Indian ships docking in the northern ports of Red sea and this may have been partly because Indian ships were not permitted beyond Ocelis.[507] The Sabaeans in South-East Arabia are said to have acted as middlemen between India and Mediterranean world, prior to the development of Roman trade.[508] Perhaps the coral reef made it dangerous to travel the long distance and to handle the situations for Indian traders.[509] The Periplus, traders, manual probably dating to the mid first ˬentury A.D. states that Aden declined as a port after Plolemaic times and this doubtless coincided with the growth of Red Sea ports such as Berenice,

Myos Hormus and Leucos Limen.[510] Strabo refers to a fleet of a hundred and twenty ships sailing from Myos Horamos to India.[511] But the Indian traders were not allowed to move freely in the Red Sea because the initiative of Indian trade was going into the hands of Egyptians hands. Ostracon inscriptions in Prakrit at Quseir and some Tamil sources point out the names of Indian merchants.[512] A much discussed Greek inscription found closer to Nile refers to an Indian, Sopho, (probably Sobhanu) who addresses prayer to the God Pan and was evidently Hellenised Indian.[513]

These were the sea routes, which were mainly connecting India and Western World. Both land routes and sea routes were fraught with dangers of pirates, attack from marauding tribes, unhealthy monsoons. The sea routes were constantly blocked by different rulers inorder to derive maximum profit out of this trade. During the days of Augustus, the Yemenities, the Nabataeans, Himyars had their share in Indian trade and therefore they greatly opposed the direct trade between Rome and India.[514] On the Somali seacoast, during this age, the Arab Africans had led the foundation of Axumite Kingdom. Perhaps they prohibited the Indians to proceed beyond the Ocelis in the strait of Bab-el-mandeb. These Axumites preferred to meet the Alexandrian Greeks at Adulis though there was a trade route between the Abyssinia and Alexandria.[515] Sometimes the traders or ship crews who spent sometime in India in suggested by a few votive inscriptions of Yavanas in western part of India and Deccan. These inscribed in Western part of India and Deccan. These inscribed in locally used languages like Prakrit. These occur in four major rock cut Buddhist monasteries known to have functioned as points along more frequented trade routes.[516] The Yavanas mention their names and places from where they come and these are places generally associated with Deccan. The frequently mentioned being Dhenukakata that is another inscription is specifically described Vaniya-gama, a community of traders.[517]

The ultimate success of the Roman trade lies with the ruin of Arab merchants. Certain other factors helped the Roman ambitions also. The new kingdom of Auxum secured the Roman alliance and trading ports of Guardafui were now free because of the quarrels of the over lands. Previously the were unrder active control of the Arabs.[518]

Transport and Communication

Means of transport and communication, being an important auxiliary to trade, have always been the backbone of trade and commerce. In ancient period the people were mainly dependent on chariots, carts and ships to carry their goods for long distance. The beasts of burden have been used as an important means of transporting goods and passengers since the earliest phase of human civilization. Beasts were employed for transporting goods of short distance and also at places where the easy approach of vehicles was not possible. Animals like horses, elephants, bullocks; Donkeys were proved to be of great use. But mainly they were used in war to carry the war materials. Patanjali refers that the bullocks, camels, horses and elephants were independently called the beasts of burden. But, at times, they pulled the vehicles, which were called Vahya or Vahana.[519] Manu refers to beasts of burden, which included the horses, elephants, donkey and camel.[520] According to his reference, it appears that the beasts of burden were properly trained and marks were endowed on them as a token of such training.[521] Kautilya in his Arthasastra also mentions about this.

The cart was the mode of transportation from the time of Indus valley.[522] Oxen mainly drew these carts.[523] The process of transportation by carts was very slow and tedious. The Lalitavistara speaks of two oxen, Syjata and Kirti, which carried the goods of two merchants.[524] We have also archaeological evidence to prove the use of carts in 1st C.B.C. Excavations at Bhita under Marshall, have yielded to the spade a number of antiquities, found on the floor level of the house, which is supposed to have been the house of Guild in 1st C.B.C. The most noteworthy of the finds are two wheels of a terracotta toycart.[525] Many other remnants of the similar carts and their riders were found in the buildings of the site. About the use of carts in the post Mauryan period evidence are found largely from the Jatakas.[526]

According to Patanjali, carts used on land were called Sakatas[527], which carried goods as well as passengers.[528] These sakatas were named after the kinds of goods or types of passengers they carried. Sakata was the name of large carts while the small carts were called as Sakati.[529] The merchants who were traveling for foreign lands were moving with large number of carts and beasts of burden.

Fortunately, for us, the art forms of 2nd century B.C., to second century A.D. present some examples of ancient Indian carts. Their representations are very useful for the structural study of the carts. The bas-relief of Jetavana monastry depicted in Barhut Sculptures shows cart.[530] Being unloaded by the men of Anathapindika. This cart was very simple in structure because it was a loading cart. It was a cart of two *isadandas* with probably a wooden floor. Both the isadandas join the yoke *(yuga)* and are tied. The wheel is not so solid and has sixteen spokes *(ara)*. Accordingly, one Amaravati sculpture in the British museum, which depicts the merchants Trapusa and Bhalla, who adore Buddha, shows their bullock cart. The same merchant passing through Uruvela is shown on the bottom panel of the southern gateway of Sanchi. Two bulls are shown, one with its tail coming on the body. A covering was spread on the poles, which raised on the sides of carts. The spoked wheel is shown, the number of spokes being 24.[531] Another scene at sculpture representing a scene from Vasantrara Jatak, shows a cart drawn by a pair of bullocks. At Goli, the same type of cart appears to see. Another Amaravati sculpture carved on a small frieze shows a similar cart but the wheels are solid.[532] At Nagarjunakonda, both solid and spoked wheels are represented. The body of the cart is covered with openings at back and front. But an interesting picture is presenting in the sculpture at Barahuta.[533] The scene depicting the caravan merchants in a desert, shows the two bulls in resting posture free from the cart. Yet there is another sculpture representing the scene of the purchase of a royal park from Prince Jeta by Anathapindaka showing a bullock cart and a cartsman lifting the yoke from the neck of animals. Here also the spokes number is sixteen.

Two oxen generally drew these carts.[534] The instances of cow and bulls are also found which were yoked to the carts.[535] But according to Panini, the oxen were suitable to cart. The word prastha was referred to a leader ox that was yoked infront of the cart along with other oxen.[536] Generally, young horses and calves were unfit to be yoken in the cart. Similarly old oxen were regarded as useless to drag a single cart.[537] The oxen were peoperely cared when they set out for a long journey and they were given kindered treatment. In a Gandhara sculpture, two carts men are shown; massaging is of the yoked oxen.[538]

There were several kinds of chariots, which were used for transportation in ancient period. Kautilya provides a very good account about these chariots. According to him, the best chariot was measured 10 purusas (i.e., 120 angulas) in height, 12 purusas in width. After this model, 6 more chariots with decreasing heights by one purusa successively down to a chariot of 6 purusuas in width, were constructed. Such chariots were named as *devaratha* (Chariot of gods) *Pusyaratha* (festal chariots) *Sangramika* (battle chariots), *Pariyanika* (traveling chariot), *Parapurabhiyanika* (chariot used for assailing enemy's stronghold) and vainayikal (training chariot)[539]

The chariot was the most speedy land vehicle of this time carrying goods and passengers.[540] The driver of the chariots was called as Praveta, Sarathi, Suta or Prajita.[541] The chariots were specially dragged on a particular type of road, which was mainly built for these were known as Rathya.[542] Sometimes the chariots had a cloth-canopy over it and the seat of the chariot was covered with the woollen cloth or with the skin.[543]

The chariots were usually named after the names the beast pulling the chariot. Patanjali refers to chariots drawn by horses *(asvaratha),* by camels *(custraratha)* and by asses *(gardabharatha)*.[544] According to Manu, the beasts of burden, engaged in pulling vehicles, should be properly trained, swift, endowed with lucky marks and perfects in colour and form and without being urged much with the good.[545]

In the sculpture of Sanchi, these vehicles can be seen. All the chariots are more or less stereotyped with two spoked wheels, two horses with front and sides closed and opened at the back. The front side is often decorated with pellet borders.[546] The number of spokes of the wheel varies in the sculptures at Sanchi, Barahut, and other places varying from 16 to 32.

The sculpture at Sanchi provides an interesting fact that the tails of two horses were tied to the front of the body. The purpose may be to avoid the contacts with wheels. In Amaravati, a festive chariot is carved with four horses and a charioteer. The representation of the Sun chariots found at Bodhgaya and at Bhaja shows the chariot was drawn by four horses, with two on the either side. It can be summed up that the different people used the various types of chariots for different purposes during this time.

Excepting the carts and chariots to carry a large amount of goods, donkey carried the small amount of goods, bull, ox, camels. The camels were specially used for roads in desert. Manpower was also used to carry the goods.[547] Goli represents a cart drawn by two men (PI-IV, Fig.2). Manpower was so important in transporting the goods that Angavijja has included man *(nara)* as also a type of sajjivajana.[548] On the east gate of Sanchi, we see a man depicted as carrying two loads on his shoulder suspended on a bamboo stick. Load- baskets were hung at the both ends of bamboo like sikya, formed by pending nets on the two ends of a strong pole. Rings of hard material, like wood or metal were provided on each end of a strong pole on which rested the pitcher.[549] Sometimes the heavy loads were carried by two persons with a strong pole on the shoulder, in a basket suspended on the middle.[550]

Water Vehicles

Water vehicles plied both on river and sea. According to Patanjali, the water vehicle was called as *nau.* The person who was incharge of sailing the boat was called as *Navika*. These water vehicles were used for carrying goods as well as passengers.[551]

About water vehicles, *Kautilya* informs us that the *navah* (boat) and *mahanavah* (large boats) were suitable for rivers with ford or without ford. The large vessels were provided with a *Sasaka* (*Captain), Aiyamaka (Steersman)* and servants to hold the sickle and the ropes and to pour out water.[552] Patanjali also furnishes a good account about the water vehicles. He used the terms like Bhastra (skin carrier), Ustanga (possibly dongi of modern days), pitaka (a bamboo carrier) Udupa (small boat) and Utapata (long fishing boats) are referred as the means to cross the rivers. Ghatika was the temporary small boats made up of pots turned down water.[553] Patanjali also informs as regarding caravans *(Sartha)* of the water vehicles. We come across the transactions of goods filled in five such vehicles.[554]

Milinda Panha informs us that a ship was pieced together with timber of all sorts.[555] About a pilot, he informs, as that he was expected test the shore inorder the guide the ship. This work shows acquaintance with ocean- going ships, freighted numerous passengers and provided with masts, anchors, straps, sails and ropes.[556]

According to Periplus, in the gulf of Bharukachcha, there were some pilot boats known as trapanga and cotymba to guide the foreign ships coming to Bharukaccha through the entrance of the river, on which the emporium of Bharukaccha or Barygaza was stood. [557] Trapponga was a large type of fishing boat and cotymba may be the modern Kotia type of boat.[558] The Angavijja also refer to kottimba and tapanga as two types of boats.[559] Periplus again says the sangara was probably made of two such canoes joined together by a deck-plat form admitting of a fair sized deckhouse.[560]

About the construction of boats, the Greek writers, informs us that the ships and boats of India were constructed from the logs of fir, pine, cedar and other types of wood.[561] In this connection, Periplus informs us that the large vessels like sangara and trapanga which carried great bulk of goods and were employed for the voyages to the ports of Ganges and to Chyrese (Malaya Peninsula). These vessels were constructed by fastening together large logs of woods.[562]

On the Eastern coast of Chola Kingdom, there were as many as three types of rafts and ships. Of these one was a very simple construction mode perhaps hollowed logs, with planks sides and out riggers.[563] This was the light boat for coastal traffic.[564] In the Pandyan kingdom, as Pliny informs us, pepper was carried down to Bacare in boats, hollowed out of a single tree.[565] The sangara type of raft was a more complicated structure and would seem to have been used merely for coastal traffic. It has been described as "very large" made of single logs bound together.[566]

From Jaina sources we know that besides nava, which was common types of water transport, there were *agatthiya, antarandakagoliya* (Conoes) Koncaviraga and boats having the shape of an elephant's trunk and leather bags (daiya) and goatskin[567] were also used to float.

There are enough evidences on Indian art and coins to corroborate the facts of literacy sources. A sculpture of Barhut, presents a big boat (PI-VI, Fig. 8) made of strong planks of joined with wooden dowels. This large boat was rowed by big four oars (tow on each side) of which only two are visible.[568] The sculpture engraved on Eastern gate way of Sanchi, represents a river or a sheet of fresh water with a canoe crossing it and carrying three men in the ascetic priestly costume, two propelling and steering, the boat, while another sculpture engraved on the Western Gateway exhibits a piece of water with a large boat floating on it whose prow is formed by a winged gryphon and stern by a fish's fail. The large boat contains pavilion overshadowing a vacant throne, over which a male attendant holds chaatr (umbrella) while another man has a chori, a third man is steering or propelling the vessel with a large paddle.[569] The Amaravati representation of a boat[570] is similar in construction to the boats reproduced at Sanchi and Barhut.

Satavahan rulers of second C.A.D. presented a scene of shipwreck in the caves of Kanheri, which is probably the oldest representation of a sea-voyaage in sculptural forms. But the most curious fact is that the boats and ships of Sanchi, Barhut and Amaravti sculptures don't show the sails and the masts. But the coins of Andra Pradesh show that the ancient Indian ships and big boats had generally two masts.[571] Alexander Rao[572] describes the coins and says that the coins of Yajna Sri bears a two masted ships, testifies the existence of a sea borne trade on the Coromondal coast in the first century of Christian era.

The above references give a good idea about shape size of boats through which the goods were carried in sea and rivers.

Both land routes and sea routes were not free from dangers. Whether Indian, South Arab or other traders came to Mediterranean world or westerners visited Eastern land, the journey was long and ardous and dangerous also. Stroms at sea and pirates could deprive the merchants and travelers of their valuable cargoes and lives.[573] Again overland caravans were slow, expensive and could be attacked by marauding tribes. In order to overcome such difficulties, the traders were sometimes taking proper precautions like knowledge about monsoon, winds, taking sufficient amount of food and water. Archers sailed abroad some of merchant ships as protection against pirates in both Ptolemaic and Roman times.[574] Military units were stationed at some (eg clysma, Abu Shaar, Lukos Limen, Leuke Kome, Berenice)[575] if not all the northern seaports were engaged in this sea trade. There may have been a Roman coast guard to protect the interests of merchants.[576] The Roman army and auxiliary units provided protection to the Caravans in the desert of Egypt. Watch towers were placed on the hills from which soldiers can supervise the attack of robbers.[577] Again Roman govt and military were also responsible for the repair or expansion of these ports or as in the case of Leukos Limen, the initial lay out.[578] But some historians don't accept this theory. According to Casson, in effect the historical records reveal no measures taken by the emperors for the promotion of sea trade and these measures were directed to protect the mines and queries in the sea.[579]

There are some inscriptions and other record from Egypt which provide adequate informations about the Indian merchants in Western lands. Two inscriptions on the Coptos-Berenice road mention that Numidius Eros returned from a trip to India in and CBC.[580] A census list of Arsinoe district mention the names of hellenized Egyptians or Greeks who lived in India because they were g ranted exemption from personal taxes.[581] A relatively recent document in this connection is a contract dated to middle of second century A.D. between a merchant from Muziris and a transporter. The papyrus is written in Greek but is partly damaged and the name of the merchant is lost. These references can be matched with those to Indians in Egypt. Dio-Chrisostom indicates that Indian merchants resided at Alexandria.[582] These are some references which increasingly points out the fact that the Indian traders were directly involved in this trade.

An interesting fact has been unearthed in1985 by Harraeuer and P. Sijpesteinj and published a papyrus, which deals with a loan agreement. The recto and verso who are more or less contemporary, mid century A.D. and both deal with shipment of goods from India. This agreement covers the transport of goods from the point of Red Sea where these goods had been unloaded no doubt in Myos Hormos or Berenice.[583] It also refers about a loan contract between the two parties and the loan in question is a maritime loan that made possible the acquisition of goods. It contains a list of goods to be transported like nard, ivory and textiles all of which prominently figure in the first of export goods from India to Rome. Again it slightly refers about the custom duty, which was to be imposed on the party.[584] But this contract paper has raised a hue and cry among the historians by interpreting the contents of paper in different directions and in different angles. However, L. Casson, finally points out that the agreement was signed to protect the goods against the brigands during the crossing. And again the costly nature of shipment had compelled the creditor to sign the document to get an assurance that his costly goods would reach the destination in good condition.[585] This type of loan contract casts a picture which is much more similar to modern day transactions

Important Trading Centres in India

The extensive trade between India and western countries facilitated to develop many trading centres in coastal area as well as by the sites of the trade routes. These points served as important marts as well as ports. Some of them were Broach Muziris, Kalyana, Sopara, Paithana and Tagara etc. these cities played a prominent role in the growth of inland and foreign trade.

1. **Barygaza:** Barygaza was the most important port, which was probably the first port of international importance.[586] Bharukaccha was the other name of Barygaza. It received the goods not only from the interior and the Narmada River, at the mouth of which it was situated but also from the coastal ports. From Barygaza, the Indian products like ivory, silk, cotton, pepper etc. were exported while wine; glass products and girdles were brought in from western towns to the port.[587] It is found that the western copper exported to Gulf was brought to Barygaza first: on this large market, the traders or sailors could have taken Roman pottery, other western items and Red polished ware also.[588]

   It also acted as a centre of redistribution of western goods. Barygaza was also a manufacturing centre and therefore imported some raw materials as well as commodities such as silver ware, wine and perfume not to mention slave girls and musicians.[589] It is generally presumed that local merchants were handling this type of trade. A bead industry which was present there and the beads were found in large quantities in all stages of manufacture.[590] It is significant that Barygaza had a direct communication route with Ujjaini in Central India which helped the merchants and traders in promoting the cause as well as the course of trade.
2. **Ujjaini:** It was called Ozene by ancient authors. It was situated at the junction of two routes, one the Barygaza-

Kausambi route and other one was coming from the Deccan. Hence Ujjaini gathered up and forwarded the trade between the N.W. India southern India and western India. Schoff says, "Ujjaini was the Greenwich of India. By its location it was trade centre of all produce imported at Barygaza where distribution was made to the Ganges Kingdom".[591]

3. **Muziris:** Due to its geographical location, Muziris gained an international significance. It is in the Malabar district, modern Cranganore. The port, according to Periplus, was situated in the kingdom of Pandya. The Periplus (54) speaks of this port. Muziris also finds place in the writings of Pliny, the naturalist, when he says, "if the wind called Hippalus be blowing, Muziris the nearest mart of India can be reached in forty days".[592] The Tamil poem speaks of the Yavana ships arriving at Indian ports with merchandise and gold, the pepper and cargoes...."[593] Muziris was one place which was well known to the merchants of Rome. According to the Peutingerian Tables (222 AD), the Romans were maintaining a force of two cohorts at Muziris to protect the trade and they had also built a temple for Augustus. But Rawlinson has remarked that, "Muziris was shunned by the travellers on account of bad anchorage and the pirates".[594] It is also found that the foreign merchants also maintained the force to protect their goods against the lootings.[595] This is perhaps indirectly confirmed by Patrripattu which refers to a Chera king Imayavaramban Neduncerelatan punished the yavanas by binding their hands behind them and pouring ghee on their head and walking along.[596]
4. **Soppara:** It was a market town during the opening centuries of Christian era. It was the capital of Konkan. Horse trading was an important trade of this locality.[597] The Periplus (52) takes it as a market town of the region which in the times of elder Saraganus became a lawful market town. The place had an intimate connection with Paithana via Kalyana.
5. **Kalyana:** It was another important town in the ancient India. Its strategic location gives it more importance and therefore it

was called as gateway of India.[598] It is situated on the bank of the river Ulhas, twenty two miles from the open sea. It is mentioned in thirteen inscriptions, eleven of such are found at Kanheri Buddha cave inscription and the remaining two at Junar. The route from Kalyana via the Nana pass is definitely established by an inscription at Kanheri, which links Sopara, Kalyana and Paithan.[599]

According to Periplus (52), the city of Kalyana was both a city and harbour. Cosmos (bk-XI) also refers to this port town and highlights its significance. But Ptolemy[600] has failed to notice this port does not mean that the port has fallen into insignificance by that time. During the early rule of Satavahana, Kalyana grew into an international trading centre. But during Second Century A.D. the importance of Kalyana started to decrease. But from fifth Century A.D. it again regained its lost importance and the Alexandrian merchants Cosmos Indicopleeustes refers to this place. He mentioned it as "a great mart of trade where copper is produced and sesame wood and materials for Press"

6. **Simylla:** The Periplus[601] mentions Symilla as a market twon pearl fishery is located by Pliny[602] at Perumala (Semylla). Now it is a fishing village of no importance, but in former times it was a great center of trade in teak and black-wood for ship building.[603] Rawlinson identifies this port with Bankot.[604]
7. **Dharanikota:** It finds place in Selarbadi inscription and once in a Kanheri Buddha cave inscription.[605] Karle inscription records it for seventeen times and this definitiely shows it was an important trading centre during the period of our study, situated on the delta of river Krishna.[606] This place has yielded the Roman wares during the excavations. Some scholars question the identification of this city either in the western coast or somewhere in the interior, east of Karle. Burgess suggests that it was somewhere in or near western coast.[607]

8. **Paithan:** According to Imperial Gazetteer,[608] Paithan was one of the oldest towns in the Deccan. Recent archaeological discoveries have enabled us in confirming us the accounts of classical literature.[609] It was most excellent and celebrated town mart in Deccan and also one of its oldest cities.[610] According to Periplus (51) Paithan was an important centre of the textile industry. Ptolemy (VII, 1.6) mentions it as the capital of Pulamayi-II, the Andhra King (A.D. 138-170). Schoff has disputed this fact and is of the view that it was probably the capital of western provinces, the seat of Andhra monarchs, having been in the eastern part of the kingdom at modern Dharanikota on Krishna River.[611]

   Fleet[612] draws our attention on an early trade route from the coast, starting from Masulipatanam, passing through Paithan and Ter to Chanore in Nasik and then crossing the Western Ghats to reach Barygaza on the western coast. Hence we may expect that the Paithan carried on smoothly through the parts of both the east and west coasts of India overseas trade with the countries of East and West. The figure of ship found in the coins of Yajna Sri Satakarni testifies to the fact that the king's power extended over the sea and carried on sea trade with the distant countries.[613]

9. **Tagora:** The modern name of Tagora is Ter which is identified by Fleet.[614] It is situated on the western bank of the Terna River in Osmanabad district of Maharastra. Tagara is one of the inland commercial enter ports from which streams of trade flowed to Barygaza in the 1st Century A.D. when Periplus[615] records: "The goods were brought down to Barygaza.... from Tagara, much common sloth, all kinds of muslins and the mallow cloth and the other merchandise brought there locally from the regions along the sea-coast". Cotton industry was the most thriving industry of this period and; Tagara and Pratisthana were the great centres of this trade.[616] Excavations at Ter have yielded many objects of Roman origin which speak of its commercial contacts with the west. It had certainly some links with the Hellenistic

world, a theory supported by the position of Ter in relation to the system of trade routes in ancient India.[617] The flourishing state of Ter was due to its position on a major trade route traversing the peninsula. The goods like common cloth, all kinds of muslins, mallow cloth and other merchandise were exported from the port of Tagora.

10. **Melizigara:** It was a small port and less important than others. At first it was a port of some size but subsequently it was dwindled into a mere fishing village. Muller and Mc. Crindle have identified it with modern Jaigarh. It was the only port on Ratnagiri coast where the Arabians directly traded. Pliny knows it as Sigerus[618] whereas Periplus (53) calls it Melizigara. Vincent Smith[619] identifies this port to the port Jayagadha.
11. **Colchi (Modern Korkiai):** It was the earliest seat of Dravidian power according to Periplus. The Periplus (58) mentions a boat that "a harbour at Comari", and it was important for pilgrimage and pear fisheries. Presently it is in the district of Tuticorin. Korkai is one of the few places of India found in the "Peutingar Tables" in the name of "Coleis Indorum". It was perhaps the chief gateway to South India for Ceylonese colonists Dr. Caldwell who carried out stray excavations in 1877 and he found the factory of manufacturing of shell ornaments such as bangles, rings, beads etc.[620]
12. **Cape Camorin:** It is an important place of Indian trade with Mediterranean region. The Periplus (58) refers to this place in the narratives. Comari which is still the Tamil pronunciation designates the cape of the southern most extremity of India. Schoff, however, points the name in the Tamil form of Sanskrit Komari, a virgin which is applied to the goddess Durga or Parvati.[621] In Southern India it was the most important pilgrimage place.[622] According to Periplus this place was not only celebrated to its sacredness but also as an emporium, importing all the commodities for commercial

purposes. It also absorbed near all varieties of goods brought from Egypt.[623]

13. **Kaveripattanam:** In the Chola empire, it was the most famous port of south India. It is known as Pumpahar in Tamil Sangam literature. Recent excavations at Kaveripattanam had proved beyond doubt that it had the colonies of Roman merchants and warriors.[624] The Indo-Roman trade had undoubtedly influenced the economic, social and cultural life of the people of that region. The "Silapaddikaram" or "the day of the Anklet"[625] bears the testimony of foreign contacts of the region. This epic points out that Pumpahar had the warehouse near the harbour and the Yavana abode also. It provides the valuable information about the foreign trade, crafts, occupations and city life of Tamil people. The early Tamil literature provides very similar reference to the brisk and very flourishing commercial activities of south India with foreign countries.[626] The harbour it is claimed was generally safe for bigger ships. They could enter the harbour without removing cargo or slackening sail and yet be quite stable, steady and safe.[627]
14. **Poduca (Pondicherry):** Poduca or Podouke mentioned in the Periplus and Ptolemy respectively may be identified with modern Pondicherry. It was an important trading centre of Indo-Roman trade on the East coast of south India. The geographical position of Arikamedu (Pondicherry) is consistent with the general indication for Podouke by the Periplus and Ptolemy.[628] Pondicherry is a European corruption of Pandu Chcheri, meaning new town.
15. **Arikamedu:** Before and after the death of Augustus, the merchants living in Arikamedu had regular contact with Roman world. The famous muslin cloth was the most important product of this place. Available evidence at Arikamedu indicates anything but a diminution of trade there after the middle of first century of the Christian era. According to Prof. N. K. Sastri,[629] "the objects found at Arikamedu have a striking resemblance with the objects

discovered at Oceo, a maritime city of Siam, connected by canal to a port once on the littoral of the east coast of the gulf of the Siam". The trading station at Arikamedu flourished between 23 B.C. and 200 A.D. and Oceo commanded a large towards the end of the period.

Recent archaeological excavations at this site have yielded notable materials of Roman origin. These include amphorae, rouletted ware, pottery, Roman lamps and coins and many other things.[630] The universal abundance of Mediterranean amphorae at this site clearly indicates a flourishing trade between India and western world at that time. Wheeler adds,[631] "Among other industries of the town was that of bead-making, gold, semi-precious stones and glass were used and two gems, curved with intaglio designs by Graeco-Roman gem cutters, suggest the presence of Western craftsmen in the region". Numerous sherds of Italian pottery of the 1st C.B.C. and of the 1st C.A.D. amphorae, Roman glass lamp, and Mediterranean wine prove that Arikamedu was a Graeco-Roman colony. The largest number of amphorae sherds has been reported from Arikamedu.[632] Wheeler reported 116 sherds from the excavations and though the twice number of that have been founded in the renewed excavations in 1990-91.[633]

16. **Masalia (Masulipatanam):** It was a great port of Andhra Pradesh region. According to Mc. Crindle, the Sanskrit name of Masulipatanam was Masula, which survives in Machulipatana. Tavernier (I, IX) describes it as the best anchorage in the Bay of Bengal and the only place from which the vessels sailed for foreign countries. At that time Bengal was famous for the cotton products like fine-hand printed fabrics, coarse printed goods. Therefore, Tavernier has opined that the supply (of cotton cloth) was never equal to the demand.
17. **Tamluk (Tamralipti):** Tamralipti was the most notable centre on the East coast because it was one important point from where the trade was carried off with mainly south-Asia.

Through this port, the Chinese silk products were also exported to western world. It was also a great seat of learning. During first and second centuries A.D. Tamralipti seems to have shared with other ports on the Indian coast trade contacts with Roman world, as witnessed by sprinkler and the profuse occurrence of the Rouletted ware, both believed to be originally coming from Rome.[634] From Bamanghatti,[635] in Singhbum district of Bihar, Roman gold coins of Constantine and Gordion have been discovered. It indicates that the region of Bamanghati must have been situated on the trade routes connecting the port of Tamralipti. A road from Tamralipti to Barhut would pass through Bamanghatim Berampur etc. all said to be ancient places to note.

These were some important trade centres in ancient India through which India was carrying its business with the western and Mediterranean countries. The Mediterranean of these places were collecting different goods from the near by regions and exporting these goods to the foreign countries to earn profits. Again the industries which were flourished mainly in the urban areas, producing goods to cater the needs of local people as well as for export purposes also. These places about which the foreign as well as indigenous literary sources give a detailed description in addition to archaeological excavations. But there are some towns which have come to the view of historians mainly due to its archaeological excavations, would be discussed with its findings. This would enable us to form an idea of the intensity of the Indo-Roman trade and its impact on Indian culture. Earlier, scholars like E. H. Warmington, M. P. Charlesworth have laboured hard to unravel the various facets of India's trade with western countries on the basis of literary sources. They could not utilise the archaeological materials as little progress was achieved in this sphere by that time. Recent archaeological excavations have widened the sphere of knowledge.

18. **Baroda:** It is located on the ancient highway connecting Gujarat, Malawa and Rajasthan. It was one of the wealthy centres of commerce during second century A.D. Various interesting things have been excavated from this place. The discovery of Roman bronze handle with the figure of Eros is remarkable.[636] Some of the Red polished ware signals that India had a good trade relation with Mediterranean region. The burnt brick houses and the use of Graeco-Roman wares indicate the prosperous city life of the people.
19. **Akota:** It is located on the bank of the river Viswamitri and four furlongs from the South Baroda. According to Desai, probably it was ancient Ankottaka proper. Many objects of Roman antiquities have been found during the excavations. Though some of the goods were not of Rome, at least the Roman technique of art and architecture is clearly visible on these goods. Fragments of wine containers or amphorae, Arrentine pottery, dishes and bowls have been found form these places.[637] It may be supposed that due to the great demand of Italian wine they were importing the wine in large extent and after the use they were throwing away the wine bottles. It is curious to observe that the fragments of pottery shred don't bear any distinct potters mark like Arikamedu pottery shreds. Therefore it may be conjectured that the indigenous potters followed the technique of Rome.

    One remarkable find deserves our attention in this regard. The find of the handle and several pieces of trefoil mouth of a jug needs our attention, as it is a unique find. Pots with trefoil mouth are common in Greek and Roman ceramics, and bronze. The most notable point in this context is the presence of relief on the handle. It represents a nude boy sitting on a bench, almost like a ploughshare and holding with both hands a rod emerging from the rectangular hole of the bench. Desai has interpreted the relief as Eros (a favourite subject of Hellenistic Roman art) posing as an oarsman on a Roman trireme or the war galley with three sets of rowers. So it may be concluded that Akota was an unimportant centre in the early centuries of Christian era and it had been definitely in touch with Rome.

20. **Broach:** It is situated on the western coast of Gujarat and was the first port of anchor.[638] Unfortunately full scale excavation has not been carried out at the site which makes it impossible to assess the importance in the real sense. The minor excavations done so far have revealed the fragments of Red polished ware in association with bead industries.[639]
21. **Bhokardan:** It was located on the trade route form Ujjaini to Paithan. It gained its importance due to its economic and artistic activities. The excavations have revealed the fragments of red polished ware, Amphorae and Megraon ware. It has also yielded rotary querns of the type recovered at Nevasa and assigned there to Indo-Roman period. The recovery of amphorae shreds is a definite indication of the demand of the Italian wine and olive oil, which was highly demanded by the Indian people. Amongst the other things, the Graeco-Roman coins, a beautiful ivory statue of a female and a bead industry also which established the Indo-Roman contacts in the first century of Christian era.[640] Fifty two sherds of Roman Polished ware have also been discovered at Bhokradan and one noteworthy feature of this ware is the occurrence of a decorated small pot which is an initiation of the Magarian ware.[641]
22. **Brahmapuri:** It is situated near modern town Kolhapur on the banks of river Panchajanya. It had certainly experienced the taste of foreign trade with western world which is clearly evident from the archaeological excavations. Several shreds, two complete vessels, imported pottery, shapes of certain glass beads and a number of foreign antiquities having Roman influence have been found at Kolhapur which shows a distinct trend of cultural migration.[642] Several clay copies of Roman coins have been excavated in addition to metal vessels like Arikamedu and Nasik.[643] It was remarkable to note that the fragments of handles of amphorae have also been detected from the Brahmapuri site by Sankalia when he revisited this

place after reviewing the report of Rawlinson.[644] The discoveries of a unique bronze Graeco-Roman statuette of Poseidon,[645] trephoil shaped bronze vessel and possibly the chariot, the spouted bronze jug and their imitations in five clay red vessels and shapes of certain glass beads bear evidence of cultural migrations.

23. **Dharanikota:** It is found in right bank of river Krishna. The excavation of this city has yielded Roman glass bangles of varying shapes, fragments of Arrentine ware, rouletted ware, amphorae etc.[646] This site is the second of its kind located on the eastern coast of India, the other being Arikamedu where structural relics of the types of wharfs (loading or unloading of vessels) and warehouses were also identified.
24. **Dwaraka:** It is surrounded by the Gomati creek on the south and by the sea on the west. It shows its natural surroundings with the region in which it is situated, Okhamandala in Gujarat. This place is associated with Krishna mythology. The prominence of Dwaraka in ancient times is due to the commercial contacts with the outside world like Red Polished wave, amphorae and typical italic ware have been excavated.[647] The shreds of Red polished ware of Dwaraka are made from very well levigated clay fired to a high temperature and oxidized completely.[648] It is believed that this ware was imported from this Roman world but no direct evidence is available as their shapes are obscure in Italy or Rome's African or Asian colonies. Dwaraka's amphorae is thick, gritty and compact in appearance and has a coarse surface. The shreds also contain resin mixture and it may well be supposed that all Indian amphorae were wine amphorae.
25. **Maheswar and Navadatoli:** Mahesawar is located on the Northern bank of river Narmada and Navadatoli is on its southern bank. The Red Polished ware excavated from this area bears a close resemblance to the Roman Samian ware and other red wares of Eastern Mediterranean area.[649] It is expected that the Roman ware instead of being imported, it was copied by the Indian craftsmen for the commercial

purpose. A large number of beads of semi-precious stones have also been found.[650] Possible Roman influence or contact is further supported by the discovery of the trowel[651] like object with a long handle form Maheswar. The earliest recorded trowel comes from the Roman levels at Troy.[652]

26. **Nevasa:** It is situated on the river Pravar, a major tributary of the Godavari. Nevasa though far in the interior, imported the Mediterranean wine in amphorae. A copper or bronze dish with an amphalos and a rotary quern confirm its affinities with extra Indian types from the Western Europe.[653] The most important feature of Nevasa was the gradual disappearance of the local ware and the emergence of the important Mediterranean wares which supporting, in turn, the theory of its link with imperial Rome.[654] Approximately three hundred shreds of Red Polished ware and a few Magrarian sherds have also been found along with the scores of pieces of glass slags and incomplete bangle pieces.[655] Two specimens of the finest, polished and transparent blue Roman glass confirm the Western contact of Nevasa with Roman region in the opening century. Six pots of copper are a brilliant recovery from this place. One of them with amphalos base has a parallel at Taxila. Marshal is of the view, "The origin can be traced to the Phiale Mesophalos,[656] of the Greek and Roman" Patera Clipeate.[657] These things clearly indicate the presence of Indo-Roman trade in the first centuries of Christian era.

27. **Nasik and Jorwe:** Nasik is located on both the banks of the river Godavari. Panini, Patanjali and Katyana refer about it. Inscriptional evidences not only throw lights on its antiquity but also depict its political, administrative, religious and economic conditions between 200 B.C. to 300 A.D. According to the excavations, period-III (A.D. 50-200) at Nasik was the most flourishing and prosperous phase and it witnessed the brick commercial activities with Roman world for sherds of Samian ware, bowls of Red polished ware and sprinklers have been found.[658]

28. **Prabhas Patna:** It is geographically situated in the Junagarh district and occupied a minor place in the history of economic activities of India with the Mediterranean world during the opening centuries of Christian era. Excavations[659] have revealed the sequence of cultural and habitations covering different periods. During the period of 100B.C- 600 A.D. this place saw an aura of Roman trade since several sherds, of course fragmentary, have been discovered which are definitions of Italian origin. One fragment of typical Roman amphorae is available to us along with some sherds of Red Polished ware to prove that it had a commercial link with the Roman Empire.
29. **Uraiyur:** It is found in Tiruchirapalli district and was actively connected with the economic intercourse of India with Imperial Rome. Due to its geographical position it played an important role in this trade. Certain sherds of foreign ware along with native ware were excavated from this site.[660] Rouletted and Arrentine wares have been unearthed from here. It is remarkable to note that some sherds of pot have been discovered containing Tamil inscriptions in the Brahmi script which is safely assigned to the first- second century A.D. During the early centuries of Christian era, the Tamil merchants seem to have acted as middlemen for Sri Lakan articles exported to the West and hence they faced the competition from indigenous (Sri Lanka) I lam Merchants.[661]
30. **Yeleswaram:** It is situated on the bank of the river Krishna of Nalganda district. It was perhaps a flourishing town at the time of Iksavakus. The place has yielded sherds of Red Polished sprinklers recovered from this site were made of well levigated clay and were probably a Samian ware or its imitation.[662] Red polished ware of Roman texture and fabric directly imported from the Mediterranean region is also available to us for analysis. "One Roman jar painted with black band at the junction or neck with a tapering body has also been discovered."

31. **Kolhapur:** In Kolhapur two large metal pots of Satavahan period have been found. In addition to these, smaller bronze vessels, statuettes lamps, mirror stands were also available there.[663] Most of the smaller objects were of Indian origin although some way show the influence of Graeco-Roman art.[664] However, at least ten of them were of Roman imports. Among the best-known Kolhapur bronze statuette, the statue of Poseidon is famous. The bronze vessels of Kohlapur have been assigned to a range of dates in Julio Claduian and Flavian periods (27 BC-98AD).[665] It is believed that most of the Kolhapur bronze products were prepared by companion of bronze workers. The Mediterranean bronzes have been found at Begram, Taxila, Ai Khoneum are most likely the evidence of overland trade rather than products of sea commerce.[666]

The above-mentioned excavations establish the fact that there was a flourishing trade between India and Rome in the early centuries of Christian era. The potteries, which were excavated at different places, point out that there were two types of potteries. One type of pottery which was directly imported from Rome with wine and olive oil; and the other one was prepared by the Indian craftsmen in imitation of the former. Wherever the Roman merchants settled or travelled in course of trade, they probably threw away the used pottery which has been discovered in course of the excavations. The find spots of Roman pot sherds from different Indian sites clearly indicate the intensity of the Roman trade and the large area covered by Roman merchants in course of their travels in India.

In the last half of Third Century, there was an increase of discovery artefacts in India. Some were of Roman origin, or of Mediterranean origin or some Indian imitations of these products. Excavations at sites of Arikamedu, Alagankulam, Kadumanal, Karur, Ter, Bhokardan, to name a few, not only register such artifacts but also bring into purviews both local circuits of exchange as well as the possible relationship of existing population to new traders.[667] Recent excavations at Arikamedu suggested that the Yavana presence dated to first century B.C.

although megalithic occupation of these sites goes further back in time.[668] Alaganakulam is located opposite to Sri Lankan Mantota on the island, some graffiti from this site being read as Sinhala, Prakrit.[669]

Here we may also refer to the other parts and market centres of the Mediterranean region which played a very vital active note in India's commercial relations with Roman world.

Adulius was an important distributing centre for semi-manufactured goods between India in one hand and Syria, Egypt on the other hand. It corresponds to the modern Zula near Massawa. As an emporium it is mentioned in Periplus possible due to its shallow harbours it gained importance. It is remarkable that Indian iron as well as muslin, cotton and other textiles, fabrics and gum were imported to this port although indirectly from Arabia.[670]

Alexandria was the chief port of Egypt for Indian commerce and trade. Before the emergence of Constantinople, the city of Alexandria was the main port of Roman Empire. It is remarkable to note that the ships from Alexandria went directly to West for articles of Egyptian grains in exchange.[671] Mainly the goods form India flooded the markets of Alexandria because the Indian goods were carried by the Indian traders to Alexandria and after that the goods were mainly carried by the Arabians, Phoenicians, Roman traders to the different parts of Rome and West Asia.[672] It was directly linked with the Roman post of Ostia.

Leukekome was an important centre in the Egyptian region and occupied a significant place in the Western trade of India and Egypt. It was the southern most emporium and port of the Nabotaeans whose caravans travelled constantly from this place to Petra.[673] It is situated on the route from Aden to Mediterranean. The Periplus (19) refers to it as a white village, from which there is a road to Petra, which is a subject of Malichas, the king of Nabotaeans.

It was probably founded on the site of earlier Milesian colony of Ampelone. Leuke Koime started to function in 1st CBC. But it is difficult to know whether it was under the occupations of Romans or Nabateans.[674]

Ophir is the most well known potential Indian name of place which is found in Bible.[675] The Bible identifies Ophir particularly with the export of gold. (II chronicles ix: 10) Although there is nothing in Bible to prove that Ophir was in India but a widely held view among the archaeologists that it was in South-Arabia. In short, no one can sure about this unless and until no further excavation evidence found on this.

Muza, the Mokha emporium is mentioned by the Geography of Ptolemy and the Periplus, it was a seaport and it was identified with modern Mocha. Muza was inhabited by Arabs acquainted with navigation and full of merchants who used to carry trade not only in the Indian wares that come from the port of Barygaza but also the products in their own country.[676] Muza imported purple cloth, saffron, muslins, cloak, spices, perfumes etc. while myrrh,[677] while stones and alabaster were the chief articles of exports.

Arabia Felix or Periplus's (26) Eudaemon Arabia is the modern Aden, which played a vital role in the Indo-Roman commerce. The town was called Felix because when voyages were not made from India to Egypt to the interior of India, all proceeded only as far as this town, which received the merchandise both of the Indians and Egyptians in the same way as Alexandria received foreign goods, which came from Egypt.[678] It was an important centre of trade where merchandise of East was trans-shipped for the Mediterranean markets during the opening centuries of Christian era. During the rule of Homeric kings, this place lost its significance but it again regained its position by the 4th Century A.D. the direct intercourse between the Romans and the Indians offered the former the opportunity for monopolising the trade of Aden and asserting their supremacy.

Another important trading centre was Cana where Egypt was actively involved in her Eastern and western trade and commerce. Cana had a fine harbour, which was protected from all winds by projecting capes on either side and by island in the offing. Cana had brisk commercial relations with India, especially with Barygaza.[679] It has been taken as the chief emporium of international trade between India and Egypt where ships from both these countries met and traded. Cana was well fortified and it was a favourable locality for oceanic navigation and extensive commerce with India. To Cana, the frankincease was conveyed as a general mart in order to be shipped to the more distant emporium of Oman and Persian ports. Corn and wine came to Cana from Egypt.[680] Indigenous products like aloe, frankincense and other articles of trade were exported.

Arsinoe-Clysme-Qolzoum was also an important port of Ptolemaic foundation. Lucian writing in about 170 A.D., indicated the ease with which a traveler could board a ship at Clysme bound for India.[681] The archaeological evidence confirms the fact and points out that the port was active till the 4th CAD. According to Periplus[682] grain, textile and viticulture were largely imported by South Arabia and India. It is likely that Roman military post at Babylone passing by canals between Clysma and Nile.[683] Probably it was the most southerly Egyptian Red Sea port which served as both exporting and importing ports for mainly – less bulky, more luxurious commodities which could more easily absorb trans desert transportation costs.

Mirbat was in inland emporium of Zafar. It probably exported frankincense, myrrh and hides in the time of Ptolemy. Syagros was also commercially important because it had a port, which was depository of all frankincense collected in these regions. Between this place and Cape Guardafue, there was an island to the south, which was very large, and this island formed the centre of trade between Egypt, Arabia and India. Schoff has identified it with Ras Fartak.[684]

Another important depot of the articles of commerce was Moscha. The articles were carried by ships, which were arriving from Limyrica (Canara) and Barygaza (Broach). The Periplus (32) has also referred to it after describing Syagrus to it as harbour where ships used to come regularly from Cana and returned to Damirica and Barygaza. But Schoff points out that Moscha was another port.[685] Wherever, the port Moscha may be but it was a great commercial harbour, there is no doubt at all.

Berenice was also a very prominent place in the commerce of Roman Empire with Eastern countries, particularly India-Berenice had a fine natural harbour and there were dangerous rocks and violent winds from the sea, as described by Strabo.[686] It was the southern most of the Egyptian Red Sea ports, which was probably the largest and most important at least in 1st CBC and 1st CAD.[687] Ptolemy –II founded the port in early 3rd CBC and named it after his mother.[688] Strabo and Pliny the elder suggest the peak activity of the trade was from 1st CBC to 1st CAD. Probably the port continued to be inhabited till 7th CAD if not used as a commercial emporium, well into Byzantine period. Another important place, Nubia, was located on the river Nile. It is identified with Begerawiyeh.[689] It received the gold from Sudan along with other things while from the Red Sea across Tigre, Myrrh, frankincense and other things came to this place.

The Petra of Periplus (19) was known a great trading centre of northern Arab in the history of Roman commerce with East. Due to its geographical position it controlled the Eastern trade from both directions. It had supremacy over land route and the route to Palmyra and the sea trade, which was diverted, to Alexandria. The importance of Petra declined in 105 AD. When Trojan established his sway over the region, Palmyra gained advantage of being supreme in the overland trade when it was revived towards the end of second century and obviously Petra had neither a place nor an effective role in the overland trade route, which she once reigned.

Ommana was an important town of Persia. Pliny (VI, 32) and Periplus (36) point out that it occupied a place of importance in the context of India's trade with western nations. It received the products of the East and reshipped them and then sent them to the Mediterranean world through land routes.[690] Myos Hormos was another important port. From 1st CBC to 1st CAD it was the peak period of activity of the port of Myos Hormos.[691] Numerous scholars since 19th century have equated Myos Hormos with Abu

Shaar. Though it is considered as a commercial centre, no commercial port site has been discovered. These facts – the late date and lack of a commercial port –threw some doubt on the association of this port site at Abu Shaar with the ancient port Myos Hormos.[692]

After discussing the important marketing centres of Egypt and the Persian Gulf, which played a dominant role in the history of India's commercial relations with the West. We shall now turn our attention to the remarkable ports and trading centres of Imperial Rome that facilitated the smooth flow of trade between India and Rome. Some of the recent archaeological excavations in Italy and Rome shed sufficient light on Indo-Roman trade. These finds also help in corroborating the evidence preserved in the classical accounts.

Pompeiopolis was a noted Cilician coastal city. The coinage of Pompeiopolis suggests that the city in the second and third century A.D. tallied with the tradition recorded in the early empire by Strabo. This harbour continued to occupy a significant place in the history of commerce of Rome.[693] Available evidence makes it clear that Hadrian had a hand in the construction of harbour installations of pompeiopolis, though its completion and inauguration was probably done under his successor. Ostia was another port of importance from navigation point of view. By the time of Augustus the flow of traffic reached at massive proportions. There were links between the storage of foodstuffs and other goods are well represented in the archaeological records at Ostia. Commercially Ostia was very active and it formed an important feature of the town life of the port city.

Pompeii was another important town of the Roman Empire. It was located in Campania in the Bay or Naples. It was a small town at the mouth of the river Sarno. It was totally destroyed by the eruption of 79 A.D. It was from this place a minor work of Indian art has been discovered in course of recent archaeological excavations.

Portus was a great harbour and a brilliant gift of Claudius. It was constructed in the middle of first century A.D. In 42 A.D., the emperor Claudius embarked on the ambitious project of building Portus harbour.[694] It was a mammoth man made port and it was only two miles up the coast from Ostia. Recent archaeological excavations have unearthed wonderful remains at the site. A canal was dug to connect it directly with Tiber and Rome had finally the harbour facilities she deserved. The remarkable by product of this newly constructed harbour was to denote the status of Puteoli from a great enter port to a provincial port, for all sea going vessels could now safely put in at Rome's new harbour.[695] There are many evidence of presence of India traders at different parts of world. The discovery of Tamil – Brahmi graffiti on typical Indian megalithic Black-Red w are pot sherds of first century A.D. excavated in the manufacturing sector Quseir-al-Qadam on the Red Sea.[696] One word has an incomplete inscription reading... atan which could have been the name of Catan well attributed in Tamil Brahmi cave inscription and in Cankam literature. A reading of graffiti on an Arikamedu sherd is also said to refer to a catan.[697] An Ostracon from Quseir carries what has been read as Prakrit inscription mentioning 3 persons with seemingly Prakrit names – Halaka, Vishudatta and Nakada – suggesting home base in the Deccan. The language and script are also influenced in some extent by South-Indian language.[698] It is also interesting that this almost incidental epigraphic evidence again underlines the links between Deccan, South-India and Red Sea.[699]

Another port Leukus Limen was important to the merchants of this period. It was closest to the Nile. Archaeological evidence both ceramic and numismatic seems to indicate that Leukus Limen was founded sometime in 1st CAD.[700] Several excavated areas of Quseir-al-Qadim attested the importance of its trade with India and South Arabia.[701] Excavations of this site produced sherds with Himamgaritic and Sabaean(South Arabian) graffiti, the former mentioning a personal name. An unearthed wooden ring indicates that the harbour had been dredged or cleared at l east once in Roman times. The site revived in the medieval Islamic period. At that time it enjoyed contacts with Africa, India and China.

In southern Arabia, three important centers as Timana, Khor Rori and Shabwa bear some Indian products and corroborates the fact that there was a flourishing trade between India and West Asia. Timna was known for incense trade and its inhabitants had access to Mediterranean lands.[702] Khor Rori in Dhofar was ancient port site dated between 1st CBC to 7th CAD. A bronze statue he has been founded at the site bearing close resemblance to female statues from Mathura, dating 2nd CAD.[703]

The excavations at Berenike have produced many things. On the paleo-botanical evidences it has been identified that there were 65 cultivated plant species.[704] Thanks to the arid conditions, botanical remains tend to be preserved by desiccation. Among the finds the most important things are: rice, coconut, amla, mung bean, teak etc. The five excavations at Berenike have clearly shown that investigating such a location contributes greatly to our knowledge of the commerce between Rome and India.[705] The port of Berenike is situated on the southern most part of Rome. Although this port had been founded by the Greeks, its use increased as soon as the Romans gained insight into the Monsoon system during the first century A.D. and got the access to the already flourishing trading networks in South Asia.[706] In addition to these trading works in the Indian Ocean, important land routes such as Silk Road and the Incense Road connected Arabia and South Asia with Roman Empire. The Red Sea ports were surprisingly squalid places. Buildings of the most part poorly constructed of sun dried bricks, field stones and chunks of coral.[707] Some of these port buildings at Leukos Limen lacked roofings.[708] It seems that the merchants built in expensive structures to keep their overhead costs down and to increase their profits. The streets intersect at right angles indicating that the site was well planned from the beginning and not laid out in a helter-skelter fashion.[709] It indicates about the participation of both govt and private parties to develop the coastal harbours.[710] The Red Sea ports were density populated only when merchants' ships left and returned from their voyages at specific times of the year.[711] These ports primarily existed due to international trade.

From the above discussions it is obvious that the different international commercial routes and trading centres helped immensely the cause of commerce both in India and Imperial Rome. The Roman control over Egypt and Iraq facilitated her in organising her commercial network on a mass scale. Due to this enlarged volume of the trade, it was but natural that several trading marts and towns in India as well as in the Mediterranean region developed.

Business Organisations

The corporate organisations, which were common in the ancient India, were the guilds. There are many references about this organisation in Ramayana, Mahabharata, Jatakas, Kautilya's Arthasastra and others. These guilds spread throughout India in the ancient times and mainly controlled the inland as well as foreign trade. Therefore without going detail into it, the description about the trade and commerce of that time will be incomplete. In the earlier chapter, the origin, spread and the mechanism of guild organisations are discussed. Hence, in this chapter the further growth of the organisations and a comparison with Roman counterpart will be drawn.

After the disintegration of Mauryan Empire, large number of tribal republics and small kingdoms raised their monstrous heads in the political arena. Therefore this period is marked by political wrangling, petty warfare in the political scene. But it is marked by the intense activity of trade and commerce while the guilds tried to strengthen their stranglehold on the economic and trade affairs taking the advantage of political laxity.[712] Literary and epigraphic evidence of this period refers to a number of guilds, their number being very much greater than eighteen met with in the early Buddhist texts.[713] But Mahavastu[714] mentions about two dozens of guilds. About sixty crafts (of which eight are connected with the workings of metal) are included among over seventy occupations referred to in Milinda Panho.[715]

There are many evidences in support of prevalence of guilds in the period of 200 B.C. to 300 A.D. The epigraphic evidence of

Sanchi, Barhut, Bodhgaya, Mathura and the sites in Deccan refer to a number of donations given by the guilds of potters, masons, weavers, gem cutters, jewellers, painters, goldsmiths, ironsmiths, brass-smiths, bronze-smiths, carpenters, sculptors, terracotta makers, glass makers, ivory makers, perfumers, leather workers, bankers-cum-merchants, caravan merchants.[716] This donation indicates the prosperity of guilds. The recording of donations on permanent materials also served as an advertisement to highlight their economic status and munificence. Though the above mentioned members are not mentioned as the guilds but it can be safely presumed that they were the members of guilds because at that time these occupations were organised into guilds. There are other references of different guilds in this period. The guilds of flour makers, weavers,[717] oil makers, potters, manufacturers of hydraulic machines, corn dealers, bamboo workers, bankers etc. also find mention in epigraphs of this period.[718]

This was the period when large number of foreigners entered into India. The Greeks, Sakas, Hunas, Parthians and Kushanas penetrated Into Indian and it developed the continuing commercial relations of India with foreign lands especially with Roman people.[719] The discovery of South-West monsson ascribed to Hippalus in 46 A.D., gave impetus to mid sea voyage, reducing to time of journey, minimizing the danger of piracy and obviating the need of middlemen in Indo-Roman trade.[720] The Indo-Roman trade reached at its peak during this period. The demand of luxury goods in an exorbitant rate gave an impetus to the growth of guilds. Because the large scale production of goods for export purposes were mainly done by the guilds whose quality was also praiseworthy.

The references about the guilds are also found in different texts like Manusmriti and Yajnavalkya Smriti etc. As Rick points out that Manu's views on loans and interests, on export through sea-borne trade and the duties on sea borne goods show that the fiscal system related to this matter had reached a higher stage of development than met with in Jataka tales.[721] From Manusmriti and Yajnavalkya Smriti it is clearly evident that in the early centuries of Christiạn era the guilds had developed considerably and their authority in the internal matters was upheld by the state. References in these two Smritis show that the guild organisations had a much more developed form in the Yajnavalkya Smriti than the Manusmriti. For the first time Yajnavalkya Smriti states that besides being the judicial authority for its members, a guild also functioned as one of the ordinary courts of law. He also mentions about the executive officers of the guild.[722] Their (the executive officers') qualifications, powers and rules regarding vocational apprenticeship are also clearly mentioned in Yajnavalkya Smriti. It further mentions that the rules of the guilds should be followed like the rules of the state.[723] This means that sometimes there was no difference between the state laws and guild laws. It indicates the powerful position of the guild. Manu mentions of agreements as one of the titles of the law. Many epigraphic evidences of this time mention about the munificent grants given by the guilds to temples or other institutions. A Nasik inscription of the time of Nạhapana makes a note of two different rates of interests which two guilds, referred to in the epigraphs, were to pay an the endowments made with them and also to their registration in the nigama sabha (traders' assembly).[724]

In the post Mauryan period the elements of state control were loosened and guilds enjoyed considerable freedom in their own spheres; yet when they were at fault royal intervention became necessary. The lawgivers justify this.[725] The view of M. V. K. Rao[726] is doubted here because he points out that some groups like guilds themselves desired that the authority of the state should be exercised over the whole social and economic life of the people. Yajnavalkya mentions that it was the duty of the king to restrain the guild members in case dissensions erupted among the members of the guild. According to Brihaspati, the king is the highest authority to pass the judgements. Again he gives very good information that if a guild cheated the king of his share of profit earned in the trade, it was to pay eight times as much and was punished if it moved to another location without the permission of the authority.[727] The king had the authority to enforce the maintenance of laws, contracts and agreements between the individual members and guilds. It is mentioned by Beniprasad that it was the duty of the guilds "to codify the usages and enunciate it on any occasion".[728] On petty grounds also the king had the authority to punish the guilds. The Nayadhammakha provides an interesting fact[729] that the king of Mithila Kumbhanga banished the guild of goldsmiths only on account of the fact that they could not repair his earrings.

Manu[730] says that a member of corporation who after entering duly an agreement if he breaks it in avarice, he was to be banished by the king from his realm. He might be fined or imprisoned also for his mistakes. Yajnavalkya[731] prescribes the forfeiture of the property and banishment as punishment for misappropriation of property of a corporation. Brihaspati enjoins that the member of a guild who falls out with his association or neglects his duty should be fined. There are the various restricts on the functions of guilds. Though they were given certain freedom, these regulations were necessary to control their authority. Every guild had its own rules and regulations on its customary rules. About the distribution of profits, Manu gives an indirect clue that the total income should be distributed among the workers in joint production.[732] In this connection, Yajnavalkya lays down some clear injunctions that when a group of traders carrying on business jointly for the purpose of making profit, the profit and loss of each shall be, either in properties to the share of the capital contributed by each, or as may have been agreed upon among themselves.[733] He further states that if any one of them is found to be crooked, they should turn him out, depriving him of any profits that he may have earned. In case a member was honestly unable to do his allotted duty, his work was allowed to be done by his substitute. These rules laid down by Yajnavalkya were equally applicable to priests, cultivators and artisans.

Guild funds were derived from various sources. The individual members are allowed to contribute by way of subscription towards the common guild stocks. Before being a member to guild, every person had to deposit certain amount of money for his or her guarantees.[734] The fairly large amount of money was in flowing to the guilds by way of gifts bestowed by the kings on members, executive officers and elder men. This was regarded as the property of the guild. Again the second most important source was the profit earned by the execution orders. Even a member of guild who earned the money by his public works was regarded as the property of the guild.[735] The guild has the authority to fine the members, who violated the laws of the guild. It also contributed a handsome amount of money to the guilds. Amongst most important source of guild fund were profits earned by their functions as banks. In doing banking business, the guilds received permanent deposits guaranteeing the regular payment of interests, which was to be utilized for the charitable objects that the donors specified.[736] Such endowments were often made by kings, officials, traders, artisans and other classes of people.

Among the expenditure, the guilds spent a quite good sum on purchase of raw materials, which they would turn into finished products and sell it at profit.[737] Considerable expenditure would have been incurred in travelling in connection with business, transport of merchandise, wages of labour and payment of different duties. A sizeable expenditure must also have been incurred by the guilds, particularly the prosperous ones, on the care and protection of treasury and merchandise and ensuring safety of the members of the guilds against robbers and irregular troops and even the exactions of unscrupulous kings.[738] The expenditure on this head usually became heavy when they maintained armed guards to protect the caravans and traders against the attack of robbers, violent tribal people etc. According to Brihaspati, a portion of the profits of the guilds was earmarked for the developmental works, charity and piety and it is found clearly in different epigraphic references.

The most important contribution of guild to the development of economic activities was the banking facilities. In the post-Mauryan phase, the minting of large amount of money facilitated the trade and commerce and money economy occupied a predominant position. Due to the changed circumstances, the essence of banks was clearly felt and guilds took the advantage of the situations. The guilds now gained such reputation for their efficiency as well as integrity in providing dependable credits and banking facilities that not only to private individuals but even high government officials began to deposit money. A Mathura inscription of the time of Huvishka (106 A.D.) refers to the charitable acts of high officials of foreign origin and a predominant endowment of 550 puranas (Silver coins) with a flour makers' guild and another guild with a view of serving one hundred Brahamans every month and distributing daily a fixed quantity of edibles to the poor out of the interest on deposits.[739] Just like this, the Nasik inscription, Junar inscription and Godhwa inscriptions also clearly exhibits the bank like functions of guilds.[740] Major part of these money deposits must have gone towards expanding and upgrading their respective trades and crafts. At times, the guilds lent out part of the endowed sum to other parties[741] obviously a rate of interest higher than the stipulated in the original endowment and earned same profit.

The guilds successfully performed their task showing internal coherence, resourcefulness, fair and honest dealing and faithful discharge of their responsibilities and obligations. The public reposed faith in them because of their high credit prestige. Therefore the royal officials and kings instead of depositing money in royal treasury, thought it prudent to deposit money on the guilds. Probably it had again increased the faith of public on the guilds.[742]

The change of membership of the guilds did not affect the terms of contract. Usually it is said that the terms of contracts of guild lasted "till the sun and moon an earth endure" and bound the guilds for generations to come. The migration of the guilds under the economic pressure or political compulsions as pointed out by Mookherjee did not affect their distinctive corporate personality or individuality, their internal cohesion or the credit, their legal relations and liabilities.[743] The guilds paid much more importance to the confidence of the people than any other things. Even after the migrations the people did not loose the confidence in them.

As per the agreements, in respect of endowments, the guilds not only provides articles they manufactured or traded in, such as supplying of cloth by the weaver's guild and oil by oilmen's guild but they also undertook other tasks of beneficence unrelated to their profession, for example,, weaver's guilds providing light meals to the monks or oil-men's guild providing medicine to them.[744] Sometimes the guilds were taking the help of other people, to complete their contract, the tasks which were beyond their capacity. Curiously enough there is also evidence to show that sometimes the guilds were giving the contract to another party if they were overburdened with the work. For example, in the Vasudevahindi, it is stated that the king Agrasena of Mathura entrusted the guild of goldsmith with the work of fashioning a golden anklet, which the guild assigned to another party.[745]

In ancient India, the guilds had a very limited scope in comparison with modern banks. It is not clear whether people were depositing money in the bank only for safety purpose or for the purpose or for the purpose to earn money, which is common in the modern banking system. Usually, from epigraphic sources, it is known that the principal (nivi) deposited with guild were everlasting and the interests were spent on religious activities. About the rate of interest our knowledge is very limited. Still then it was highly praiseworthy because thousand years back a system, which was evolved for smooth transactions of money and is quite similar to our modern banking system.

The multifarious activities of the guilds were quite helpful for the traders to facilitate the trade and commerce in a very smooth and steady manner. It not only provided the social security to the artisans but also checked the fraudulent practices by controlling the quality. It was an obvious reason for which the high quality goods of India were much liked in the foreign lands. Now the Indian guilds may be compared with Roman guilds of more or less the same period and it will show what an extent such a comparison holds good.

Roman guilds have been assigned to periods from the days of First Republic Circa 509 B.C.,[746] but their variety and formation became the features of Roman economic life in 2nd Century A.D. in India, however, the origin of the guilds can be traced from the period of Rig Veda, prior to 800 B.C. and considerable light can be thrown on this from 4th Century B.C. On the basis of Kautilya's Arthasastra. From that time until 7th Century A.D., the guilds became an integral part of the Indian system and continued to be so for a thousand years hence. The chief reason for this early development must have been the earlier commercial connections of India with the other trading centres like Babylonia, Assyria, Egypt, and Persia etc.

In India, the guilds were primarily organized on the basis of caste system while the Roman guilds organized the guilds on the line of citizenship, religious and political considerations and on the basis of trade and profession.[747] Again guilds in India could hardly have been established for only social purposed for they were bodies intended mainly if not entirely, for commercial undertakings. They appear to have had little to do with social objectives for Indian society unlike the Roman.[748]Again the profit orientation was the sole concern of Roman guilds while the Indian counterparts were devoid of this. The prices were fixed by the guild, which was careful about the interests of consumers.

About the strength of members of guild a faint comparison can be drawn. The Roman carpenter's guilds in 3rd Century A.D. were reputed to have had 60 officers with about 1500 members. About the strength of Indian guilds, we have no conclusive evidence but it can be assumed that the Indian guilds had never so many members in comparison with Roman counterparts.[749] The guilds of Rome were also undertaking various organizational and other activities owing to their affluent circumstances, raised memorial structures and temples with their funds. The baker's guild raised a huge marble monument through the agency of its high officers in 144 A.D. in honour of Antonius Pius.[750]The guild of perfumers, during Augustus, built and dedicated a temple to Jupiter.[751]They could also make advances from their own finances. Suetonius tells us that, during Augustus, when his palace at Palatine was burnt down, the guilds of minor officers, the city tribes and the people of every description contributed to their mite.[752] These types of munificent contributions were given by the Indian guilds, which are clearly evident from the donations of Lata's Silk weavers' guild, and the inscriptions of Sanchi, Barhut, and Budhgaya clearly give the evidence of their generous contributions.[753]

There were a large number of guilds, which had mushroomed in the whole western lands. Sometimes there were some famous guilds that had established their guilds throughout the country. But in Indian context, there was no lack of guilds, which were prevalent invariably in all major cities of ancient India. In the matter of functions and working patterns, there were not much more differences between these organisations in India and Rome. These organisations were working to channelize the resources, labours and were providing smooth progress to trade and commercial activities.

Cultural Contacts

Geographically India and Roman Empire were far away from each other in ancient times but a close commercial and diplomatic ties were established which resulted in significant changes.[754] The exchange of embassies further strengthened the relations between the two sub-continents. In 25 B.C., Augustus Caesar received an Indian embassy, which gave the foundation to the indo-Roman relations. A three-man delegation arrived at Antioch with slaves and tropical animals and an ascetic from Broach who ritually burned himself alive.[755] In another instance, Augustus received the embassies in 21B.C. 17 B.C. and 14 B.C. and they brought with them the gems, pearls, elephants and tigers.[756]It is providing an indication that there was a marked increase in trade and commerce between India and Rome. According to an ancient map, there was a temple of Augustus on the Indian coast near Calicut.

A custom collector of the Emperor, in 45 A.C., was driven off and he came to Ceylone. He learned the native language in 6 months and was then able to inform the king about Rome and Caesar. The Sinhalese ruler was duly impressed, especially by the stall weight of denarrii. In exchange the Roman Emperor also sent three people, one of them met Pliny and he was interrogated.[757] Pliny writes that the reliable knowledge of the annual use of South East monsoon and the voyage of Egyptians to Muziris and Nelycinda in two days.[758] About the knowledge of monsoons Indians were well aware before Hippalus' knowledge of monsoon, which gave an advantage to the Arabian and Roman sailors.

There are enough evidences about the Indo-Roman trade which clearly indicates that Indo-Roman trade was in a flourished condition at that time. One vestige of this trade is an ivory statuette of an Indian goddess (a Lakshmi)(see figure-6) at her toilet, it was discovered in 1938 in Pompeii and must date before the destruction of the city in 79 A.D.[759]Again cotton was found in the north cemetery of Meroe in Sudan and there are features in iconography of Sudan in the 1st B.C. Such as gods with triple heads and two pairs of arms and gods with elephant trunks which are typical only of India.[760] On Novembers 30 1959, it was announced that a Graecian urn of copper having dolphins and three bronze handles and dating from 3rd and 2nd century B.C. was accidentally dug up at Charasda in the North- Western Frontier.[761]

There is a whole group of Yavanas mentioned in the cave inscriptions of Western India. Apart from the Yavana, Irila who has a foreign name, the others are all native Buddhists who have made architectural donations in the construction of monasteries and Chaityas of Junnar, Karle and Nasik. The only sense in which these Yavanas can be regarded as Greeks is that they may have been Greek citizens or Indian traders with Greek affiliations.[762] In additions, to the gifts at Nasik mentioned above, other Yavanas donated the following gifts: - five gave pillars, one a hall front, and another refractory for the monastic community.[763]

According to Fergusson,[764] the Chaityas of India bear a remarkable resemblance to the early Christian church. Behind both of them lies a common tradition- the private basilicas of Roman Emperors. The plans of Caitya halls at Bhaja and Karle bear similarity with the private basilicas of the Palatine, of Porto, of Kremna and of Aspedos.[765] In each case the structure is longitudinally disposed, with triple arisles and terminates in a semi-circular apse. It is expected that in the construction of these Caityas, the Yavanas might have been employed. It is already noticed a Chola King employed Yavana architect. There is also legend, for what it is worth, of St. Thomas voyaging India to offer services as a carpenter or architect to King Gondphornes (reigned 19-45 A.D.). St. Thomas claims ability to fashion in stone, "pillars, temples and courthouses, for kings".[766]

Now a days the scholars point out that the Gandhara art not only derived purely from Greek but also from Roman art. These include the pilasters each with a panel upon it and quasi-Corinthian capitals. In the Greek architecture the fluted columns are absent and they could be traced to the Roman modillions.[767] In Roman Palmyra for example we find such pilasters with panels and flute less columns. Another feature of the classical origin used decoratively at Taxila was the gable. It is used over the false doorways in the shrine of the double headed eagle at Sikap and in the Jaulian Stupa.[768] The broken pediment is found in the plinth of the Dharmajika stupa.[769] Lastly the alternation of semi-circular and three sides framing arches on the plinth of the North-Western stupas seems to be derived from the Roman or Byzantine alternation of semi-circular arches and pediments.[770] In another context the presence of Roman influence can be traced; the motifs of Buddhism sometimes borrow fabulous animals from the classical sources purely decorative purposes and without attempting to explain them through a mythology of their own construction. The very absence of explanations of tritons, centaurs, hippocamps and sphinxes which are to be found in the art but not in the literature and it provide the conclusive proofs of their foreign origin.[771]

We know from some inscriptions that the indo-Greeks both patronized the art in India and were the owners of artistic objects.

And the epigraphic evidence point out that Indians owned the western type objects. The Phialo-mesomphalos (round silver dish with a raised central boss) from Taxila has the name of the owner, Mimjukritasa,[772] as against another silver boul from the same site which is inscribed with the name of Thedorus son of Thavara.[773] This verifies the statement of the Periplus noted earlier, that among the western imports at Barbaricum were silver plates and the glass vessels. The sea green translucent flasks from Taxila are typically Roman blown glass[774] and the glass ware excavated at Begram in Afghanistan (assigned to 3rd quarter of 1st century A.D.) was primarily believed to have been made in Roman Syria.[775] Even some furniture and utensils at Taxila were of western type, including an iron folding chair with crossed legs and an iron candelabra and for the bronze ladles and spoons and a gadrooned flat copper saucer, Roman prototypes have been cited.[776] Another imported object was the copper incense burner from Sirkap whose handle is in the shape of a horned and a winged lion. These types of objects were originated in Iran. It is found at Palmyra and Hatra.[777] There are indications that the imported objects of Taxila, arrived by sea not overland first, an oval seal engraved with cupid and cock,[778] of which a similar intaglio was found at Arikamedu.[779] And in another example a flat bowel of bronze with a ram's head handle terminal from Taxila of which an example has now been found in a cave near the Red Sea.[780] These objects establish the trade contacts as well as cultural contacts between India and western Asia.

The impact of Iran people is also found in different spheres of the ancient Indian life. It has been suggested that Pushyamitra may have been an Iranian, a worshipper of the Sun Mithra.[781] The fact that according to Kalidasa, he revived the asvamedha or horse sacrifice in India[782] would at first seem to suggest that he sought his inspirations in the Vedas where the horse sacrifice is attested (Rig Veda, p. 162) and if this is true then his ruling deity would be the Vedic Mitra instead of Avestic Mitra. The Persian influence is also expected when they dominated the North- West India. In the coins of North West India, the Parthian names and portraits were found. Gandphornes seems to have copied a unique silver coin of Mithridates II (88 B.C.), having a one side the seated king holding an eagle and crowned by a city and he also uses an epithet found only on Parthian coins.[783] The Parthian interlude in India must have been of short duration. When Kushanas occupied this region, they also adopted some Greek and Iranian gods on the coins. The Iranian angels Sraosha and Rashnu of Avesta can be recognized in the doorkeepers of Mihira- Rajna and Srausha who were worshipped by the Magas in India, according to Bhavishya Purana.[784]

It is observed that the worship of Sun was introduced in India by the Persians.[785]The earliest Sun temple in India may be that of Jandial in Taxila[786] and it is certainly related to a Persian Fire Temple in plan, including its pradakshina patha or the passage which forms an ambulatory around the cella, a feature which we find already at the Ayadana (place of adoration) at Susa of Artoxerxes II (405-385 B.C.).[787] The ambulatory at Taxila may have been of Persian inspiration but circumambulation itself is a widespread Aryan practice.[788] But the possibility of Jandial temple being intended for a fire cult is strengthened by a deep foundation for a tower with the steps at the back of the sanctuary on the summit of which a fire must have burned judging from the Iranian analogies. There is no doubt that Taxila was more or less influenced by the Persians. According to Strabo (XV, 714), Aristobulus saw that the corpses in Taxila were exposed to vultures. These types of practices are not allowed in India. Therefore, it might be the impact of Persians who did these things and Wei Shu reported it.[789]

The interactions between India, Persian and Iranians continued during the Sassanian period also. During the reign of Ardashir (226-241 B.C.), the indo-Muslim writer Feristha claimed that Adarshir reached as far as Sarhiad in his march on India.[790]At any rate, as, we have seen it was Adarshir's reign that Mani made his voyage to India for preaching his religion. It is suggested that Mani had borrowed his belief in metempsychosis from Buddhism.[791] Again a relief carved on the cliff of Shahapur represents the triumph of a king (possibly Shapur-I) over an Indian people. Some of the Hindu books on grammar and horoscopy were regarded a holy books in Shapur's court. The Sassanian state manual, the lost Ayinnameh, which survives in Arabic references might in same manner have drawn on Arthasastra for certain features of military tactics advocated although an opposite borrowing has been suggested.[792] The coins issued by Hormazd-I (272-273 A.D.) and Peroz (294-301 A.D.) present the figure of Buddha.[793] These evidences point out the intercourse between India and western world.

Though India and Roman Empire were far removed from each other geographically, close commercial and diplomatic ties were established which resulted in significant exchanges.[794]India sent an embassy to Augustus Caesar in 25 B.C. A three men delegation arrived at Antioch with slaves and tropical animals and an ascetic from Broach who ritually burned himself alive. Again Augustus received further embassies in 21, 17, and 14 century B.C.[795]They ambassadors brought with them gems, pearls, elephants and tigers. Florus in 110 A.D. says that among the foreign ambassador received by Augustus were "Seres and Indian living right under the sun, bringing elephants, as well as gems and pearls among their gifts" and having been four years on their journey.[796] Dio cassius (XXVIII, 156) mentions about the embassies in the reign of Trojan (98-117A.D.). He says that upon Trojan's return to Rome in 106 A.D. the emperor received many embassies from barbarian courts and particularly from the Indians. Then the emperors like Hadrian (117-138A.D.)[797] and Antoninus Pius (138-161 A.D.) also received the embassies from the Indian Territory. The Indian embassies also reached in Syria in 218 A.D. to welcome the emperor Dandamis, who was the source of Bardesanes on the Indian gymnosophists.[798] Among the ambassadors received by Aurelian (270-275 A.D.) at his triumph in 274 A.D. were Indians, not to mention Arabians, Persians, Bactrians and Chinese.[799] This exchange of embassies is further indicative of a growing trade relationship between India and West-Asia.

Conclusion

India's trade relations with West Asian region and Rome reached at its pinnacle of growth during the post-Mauryan period. The two sub continents of ancient world met each other not only on the commercial front but also on the cultural plane. When Rome was at its height of glory, India (both North and South) already enjoyed peace and prosperity under different dynasties. Peaceful conditions, surplus wealth and the commodities made the situations favourable to an effective foreign trade and both countries utilized the opportunity to the fullest extent with their capacity and resources. Kushanas established peace and stability in India in north and Satavahans in Andhra region became the potent factor for the prosperous trade. From the other side, the prosperity of Romans increased the demand of luxurious goods to suffice their inordinate ambitions to maintain a comfortable life. They tried to carry ahead this with feverish haste and great display. The Indian goods were the focal point of their attraction because of its quality and the availability. The products like pearls; drugs, spice, condiments, incense, ghee, jewels, perfumes, cosmetics, dyes and others were directly imported from India. Sometimes the Indian merchants were also carrying the goods of Sri Lanka and China to the western countries.

Various foreign accounts like Pliny's Natural History, the Periplus of Erythrean Sea, Strabo's Geography, Arrian's Indika and Indika of Ctesias throw much more light of this trade and provide a good knowledge about the geographical condition of India. But one of the greatest lacunae of these accounts are they primarily depended on the secondary sources to construct the history of India. Some recent excavations have cleared the clouds of suspicion and widened the sphere of knowledge. Again the validity of archaeological facts is beyond the question mark. About the cultural contacts between these lands may be constructed more on the findings of excavations than the literary sources. So, the archaeological sources have taken a commendable task to present the picture of Indo- Roman trade.

The Indo-Roman trade was favourable to India; it was commented by most of the ancient authors. The long list of exports exceeds the list of import in quantity and this clearly indicates that India had occupied a prominent position in this trade. The vast geographical boundary of India was producing various types of goods to cater the needs of indigenous as well foreign people. Excepting some luxury items like wine, liquid storax, lead, glass, copper etc. the Indians were not demanding more goods and this placed India in a favourable position. The comments of Pliny about the drain of wealth to India again strengthen the statement. But many historians on different grounds doubt on Pliny's statements. The mention of Pliny about 550 million sesferecs which was drained by India; is representing the whole East Asia instead of India only. It has been rightly observed that, if the sums represented the whole value of imports the value of trade had been very small. But in order to evaluate the money value of Roman imports it is essential to know the total annual quantities of Roman exports, which must have partly paid for them. Again the price of Roman currency should be determined before making any comments on the statements of Pliny. If we accept the statements of Pliny as correct, then there are various reasons to justify the statements. First of all the Romans demand for Indian goods were much higher than the availability and this was the reason, which raised the prices. Secondly, the whole profits of this trade was not coming to the hands of Indians because the agents like Arabians, Parthians, Jews, indo-Greeks had played their own role to raise the prices. Thirdly, the distance through the land and sea routes which was invariably so lengthy, arduous and expensive, must have contribute in no small measure in enhancing the total cost of goods which came through such routes. Finally there appears to have been hardly any effective price control mechanism in Roman Empire to check the inflation of prices of goods and the greedy traders had taken the undue advantage of the prevailing situation to garner more profits.

The transportation system in post-Mauryan period was not so well developed. During the Mauryan period the Grand Trunk Roads were constructed which specially helped the traders to carry their goods easily. But in the post-Mauryan period the construction of the roads were not maintained properly. It created the problems not only for the traders but also for the Silk Route which was famous for its trade that became the focal point of attention of traders who were carrying the goods by land routes. Lacks of scientific progress in the transportation system and the continuance of the age-old systems of chariots and carts drawn by the animals was the greatest misery of trades. Again the land routes were not safe because the wild beasts in the jungle and wild tribes, robbers constantly troubling the traders. In order to protect their goods form these attacks the guild was providing the armed men to the traders and sometimes the traders were also organising the armed men on their own. Equally dangerous was the sea route where the pirates were constantly looting the traders at the slightest opportunity. It was the duty of the kings to take the interests of the traders into account and; to maintain the law and order, but their apathetic attitude towards this caused a great hardship to the traders. The Indian ships were not were built enough like the Roman and Arab counterparts face the storms in the sea. In order to face the turbulence of South West monsoon, the ships of Roman Egypt had supremely strong hulls which were fitted with a rig- meant primarily for safety and not for speed. Moreover, such ships were big and sturdy enough to use against southwest monsoon over open water. The use of big ships for indo-Roman trade had tremendous economic implications. Since Indian goods that attracted the Romans were not bulky and cheap commodities, rather compact and costly merchandise, a cargo of such goods would have represented huge investments. Possibly the use of small ships by the Indians became the main cause which did not permit the traders to carry their goods for a long distance. Therefore large share of profits were going to the pockets of Arabs, Romans and other traders who were acting as middlemen in this trade. But the knowledge of monsoons by the

Indian people much before the discovery of Hippalus provided an advantage to the Indian traders. The deplorable conditions of transportation system had a very adverse effect on the trade and commerce.

The growth of trading centres at the different parts of India as well as along the routes connecting India and West Asia is clearly indicative of growth of trade and commerce. Literary evidence and the inscriptions show that the construction and restoration of harbours was a part of broad policy of Imperial Rome. In contrary, the Indian kings did not formulate any strong measures for the upliftment of trade centres and mart towns. But the long coastline of India had naturally provided the good harbours and trader enter ports through which the trade of India was mainly carried out. Along the land routes the trade centres also grew up to facilitate the commercial activities. The goods from distant villages were coming to these trade centres and from these places the traders were collecting the goods. The descriptions provided about the trade centres in different classical accounts portray a good picture of flourished condition of trade and commerce.

Among the business organizations in ancient India, the guilds were playing a predominant role. It was supplying the qualitative goods to the international markets and it was probably one cause of highly appreciation of Indian goods in international markets. The technical know how was imparted by this organizations to the people and produced a large quantity of goods, mainly for export purpose. The most important function of the guild was the bank like functions. Though it was not a modern bank, it was keeping the money of the people by paying the interests. It was investing money in different commercial activities. Sometimes it was providing finances to the trading organizations. These multifaceted functions of guilds provided a leeway to the progress of commerce and trade. Besides this, the guilds were also involved social activities.

A trade and commercial activities should not be viewed only from the angle of export and import of goods. The cultural intermingling and transportation also provides enough indications of smooth trade. The impacts of Greeks, Romans, Arabs and Iranians on different walks of Indian life, ranging from art, architecture, language, coins etc. were enough to prove that there was a thriving trade among these countries. Again the excavations of some mounds of coins in different places of India points out the fact that the trade was in favour of India though some scholars challenge this theory on different grounds. It again unravels the fact that the Indian religious system was much more influenced by the western counterpart.

In the third century there was a falling off in the trade and for a time India, though much written about it in the West, faded away into a land of fancy and fable. The collapse of Roman Empire and the rise of Parthians gave a jolt to the Indo-Roman trade. Again the direct link of Chinese people with Western people through the Silk routes kept the Indian traders in abeyance. Taking the prevailing situation into account the Indian traders diverted their attention towards South-East Asia, which provided much greener pastures. India's trade with West Asian countries passed into the oblivion for a short time and again it revived in 11th century A.D. with the upcoming of Sindh merchants.[800]

End Notes

---

[1] Chakraborty, Haripada, *Trade and Commerce in Ancient India*, p. 1.
[2] Paul Louis, *Ancient Rome at Work*, p. 235.
[3] Singhal, D.P., *India and World Civilization*, p. 79.
[4] Pliny, *Natural History*, VI, p. 26.
[5] Tacitus, *The Annals of Imperial Rome*, II, 33; 53.
[6] Rawlinson, H.G., *Intercourse between Indian and Western World*, pp.124-151
[7] Ancient Indians, it appears originally used the term Yavana for the Ionian-Greeks, but later for all foreigners from the West. Somewhat in a similar manner, modern Indians use the term Angrez, the English for all westerners.
[8] Wheeler, Mortim, *Rome Beyond the Imperial Frontiers*, p. 209.

[9] Dion Chrysostom, *Orations XXXII*, p. 373. In another oration he mentions that the Indian Brahmins excel in self-control, righteousness and love of God.
[10] Singhal, D.P., op.cit., p. 81.
[11] Romanis, F. De and A. Tehernia, *Crossings: Early Mediterranen contacts with India*, pp. 14-15.
[12] Ibid.
[13] Ibid, p. 83.
[14] Grostier, B.P., *Indo-China*, p. 49.
[15] Saletore, B.A., *Indian's diplomatic relations with India*, p. 46-62.
[16] Jairazbhoy, R.A., *Foreign Influence on Ancient India*, pp. 143-148.
[17] Bunbury, E.H., *A History of Ancient Geography among the Greeks and Romans from the Earliest Ages to the fall of Roman Empire*, pp.42-49.
[18] Warmington, E.H., *The Commerce Between the Roman Empire and India*, p. 2.
[19] Chandra, Moti, *Trade and Trade Routes in Ancient India*, p. 109.
[20] Ibid.
[21] Adhya, G.L., *Early Indian Economics*, pp. 34-62.
[22] Singh, Ajay Kumar, *Indo-Roman Trade*, pp. 2-4.
[23] Saletore, R.N., *Early Indian Economic History*, p. 185.
[24] Ezekiel, XXVIII, 15, quoted from Chakrovarty, H.P., *Trade and Commerce in Ancient India*, p. 238.
[25] Warmington, E.H., op.cit., p. 213.
[26] Chakraborty, H.P., op.cit., p. 238.
[27] History of Plants, IV, iv, p. 6.
[28] Periplus, p. 36, quoted from, Srivastav, Balaram, *Trade and Commerce in Ancient India*, p. 260.
[29] Pliny, XII, 8, p. 9.
[30] Ibid.
[31] Saletore, R.N., op.cit., p. 186 and Chakrovarty, H.P., op.cit., p. 239.
[32] Schoff, *Periplus*, p. 153.
[33] Saletore, R.N., op.cit., p. 187.
[34] Ibid.
[35] Pliny, *Natural History*, III, BK-III, Ch. 9, p. 109.
[36] Ibid.
[37] Saletore, R.N., op.cit., p. 187..
[38] Watt, George, *Dictionary of Economic Products of India*, pp. 148-53.
[39] Periplus, 36, p. 36.

---

[40] Saletore, R.N., op.cit., p. 186.
[41] Ibid.
[42] Chakrobarty, H.P., op.cit., p. 239.
[43] *Theophrastus*, V. 47.
[44] Warmington, E.H., op.cit., p. 214.
[45] *Periplus*, p. 36.
[46] *Imperial Gazetteer*, VI, p. 383.
[47] Chakrovarty, H.P., p. 240.
[48] Ibid, p. 240.
[49] *Periplus*, p. 36.
[50] *Imperial Gazetteer*, XIV, p. 322.
[51] Raichoudhury, H.C.,*Political History of Ancient India*, p. 483.
[52] Saletore, R.N., op.cit., p. 189.
[53] Saletore, R.N., op.cit., p. 189.
[54] Rawlinson,H.G., *History of Phoenicia*, pp. 420-32.
[55] Brain, Weinstein, "Biblical evidence of spice trade between India and the land of Israeli. A historical analysis." *The Indian Historical Review*, vol. xxvii, No. 1, January 2000, pp. 18-22.
[56] Joseph, P., "Algummim or Almuggim" Of the Bible: An attempt at identification, in Tamil culture, vol. vii, no. 2, April 1957, pp. 133-138.
[57] *Periplus*, (36), p. 36.
[58] Chakrobarty, H.P., op.cit., p. 240.
[59] Champaklakshmi, R., *Trade, Ideology and Urbanization*, p. 18.
[60] Sino-Iranicaa, p. 552.
[61] Watt,G., *Commercial Products of India*, p. 978.
[62] Ray, H.P., *The Winds of change*, pp. 52-58.
[63] *Arthasastra*, BK-II, Ch. XI, p. 79.
[64] Saletore, R.N., op.cit., p. 190.
[65] Ibid.
[66] Chakraborty, H.P., op.cit., p. 240.
[67] Chakravarty, H.P., op.cit., p. 242.
[68] Ibid.
[69] Lauffer, *Sino-Iranica*, p. 535.
[70] Pliny, *Natural History*, XVI, ixv.
[71] **Ibid.**
[72] Saletore, R.N., op.cit., p. 191 & Mc. Crindle, *Ancient India Described in Classical Literature*, pp. 126-127.
[73] Ibid, p. 202.

[74] Chakraborty, H.P., op.cit., p. 234.
[75] *Brihat Samhita*, VIII, p. 30.
[76] Saletore, R.N., op.cit., p. 202.
[77] Ibid.
[78] Beal, op.cit., p. 200.
[79] Strabo, XV. 1, p. 20.
[80] Chakrobarty, H.P., op.cit., p. 235.
[81] *Milinda*, IV. 37.
[82] Srivastav, Balram, *Trade and Commerce in Ancient India*, p. 262.
[83] Rostovzeff,J., *Socio-economic History of Rome*, vol. II, p. 1167.
[84] *Jataka*, II (doddaru), no. 172, p. 66.
[85] Ibid, I, Puppaharatta, no. 147, p. 313.
[86] *Periplus*, (8), p. 25.
[87] Watt,C., op.cit., p. 146.
[88] Saletore, R.N., op.cit., p. 193.
[89] Ibid.
[90] Chakraborty, H.P., op.cit., p. 231.
[91] Saletore, R.N., op.cit., p. 193.
[92] Ibid, p. 193.
[93] Saletore, R.N., *Life in Gupta Age*, p. 416.
[94] Ibid.
[95] Pliny, *Natural History*, III, BK XXXV, Ch. 25, p. 241.
[96] Ibid.
[97] Ibid, p. 143.
[98] Saletore, R.N., op.cit., p. 195.
[99] Ibid.
[100] Warmington, E.H., *The Commerce between the Roman Empire and India*, p. 362.
[101] Chopra, R.N. & Others, *A Glossary of Indian Plants*, p. 141.
[102] Ray, H.P., *The winds of change*, pp. 51-62.
[103] Cunningham,A., *Geography*, pp. 337-39.
[104] Brain, Weinstein, "Biblical evidence of spice trade between India and the land of Israel. A historical analysis", *The Indian Historical Review*, Vol. xxvii, No. 1, January 2000, pp. 12-28.
[105] Ibid.
[106] Rathanvel, I.K., "The Indian circumnavigator of the past" in, *Journal of Tamil Studies*, vol. 04, Dec 1973, p. 27.
[107] Brian, Weinstein, op.cit, p. 24.

---

[108] Saletore, R.N., op.cit., p. 196.
[109] Chakrobarty,H.P., op.cit., p. 216.
[110] Saletore, R.N., op.cit., p. 197.
[111] Pliny, *Natural History*, II, Book-IX, Ch. 64(40), p. 448-49.
[112] Sayce, *Babylonian & Assyrian Life*, p. 107.
[113] Saletore, R.N, op.cit., p. 199.
[114] Ibid.
[115] Saletore, R.N., op.cit., p. 204.
[116] Ibid.
[117] Saletore, B.A., *India's Diplomatic Relations with West,* p. 222.
[118] Strabo, *Geography,* III, BK-XV, p. 117.
[119] Ibid.
[120] McCrindle, *Ancient India as Described in Classical Literature*, p. 78.
[121] Suetonius, *Twelve Caesars,* IV, 23, p. 160.
[122] Saletore, R.N., op.cit., p. 205.
[123] Ibid.
[124] Mc Crindle, *Ancient India as described in Classical Literature*, p. 75.
[125] Saletore, R.N., *Early Indian Economics*, p. 206.
[126] Ibid.
[127] Pliny, *Natural History*, II, Ch. (8), p. 255.
[128] Chakrobarty, Haripada, *Trade and Commerce of Ancient India,* p. 230.
[129] Pliny, *Natural History*, II, BK-VIII, Ch.(7), p. 254.
[130] Pliny, *Natural History,* II, BK VIII, ch. (10), p. 259.
[131] Ibid.
[132] Srivastav, Balaram, *Trade and Commerce in Ancient India,* p. 240.
[133] Saletore, R.N., op.cit., p. 212.
[134] Warmington, E.H., *The Commerce between the Roman Empire and India*, p. 156.
[135] Ibid.
[136] Pran Nath, *The Economic Condition of Ancient India,* p. 264.
[137] Warmington, E.H., *The Commerce between Roman Empire and India,* p. 166.
[138] Ibid.
[139] Dhar, M.K. and Mehta, R.L., *Social and Economic History of Ancient India,* pp. 56-58.
[140] Warmington, E.H., op.cit., p. 167.
[141] Saletore, R.N., op.cit., p. 262.
[142] Mc Crindle, *Ancient India as described in Classical Literature*, p. 79.

[143] Saletore, R.N., op.cit., p. 263.
[144] Ibid.
[145] Warmington, E.H., op.cit., p. 169.
[146] Pliny, *Natural History*, II, BK-IX, Ch. (54), p. 430.
[147] Das,S.K., *Economic History of Ancient India, p. 65.*

[148] Romanis, F. De and A. Tcharnia, op.cit, pp. 26-27.
[149] Chakrabory, Haripada, op. cit., p.129.
[150] Pran Nath, *Early Indian Economics*, p.148
[151] Warmington, E.H., op. cit. P. 181.
[152] Ibid
[153] Oppert G., *Ancient Indian Economy,* p. 152.
[154] Thapar, Romila, *Cultural Pasts*, p. 567.
[155] Pliny,op.cit, 12. 14.28. Four denarii per pound for black pepper and seven and fifteen respectively for white and long pepper.

[156] Ibid.
[157] Champaklakshmi, R., op.cit, p. 184.
[158] Ibid.
[159] Brian, Weinstein, op.cit., p. 22.

[160] Saletore, R.N., op.cit., p. 221.
[161] Romanis, F. De and A. Tcharnia, op.cit, pp. 26-27.
[162] Ibid.
[163] Srivastav, Balram, op.cit., p. 172.
[164] Romanis, F. De and A. Tcharnia, op.cit, pp. 26-27.
[165] Pliny, *Natural History,* XI, BK-XII, ch. (41), 18, p. 137.
[166] Pliny, *Natural History*, III, fn. 54, p. 113.
[167] Warmington, E.H., op.cit., p. 200.
[168] Ibid.
[169] Samaddar, J.N., *Economic Conditions of Ancient India*, p. 137.
[170] Saletore, R.N., op.cit., p. 225.
[171] Ibid.
[172] Champaklakshmi, R., Op.cit., p. 187.
[173] Ibid.
[174] Ibid.
[175] Miller, J., *The Spice Trade of Roman Empire, 29 BC to 641 AD*, p. 89.
[176] Brain, Weinstein, op.cit, p . 21.

[177] Rawlinson, H.G., op.cit., p. 138.
[178] Pliny, *Natural History,* III, B.K-XII, Ch. (25), p. 119.
[179] Saletore, R.N., op.cit., p. 227.
[180] Das, S.K., *Economic History of Ancient India*, p.62.
[181] Ibid
[182] Brain, Weinstin, "Biblical evidence of Spice trade between India and the land of Israel: A historical analysis", *The Indian Historical Review*, vol. xxvii, no. 1, Jan- 2000, p. 12-28.
[183] Miller, Jonnes, *The Spice Trade of Roman empire 29B.C.-641A.D.* p. 69.
[184] Ibid., p. 70.
[185] Warmington, E.H. op. cit, p.185.
[186] Champaklakshmi, R., op.cit, p. 184.
[187] Ibid.
[188] Romanis, F. De and .A. Tcharnia, *Crossing, Early Mediterranean contacts with India*, New Delh, , pp. 26-27.
[189] Ibid.
[190] Ibid.
[191] Chakrobarty, Haripada, op. cit, p.46.
[192] Rawlinson, H.G., op.cit., p. 133.
[193] Brain,Weinstin, "Biblical evidence of Spice trade between India and the land of Israel: A historical analysis", *The Indian Historical Review*, vol. xxvii, no. 1, Jan- 2000, p. 18.
[194] Miller, J.Innes, *The Spice trade of Roman empire 29 BC to 641 A.D.* pp. 65-96.
[195] Periplus (24), p. 30.
[196] Saletore, R.N., op.cit., p. 237.
[197] Ibid.
[198] Srivastav, Balaram, op.cit., p. 131.
[199] Pliny, *Natural History*, III, BK-XIII.
[200] Saletore, R.N., op.cit., p. 240.
[201] Rawlinson, H.G., op.cit., p. 86.
[202] Ibid.
[203] Periplus (14), p. 27.
[204] Saletore, R.N., op.cit., p. 242.
[205] Warmington, E.H., op.cit., p. 209.
[206] Warmington, E.H., *The Commerce between Roman Empire and India,* p. 258.
[207] *Indian Antiquary*, IV, p. 225-232.

[208] Saletore, R.N., op.cit., p. 247. Mortim
[209] Wheeler,M., *Rome Beyond the Imperial Frontiers,* p. 118.
[210] Ibid.
[211] Warmington, E.H., op.cit., p. 268.
[212] Warmington, E.H., op.cit., p. 268.
[213] Ibid.
[214] Saletore, R.N., op.cit., p. 248.
[215] Ibid.
[216] Haripada, Chakraborty, op.cit., p. 123.
[217] Pliny, *Natural History*, VI, Ch. (9), p. 326.
[218] Ibid, p. 169.
[219] Saletore, R.N., op.cit., p. 243.
[220] Mitra, R., *Antiquary of Orissa,* I, p. 101.
[221] Warmington, E.H., op.cit., p. 248.
[222] Saletore, R.N., op.cit., p. 251.
[223] Ibid.
[224] Ibid.
[225] Chandra, Moti, *Trade and Trade Rroutes in Ancient India*, p. 111.
[226] Ibid.
[227] Buch, M., *Economic Life in Ancient India,* p. 63.
[228] Champaklakshmi, R., *Trade, ideology and urbanization*, p. 183.
[229] Watt, G., *The commercial products of India*, p. 556.
[230] Champaklakshmi, R.,*Trade, ideology and urbanization*, p. 183.
[231] Saletore, RN., op.cit., p. 254.
[232] Ibid.
[233] Pliny, *Natural History*, VI, BK-XXXVII, Ch. (31), p. 426.
[234] Ibid.
[235] Warmington, E.H., op.cit., p. 238.
[236] Warmington, E.H., op.cit., pp. 251-252.
[237] *God, Child, Precious Stones*, p. 240.
[238] Schoff,W.H., op.cit., p. 171.
[239] Chakraborty ,Haripada, op.cit., p. 251.
[240] Ibid.
[241] Beal, I, p. 11.
[242] Pliny, *Natural History,* VI, BK-XXXVII, Ch. (54), p. 440.
[243] *Periplus*, (48-49), p. 42
[244] Warmington, E.H., op.cit., p. 240.
[245] Singh, Ajay Kumar; *Indo Roman Trade,* p. 145.
[246] Saletore, R.N., op.cit., p. 257.

[247] Champaklakshmi, R., op.cit., p. 184.
[248] Ibid.
[249] Warmington, E.H., op.cit., p. 245.
[250] Ibid.
[251] Chakraborty, Haripada, op.cit., p. 245.
[252] Ibid.
[253] Ibid.
[254] Ibid.
[255] Watts,G., *Commercial Products of India*, Ch. III, pp. 93-101.
[256] Singh,Ajay, op.cit., p. 145.
[257] Saletore, R.N., op.cit., p. 259.
[258] Warmington, E.H., op. cit., p. 263.
[259] Pliny, *Natural History*, XVI, BK-XXXVII, Ch. (56), p. 445.
[260] Warmington, E.H., op.cit., p. 264.
[261] Saletore, R.N., op.cit., p. 260.
[262] Saletore, R.N., op.cit., p. 261.
[263] Ibid, p. 262.
[264] Arrian, *Indika*, Ch. (38), pp. 760-61.
[265] Chakraborty, Haripada, op.cit., p. 256.
[266] Ibid.
[267] Saletore, R.N., op.cit., p. 264.
[268] Champaklakshmi, R., op.cit., p. 184.
[269] Ibid.
[270] Ibid.
[271] Pliny, *Natural History,* VI, BK-XXXVI, Ch. (65), p. 379.
[272] Warmington, E.H., op.cit., p. 271.
[273] Ibid, p. 272.
[274] Begley, Vimala, op.cit., p. 114.
[275] Ibid.
[276] Ray, H.P., *The winds of change*, pp. 70-76.
[277] Francis, P., *Bead Emporium: A Guide to the beads from Arikamedu in the Pondicherry Museum*,.
[278] Stern, E. M., *On Glass industry of Arikamedu* in Newby, M. and Painter, K. (ed.) *Roman glass: Two centuries of art and invention*, pp. 141-54.
[279] Kautilya, *Arthasastra,* II, BK-XXIII, Ch. (106), p. 114.
[280] Saletore, R.N., op.cit., p. 266.
[281] Ibid, p. 266.
[282] Chandra, Moti, *Trade and Trade Routes in Ancient India,* p. 126.

[283] Ibid.
[284] Champaklakshmi, R., *Trade, ideology and urbanization*, , p. 182.
[285] Silapapadikaram, 6, 88, Quoted from Champaklakshmi, op.cit, p. 183.
[286] Saletore, R.N., op.cit., p. 267.
[287] Chakraborty, Haripada, op.cit., p. 222.
[288] Chandra ,Moti, *Trade and Trade Routes in Ancient India*, p. 125.
[289] Chakraborty, Haripada, op.cit., p. 222.
[290] Mehta, R. N. and Shah, D. R., *Excavations at Nagara*,.
[291] Ray, H.P., *The Winds of change*, p. 76.
[292] Boulnois, L., *The Silk Road*,.
[293] Champaklakshmi, R., *Trade, ideology and urbanization*, pp. 181-183.
[294] Ibid.
[295] Salles, Francois Jean., *Athen, Aden, Arikamedu*, pp. 130-151.
[296] Saletore, R.N., op.cit., pp. 108-112.
[297] Pliny, *Natural History*, II, BK-VII, Ch. (32), p. 128.
[298] Chakraborty, Haripada, op.cit., pp. 266-70.
[299] Chakraborty, H.P., op.cit., p. 247.
[300] *Encyclopedia of Britannica*, 11th ed., Vol. XI, p. 23.
[301] Ray, H.P., *The winds of Change*, pp. 51-60.
[302] Chakraborty, H.P., op.cit., pp. 267-269.
[303] Warmington, E.H., op.cit., p. 266.
[304] Pliny, *Natural History*, XII, p. 32.
[305] Schoff,H., *Periplus*, p.65.
[306] Ibid, p.66.
[307] Saletore, R.N. op. cit., pp.112-114.
[308] Chakraborty, Haripada, op. cit., p.267
[309] Pliny, *Natural History*, XII, p.32.
[310] Periplus (28), p.33 quoted from Haripada, Chakraborty, op. cit., p.268.
[311] Warmington, E.H., op. cit., p.266.
[312] Saletore, R.N., op. cit., p. 113.
[313] Ibid, p. 114.
[314] Ibid
[315] Schoff, Wilfred H., *The Periplus of the Erythrean Sea*, p. 191.
[316] Pliny, *Natural History*, IV, Bk-XVIII, p.265.
[317] Saletore, R.N., op. cit., p.125.
[318] Chopra, R.N., Nayar, S.L. and Chopra, I.C., *A Glossary of Indian plants*, p.75.

---

[319] Saletore, B.A., *India's Diplomatic Relations with the West*, p.220.
[320] Saletore, R.N., op. cit, p.125.
[321] Ibid
[322] Chopra, R.N., op. cit., p.75
[323] Saletore, R.N., op. cit., p. 128.
[324] Saletore, R.N., op. cit., p. 129.
[325] *Periplus* (Schoff) (13), p.27
[326] Strabo, *Geography* - I, Bk-II, Ch (13), p. 111
[327] Saletore, R.N., op. cit., p. 117.
[328] Pliny, Natural History, III, Bk-XII, Ch (5), p. 168.
[329] Mc. Crindle, *The invasion of Indian by Alexander the great as described by Arrian,* p. 342-47.
[330] Driver and Milles, *The Babylonian Laws*, I (237), p. 85.
[331] Saletore, R.N., op.cit., p. 145.
[332] Champaklakshmi, op.cit, p. 188.
[333] Ibid.
[334] Kanakasabhai, Pilai, V., *The Tamils Eighteen hundred years ago*, Tirunelveli, 1966, p. 18-34.
[335] Champaklakshmi, R., op.cit., p. 189.
[336] Chakraborty, Haripada, op.cit., p. 265.
[337] Strabo, XIV, I. p.15
[338] Ibid
[339] *Sino-Iranica*, p. 220 quoted from Chakrobarty Haripada, op. cit., p.265.
[340] Ibid
[341] Warmington, E.H., op.cit., pp.264-270.
[342] *Journal of Indian Society of Oriental Art*, vol. XVI, 1948, p.45
[343] Pliny, *Natural History*, XIV, p.102.
[344] Ray, H .P., *The winds of change*, pp. 78-79.
[345] Herodotus, *Persian Wars,* I, BK-II, Ch. (6), p. 68.
[346] Ibid.

[347] Saletore, R.N. Op.cit, p.148,
[348] Ibid.
[349] Warmigton, E.H., Op.cit, p.268.
[350] Pliny, *Natural History*, VI, BK-XXXIV, Ch (2) p. 149.

[351] Saletore, R.N., Op.cit, p.149.

[352] Pliny, *Natural History*, XXXIV, p.17 quoted from Haripada Chakrabarty, Op.cit, p.273
[353] Chakrabarty, Haripada, Op.cit, p.273
[354] Marshall, *Taxila*, Vol-II, p.565.
[355] *Encyclopeadia of Britannica*, Vol., XIV, p.314
[356] Pliny, *Natural History*, XXXIV, p.17.
[357] Periplus, (36), p.49
[358] *Encyclopaedia of Britannica*, Vol-X, p.482.
[359] Saletore, R.N., op.cit, p.151.
[360] *Chakrobarty*, Haripada, *op.cit*, p.272
[361] Marshall,J., *Taxila*- II, p.620
[362] Tarn, W.W., *The Greeks and Bactrains in India*, p.104.
[363] Chakrabarty, Haripada, *Trade and commerce in Ancient India*, p.272
[364] Ibid.
[365] Marie, Francois Boussac, and others (ed), *Athens, Aden, Arikamedu*, p. 111.
[366] Ibid.
[367] Saletore, R.N., *Op.cit*, p.152.
[368] Ibid.
[369] Periplus (10) p.26
[370] Chakrabarty, Haripada, op.cit, p.282,.
[371] Ibid.
[372] Rostovzeff,J., *Socio, Economic History* II, p.1211.
[373] Pliny, *Natural History*, XXXVI, p.65
[374] *Encyclopaedia Britannica*, Vol. X, p.410.
[375] Marshall, J.,*Taxila*, Vol-II, pp.685-7
[376] Saletore, R.N., op.cit,., p.157.
[377] Pliny, *Natural History*, VI, BK-XXXV ch(29) p.251.
[378] Singh, Ajay Kumar, op.it, pp.154-159
[379] Periplus (49)p.42, also see (56) p.45 of Schooff,J.
[380] Saletore, R.N., Op.cit, p.161.
[381] Ibid.
[382] Pliny, *Natural History*, VI, BK-XXXIII, Ch (35) pp.115-116.
[383] Periplus, (39) p.47.
[384] Pliny, *Natural History*, VI, BK-XXXII Ch(22) p.118.
[385] Ball, *Economic Geography*, p.162
[386] Chakrabarty, Haripada, op.cit., p.277.
[387] Saletore, R. N., op. cit., p. 163-165.
[388] Pliny, *Natural History*, XXXIII, p. 34.

[389] Saletore, R.N., op. cit, p. 163.
[390] Ibid.
[391] Pliny, *Natural History*, V1, BK- XXXVII, ch (32) pp 426-27.
[392] Singh,Ajay, op. cit., p. 158.
[393] Schoff,J., *Periplus*, p. 156.
[394] Ibid.
[395] Pliny, *Natural History*, VI, BK- IX, p. 56.
[396] Pliny, *Natural History* XXXII, p. 11.
[397] Chakraborty, Haripada, op. cit., p. 284.
[398] Ibid.
[399] *Periplus*, (39), p. 33.
[400] Ray, H.P. *The winds of change*, p. 77.
[401] Cousen, H., "Buddhist stupa at Mirpur Khas in Sindh," *Archaeological Survey of India, Annual Report*, 1909-10, pp. 80-90.
[402] Marshall, J., *Taxila*, vol. III, 1951, p. 249.
[403] Ibid
[404] Samsastry, *Arlhasastra* (Kautilya) II, BK – XI, p. 78.
[405] Kangle, R.P., *Kautilya Arthasastra*, p. 100.
[406] Chakraborty, Haripada, op. cit., p. 285.
[407] Watt,G., *Commercial products of India*, p. 532.
[408] Saltore, R. N., op cit., p. 175.
[409] Ibid.
[410] *Periplus* (3-6) pp. 22-24.
[411] Saletore, R.N., op cit., p. 179.
[412] Ibid.
[413] Champaklakshmi, R., *Trade, ideology and urbanization*, pp. 184.
[414] *Pattanipallai*, I, p. 185.
[415] Kailaspathy,R., *Tamil Heroic poetry*, pp. 220-1.
[416] Aiyanger,S., *History of India*, p. 66. Quoted from Chakrobarty, Haripada, op. cit., p. 259.
[417] Saletore, R. N., op. cit., p. 180.
[418] Ibid
[419] *Encyclopaedia of Britannica* 11th ed. Vol-XXV, p. 217.
[420] *Periplus* (36) Schoff,J.
[421] Strabo, *Geography*, II, 5, p. 12.
[422] Chakraborty, Haripada, op. cit., p. 258.
[423] Tarn, W.W.,*Greeks and Bactrias in India*, p. 355.
[424] Chakraborty, Haripada, op. cit., p. 259.

[425] Champaklakshmi, R., *Trade, ideology and urbanization*, , p. 178.
[426] Ibid.
[427] Subrahmanian, N., *Sangam Polity, The Administration and Social life of Sangam Tamils*, pp. 18-29.
[428] Saletore, R.N., op. cit., p. 272.
[429] Pliny, *Natural History*, IV, BK-XII Ch. 41(18) p. 197.
[430] Tacitus, *Annals III*, p. 102.
[431] Saletore, R.N., op. cit., P. 273
[432] Saletore, B.A., *Ptolemy and Western India*, p. 113.
[433] Warrington,E.H.,"The commerce between the Roman empire and India, pp. 273-276.
[434] Begley, Vimala, and Richard, Daniel, De Puma, *Rome and India: The Ancient Sea trade*, Bombay, 1992, p. 23.
[435] Ibid.
[436] Mac, Dowell, *Finds of Roman coins in South Asia: The problem of interpretation of Ancient Ceylone*, 1990, quoted from F. De. Romanis and A. Tchernia, *Crossings: Early Mediterranean contacts with India*, p. 18.
[437] Romanis, F. De and A. Tchernia, op.cit, p. 18.
[438] Berghaus, P., "Roman coins in India and their imitations", in Jha, A.K. (ed.) *coinage, trade and economy*, 3rd Int cologuim, Naik, 1991, pp. 108-121.
[439] Romanis, F. De, op.cit, p. 28.
[440] Ibid.
[441] Chandra, Moti, *Trade and trade routes in Ancient India*. P. 109.
[442] Ibid.
[443] Chakrobarty, Haripada, op. cit, p. 4.
[444] *Annual Bibliography of Indian Archaeology*, vol. XIII, 1938.
[445] Romanis, F. De., and A. Teharnia, *Crossings: Early Mediterranean contacts with India*, pp. 15-17.
[446] Ibid., p. 17.
[447] Saletore, R.N., op. cit., p. 379
[448] Strabo,*Geography*, v, p. 35.
[449] Chakraborty, Haripada, op. cit., p. 5.
[450] Ibid.
[451] Warmington,E.H., *The commerce between the Roman empire and India*, p. 5.
[452] Chakrobarty, Haripada, op. cit., p. 6.
[453] Strabo, VII, p. 74.

---

[454] Strabo, XVI, Ch(4) p. 5.
[455] Pliny, *Natural History*, VI, pp 101-104.
[456] Chakraborty Haripada, op. cit., p. 8.
[457] Rawlinson,H.G., *History of Ancieat Egypts*_II, pp. 297-98.
[458] Pliny, *Natural History*, VI, pp. 165-168.
[459] Chakraborty, Haripada, op. cit., p. 10.
[460] Saletore, R.N., op. cit, pp 362-6.
[461] Rostovzeff,J., *Social and Economic History*, vol. II, pp 867.
[462] Pliny, *Natural History*, vol-VI, pp 96-100.
[463] Chakraborty, Haripada, op. cit., p. 12.
[464] Tarn, W.W.,*Greeks and Bactrians of India*, pp. 368-370.
[465] Pliny, *Natural History*, vol-VI, pp. 99-101.
[466] Chakrobarty, Haripada, op. cit., o. 19.
[467] *Cambridge History of India*, vol-I, pp. 27-29.
[468] Strabo, *Geography* – II, ch (1) p. 15.
[469] Ibid.
[470] Pliny, *Natural History*, vol-XI, ch (7) p. 3.
[471] Strabo,*Geography*, XI, 2, pp. 14-19.
[472] Pliny, *Natural History*, II, p. 170.
[473] Strabo, *Geography*, XI, pp. 1-4& 6-7. It is interesting to note that Bactria received gold from Siberia. Some specimen of jewellery found in Siberia and South Russia, are believed to have been made by the Greeco-Iranian artists. Hence it may be assumed that if was made in Bactria and was transferred to Siberia or Russia along the routes of Caspian sea. (Rostovzeff,J., *Socio-Economic History* vol- IV, p. 546.
[474] Begley, Vimala, and Richard, Daniel, De Puma, *Rome and India: The Ancient Sea trade*, p. 12.
[475] Charlesworth, M. P., *Trade routes and commerce of the Roman Empire*, pp. 97-111.
[476] Sidebotham, S.E., *Roman Economic policy in the Erythra Thalassa, 30 BC – 217 AD*, pp. 71-86.
[477] Begley, Vimala, op.cit, p. 12-16.
[478] Charlesworth, M.P., op.cit, pp. 63.
[479] Singh, Ajoy Kumar, *Indo- Roman trade*, p. 44.
[480] Ibid.
[481] Saletore, R.N., *Early Indian Economic History*, pp. 364-365.
[482] Ibid.
[483] Strabo, *Geography*, BK-CI, ch (27) p. 158.
[484] Bunbury,H., *Ancient Geography*, I, p.254

[485] Samasastry, (Kautilya's) *Arthasastra*, p.142
[486] Ibid.
[487] *Periplus* (14) p.27.
[488] Ibid (57) p.45
[489] Saletore, R.N., op.cit., p.283.
[490] Ibid.
[491] *Periplus* (6) p.24
[492] Thapar, Romila, *Cultural Pasts*, p. 559.
[493] Pliny, *Natural History*, 6, 26, p. 106 quoted from Thapar, Romila, op.cit, p. 559.
[494] Thapar, Romila, *Cultural Pasts*, p. 559.
[495] Ibid.
[496] Ibid.
[497] Strabo,*Geography* ,Vol-VIII, p.119.
[498] Ibid.
[499] Schoff, H., *The Periplus of Erythrean Sea* p.32
[500] Singh, Ajay Kumar, *Indo-Roman Trade*, p.21.
[501] Saletore, R.N., Op.cit., p.294.
[502] Strabo, *Geography*, III, p.244.
[503] Herodotus, *The Persian Wars*, BK-I, Ch-I, p.37
[504] Saletore R.N., Op.cit, p.307.
[505] Chandra, Moti, *Trade and Trade routes in Ancient India*, p.110.
[506] Strabo, XVI, IV, p.24, quoted from Ajay Kumar Singh, *Indo-Roman trade*, p.23.
[507] Thapar, Romila, *Cultural Pasts*, p. 563.
[508] Fraser, P.M., *Ptolemaic Alexandria*, I, p. 543. quoted from Thapar, Romila, *Cultural Pasts*, p. 563.
[509] Ibid.
[510] *Periplus*, pp. 18-19, 26, Strabo, 16, 4, 22-24.
[511] Thapar, Romila, *Cultural Pasts*, p. 563.

[512] Salomon, R., "Epigraphic remains of Indian traders in Egypt", *Journal of the American Oriental society*, 3, (1991), pp. 73-6, quoted from Romila Thapar, *Cultural pasts*, p. 564s.
[513] Ibid.
[514] Chandra, Moti, *Trade and Trade routes in Ancient India*, p.110
[515] Warmington, E.H., op.cit, pp.10-16.

[516] Heizman, J., *Early Buddhist trade and empire* in Kenedy, K.A.R., and Possel, G.L. (eds). *Studies in archaeology and paleoanthropology of South Asia*, pp. 121-38.
[517] Romanis, F. De and A. Tcharnia, *Crossings. Early Mediterranean contracts with India*, pp. 28.32.
[518] Singh, Ajay Kumar, *Indo-Roman Trade*, p.21
[519] Patanjali, VI, 2, 40-41 quoted from Shyamsundar, Nigam, *Economic Organizations of Ancient India*, p. 196.
[520] Manu, IV, p.120.
[521] Ibid, IV, pp.67-68.
[522] Srivastav, Balaram, *Trade and Commerce in Ancient India*, p.137.
[523] Ibid, p.138.
[524] Chakraborty, Haripada, op.cit, p.77.
[525] *Archaeological survey of India Report*, 1911-12, p.32.
[526] Chakraborty, Haripada, op.cit, p.8
[527] Patanjali, I, 2, 24.
[528] Nigam,S.,op.cit, p.196.
[529] Ibid.
[530] Cunnigham, A., *Barhut*, P1, XXVIII, B.M., Barua, Barhut, Fig.45
[531] Rao, Prabhakar, P., "Vehicles in Ancient India", *Nagpur University Journal* XV, I, pp.50-53
[532] Ibid,
[533] Nigam,S.,op.cit, p.197.
[534] Smith, V.A., *Jaina Stupa and other Antiquities of Mathura*, PI, p.5
[535] Srivastava, Balaram, op.cit, p.143.
[536] *India as known to Panini,* p.153
[537] *Jataka*, Vol.I, pp.194-95
[538] *Archaeological survey of India report*, 1907, PI, XLV.
[539] *Arathasastra,* II, p.33.
[540] Patanjali- I, p.70
[541] Nigam,S.,op.cit, p.197
[542] Ibid.
[543] Ibid.
[544] *Sacred Book of the East*, XXV, p.43.
[545] Manu, IV, p.68
[546] Rao, Prabhakar, "Vehicles in Ancient India", *Nagpur University Journal,* pp.49-50
[547] Srivastav, Balaram,op.cit, p.145.
[548] Ibid.

[549] Marhsall, J., *Monuments of Sanchi*, PI, LII, Lowest panel, Barhut Fig.95, Barhut PI, XLIV, Goli, PI, 6g.
[550] Barhut, Fig. 137, Quoted from Srivastav, Balaram, Op.cit, p.146.
[551] Agnihotri, P.D., Patanjali Kalina Bharat, p.240
[552] Arthasastra, II, p.28, quoted Nigam,S., *Economic organization in Ancient India*, p.199.
[553] Agnihotri, op.cit, p.240-241
[554] Agnihotri, *op.cit*,. p.240-1.
[555] *Sacred book of the east*, xxxv, p.227, quoted from Nigam, op.cit, p.199.
[556] Sastri, Nilakantha, *A Comprehensive History of India*, II, p.441.
[557] Periplus, (44).
[558] Ibid, p.181.
[559] Srivastav, Balaram, op.cit, p.153
[560] Periplus (60) p.243.
[561] Majumadar, R.C., *The Classical Accounts of India*, p.258.
[562] Nigam, Shyamsundar, *Organizations in Ancient India*, p.200.
[563] Periplus,op.cit, Sastri N.K., *Colas*, Vol., I, p.85.
[564] Ibid, Vol., I,p.60.
[565] Pliny, VI, p.26
[566] *Journal of Asiatic society of Bengal*, Jan1847, pp.1-78.
[567] Jain, J.C., *Life in Ancient India as depicted in the Jaina Canons*, p.118
[568] Srivastav, Balaram,op.cit, p.154.
[569] Maisley, F.C., *Sanchi and Its remains*, p.42-43.
[570] Fergusson,*Tree and Serpent Worship*, PI, LXVIII, quoted from Srivastav, Balaram, op.cit, p.154
[571] Srivatav, Balaram, op.cit, p.154
[572] *Archaeological Survey of Indian Annual Report* (New Imperial series) Vol. XV, p.29.
[573] Begley, Vimala, op.cit, p. 23.
[574] Pliny, *Natural History*, 6.26, p. 101.
[575] Begley, Vimala, op.cit, p. 23.
[576] Sidebotham, S.E., *Roman Economic policy in the Erythra Thalassa 30BC-217AD*, pp. 68-71.
[577] Begley, Vimala, op.cit, p. 23.
[578] Ray, H.P., *The Winds of change*, pp. 64-68.
[579] Cason, L., The *Periplus Maris Erythraei*, p. 39.
[580] Ray, H.P., op.cit, p. 65.

[581] Ibid.
[582] Rasche,M.G., *Papyrological evidence for Ptolemaic and Roman trade with India.* Proceedings of xiv International congress of Papyrologists, London, 241-6.
[583] Chakrabarty, Ranabir, *Trade in early India*, pp. 228-29.
[584] Ibid.
[585] Ibid., p. 242.
[586] Margabandhu, C., "Trade Contacts between the Western Asia and Graeco-Roman World in the Opening Centuries of Christian era", *Journal of Economics and Social History of Orient*, Vol. VIII, 1965, p.3.
[587] Singh, Ajay Kumar, op-cit, p.28.
[588] Mamrrie, Francos Boussac, *Athen, Aden, Arikamedu*, p. 138.
[589] Thapar, Romila, *Cultural Past*, p. 564.

[590] Ray, H.P. , *The Winds of change*, pp. 48-55.
[591] Scoff, H., *The Periplus of the Erythraean Sea*, p.188.
[592] Crindle, M. C., *India Described in Classical Literature*, p. 111.
[593] Charlesworth, M.P., *Trade Routes and Commerce of the Roman Empire*, p. 69.
[594] Rawlinson, H.G., *The Commerce Between India and Western World*, p. 120.
[595] Champaklakshmi, R., Trade, Ideology and Urbanization, p. 179.
[596] Ibid.
[597] Chakravarty,Haripada, *Trade and Commerce in Ancient India*, p.101.
[598] Comes, Henry, "Kalyana: The Ancient gateway of India", *Indica-I*, March 1968, pp.1-23,
[599] Singh, Ajay Kumar, op-cit, p. 30.
[600] Chakraborty, Haripada, op-cit, p.105.
[601] *Periplus (42)*
[602] Pliny, *Natural History*, VI, p.54.
[603] *Imperial Gazzettier*, VI, p.383, Schoff, W.H., *Periplus*, .201
[604] Rawlinson, H.G., *The Commercial intercourse between Indian and the Western World*, p.119
[605] *Indian Archaeology: A Review*, p.1.
[606] *Gazetteer of Bombay Province*, 14 (ii), p. 147.
[607] *Indian Antiquary*, Vol. II, p. 97.
[608] *Imperial Gazetteer*, Vol. XIX, p. 317.
[609] *Annual Report of Archaeological Department*, Nizam's Dominion 1936-37.

[610] *Imperial Gazetteer*, Vol. XIX, p. 317.
[611] *Imperial Gazetteer*, op-cit.
[612] Ibid.
[613] Rapson, *The coins of Andhra Dynasty*, p.22
[614] Chapekar, B.N., *Report on excavations* at Ter.
[615] Schoff, W. H., op-cit, p.51.
[616] *Indian History Congress*, 1951, Altekar,A.S., p.28.
[617] Singh, Ajay Kumar, *Indo-Roman Trade*, p.33.
[618] Pliny, *Natural History*, VI, Ch (23), p. 26.
[619] Singh, Ajay Kumar, op-cit, p.33.
[620] *Archaeological Survey of India Report*, 1936-37, p.64.
[621] Schoff, W.H., "*The Periplus of the Erythraean Sea*", p. 201.
[622] Ibid., p. 235
[623] Singh, Ajay Kumar, op-cit, p. 35
[624] Raman, K.V., "Excavations at Pumpuhar", *P. I. C. on Tamilkam Studies*, 1968.
[625] Dikshitar, V.R. R. (tr) "*The Silappadikaram*" (OUP, 1939).
[626] Champaklakshmi, R. Trade, ideology, urbanization, p. 179.
[627] Ibid., p. 181.
[628] Wheeler, M.E.D., "Ancient Name of Arikamedu", *Ancient India*, No.2, 1946.
[629] Sastri, N.K., *Indo-Asian Culture*, Vol.1, No.1, 1952, p. 45, quoted from Chakrobarty, Haripada, op-cit, p. 139.
[630] Chakrobarty, Haripada, op-cit, p. 132.
[631] Wheeler, *Ancient Indian Bulletin of Archaeological Survey of India*, No. 2, July 1946.
[632] Marie, Francois, Boussac, and others (ed.) *Athens, Aden, Arikamedu*, p. 102.
[633] Ibid.
[634] *Indian Archaeology: A Review*, 1954-55, p.20.
[635] Cunningham's A.S.I.R., Vol. XIII, pp.72-73.
[636] Subbarao, B., *Baroda through the Ages*, M. S. University of Baroda, 1953.
[637] Desai, M.D., "Some Roman Antiquities from Akota near Baroda", *Bulletin of Baroda Museum and Picture Gallery*, Vol. 7, Part-I and Part-II, 1949-50.
[638] Margbandhu, C., "Trade Contacts between the Western Asia and Graeco-Roman World in the opening of Centuries of Christian era", *Journal of Economic and Social History of Orient*, Vol. VIII, 1965, p.3

[639] Singh, Ajay Kumar, op-cit, p.77

[640] Deo, S. B. and Gupta, R.S., *Excavations at Bhokardan*,pp.14-39.

[641] Ibid.

[642] Sankalia, H.D. and Dixit, "*Excavations at Brahmapuri*", (Kolhapur), Deccan College Monograph Series, 5, p.207.

[643] Ibid.

[644] *Journal of Royal Asiatic Society*, London, 1957, p. 207.

[645] Shankalia, H.D., op-cit, p. 150.

[646] *Indian Archaeology: A Review,* 1962-63, pp. 1-2

[647] Ansari Z.D. and Mate, "Report on excavations at Dwaraka (Poona 1966) I.A.R., 1962-63, p.12.

[648] Sankaalia, H.D., Suba Rao, Deo, S.B., "Report on the excavations at Maheshwar and Navadatolli",

[649] Sankalia, H.D., Subba Rao, Deo, S.B., "Report on the Excavations at Maheshwar and Navadatoli",

[650] Ibid.

[651] A flat or scooped shaped tool with a handle for plastering **and** gardening purposes.

[652] Petris, F, *Tools and weapons.*

[653] Sankalia, H.D., and others, *From History to Pre-History at Nevasa*, I. A. R., 1959-60, pp. 1254-55

[654] Singh, Ajay Kumar, op-cit, p.87.

[655] Ibid.

[656] Around flat dish, especially for receiving a sacrificial libation (pouring of wine other liquids in honour of Gods) among the Romans.

[657] Deo,S.B.,and Dhavolkar,M.K., *Paunar Excavation*, 1967.

[658] Sankalia, H. D., and Deo, Report on Excavations at Nasik and Jorwe (1950-51), (*Deccan College Monograph Series 13*), Poona, 1955.

[659] *I. A. R.*, 1971-72, pp.12-13.

[660] *I. A. R.*, 1964-65, 1966-67

[661] Champaklakshmi, R., op.cit, pp. 184-186.

[662] Ibid.

[663] Begley, Vimala and Richard Daniel De Puma, *Rome and India: Ancient Sea trade*, pp. 82-85.

[664] Ibid.

[665] Ibid., p. 90.

[666] Ray, H.P., *The winds of change*, pp. 70-76.

[667] Romanis, F. De and A Tchernia, *Crossing: Early Mediterranean Contacts with India*, p. 2 1.

[668] Begley, Vimala, "New Excavations at the port of Arikamedu", *Journal of Roman Archaeology*, 6, pp. 93-103.

[669] Mahadeven, I., "Old Sinhalese inscriptions from India ports: New evidence for Ancient India – Sri Lankan contacts, In Epigraphia Zeylanica" – *Journal of Institute of Asian Studies*, xv, 1996, no. 1, pp. 55-68.

[670] Singh, Ajay Kumar, *Indo-Roman Trade*, pp.45-47.

[671] West, L.C., "Phases of Commercial Life in Roman Egypt", *Journal of Royal Asiatic Society*, Vol. 7, 1917, p. 46.

[672] Saletore, R.N., op-cit, pp. 146-149

[673] Begley, Vimala, and Ricahrd, Daniel De Puma, *Rome and India : The Ancient sea trade*, pp. 20-26.

[674] Ibid.

[675] Brian, Weinstein, "Biblical evidence of spice trade between India and the land of Israel: A historical analysis", *The Indian historical Review*, vol. xxvii, no. 1, Jan 2000,pp. 11-28.

[676] Schoff, W.H., *The Periplus of Erythraean Sea*, p. 106.

[677] A transparent gum excluded from the bark of a small tree native in south Arabia and some extent in Oman and the Somali coast.

[678] Retatsek, E., "Emporia", *J.R.A.S, Bombay Branch*, XV, 1883, p. 117.

[679] Singh, Ajay Kumar, op-cit, p. 50

[680] Chakraborty, Haripada, op-cit, p.138.

[681] Begley, Vimala and Richard Daniel De Puma, *Rome and India: Ancient Sea trade*, p16.

[682] *Periplus, Maris Erythrae*, p. 24.

[683] Begley, Vimala, op.cit, p. 17.

[684] Schoff, W.H., op-cit, p. 133.

[685] Schoff, W.H. op-cit, p.140 and 143

[686] XVI. IV, 6 (loeb)

[687] Begley, Vimala and Richard Daniel De Puma, *Rome and India: Ancient Sea trade*, pp. 20-21.

[688] Ibid.

[689] Schoff, W.H., op.cit, p. 107.

[690] Singh, Ajay Kumar, op.cit, p.53

[691] Begley, Vimala, op.cit, p. 19.

[692] Ibid.

[693] Boyce, A.A., "The Harbour of Pompeiopolis", *A. J. A.* (NY), Vol. 62, 1958, pp. 67-68

[694] Archaeology, XVII, (1994), pp.173-179
[695] Singh, Ajay Kumar, op.cit., p. 55
[696] Romanis, F. De., and A . Tcharnia, *Crossings: Early Mediterranean contacts with India*, p. 22.
[697] Wheeler, R. E. M., A Ghosh and Deva, K., *Arikamedu: An Indo Roman trading station on the East-coast of India*, in Ancient India, 2, pp. 77-124.
[698] Salomon, R., "Epigraphic remains of Indian traders in Egypt", *Journal of the American Oriental society*, 3, 4, 1991, pp. 731-7.
[699] Romanis, F. De., op.cit, p. 22.
[700] Begley, Vimala and Richard Daniel De Puma, *Rome and India: Ancient Sea trade*, p.19.
[701] Ibid.
[702] Ray, H.P, *The Winds of change*,p. 72.
[703] During, Caspers, "Contacts between India and West during early historical times", *Indian Museum Bulletin*, 21, pp. 22-23.
[704] Ray, Himanshu Prabha, *Archaeology of Sea faring*, pp.56-62.
[705] Ibid.
[706] Ray, H.P., *The Winds of Change: Buddhism and Early Time Links of South Asia* pp. 32-38.
[707] Beglay, Vimala, op.cit, p. 27.
[708] Sidebotham, S.E., op.cit, p. 56.
[709] Ibid.
[710] Begley, Vimala, op.cit, p. 27.
[711] Ibid.
[712] Thaplyal, Kiran Kumar, *Guilds in Ancient India*, p. 29
[713] G.L. Adhya, *Early Indian Economics*, p. 82; R.S. Sharma, *Perspective in Social and Economic History of Early India*, p. 140.
[714] Mahavastu (trans) III, p. 110; See also R.S. Sharma, *Shudras in Ancient India*, p. 200.
[715] Adhya, G. L., op.cit, p. 82; See R. S. Sharma, *Perspective of Social and Economic History of Early India*, p. 140.
[716] For Detailed reference see, Mookharjee, R. K., *Local Government in Ancient India*, pp.88-91, Ray, H.P., *Monastery and Guild: Commerce under Satavahans,* pp.112-113.
[717] From Mathura, Epigraphica Indica, XXI, p. 55.
[718] Deshpande, M.N., Ancient India, R.C. Majoomdar, *Classical Literature Ancient India.*
[719] Thaplyal, Kiran Kumar, *Guilds in Ancient India*, p.30.

---

[720] Sirvastav, Balaram, *Trade and Commerce in Ancient India*, p.105.
[721] Rick, R., *Social Organisation in North-East India in Buddha's Time*.
[722] Thaplyal, Kiran Kumar,op.cit, p.31,
[723] Ibid., p. 32
[724] Jain, B., *Guild organizations in North India*, p. 50, *Jain takes Nigama Sabha of the Nasik inscription as town hall but at another place* (p.51) he takes nigama as in the sense of guild of merchants.
[725] Srivastava, Balaram, *Trade and Commerce in Ancient India*, pp. 215-221
[726] Rao, M.V.K., *Studies in Kautilya*, p. 67.
[727] Thaplyal, Kiran Kumar, op.cit., p. 131.
[728]Beniprasad, *Theory of Government of Ancient India*, p.310.
[729] Nayadhammakha, p. 105, as referred to in J.C. Jain, *Life in Ancient India as depicted in Jain Canons*, p. 90.
[730] Manu, VIII, p.219, quoted from Thaplyal K. K., op.cit, p. 131.
[731] Yajnavalkya, II, p. 187.
[732] Manu, VIII, p. 210
[733]Nigam,Shyamsundar,*TheEconomicOrganizations of Ancient India*, p. 121.
[734] Bandopadhyaya, N. C., *Economic Life and Progress in Ancient India*, p. 226
[735] Thyplyal, K. K., op.cit, p. 70.
[736] Altekar, A.S., and Majumdar, R.C., *A New History of Indian People*, p. 355.
[737] Ibid.
[738] Brihaspati, XVI, 5-6.
[739] *Epigraphica Indica,* XXI, p. 60 ff, D.C. Sircar, Select Inscriptions, I, p.55.
[740] Thaplyal, Kiran Kumar, op.cit, p. 94.
[741] Ibid.
[742] Ibid.
[743] Mookherjee, R. K., *Local Government in Ancient India*, p. 120.
[744] Thaplyal, Kiran Kumar, *Guilds in Ancient India*, p. 95.
[745] Jamkhedkar, A. P., *Vasudevahindi: A Cultural Study*, p. 142. The reason for such may be that the guilds were generally taking up many contracts for their popularity. But if they thought that it was impossible them to complete within stipulated time, then they gave that contract to other guilds.
[746] Saletore, R. N., op.cit, p. 593

[747] Frank,R., *Rome and Italy of the Republic*, I, p. 13,
[748] Ibid.
[749] Saletore, R. N., *Early Indian Economics*, p. 596
[750] Day, *Agriculture in the life of Pompeii*, p. 192 (Yale Classical Studies, III)
[751] Ibid.
[752] Seutonius, Twelve Caesars (57), p. 83.
[753] Thaplyal, Kiran Kumar, op.cit., p. 94.
[754] Jairazbhoy,R.A.,*Origin and Spread of Ancient Civilisation,* p. 134,
[755] Jairazbhoy, R.A., The First Goddess of Indo-Pakistan Sub-continent, *A New Theory*, p.9
[756] Ibid
[757] Ibid.
[758]Singh,Ajay Kumar, *Indo-Roman Trade*, pp.49-65
[759] Jairazbhoy,R.A., *Origin and Spread of Ancient Civilisation*, p. 134-137
[760]Ibid.
[761]The Dawn, December 1, 1959, The *urn covered by a slate stone lid contained a complete corpse*.
[762] Jairazbhoy,R.A., *Foreign influence in Ancient India* , p.126
[763] Bhandarkar, D. R., "Foreign Elements in the Hindu Population", *Indian Antiquary*, XL, p.7.
[764] Fergusson,J., and J. Burgess, *Cave Temples of India*, 1880, *PIS* IX and X,
[765] *Lalit Kala,* 1957, nos. 3-4, p. 23
[766]James,M.R., *The Apocryphal New Testament*, pp. 366, 371.
[767] Simpson, W., "The Classical Influence in the Architecture of the Indus Region and Afghanistan", *Journal of Royal Institute of British Architects*, 1894, pp.107,108
[768] Marshall, J., *Taxila, II,* Pls. 28, 30,
[769] Ibid
[770] Jairazbhoy, R. A., *Foreign Influences in Ancient India*, p.130
[771] Marshall, J., Taxila, II, p. 612, Class V.
[772] Ibid.
[773] Ibid
[774] Ibid
[775] Jairazbhoy, R. A., *Foreign Influences in Ancient India*, p. 140.
[776]Ahmad Nizamuddin, *The history and Archaeology of Taxila*, p.234
[777] Jairazbhoy, op.cit, p. 140

[778] Marshall, J., op.cit, p. 679, No.14.
[779] Wheeler, R.E.M. *In Ancient India*, No. 2 , Pl. XXXIII, B.11, 12.
[780] *Daily Telegraph*, July 22, 1960, p. 18, quoted from Jairazbhoy , op.cit, p. 140.
[781] Smith, V. A., The *Oxford History of India*, p. 118.
[782] *Indian Antiquary*, 1932, p. 203
[783] Jairazbhoy,R.A., op.cit, p.151.
[784] Hodivala, S. K., *Parsis of Ancient India*, 1920, pp. VIII and 90.
[785] Bhandarkar, G. R., *Vaishnavism, Shaivism and Minor Religious Systems*, 1913, pp. 153-155.
[786] Marshall, J., Taxila, 1951, p. 222.
[787] Jairazbhoy, R., *Foreign Influence in ancient India*, p.154
[788] Hasting, *Encyclopaedia of Religion and Ethics*, 1910, III, p.658.
[789] Hori, K., *Speigel Memorial Volume*, 1908, pp.246-250.
[790] Elliot and Dowson, *History of India as told by its own historians*, VI, p. 55
[791] Jackson, A.V.W. *Journal of American Oriental Society*, Vol. 45, p. 246.
[792] Heichelheium, F. M., *in Economic History*, February 1938, pp.5-6
[793] Stein, A., *Innermost Asia*, 1928, II, p. 913.
[794] Jairazbhoy, R. A., *Origin and Spread of Ancient Civilisations.*, p.134.
[795] Ibid.
[796] Florus, *History of Rome*, IV, p.12
[797] Warmington, E. H., *The Commerce between Rome and India*, p. 98.
[798] Jairazbhoy,R.A., *Foreign Influence in Ancient India*, p.112
[799] Warmington, op.cit, p. 138.
[800] Ibid

5

Conclusions

The relationship between India and Roman Empire had become a matter of discussion among the historians in the recent years. The commercial connection between the two lands is corroborated by many archaeological, literary and numismatic sources. But in our survey, India's commercial relations with Western Asia has become a predominant factor which provides Indo-Roman commercial intercourse a suitable place because at that five time of the west Asian regions were occupied by the Romans. But attempt has been made not to dilute the whole trade connections as Indo-Roman but as Indo-West Asian commercial intercourse by making threadbare discussions of trade with different regions. But the constraints are the lack of sufficient evidences to prop up our work. The paucity of archaeological evidences does not provide a clear picture of trade. In this connection, the contribution of foreign writers, geographers and historians are immense and are supported further by our internal literary evidences.

Indian literary sources about this trade are quite inadequate because most of the literary sources were religious and Hindu religion was not permitting that type of foreign trade due to fear of losing caste. Again the wealth earned by the trade was regarded as the black wealth. The numismatic sources are quite helpful in this regard to construct the history. A large number of hoards of Roman coins, Persian coins provide a good idea about the trade and clearly symbolizes that the trade was in favour of India. Some of the recent excavations in West Asian regions like, Ostia, Pompeiopolis, Portus, Alexandria, Cana, Bernice etc have enriched our knowledge in this matter. The excavations at Arikamedu in India brought a complete revolutionary change in the Indo-Roman trade connections. The excavated materials indicate the exactness and reliability of the information furnished by Greek and Latin geographers. Excavations carried out at a number of places in Western and Southern India have yielded significant materials to show their affinity with the Mediterranean region.

The places like Broach, Maheshawara, Navadatoli, Paithana, Nevasa, Naski, Kondapur, Dwaraka, Yelleswaram etc. have given us the objects of West Asian origin to confirm the literary version of classical authors. The excavation reports and archaeological evidences were handicapped because most of the products, which were exported from India, were perishable and it is the reason which leave no trace of archaeological evidence of these products. Still then, with the help of foreign accounts, indigenous literary sources and epigraphic sources, an attempt has been made to construct the trade relations between two ancient lands, having a hoary past.

The archaeological remains in India are indicative of the fact of commercial relations between two sides, which was very close and prosperous. But one thing, which creates the greatest hurdle to draw conclusion, is the non-availability of Indian goods profusely in West Asian region. It has been explained by Warmington, who is of the view that the Roman subjects constantly visited India but Indians seldom visited the Roman Empire excepting Alexandria and Asia Minor. The Persian and Arab merchants were playing the role of intermediaries and were carrying the Indian goods to West Asian regions and Roman markets also. Again the perishable nature of Indian goods hardly leaves any trace. In this connection it may be expected that the further excavations in the West Asian region will add more facts to bridge up the gap in the relations.

It is usually observed that the trade relations between the two territories are largely dependent on the political relation. Unless and until a cordial political relation is not established between the two lands, the trade and commercial intercourse may not flourish well. From ancient times Indians have been accused of insularism, isolation, and utter lack of any contact with contemporary world.

Through this statement does not contain much water but for the first time the wall of separation was broken by Cyrus who occupied Gandhara and collected the tribute. This political invasion opened the floodgates of trade opportunities. Though the trade relations between India and western Asia was continuing from the Indus Valley Civilization, it got a boost with the establishment of political relations. Again Darius dispatched Skylax to explore lower Indus. In course of the voyage the fleet of Skylax touched the Egyptian ports on the Red Sea thus ensuring the safety of ports on the West Asian coast as well. In this set up, the trade relations between India and Western Asia increased in a considerable extent, which is clearly evident from Susa inscription. Herodotus observed that the Persians had a saying that Darius was a tradesman and in view of this admission, his real intention of discovering the sea-route to Indian may be well realized. Again the invasion of Alexander is claimed to have "laid open" to the Greeks "the passage of Hells Pont".

His one objective appears to have been to extend the Persian commerce to the Greeks of his generation, not only by discovering the arduous land routes but also by opening up the sea-ways,' with the result the Greek commercial colonists penetrated almost every possible areas of world. With the coming of Mauryas, the trade relations attained a new height. The cultural contacts between India and West Asia symbolize the cordial commercial relations. Though literary sources, archeological evidences and numismatic sources don't throw much light about the commerce of Mauryas but the elaborate offical arrangement of Mauryas to control the trade clearly signals about the developed trade relations between India and West Asia. Ashoka's good relations with the rulers of Syria, Egypt and Macedonia and Cyrene also acted as a boon for trade and commerce. His desire to spread Buddhism gave a boost to foreign trade and commerce.

The migration of Sakas, Hunas and Kushanas changed the chemistry of relations. Peace and stability brought by Satavahanas, Kushanas and Augustus to Rome was primarily responsible for commercial contacts, which touched its peak. The exchange of embassies further improved the political as well as commercial relations. The peaceful rule of Cholas, and Pandyas in south Indian region created a conducive atmosphere for trade and commerce. Analyzing these things it may clearly be concluded that a good political relation, peace and stability in the region provided a helping hand to trade and commercial relations. In a bad political atmosphere, the trade relations may not prosper well without the political backings, which is an essential ingredient for a developed commercial intercourse.

The trade and commercial interactions between India and West Asia facilitated the cultural intermingling and enriched the mosaic culture of India. The traders were the cultural ambassadors who carried the cultural elements to distant lands in addition to their commercial goods. And this is clearly visible in Ancient Indian administration, culture, way of living, art, architecture etc. In the sphere of administration, Mauryan administration bears close resemblance with Greeks, and Iranian counterparts. The impacts on art and architecture are widely felt in different spheres but it creates confusion among the historians to trace out the origin of every part. Religion and rituals practised by Indians have a close nexus with West Asian counterpart and the possible reason of this close connection may be they were the two branches of Indo-European stock. If a microscopic study will be made, it may be found that there is no such area in Indian culture where the impacts of West Asian people were not found in ancient period. So, it symbolizes again that there was a close commercial connection between the two lands in different periods despite unsteady political connections. The cultural immigration took a new turn with the foreign invasions and Ashoka's new initiative to spread the Buddhism in distant lands. A fertile ground was prepared by these political interactions and commercial intercourse on which the seeds of foreign cultural elements sprouted freely.

In this connection it is very difficult to decide the extent of cultural mobilization because not only West Asian region contributed a lot to the Indian culture but also India had enriched their culture in different dimensions. The Indian philosophies, drama, literature had created a stir among the intellectuals to explore the cultural horizon of India. Therefore, the flow of cultural elements was a two way process and it is difficult to determine who had contributed how much. Sometimes the historians get confused to decide the origin of archaeological products excavated at different places. This confusion became strong, when the Indian people started to produce the Roman goods in imitation, which creates difficulty to segregate the original Roman products from the Indian imitation of Roman products. For an example, from a series of recent studies it is becoming increasingly clear that many of the supposed finds of Roman pottery are infact indigenous Indian ceramic products. The Red Polished Ware (RPW), once considered a Roman import is infact an Indian product that was originated in Gujarat. At Amreli, Black Polished Ware precedes RPW in the First Century B.C., identical with RPW in composition and technique and differing from it only in colour.

As the technique of production, which was used in Gujarat, was prior to the Roman imports in the region, it is reasonable to conclude that RPW is not a direct imitation of Roman Samarian ware which it superficially resembles. The Rouletted ware found in India is a regional product of South-East and has been dated from the second century B.C. to First Century A.D. at Arikamedu, as Vimla Begley's excavation report points out. Mould Made ware of the Western Deccan has clear analogies in shape and decoration with Hellenistic pottery and metal work. The Mould Made ware from Nevesa is dated to first century B.C. So the foreign prototypes must be earlier and antidate Roman imports. Therefore, it may be concluded that MW is itself a local product made in Western India. Similarly the Roman coins, Roman bronze have been questioned about the origin.

The Indian coins were also not left untouched by the foreign influence. Until the beginning of 2nd century B.C., the extensive modification of Indian coinage was caused by the foreign influence. Although foreign influences can't be said to have affected Indian coinage very extensively even from that date still its faint influences can be traced in some respects from much earlier times on certain though not on all types of Indian coins. The main alien influences, which affected the Indian currencies, were Greek, Graceo-Bactrian, Persian, Parthian, Roman and Sassanion. Among them the impact of Roman and Greek currencies are largely felt on Indian currencies. Sometimes there coins were brought from the respective countries in exchange of goods and sometimes these types of coins were produced in India, imitating the foreign coins. It may be concluded that the Indian coin was greatly modified by coming in contacts with the coins of West Asian Countries in general and Roman coins in particular.

India's trade with West Asian countries provided an ample opportunity to the traders to earn their fortune by exporting various goods which these countries desperately requiring due to their geographical compulsions. The unfavourable climate, barren lands of West Asian countries made the hard working people handicapped to meet their needs. But in contrary, the fertile soil, the suitable climate, rich flora; and fauna and strong centralized peaceful govts, under different dynasties in India provided a conducive climate for India's trade with West Asian Countries. The natural harbours and the geographical continuity with West Asian countries became an added advantage in this connection. Inspite of so many advantages, the Indian trading systems was crippled under heavy cultural scrutiny. The Indian caste system put a stigma on trade, fearing the loosing of caste system by coming in contact with foreigners. Again the fearful Brahmins were casting aspersions on Vaishyas by depicting the wealth accumulated through trade as black wealth.

The Indian caste system did not permit the other castes except the Vaishyas to conduct the trading activities. Hence the trading activities did not get a proper boost from the cultural set up instead of geographical advantages. These cultural barriers became the stumbling blocks on the path of trade and commerce.

Various economic organizations sprang up to cater the needs of trading communities. Among them the guild was an important organization, which played its pivotal role in the commercial transactions. It fixed the prices of goods not providing an opportunity to the unscrupulous traders to manipulate the prices in internal as well as international markets. It's function like banks i.e. giving loans to the businessman, taking mortgage etc., facilitated the transactions in trade. The spread of technical know-how to the coming generation in the caste line is regarded another advantage in the guild system. But the most important contribution of guild was – it was producing huge quantity of qualitative luxurious goods to satiate the needs of foreign people as well as rulers who were demanding these goods in a vast quantity. In the absence of guilds, to meet the needs of these people might be a difficult problem. Again it provided an opportunity to prepare qualitative goods in an organized way, which might be impossible for the individual worker.

The products which were mainly exported from India to West Asian countries were-food products, textiles, copal, indigo, lac, animal stock etc.. But the goods, which were mainly demanded by India from Western Asia, were quite less in comparison to goods exported in quantity. Arabian incense, storax, sweet clover, figs, dates, wine, tin, lead, glass, orpiment etc. were the main products, which were imported into India. Again the horses of West Asian countries and slaves were also imported into India. Taking these goods into account it can be presumed that the trade was infavour of India. The hoards of coins found at different places in India substantiate the fact that the west Asian countries were paying heavy prices for their exorbitant needs for Indian luxurious goods. And that is the only reason why Pliny wailed for the drain of Roman wealth in exchange of Indian luxury products. But the Arabs, Parthians, Jews, Indo-Greeks and Persians took a large chunk of the profit of this transaction because they were the intermediaries of this trade.

These unscrupulous traders took the advantage of lack of price controlling mechanism in the West Asian markets and dictated the price of luxurious goods which were in heavy demands in their markets. Again Pliny did not take into account the market prices of their goods in their respective countries and the difficulties of traders who were traversing a long distance braving the dangers in the long routes. Whatever may be the situation, it clearly establishes the fact that the trade was in favour of India. Sometimes the barter system was prevalent in spite of money economy though Kautilya refers it as a despicable thing. It was a prevalent from of exchange of goods. In internal as well as external trade this practice was followed though it was rare in its occurrence. During the Mauryan period, the Superintendent of Commerce was scrutinizing and ascertaining the value of local goods before an exchange with foreign goods. Otherwise the money economy was the widely prevalent form of exchange. And that's why India had accumulated huge amount of foreign coins in exchange of its goods in the foreign markets.

The trade routes followed by the traders were not always smooth. In the land routes they were facing the dangers from the tribal people, pirates, and jungle animals. They were paying heavy taxes at different places and constantly getting harassed under different rulers. Again the Indian traders were carrying their goods through the traditional carts and chariots dragged by oxen, camels etc. This traditional mode of transportation encumbered the traders to carry a huge amount of goods for a long distance. The caravan traders, therefore, moving united with armed guards and taking the help of experienced men to guide in the routes. The sea-routes were not totally trouble free because the unruly behaviour of monsoon and dangers posed by the pirates. The greatest obstacle of the traders who were carrying the goods through sea routes was the ship that was not capable enough to bear the brunt of storms and winds. But in contrast, the ships and boats of Arabs & Romans were strong enough in comparison to Indian ships. Therefore, the Indian merchants were carrying the goods up to the port of Alexandria from which the Arabs, Parthians, Greeks carried the goods to west Asian as well as Roman markets. Through the Indian merchants had a good knowledge of monsoon; their inferior quality of shipbuilding did not permit them to traverse a long distance to earn the better fortunes. Usually the traders preferred the land routes than the sea routes to carry their goods to distant lands.

The traders followed different routes taking their convenience into consideration. These traders often exchanged their goods and buy the local products on the routes to sell in the distant lands. Again peace and stability in the region attracts the Caravan traders to pass through those regions where they were provided with all types of opportunities and facilities. The peace, stability and prosperity of the region stimulated their business transactions and that is the reason why they prefer the routes, which passed through the prosperous regions with political stability. And it was the duty of rulers to maintain the law and order situation in the region and to provide security to traders who were giving a large sum of money as tax to their exchequer. During the reigns of Mauryas, Kushanas, Satavahanas, they took the utmost care of traders and provided every opportunity to flourish the commercial activities to a great extent. The south Indian rulers like Cholas, Pandyas and Chalukyas were many steps ahead in this direction. They not only provided active support to the trading activities but also participated in these commercial activities. The huge profits amassed out of trade attracted even some Brahmins throwing the stigma attached behind this. It clearly represents that the trading activities and the wealth accumulated out of this trading activities was not considered reprehensible equally in all parts of India.

India's trade with West Asian countries passed through many ups and downs under different rulers, and in different circumstances. In the cultural front, the Mauryan rulers took the greatest advantage by mingling the western culture with traditional Indian culture and it produced a composite culture, which continued forever. But in the economic front the Kushanas extracted much more benefits than any other regimes. The Kushanas by their unifying conquests helped to open commerce by land between Western Asia and India and gained due prominence in this trade for north-west of India within easy reach from several directions.

The decline of trade initiated during the second century A.D. when the Roman Empire started to disintegrate and Parthians rose their monstrous head. Again the Chinese traders established the direct link with the Roman people by ending the intermediary role of Indian traders. In the third century A.D., there was a falling off in the trade and for a time India, though much written about it in the west, faded away into a land of fancy and fables. The changed scenario of trade compelled the Indian traders to divert their attention towards South East Asia, which provided much greener pastures. The Indo-West Asian trade though passed into oblivion for a short period, again it revived with the upcoming of Sindh merchants in the 11th century A.D.

Bibliography

Bibliography

PRIMARY SOURCES

Archaeology

Calvet,Y., "French excavations at Failaka 1984",*Proceedings of the Seminar for Arabian Studies*, 15,1985,pp.11-26.

Comfort,H., "Some imported pottery at Khor Rori(Dhofar)", *Bullentin of the American School of Oriental Research*,160,1960,15-20.

Comfort, H., "Terra Sigillata at Arikamedu", in Begley, V. and De Puma, R.D. ed., *Rome and India: the Ancient Sea Trade*, Wisconisn and Delhi: 134-50.

Comfort, H., "Imported Pottery and Glass from Timna", in Bowen, R. Le Baron ed., *Archaeological Discoveries in South Arabia,* Baltimore: 199-212, 1958.

Dasgupta, P. C., "*The Archaeological Treasures of Tamralipti*, Midnapore, 1975.

Raghvachari, K., "Dharanikota" in Ghosh, A. (ed.) *An Encyclopaedia of Indian Arcaeology*, II, New Delhi,1989.

Rao, S.R., *Excavations at Amreli*, Baroda,1966.

Sali,S.A., Diamabad (1976-79) *Memoirs of Archaeological Survey of India*,83, ASI, Delhi,1986.

Sankalia, H.D. et al., *From History to pre-History at Nevesa*, Poona,1963.

Sankalia, H.D. et al., *The Excavatians at Maheshwar and Navdatoli,*1952-53, Poona,1958.

Epigraphic Sources

Hultszch, E., *Corpus Inscriptionum Indicarum* (Inscription of Asoka),I,London, 1912.

Sculptures and Inscriptions of Darius the Great on the Rock of Behistun in Persia, London,1907.

Tolman,H.C., *Persian Inscription*, New York,1893.

Sircar, D.C., *Inscriptions of Ashoka*, 3rd edition, New Delhi, 1975

Sircar, D.C., *Select Inscriptions Bearing on Indian History and Civilisation*, I, Calcutta, 1942.

Literary Sources

Aitareya Brahamana-trans. ByMartin Haugh, Allahabad, 1922. Black *Yajur Veda*, text and trans. By A.B. Keith, *Atharva Veda*, trans. by W.R. Whitney, Harvard Oriental series, VII, Cambridge,1905, 2 vols.

Appian. *Roman History*, trans. By H. White. 2 vols, New York, 1899.

Arrian. *Anabasis of Alexander*, trans. By E.I. Robinson, Loeb's Classics, New York 1921.

Indika, translated by J. Chinnock-included in The Greek Historian, edited by Francis R.B. Godolphin, New York,,1942,2 vols. Also trans. by J.W McCrindle, London,1877.

Jataka. Text. Edited by V. Fausboll. 7 vols, London, 1877-79, also text, edited by V. Trenckner, Royal Asiatic Society, London, 1928, Trans, by E.B. Cowell and others, 6, vols., Cambridge,1895-1907.

John, W, McCrindle, *Ancient India as described in classical Literature*, Delhi,1979.

John, W., McCrindle, *Ancient India as described by Megasthenes and Arrian*, London,1887.

John,W. McCrindle, *Ancient India as described by Ktesias*, Calcutta, 1896.

John,W. McCrindle, *The commerce and Navigation of the Erythraean Sea,* Amsterdam, 1973.

Karttunen,K.,*India in Early Greek Literature*, Helsinki, 1989.

Kautilya, *Arthasastra* (6th Edition) Shama Shastri, R(tr.),Mysore,1960.

Kautilya, *Arthasastra*, Part-II,Kangle, R.P.(tr) Bombay,1963.

Lango Adigal. *Silappadikarram*, Edited and translated by V.R. Ramachandra Dikshitar, Madras,1939.

Manu, *Manu-Smriti*, Buhler,G.,(trans),Delhi,1964.

Pliny, The Elder. *The Natural History*, translated by J.Bostock and H.T. Riley, 6 vols. London, 1855-57.

Polybus. *The Histories*, trans. By W.R. Paton, Loeb's Classics, 6 vols, New York, 1922-27.

Procopius. *The History of the Wars*, trans, by H.W. Dewing,London, MCMXIV, 6 vols.

Scoff, W.H., *The Periplus of the Erythraean Sea*, Delhi, 1974.

Numismatics

Altekar, A.S., "Origin and early history of coinage in Ancient India", *Journal of Numismatic Society of Indiab,* pt.I, XV,pp.1-26.

Berghaus, P. "Roman coins from India and their imitations" in Jha A.K. (ed.) *Coinage, Trade and Economy*, Nashik,1991.

Elliot, Walter., *Coins of Southern India, International Numismatic Orientalia*, London, 1886.

Gupta, P.L., "The coinage of Satavahanas:Types and their regional distribution" in Shastri, A.M. (ed.)*Coinage of Satavahanas and coins from excavations*, Nagpur, 1972,41-61.

Gupta, V.S., "Numismatic data in the Arthasastra of Kautalya", *Journal of Numismatic Society of India*XXII,pp.13-37.

Hill, G.F., "Roman Aurae from Pudukota, South India", *Journal of Numismatic Society of India,* 1898,pp. 304-320.

Mitterwalner, G.V., *Kushana coins and Kushana sculptures from Mathura*, Mathura, 1986.

Mukherjee, B.N., *Kushana coins of the land of five rivers*, Calcutta,1978.

Narashimha, Murthy, A.V.(ed.)*Studies in South Indian Coins*, Vol-I,II,III, Madras, 1991-93.

Rapson, E.J., *Indian Coins*, Strassburg, 1877.

Rapson, E.J., *Catalogue of coins in the British Museum,* London,1908.

Rojers, Charles J., *Catalogue of coins in the Indian Museum*, Pt. III, Calcutta, 1895.

Sarma, I.K., *Coins of the Satavahana Empire*, Delhi,1980.

Sircar,D.C., "Kautilya and Indian Numismatics", *Journal of Numismatic Society of India,* pt.XV, pp. 128-143.

Smith,Vincent A., *Catalogue of Coins in the Indian Museum*, Calcutta,1906.

SECONDARY SOURCES

Books

Abbot, C.F., *Common People in ancient Rome,* New York,1917.

Abrahams, E.B., *Greek Dress,* London,1908.

Adams, J. Mckee, *Biblical Backgrounds,* Nashville, Tenessee,1946.

Adhya, G.L., *Ancient Records and the Bible*, Tenessee, 1946.

Adhya, G.L., *Early Indian Economics*, Bombay,1966.

Agrawal R.S., *Trade centres & routes in Northern India, Delhi, 1982,*

Agrawala, V.S., *India as known to Panini*, Lucknow, 1953.

Albright, W.F., *Archaeology and the Religion of Israel*,London, 1953.

Allchin, B. and Allchin, F.R., *The Birth of Indian Civilization* London, 1968.

Anderson, P., *Passages from Antiquity to Feudalism*, London, 1974.

Appadorai, A., *Economic Conditions in Southern India*, 2 Volumes, Madras, 1936.

Arne, T.J., *Excavations at Shah Tepe, Iran*,Stockholm, 1945.

Ayangar, V.K.R., *Aspects of Ancient Indian Economic Thought,* Banaras, 1934.

Baike,J., *Sea Kings of Crete*, 4th Edition, London,1926.

Balcroft, A. K. and Mason, W.F., *A History of Greece, 404-362 B.C.*, London, 1912.

Ball,V., *A Manual of Economic Geology*, Part III, Calcutta, 1936.

Balsara, P.P., *Ancient Iran-its contribution to Human Progress,*Bombay, 1936.

Bandopadhyaya, N.C., *Economic Life and Progress in Ancient India,* I, 2nd edition, Cacutta, 1945.

Banerjee, G.N., *Hellenism in Ancient India*, IIIrd edition, Delhi, 1961.

Banerjee, Gauranganath., *India as known to the Ancient World or India's Intercourse in ancient times with her neighbours,* London,1921.

Banerjee, N.R., *Iron Age in India,* Delhi, 1965.

Bapat, P.V. (ed.), *2500 Years of Buddhism*,Delhi, 1971.
Barnett, L.D., *Antiquities of India,* London, 1913.
Barrios, A.G., *Manual d'archaelogie Biblique,* Ist vol,1939, Iind vol,1953.
Basham, A.L., *The Wonder that was India,* London, 1954.
Baynes, Norman., *The Hellenistic Civilisation and East Rome,* London,1940.
Beazley, C. Raymond., *The Dawn of Modern Geography,* London,1897.
Behera, K.S., *Maritime Heritage of India*, New Delhi, 1999.
Bhandarkar, D.R., *Asoka* (2nd edition) Calcutta 1932.
Biecker, W.A., *Gallus or Roman Scenes of the times of Augustus,* New edition, London 1898.
Bient, J. Theodore, *Southern Arabia,* London, 1900.
Bierriman, A.E., *Historical Metrology*, London, 1953.
Bigchi, P.C., *India and China,* Calcutta, 1944, 2nd ed. Bombay, 1950.
Bihandarkar, Sir R.G., *Early History of the Decan*, Bombay, 1st ed.1884, 2nd ed. 1896.
Bihandarkar, D. R., *Lectures on the Ancient History of India,* Carmichael Lectures, Calcutta, 1918.
Biley,C., *The Legacy of Rome,* Oxford, 1921.
Blummer, H., *Home Life of the Ancient Greeks,* 3rd ed.,New York,1910.
Bongard, Levin, *G.M., Mauryan India*, Bangalore 1985,
Bose A.N., *Social and Rural Economy of Northern India*, 2nd vols. Calcutta, 1942-45.
Botsford, G.W., *History of the Ancient World*, New York,1921.
Botsford, G.W., *Hellenic Histroy,* New York,1924.
Bowen, R.L., *Archaeological Discoveries in Southern Arabia,*Baltimore, 1958.
Braidwood, R. J. and Howe, B., *Prehistoric Investigations in Iraqi Kurdistan*, Chicago, 1960.
Breastead, J. H., *A History of Egypt from the earliest times to the Persian conquest,* New York 1916.
Breastead, J. H., *Ancient Times,* 2nd revised edition , Boston, 1925.

Breasted, J., *Ancient Records of Egypt*, 5 vols, University of Chicago Press, 1906-7.

Buch, M. A., *Economic Life in Ancient India*, Baroda, 1924

Buddha Prakash., *Indian and the World* ,Hoshiarpur, 1964.

Bunbury, E.H., *A History of Ancient Geography* ,2nd vols. London, 1883.

Burrows,M., *What Mean These Stones*, London, 1941.

Bury, J.B., *A History of the Roman Empire, (27B.C.-680A.D.)*, London,1893.

Caldwell R., Caldwell R., Cook S.A., Adcock, F.E., Charlesworth, *Grammar of the Dravidians Language* (Madras, 1956).

Calhoun, G.M., *Business Life of Ancient Athens*, Chicago Press, 1926.

Carleton, P., *Buried Empires*, Oxford , 1939.

Casey,M. and Warmington, E.H., *The Ancient Explorers,* London,1939.

Casson, L., *Ships and Seamanship in the Ancient World*, Princeton, 1973.

Chakrabarty, Dillip.K., *The Archaeology of Ancient Indian Cities*, Delhi, 1995.

Chakrabarty, Ranabir, *Trade in Early India*, New Delhi, 2000.

Chakrabarty, Ranabir, *Warfare for Wealth*: *Early Indian Perspective*, Calcutta, 1986.

Champakalakshmi, R., *Trade, Ideology and Urbanisation*: *South India 300 BC to AD 1300*, Delhi, 1996.

Charlesworth, M.P., "Roman Trade with India: A Resurvey", in Coleman-Norton, P.R. ed., *Studies in Roman Economic and Social History*", Princeton, 1951

Chattopadhyaya, B.D., *Coins and Currency Systems in South India*, Delhi, 1977.

Chattopadyaya, Sudhakar., *Achemenids and India*,Delhi,1964.

Chattopadyaya, Sudhakar., *Social Life in Ancient India,* Calcutta,1965.

Chaudhrui, K.N., *Trade and Civilisation in the Indian Ocean*, Cambridge University Press, 1985.

Childe, V. Gordon., *New Light on the Most Ancient East,* 4th edition, London,1952.

Chopra, R.N. Nayar, S.L., and Chopra, I.C. *A Glossary of Indian Plants*, New Delhi,1956.

Conteneau, Georges., *Every-day Life in Babylonia and Assyria,* London, 1954.

Cooke, Stanley, Arthur, and others.,*The Cambridge Ancient History,*IX-XI, New York,1932-36.

Cunningham, A., "Ancient Geography of India", ed. By S.N. Majumdar, *Archaeological Survey of India: Annual Report,* Vol. V, 1924.

Cunningham, Sir,Alexander., *The Ancient Geography of India,* edited with notes by S.M. Sastri, Calcutta., 1924,also 1st edition, London,1871.

Curtin, P.D., *Cross-Cultural Trade in World History*, Cambridge,1984.

Dales, G.F., "Early Human Contacts from the Persian Gulf through Baluchistan and Southern Afghanistan", in McGinnies, W.G. et al. ed., *Food, Fiber on the Arid Lands*, Tucson: 145-70, 1971.

Das Gupta, P.C., *The Archaeological Treasures of Tamralipta*, Midnapore, 1975.

Datta, A., "Chalcolithic Culture in West Bengal-A Study on Settlement and Transition", in Ray, A. and Mukerjee, S.ed., *Historical Archaeology in India,"* Delhi: 78-79, *1990.*

Davar, F.C., *The Excavations of Pandu-Rajar-Dhibi,* Calcutta, 1964.

De Puma, R.D., "The Roman Bronze from Kohapur", in Beley. V. and De Puma, R.D. ed., *Rome and India; The Ancient Sea Trade*, Wisconsin and Delhi: 82-112, 1992.

De,Nundo Lal., *Geographical Dictionary of Ancient and Medieval India,* London,1927.

Deo, S.B., "The Megaliths: Their Culture, Ecology, Economy and Technology", in Deo, S.B. and Paddayya, K. ed., *Recent Advances in Indian Archeology,* Poona: 89-99, 1985.

Desai, D.,"Mother Goddess", in *Ghosh, A. ed., Encyclopaedia of*

Indian Archaeology, New Delhi: 267-9, 1989.

Dey, M.L., *Geographical Dictionary of Ancient and Medieval India,* Calcutta, 1899.

Dill, S., *Roman Society in the Last Century of the Western Empire,* London, 1921.

Ehrichs, R.W., *Chronologies in Old World Archaeology,* Chicago, 1965.

Fairservis, W.A., *Archaeological Studies in the Seistan Basin of South Western Afghanistan and Eastern Iran,* New York, 1961.

Fairservis, W.A., *The Roots of Ancient India,* London, 1971.

Fedlander,L., *Roman Life and Manners under the Early Empire,* 2nd edition. New York, 1909-1928.

Fick, R., *The Social Organisation in North-Eastern India in Buddha's time*, translated by S.K. Maitra, Calcutta, 1920

Finegan, J., *Light from the Ancient past* ,2nd edition Princeton, 1959.

Finley, M.I., *The Ancient Economy*, London and Berkeley, 1973.

Francis, P., *Bead Emporium: A Guide to the Beads from Arikamedu in the Pondicherry Museum*, Pondicherry, 1987.

Frank, T., *Economic History of Rome*, 2nd edition, John Hopkins Press, 1927.

Gajjar, I.N., *Ancient Indian Art and the West,* Bombay, 1971.

Gereni, *Researches on Ptolemy's Geography of Eastern Asia,* Vol. I, London, 1909.

Ghosh, A.(ed.), *An Encyclopaedia of Indian Archaeology*, 2 Vols., New Delhi,1989.

Gode,P.K., *Studies in Indian Cultural History,* I., Hosiarpur 1961.

Greenhill, B., *Archaeology of the Boat*, London, 1976

Greenhill, B., *Boats and Boatmen of Pakistan*, Newton Abbt, 1971.

Gregory, C.A., *Gifts and Commodities*, London, 1982.

Groom, N., *Frankincense and Myrrh, A Study of the Arabian Incense Trade*, London, 1981.

Hall,R.R., *The Ancient History of the Near East from the Earliest times to the battle of Salamis,* 7th ed London, 1927.

Harper, *Dictionary of Classical Literature and Antiquities*, edited by Reck, H.T., New York, 1896,,1923.

Heichelhein, F.M., *An Ancient Economic History*, Vol. I, Leiden, 1958.

Hopkins, E.W., *Religions of India,* Boston, 1895.

Hornell, J., *The Sacred Chank of India*, Madras, 1914.

Hornell, J., *Water Transport*, Newton Abbot, 1970.

Horridge, G.A., *The Lashed-Lug Boat of the Eastern Archipelago*, Greenwich, 1982.

Htti, P.K., *History of the Arabs*, London, 1937.

Hultszch, E., *Corpus Inscriptionum Indicarum* (Inscription of Asoka),I,London, 1912.

Huntingford, G.W.B., *The Periplus of the Erythraean Sea*, London, 1980.

Husaini, S.A.Q., *Economic History of India,* Vol, I, Calcutta, 1963.

Isaac, B., "Trade-Routes to Arabia and the Roman Army", in Hanson, W.S. and Keppie, L.J.F. ed., *Roman Frontier Studies*, 1979,pp889-901

Jain, J.C., *Life in Ancient India as Depicted in the Jaina Canons,* Bombay, 1947.

Jairazbhoy, R.A., *Foreign Influence in Ancient Indian,* Bombay, 1963.

Jasfrow, M., *The Civilisation of Babylonia and Assyria,* New York,1911.

Johnstone, P., *The Roman Economy*, Oxford, 1974.

Johnstone, P., *The Sea-craft of Prehistory*, Harvard, 1980.

Jolly, Julius, *Hindus Law and Custom,* Calcuta, 1928,trans. By S.K. Das from the German Edition of 1896.

Kane, P.V., *History of the Dharma Sastras*, 5 vols Poona, 1930-58.

Karttunen, R.P., *The India in Early Greek Literature*, Helsinki, 1989.

Khan, A.W., *Yelleswaram Excavation,* Hyerabad, 1963.

Khan, F.A., *Indus Valley and Early Iran* , Karachi, 1964.

King, L.W., *History of Sumer and Akkad*, Vol. I , London, 1910.

Kolta, N.S. *India as described by Meghasthenes*, Delhi, 1978,

Konow, S., ed., *Kharoshthi Inscriptions*, I, Varanasi (reprint) 1969.

Konow, S., *Indian Numismatics*, Delhi, 1981.

Lagdon, S., *Excavations at Kish,* Paris, 1924.

Lamberg Karlovsky, C.C., "*Excavations at Tepe Yahya, Iran* 1967-69, Progress Report I American School of Prehistoric Research Bulletin, Cambridge, 1970.

Laufer, Berthold, *Sino-Iranica,* Chicago, 1919.

Law, B.C., *Historical Geography of Ancient India*, Paris, 1954.

Law, B.C., *India as Described in Early Text of Buddhism and Jainism,* London, 1941.

Leemans, W.F., *Foreign Trade in the Old Babylonian Period,* Brill, Leiden, 1960.

Leemans, W.F., *The Old Babylonian Merchant,* Leiden,1960.

Liu, X., *Ancient India and Ancient China*, New Delhi, 1988.

Louis, P., *Ancient Rome at Work*, London 1927.

Lowick, N., "Trade patterns on the Persian Gulf in the Light of Recent Coin Evidence" in Konynijian, N. ed., *Near Eastern Numismatics, Iconography, Epigraphy and history: Studies in Honour of George C. Miles*, Beirut: 319-33, 1974.

MacDowall, D.W., "Indian Imports of Roman Silver Coins", in Jha, A.K. ed., Coinage, *Trade and Economy*, Nashik: 145-64, 1991

Maitra, A.K., Editor, *Gaudalekhamala* (Inscriptions of Bengal).

Mandal, P.K., *Interpretation of Terracottas from Tamralipta,* Tamluk, 1987.

Margabandhu, C., "Censers", in Ghosh, A .ed., *An Encyclopardia of Indian Archaeology*, Delhi, 1989.

Marshall, J., *Taxila*, vols. I-III, Cambridge, 1951.

Mcclees, H., *Daily Life of the Greeks and Romans as illustrated by the Classical Collection,* New York, 1925.

McCrindle, *Ancient India as described by Meghasthenes and Arrian*, Calcutta 1877,

McDaniel, W.B., *Roman Private Life and Its Survivals*, New York, 1927

McPherson, K., "Traditional Indian ocean Shipping Technologies", Bandaranayake, S. ed., *Sri Lanka and the Silk Road of the Sea, Colombo*, 1990.

Mehta, R.N., and Shah, D.R., *Excavation at Nagara*, Baroda, 1968.

Meiggs, R., *Trees and Timber in the Ancient Mediterranean World*, Oxford, 1982.

Miller, J.I., *The Spice Trade of the Roman Empire*, Oxford, 1969.

Mitchiner, M., *The Origins of Indian Coinage*, New Delhi, 1973.

Mitra, S.K. *India's Cultural Empire and Her Future*, 2nd ed. ,Madras, 1947.

Mitterwalner, G.V., *Kusana Coins and Kusana Sculptures from Mathura*, Mathura, 1986.

Mode, H., *Harappa Culture and the West,* Calcutta, 1961.

Muckelroy, K., *Maritime Archaeology*, Cambridge, 1978.

Mukerjee, R.K., *A History of Indian Civilization,* Bombay, 1956.

Mukherjee, B.N., *Kushana Coins of the Land of the Five Rivers*, Calcutta, 1978.

Mukherjee, B.N., *The Economic Factors in Kushana History*, Calcutta, 1970.

Mukherjee, B.N., *Nana on Lion*, Calcutta, 1969.

Mukhopadhya, G., *History of Indian Medicine*, Caclutta, 1923.

Myers, B.S., *Cambridge Ancient History*, Vol. I , Cambridge, 1924.

Nagaswamy, R., and Abdul Majeed, "Alagankulam: An Indo-Roman Trading Port", in C. Margabandhu et al. (eds), *Indian Archaeological Heritage* (K.V. Soundararajan, Felicitation Volume), Delhi, 1991

Nagaswamy, R., *Kaverippattinam-A Guide*, Madras: Tamil Nadu State Department of Archaeology, 1973.

Nainar, S.M.H., *Arab Geographers' Knowledge of South India*, Madras, 1942.

Narain,A.K., *The Indo-Greeks*, Oxford,1957.

Nilakanta Sastri, K.A., *Foreign Notices of South India,* Madras,1939

Olmstead, A.T., *History of the Persian Empire*, Chicago, 1943.

Olmstead, A.T.E., *History of Assyria,* New York, 1923.

Oman, Sir C.W.C., *The Byzantine Empire*, London, 1922.

Peacock, D.P.S., and Williams, D.F., *Amphorae and the Roman Economy*, London, New York, 1986.

Peacock, D.P.S., *Pottery in the Roman World: An Ethnoarchaeological Approach,* London, New York, 1982.

Petrie, W.M.F., *Ancient Gaza IV* , London, 1931-34.

Piggott, S. (ed.), *The Dawn of Civilization*, London, 1961.

Pococke,E., *India and Greece*, London, 1852.

Polanyi, K. ed., "Trade and markets in the Early Empires", in *Economics in History and Theory*, New York, 1957.

Potts, D., *The Arabian Gulf in Antiquity*, Oxford, 1990.

Pran Nath. *A Study in the Economic Condition of Ancient India*, London, 1929.

Preston, H.W. and Dodge, L., *Private Life of the Romans,* Chicago, 1900.

Pritchard, J.B., *Ancient Near-Eastern Texts Relating to the Old Testament.* Princeton,1950.

Raman, K.V., *Excavations at Uraiyur* (*Tiruchirappalli*), 1965-9, Madras, 1975.

Rao, S.R., "Shipping in Ancient India": In *India's Contribution in World Thought and Culture*, Madras: pp.83-107, 1970.

Rapson, E.J., *The Cambridge history of India*, Vol. I, *Ancient India,* Delhi, 1955.

Ratnagar, S., *Encounters: the Westerly Trade of the Harappan Civilization*, New Delhi, 1981.

Ray Chaudhary, H.C., *Studies in Indian Antiquities,* Calcutta, 1932.

Ray, H.P., *Monastery and Guild: Commerce under the Satavahanas,* New Delhi, 1986.

Ray, H.P., and Jean Francois Salles (ed.) *Tradition and Archaeology:Early Maritimes Contacts in the Indian Ocean,* New Delhi, 1996.

Ray, H.P., (ed.) *Archaelogy of Sea-Faring:The Indian Ocean in the Ancient Period,* New Delhi, 1999.

Ray, N.R., *Maurya and Sunga Art,* Calcutta, 1945.

Renfrew, C., "Trade as Action at a Distance", in Sabloff, J.A., and Lamberg-Karlovsky, C.C. ed., *Ancient Civilization and Trade*, New Mexico, 1975.

Rowland, B., *The Art and Architecture of India*, 2nd edition , London,1948.

Saggs, H.W.F., *The Greatness that was Babylon*, London, 1962.

Saletore, B.A., *India's Diplomatic Relations with the West*, Bombay, 1958.

Saletore,R.N.,Early *Indian Economic History*,Bombay,1973.

Salles, J.F., "The Arab-Persian Gulf under the Seleucids", in Kuhrt, A. and Sherwin-White, S. ed., *Hellenism in the East*, Duckworth, pp.75-184, 1987.

Salles, J.F., *The Periplus of the Erythraean Sea and the Arab-Persian Gulf*", Paper presented at the UNESCO Seminar on "Integral Study of the Silk Roads: Roads of Dialogue", Madras, 1990.

Salles, J.F.,*Athen,Aden and Arikamedu*,New Delhi,1995.

Sankalia, H.D. and Deo, S.B., *The Excavations at Maheshwar and Navdatoli*, Poona, 1960.

Sankalia, H.D., *The Prehistory and Protohistory of India and Pakistan*, Bombay, 1962 (Revised Edition, 1974).

Sastri, K.A.N., *Age of the Nandas and Mauryas*, 1st ed., Banaras, 1952.

Sayce, *A.H., Babylonians and Assyrians,Life and Customs*, New York, 1899

Sayce, S., *Records of the past*, 6 vols, London, 1889-1893.

Schoff, Wilfred, H., *The Ship "Tyre", a Study in the commerce of the Bible*, New York, 1920.

Sedlar, J.M., *India and the Greek World*, Totowa, 1980.

Semple, E.C., *The Geography of the Mediterranean Region:its relation to Ancient History*, London, 1932.

Sewell, R., *Historical Inscriptions of Southern India*, edited by S. Krishna Swami Aiyangar, Madras. 1932.

Shaffer, J.G., "Harappan Commerce: An Alternative Perspective", in Pastner, S. and Flam, L. ed., *Anthropology in Pakistan: and Recent Socio-cultural and Archaeological Perspective*,

Cornell: pp.166-210, 1982.
Sharma, R.S., *Material Culture and Social Formations in Ancient India*, New Delhi, 1983.
Sidebotham, S.E., "Ports of the Red Sea and the Arabia-India Trade", in Begley, V. and De Puma, R.D., ed., *Rome and India-the Ancient Sea Trade*, Wisconsin and Delhi,pp. 82-112, 1992.
Sidebotham, S.E., *Roman Economic Policy in the Ertythra Thalassa*, Leiden, 1986.
Singh, A.K., *Indo-Roman Trade*, Patna, 1988.
Singh, R.N., *Ancient Indian Glass*, Delhi, 1989.
Singhal, D.P. *India, and the World Civilization* , New York, 1969.
Sircar, D.C., *Cosmography and Geography in Early Indian Literature*, Calcutta, 1967.
Sircar, D.C., *Indian Epigraphy,* New Delhi, 1965.
Speiser, E.A., *Excavations at Tepe Gawra*, Vol. I , Philadelphia, 1935.
Stein, A., *Ancient Khotan,* Oxford, 1907.
Stern, E.M., "Early Exports Beyond the Empire", in Newby, M. and Painter, K. ed., *Roman Glass: Two Centuries of Art and Invention*, London: pp.141-54, 1991.
Stern, E.M., "On the Glass Industry of Arikamedu (Ancient Podouke)", in Bhardwaj, H.C., ed., *Archaeometry of Glass*, Calcutta, 1987.
Subba Rao, N.S., *Economic and Political Condition in Ancient India*, Mysore, 1911,
Suresh, S., "A Study of the Roman Coins and Other Antiquities in Indian with Special Reference to South India", Ph.D. Dissertation, New Delhi: Jawaharlal Nehru University, 1993.
Swamy, L.N., *Maritime Contacts of Ancient India*, New Delhi, 2000.
Sykes, Sir P., Molesworth ,*Hellenistic Civilisation,* London,1930.
Sykes, Sir P., Molesworth., *History of Persia*, London, 1915.
Tarn, W.W. and Griffiths, *Hellenistic Civilization,* London, 1952.
Tarn, W.W., *Greeks in Bactria and India,*2nd ed.,Cambridge,1951.
Thapar, Romila, "Epigraphic Evidence and some Indo-Hellenistic

Contacts during the Mauryan Period", in S.K. Maity and Upendra Thakur (ed.), *Indological Studies,Professor D.C. Sircar Commemoration Volume,* pp.15-19,New Delhi,1978.

Thapar, Romila,*The Mauryas Revisited*,Calcutta1987.

Thapar, Romila,*Ashoka and the decline of Mauryas*,London,1961.

Thomas, P. , *Story of the Cultural Empire* , Ernakulam,1967.

Thompson, *A Dictionary of Assyrian Botany,London* , 1949.

Tilak, B.G., *The Arctic Home in the Vedas* ,Poona, 1956.

Toussaint, A., *History of the Indian Ocean*, London, 1966.

Treble, H.A. and King, K.M., *Everday Life in Rome,* Oxford, 1930.

Turner, R., *The Great Cultural Tradition*, Vol. I, First edition ,London, 1941.

Varadarajan, L., "Maritime Encounter of East and West:Indian Ship Building Techniques", Paper presented at the UNESCO Seminar on "An Integral Study of the Silk Roads: Roads of Dialogue", Goa, 1990.

Varadarajan, L., forthcoming, "The Sailing Craft of India", in Joshi, M.C. ed. *Personality of Indian Archaeology: Essays in Honous of Shri B.K. Thapar*, New Delhi,1990.

Vogelsang, W., "The Achaemenids and India", in Sancisi-Weerdenburg, H. and Kuhrt, A. ed., *Achaemenid History*, IV, Leiden: 93-110, 1990.

Waddell, L.A., *Report on the Excavations at Pataliputra,* Calcutta, 1903.

Walburg, R., "Late Roman Copper Coins from Southern India", in Jha, A.K. ed., *Coinage, Trade and Economy*, Nashik: 164-7, 1991.

Walker, M.J. and Santoso, S., "Romano-Indian Rouletted Pottery in Indonesia", *in Van de Velde, P. ed., Prehistoric Indonesia-A Reader*, Dordrecht , pp.376-83, 1984.

Ward, W.H., *The Seal cylinders of Western Asia* ,Washington, 1910.

Wheeler,R.E.M., Ghosh, A. and Krishna Deva, "Arikamedu: An Indo Roman Trading-station on the East Coast of India", in *Ancient India*, 2: pp.17-124, London, 1946.

Wheeler,R.E.M., Ghosh, A. and Krishna Deva, *Charsada*, London, 1962.

Wheeler,R.E.M., Ghosh, A. and Krishna Deva, *Rome Beyond the Imperial Frontiers*, Harmondsworth, 1955.

Whitcomb, D.S. and Johnson, J.H., *Quseir al-Qadim 1980*, Preliminary Report Malibu, 1982.

White, K.D., *Greek and Roman Technology*, London, 1984.

Wilon, H.H.,*The Persian Gulf,* Oxford, 1928.

Woolley C.L., *Development of Sumerian Art,* London, 1935.

Woolley C.L., *The Sumerians,* Oxford, 1929.

Woolley C.L., Ur Excavations,Vol. II, *Royal Cemetery,* London, 1934.

Woolley C.L., *Ur Excavations*, Vol. I, London, 1927.

Woolley C.L., *Ur of Chaldees,* London, 1929.

Woolley, C.L.,*Ur Excavations V., the Ziggurai and its surroundings,* London, 1939.

Woolley, C.L.,*Ur of the chadees,*1954.

Wright, F.A., *Greek Social Life,* New York, 1952.

Zimmer, H., *The Art of Indian Asia,* New York, 1955.

Research Articles

Agrawal, D.P., "New Evidence for a shorter Chronology", *Current Science*, Vol. 143, no. 3609, 1964, pp. 950-52.

Agrawal, D.P., "The Ancient Indian Style seals from Bahrain", *Antiquity*, Vol. 32, London, 1958, pp. 242-246.

Basu, K.K., "An Account of the early indigo planters in Bhagalpur", *Indian Historical Review,* XII, pp.67-73.

Billimoria, N.M., "The Iranians in Ancient India, Especially in Sindh and the Punjab", *Journal of Sindh Historical Society,* vol. I, Pt. I, 1936.

Bongard-Levin, G., "Indians in ancient Armenia", *Indian Historical Review.*, XXXV,1960,pp.56-58.

Bose, Abindra Nath, "Early Industrial Organisation in Northern India", *Indian Historical Quarterly*,XX,pp.76-81

Bowen, R.L., "Primitive Watercraft of Arabia", *American Neptune*, XII, 3: 1952,pp.186-221.

Buddha Prakash, "Vyasa (A Study of Indo-Bablonian

CulutralContacts)", *Journal of Bihar and Orissa Research Society*, vol. 37, 1951.

Burges, J., Report on the Elora Cave Temples and the Brahminical and Jaina Caves in Western India, Archaeological Survey of Western India, V, 1883.

Burges, J., List of Antiquarian Remains in the Bombay Presidency, Archaeological Survey of Western India, XI, 1885.

Burges, J., and Indraji, B., *Inscriptions from the Cave Temples of Western India*, Archaeological Survey of Western India, IV, 1976.

Calvet, Y. "French Excavations at Failaka 1984", Proceedings of the Seminar for Arbabian Studies, 15: 1985, pp.11-26.

Carter, H.J., "Geography of the South-West Coast of Arabia", *Journal of Bombay Branch, Royal Asiatic Society*, Vol. III, Pts. I, and II, 1847-56, 262 ff.

Carter, M.,"Dionysiac Aspects of Kushan Art", *Arts Orientalis*, VII: 1968, pp.121-46.

Casson, L., "Rome's Trade with the East: The Sea Voyage to Africa and India", *Transactions of the American Philological Association*, 110: 1980, pp.21-36.

Casson, L., "Rome's Trade with the eastern Coast of India", *Cahiers d'histoire* , 1988, pp303-8.

Chakrabortty, S.K. "The Persian and Greek Coins and their imitations in Ancient India", *Indian Historical Quarterly*, Vol. 10, 1934.

Chanda,R.P., "The Beginning of Art in Eastern India," *Memoirs of Archaeological Survey of India*, no. 30, p. 12

Charles, J.A., "Where is the Tin?", *Antiquity*, XLIX: 1975,pp.19-24.

Chattopadhayaya, S., "Megaliths", *Ancient India*, No. 4, 1947-8,pp. 4-13.

Chattopadhayaya, S., "Foreign Notices of Achaemenid India", *Indian Historical Quarterly*, Vol. 26, 1950.

Childe, V.G., "India and the West Before Darius", *Antiquity*, Vol. XVIII, 1939.

Comfort, H., "Some Imported Pottery and at Khor Rori (Dhofar)", *Bulletin of the American School of Oriental Research,* 160: 1960,pp. 15-20,

Cunningham, A., *Annual Report, Archaeological Survey of India,* III: 1871-2,pp.13-46.

Deb, H.K., "Vedic India and the Middle West", *Journal of Royal Asiatic Society,* Bengal, Vol. XIV, no. 2, 1948.

DeCardi, B., "New Waresand Fresh Problems from Baluchistan", *Antiquity,* Vol. XXXIII, 1959, pp. 15-28.

Deloche, J., Geographical Considerations in the Localization of Ancient Sea-ports of India", *The India Economic and Social History Review* , 20, 1983., pp.439-48.

Devasahayam, N., "Roman Jewellery from Vellalore Site during the Sangam Period, *Lalit Kala,* XXI: 53, 1985.

Dihle, A., "The Conception of India in Hellenistic and Roman Literature", *Proceedings of the Cambridge Philological Society,* N.S. 190: 1964,pp.15-23.

Dohrenwend, D., "Glass in China", *Oriental Art,* XXVI, 4: 1980,pp.426-46.

During-Caspers, "New Archaeological Evidence for maritime trade in the Persian Gulf during Protoliterate Period", *East and West,* Vol. 21 (I-2), 1971, pp. 21-44.

During-Caspers, "Etched Carnelian Beads", *British Institute of Archaeology,* no. 10: 1972, pp. 83-98.

During-Caspers, "Further Evidence for Cultural Relations between India,, Baluchistan and Iran and Mesopotamia in Early Dynastic Times", *Journal of Near Eastern Studies,* Vol. XXIV, 1-2, 1965, pp. 53-55.

During-Caspers, E.C.L., "Contacts between India and the West during Early historical Times", *Indian Museum Bulletin,* 21: 1986.pp.22-33.

Francis, P., "Glass Beads in Malaya", *Journal of the Malayan Branch of the Royal Asiatic Society,* LXIVL: pp.97-118.

Frankfort, H., "Iraq Excavations of the Oriental Inst., 1932-33", *Oriental Institute of Communication,* no. 17, 1934.

Frankfort, H., "Tell Asmar and Khafaja", *Oriental Institute of*

Communication, no.13, 1930-33.

Gadd, C.J., "Seals of Ancient Indian Style found at Ur", *Proceedings of the British Academy*, Vol. XVIII, 1932.

Ghosh, A., "The Indus Civilization: Its Origin, Authors, Extent and Chronology", *Indian prehistory*: 1964, pp. 113-136.

Ghosh, J.C., "Some Additional Notes on Foreign elements in the Hindu Population", *Annals of Bhandarkar Oriental Research Institute*, Vol. XII, 1930-31, p. 167.

Gordon, D.H., "Sialk, Giyan, Hissar and the Indo-Iranian Connections", *Man in India*, Vol. XXVII, 1947, pp. 195-241.

Gupta, C., "Horse Trade in North India", *Journal of Ancient Indian History*, XIV, 1-2: 1984, pp.186-206.

Gupta, S.P., "Gulf on Oman: The original Home of Indian Megaliths", *Puratattva*, no. 4, 1970-71, pp. 4 ff.

Heichelheim, F.M., "New Light on the influence of Hellenistic Financial Administration in the Near East and India", *Economic History*, Feb, 1938,

Heitzman, James, "Early Buddhism, Trade and Empire", *Journal of South-east Asian Studies*, xx, no. 1, March, 1989.

Helfer,T.W., "On the Indigenous silk-worms of India", *Journal of Royal Asiatic Society*, 1837, VI(1), pp. 38-44.

Hoernle, R., " Ancient Indian Medicine", *Journal of Royal Asiatic Society*, 1898.

Honnell,James., "A Review of our Knowledge of Ancient Sea Trade with India,the Origins and Ethnological Significane of Indian Boat Designs",Memoir of the Asiatic Society of Bengal 7,1920, pp.191-206

Hornell, J., "The Origins and Ethnological Significance of Indian Boat Designs", *Memoirs of the Asiatic Society of Bengal*, VII: pp.139-256.

Hourani, G.F., "Direct Sailing between the Persian gulf and China in pre-Islamics time", *Journal of Royal Asiatic Society*, 1947, pp.157-60.

Jayaswal, K.P., "Ethnic Origin of Tamralipti", *Indian Antiquary*, XLIII,1914, p.64

John Irwin, "Asokan Pillars: A reassessment of the Evidence",

Burlington Magazine, Vol. CXV, Nov. 1973, pp. 706-720.

John Irwin, "The Heliodorus Pillar: A fresh Appraisal", *Art and Archaeology Research Papers*, no. 6, 1974, pp. 1-3.

Johnstone, E.H., "Two Notes on Ptolemy's Geography of India", *Journal of Royal Asiatic Society*, 1941, p.208.

Kaikini, V.N., "Ancient Indian and the Outer World", *Proceedings of Indian History Congress.*, Vol. X, Allahabad, 1947.

Kaye, G.R., "Hindu Astronomy", *Memoirs of Archaeological Survey of India*, no. 18, 1924.

Kennedy, J., "The EarlyCommerce of Babylon with India", *Journal of Royal Asiatic Society*, 1898.

Kenoyer, J.M., Vidale, M. and Bhan, K.K., "Contemporary Stone Bead-making in Khambat, India", *World Archaeology*, 23, 1991,pp.44-63.

Konow, S., "Mathura Brahmi Inscriptions of the Year 28", *Epigraphia Indica*, XI: 61, 1931-2.

Lamberg Karlovsky, C.C., "The Cairn Burials of South-Eastern Iran", *East and West*, NS, Vol. 18 (Nos. 3-4), 1968, pp. 269-76.

Lewy, Julius, "Some Aspects of Commercial Life in Assyria and Asia Minor in the 19th pre—Christian Century", *Journal of the American Oriental Society.*,78,1958, pp.89-101.

Lueders, H., "A List of Brahmi Inscriptions," Appendix to *Epigraphia Indica*, X, 1912.

Mahadevan, I., "Arikamedu Graffiti: A Second Look", *Damilica*, II, 1981.

Mahadevan, I., "An Old Sinhalese Inscriptions from Arikamedu", *Seminar on Epigraphy*, Kuppuswami Sastri Birth Centenary: Madras, 1981.

Mahadevan, I., "Ancient Tamil Contacts Abroads: Recent Epigraphic Evidence', Reverend Fr. X.S. Thani Nayagam Memorial Lecture, Thani Nayagam Foundation Trust, Colombo, *Journal of the Institute of Asian Studies*, vol. Xii, no. 1, 1994, 136-55.

Mahadevan, I., "Corpus of Tamil Brahmi Inscriptions", *Seminar on Inscriptions*, Madras, 1966.

Mahadevan, I., "The Ancient Name of Arikamedu", N. Subrahmanian (ed.), *Surya Narayana Sastri Centenary Volume*, 1970.

Majumdar, R.C., "Achaemenian Rule in India", *Inidan Historical Quarterly*, Vol. 25, 1949.

Malhotra, S.L. "Commercial Rivalry in the Indian Ocean in Ancient Times", *Journal of Asiatic Society Bengal*, Vol. 33, NS, 1958.

Mallowan, M., "The Mechanism of Ancient Trade in Western Asia", *Iran*, Vol. III, America, 1955, pp. 1-9.

Manickam, V., "Some Trade Guild Epigraphs and Sculpture", *Journal of the Institute of Asian Studies*, Vol. I, September. 1908.

Marshall, J., "Archaeological Exploration in India, 1906-7", *Journal of Royal Asiatic Society*, 1907.

McGrail, S., "Towards a Classification of Water Transport", *World Archaeology*, 16, 1985, pp.289-303.

Mishra. Sri Vijayakanta, "Sea and Land Routes as revealed in Buddhist literature", *Journal of Indian History,* XXXII, 1972, pp.117-127.

Mitra, P. "Prehistoric Trade Routes and Commerce", *Indian Culture*, Vol. II, 1935-36.

Mukherjee, B.N., "Kharoshti and Kharoshti-Brahmi Inscriptions in West Bengal (India)", *Indian Museum Bulletin*, XXV, 1990.

Oates, David, "The Roman Frontier in Northern Iraq", *Geographical Journal*., 122, 1956, pp.190-99.

Oppenheim, A.L., "The Sea Faring Merchants of UR", *Journal of American Oriental Society*, Vol. LXXIV, 1954.

Pincott, Fredric., "The Route by which Alexander entered India", *Journal of Royal Asiatic Society* ,(N.S.),1894,pp.677-89.

Priaulx,Osmond, De, "On the Indian Embassies to Rome from the regin of Claudius to the death of Justinian" *Journal of Royal Asiatic Society*, XIX,pp.274-312.

Priaulx,Osmond, De, Beauvoir, "On the first Indian Embassy to

Augustus", *Journal of Royal Asiatic Society*,XVI, pp.309-321.

Priaulx,Osmond, De, Beauvoir, "On the Second Indian Embassy to Rome", *Journal of Royal Asiatic Society*,XVIII,pp.345-361.

Prins, A. H. J., "The Persian Gulf Dhows: Two Variants in Maritime Enterprise", *Persica*, 2, 1965,1-18.

Puri, B.N., "Indian Religion and Philosophy as known to Greek history", *Proceedings of Indian History Congress.*, Allahabad, 1938, 2nd Sessions.

Pusalker, A.D., "Cultural Interrelations between India and the outside World", *Cultural Heritage of India*, Vol. I, Calcutta, 1958.

Ralmer, J.A.B., " The identification of Ptolemy's Dounga", *Journal of Royal Asiatic Society*,1946,pp. 165-173.

Ramachandran, K.S., "Gulf of Oman : Original home of the Indian Megaliths, a Reappraisal", *Puratattva*, no. 6, 1972-73, pp. 20-26.

Ramachandran, K.S., "Roman Jewellery and Coins from Karur", *The Hindu*, 14 March, 1993.

Ramachandran, T.N., "Buddhist India and the Rest of the World", *Journal of the Andhra History Society*, Vol. XVIII, 1947-48.

Ramsay, William Mitchell, "Ptolemy and Western India", *Journal of Indian History*, XL. 1962,pp.41-84.

Rapson, E., "Counter-marks on early Persian and Indian Coins", *Journal of Royal Asiatic Society*, 1895,

Rawlinson, H.G., "Foreign Influences in the Civilization of Ancient India", *Journal of Bombay Branch, Royal Asiatic Society*, Vol. 23, 1914.

Ray, H.P., "Early Historical Settlement in the Deccan: An Ecological Perspective", *Man and Environment*, XIV, 1989, pp.103-08.

Ray, H.P., "Early Historical Trade: An Overview", *Indian Economic and Social History Review*, XXVI, 4,1989pp,437-58.

Ray, H.P., "Seafaring in the Bay of Bengal in the Early Centuries

AD", *Studies in History*, Vol. VI, no. 1, 1990, pp. 1-14,

Ray, H.P., "Early Trade in the Bay of Bengal", *Indian historical Review*, XIV, 1987-8,pp.79-89.

Ray, H.P., "East Coast Trade in Peninsular India, C. 200 BC to AD 400", Paper presented at the XI Congress of South Asian Archaeologists, Berlin, 1991.

Ray, H.P., "Inscribed Potsherds: A Study", *Indica*, XXIV, 1,1987, pp.1-14.

Ray, H.P., "The Yavana Presence in Ancient India", *Journal of the Economic and Social History of the Orient*, XXXI,1987, pp. 311-25.

Ray,J.C., "Textile Industry in Ancient India", *Journal of Bihar and Orissa Research Society.*,VII,pp.35-54.

Samaddar, J.N., "Industrial and Trading Organisation in Ancient India", *Journal of Bihar and Orissa Research Society.*,VII, pp.35-54.

Sankalia, H.D., "Iranian Influence on Early Indo-Paksitan Cultures" *Central Asia*, 1970.

Sankalia, H.D., "Review of The City in Early Historical India", *Puratattva*, no. 7, 1974, pp. 108-110.

Sankalia, H.D., "Navdatoli Dancers", *Antiquity*, Vol.XXI, 1955.

Sankalia, H.D., "Spouted vessels from Navdatoli and Iran", *Antiquity*, vol. XXIX, 1955.

Sastri, K.N., "New light on the Indus Civilization and Early contacts with Iraq and Iran", *Paper read at the International Conference on Asian Archaeology*, New Delhi, 1961.

Satya Prakash, "Indo-Persian Relation in Ancient India", *Modern Review*, Vol.84, 1940.

Saxena, K.K., "Ancient contacts betweens India and countries across the Arabian Sea", *Indo-Asian Culture*, vol. XV, no. 1, 1966.

Sayce, A.H., "The names of Vedic Deities on a Hittite tablet" *Journal of Royal Asiatic Society*,1909,pp.1106-7.

Schoff, "W.H., Some Aspects of the overland Oriental Trade in the Christian Era", *Journal of the American Oriental Society.*,35, 1915, pp. 31-41.

Schoff, W.H., "Navigation to the Far East Under the Roman Empire", *Journal of the American Oriental Society,* 37,1917,pp.240-249.

Schoff, W.H., "The Eastern Iron Trade of the Roman Empire", *Journal of the American Oriental Society,*1915,pp.pp. 224-239.

Schwarz, F.F., "Arrian's Indike on India: Intention and Reality" *East and West,* N.S. 25, 1975,pp181-200.

Sen, A.C., "Ashoka's Foreign Policy", *Proceedings of Indian History Congress,* vol. XI, Delhi, 1948.

Senart, E., "The Inscriptions in the Caves at Karle", *Epigraphia Indica,* VII: 1902-3,pp 17-74.

Senart, E., "The Inscriptions in the Caves at Nasik", *Epigraphia Indica,* VIII: 1905-6,pp 59-96.

Sewell, R., "Roman Coins Found in India", *Journal of the Royal Asiatic Society*: 1905-6, pp591-637.

Sidebotham, S.E., and Riley, J.A., "Survey of the Abu Sha'ar-Nile Road", *American Journal of Archaeology,* 95 no. 4: 1991,pp571-622.

Smith, V.A., "Graeco-Roman Influence on the civilization of ancient India", *Journal Of Asiatic Society Bengal.*, LXI,pp. 50-76.

Spooner, D.B., "Mr.Ratan Tata's Excavations at Pataliputra", *Archaeological Survey of India: Annual Report,* 1912-13.

Stein, A., "An Archaeological Tour in the Ancient Persia", *Iraq,* no. 3, 1936.

Stein,Sir Marc Aurel, "The Ancient Harbours of Tyre". *Geographical Journal,* 94,1939,pp.330-333.

Sten-Konow, "Indo-European Religious Ideas in Ancient India", *Annals of Bhandarkar Oriental Research Institute,* VI, part II, 1925.

Tarn, W.W., "Demetrius in Sind", *Journal of Royal Asiatic Society,* 1913,pp.179-193.

Thomas, J.W., "A Passage in the Periplus", *Journal of Royal Asiatic Society,* 1913, pp.420-421.

Thomas, J.W., "The Date of Kaniska", *Journal of Royal Asiatic*

Society, 1913,pp.627-650.

Unvala, J.M., "Political and Cultural Relations between Iran and India", *Annals of Bhandarkar Oriental Research Institute*, Vol. XXVIII, 1947.

Varier, M.R. Raghava, "Marine Technology in Ancient Tamilakam", *Proceedings of the Indian History Congress*, 49th Session, Dharwad, 1989.

Visvanath, S.V.S., "Routes of Traffic in Ancient India", *Modern Review*, 1923,pp.294-297.

Weinstein, Brian, "Biblical evidence of spice trade between India and the land of Israel:A historical analysis" *The Indian Historical Review*,Vol-xxvii,No-1,Jan,2000.

Wheeler, R.E.M., "Iran and India in Pre-Islmaic Times", *Ancient India*, no. 4, 1947-48, pp. 41-84.

Whitehouse, D., "The Periplus Maris Erythraei", *Journal of Roman Archaeology*, 3: 1990,pp489-93.

Whitehouse, D., and Williamsons, A., "Sassanian Maritime Trade", *Iran*, 11, 1973,pp29-49.

Winternitz, M., "Surunga and the Kautilya Arthasastra", *Indian Historical Quarterly*, Vol. I, 1925.

Woolley, C.L., "Excavations at Ur, 1926-27", *Antiquaries Journal*, Vol. VIII, London, 1928.

Woolley, C.L., "Excavations at Ur, 1929-30", *Antiquaries Journal*, Vol. X, 1930-, pp. 331-389.

Woolley, C.L., "The Excavations at Ur, 1925-26", *Antiquaries Journal*, vol. Vi, No. 4, 1926, pp. 365-401.

List of Research Journals and Periodicals

American Anthropologist, Chicago.

Ancient India, New Delhi.

Ancient Pakistan, Peshawar.

Annual Bibliography of Indian Archaeology, Kern Institute, Leiden.

The Anthropologist, Delhi.

Anthropology Papers of American Museum of Natural History, New York.

Antiquaries Journal, London.

Archaeological Survey of India: Annual Report, New Delhi.
Archaeological Survey of Western India, Bombay
British Institute of Archaeology, London.
Bulletin of the Deccan College Research Institute, Poona.
Bulletin of the Museum of Far Eastern Antiquities, Stockholm.
Bulletin of the Prince of Wales Museum, Bombay.
Bulletin of the School of Oriental and African Studies, London.
Cultural Heritage of India, Calcutta.
Current Science, Bangalore.
Damilica, Madras
East and West, Rome.
Expedition Philadelphia, Pennsylvania.
Illustrated London News, London.
Indian Archaeology: A Review, New Delhi.
Indian Culture, Calcutta.
Indo-Asian Culture, New Delhi.
Journal of the American Oriental Society, New Haven.
Journal of Bombay Branch, Royal Asiatic Society, Bombay.
Journal of Field Archaeology, Chicago U.S.A
Journal of Greater India Society, Calcutta.
Journal of Near Easter Studies, Chicago.
Journal of Numismatic Society of India, Varanasi.
Journal of Royal Asiatic Society Bengal (Letters), Calcutta.
Journal of Royal Asiatic Society Great BritainAncient Indian and Ireland, London.
Journal of the University of Gauhati,. Gauhati.
Journal of Uttar Pradesh Historical Society, Lucknow.
Memoirs of Archaeological Survey of India, Calcutta.
New Indian Antiquary, Bombay.
Oriental Institute of Chicago Communications, Chicago.
Pakistan Archaeology, Karachi.
Proceedings of British Academy, London.
Proceedings of Indian History Congress.
Sino-Indian Studies, Calcutta.
Surya Narayana Sastri Centenary Volume, Madurai,
Visheshwarananda Indological Journal, Hoshiarpur.